Acrobat™ PDF
AND WORKFLOW *In Detail*

ISBN 0-13-088948-2

90000

PRENTICE HALL PTR
IN DETAIL SERIES

Frank Romano   *InDesign InDetail*

Frank Romano   *Acrobat PDF and Workflow InDetail*

Acrobat™ PDF
AND **WORKFLOW** *In Detail*

FRANK ROMANO

PH
PTR

PRENTICE HALL PTR, UPPER SADDLE RIVER, NJ 07458

Library of Congress Cataloging-in-Publication Date

Romano, Frank J.
  Acrobat PDF and workflow in detail/Frank Romano.
       p.   cm. (Prentice Hall PTR in detail series)
    Includes bibliographical references (p.) and index.
    ISBN 0-13-088948-2
    1. Adobe Acrobat. 2. Protable document software. I. Title. II. Series.

  QA76.76.T49 R638 2000
  005.72--dc21   00-033982
                                                     CIP

Editorial/Production Supervision: *Kerry Reardon*
Project Coordinator: *Anne Trowbridge*
Acquisitions Editor: *Tim Moore*
Editorial Assistant: *Julie Okulicz*
Manufacturing Manager: *Alexis R. Heydt*
Buyer: *Maura Goldstaub*
Art Director: *Gail Cocker-Bogusz*
Interior Series Design: *Meg Van Arsdale*
Cover Design: *Anthony Gemmellaro*
Cover Design Direction: *Jerry Votta*

© 2000 Prentice Hall PTR
Prentice-Hall, Inc.
Upper Saddle River, NJ 07458

The publisher offers discounts on this book when ordered in bulk quantities.
For more information, contact

   Corporate Sales Department,
   Prentice Hall PTR
   One Lake Street
   Upper Saddle River, NJ 07458
   Phone: 800-382-3419; FAX: 201-236-7141
   E-mail (Internet): corpsales@prenhall.com

Printed in the United States of America

10 9   8   7   6   5   4   3   2   1

ISBN 0-13-088948-2

Prentice-Hall International (UK) Limited, *London*
Prentice-Hall of Australia Pty. Limited, *Sydney*
Prentice-Hall Canada Inc., *Toronto*
Prentice-Hall Hispanoamericana, S.A., *Mexico*
Prentice-Hall of India Private Limited, *New Delhi*
Prentice-Hall of Japan, Inc., *Tokyo*
Pearson Education Asia, Pte. Ltd.
Editora Prentice-Hall do Brasil, Ltda., *Rio de Janeiro*

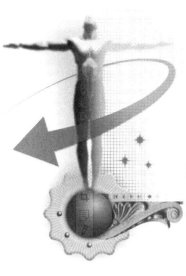

CONTENTS

One Workflow Model   149

22 Adobe Capture   461

How Capture Works   462

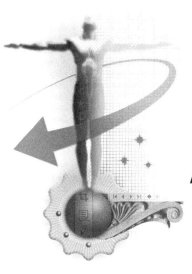

ACKNOWLEDGMENTS

Thanks to Dave Broudy, David Peters, Eric Lehman, and the gang at RIT.

Thanks to Amie Howard, Bill Eisley, Mattias Anderson (all now with Adobe Systems), and Mark Witkowski—all of whom worked on the first major book on PDF workflow.

Thanks to Kerry Reardon of Laurel Road Publishing Services, Tim Moore and the gang at Prentice Hall.

Thanks to Robert and Richard Romano.

Thanks to Joanne Romano.

This sounds like an Oscar acceptance speech.

INTRODUCTION

PDF is a phenomenon. Adobe's Portable Document Format, known as "that cross-platform utility," is also the cross-media utility. It is profoundly changing the the print industry. It is also helping to evolve electronic publishing. If you are a graphic designer, a prepress specialist, a printing company, an art director, a production person, a Web publisher, or a publishing professional—you had better stay up-to-date on Acrobat.

Acrobat 4 has features of interest to the high-end printing industry. It is designed to be the sub-atomic particle of new digital workflows. Workflow is more than moving electronic files around. It is the "glue" that links the creative professional to the information consumer.

A PDF-centric workflow uses a complete, self-contained file as a component in a production workflow or the final document in a publishing workflow. Designers and their printers send PDFs to their clients for soft-proofing on screen or hard copy printouts on their printer. Fonts and graphics are already embedded in the PDF file (if all went well). They don't need the page-layout program the designer used, because they can view and print the PDF with the free Acrobat Reader. With the full version of Acrobat, the client can annotate revisions or approvals with notes, sound files, strikethroughs, drawings, or highlights—right in the PDF.

For publishing purposes it is the one format that preserves the form and content of the information and is universally accessible. Every day, thousands of people around the world, using every major computer platform, download the free Adobe Reader from adobe.com.

A decade ago, when Acrobat was introduced, it was seen as the replacement for print. Today, it is seen as the salvation of print. It makes printing production more effective and engenders new workflows. It has a natural place on the Web and disk-based information distribution.

Adobe Acrobat is the product. PDF is the file format. This book is about both and the way you work with this unique program in digital systems.

Frank Romano
Rochester, NY
April, 2000

Intellectual Property

Adobe, the Adobe logo, Acrobat, the Acrobat logo, Acrobat Catalog, Acrobat Capture, Acrobat Exchange, Acrobat Distiller, Acrobat Reader, Acrobat Search, Adobe Accurate Screens, Adone Extreme, Adobe Type Manager, Adobe Type Set, Adobe Illustrator, Adobe InDesign, Aldus, ATM, the ATM logo, InProduction, Display PostScript, PageMill, the PageMill logo, Photoshop, the Photoshop logo, PrintMill, Pixelburst, PageMaker, PostScript, and the PostScript logo are registered trademarks of Adobe Systems Incorporated.

Agfa, the Agfa rhombus, Agfa Balanced Screening, Mainstream, AgfaType, AccuSet, Alliance, Alto, Apogee, Arcus, Avantra, ChromaPost, Chromapress, ChromaWatch, ChromaWrite, Cobra, CristalRaster, DuoProof, FotoLook, FotoTune, Galileo, Horizon, IntelliTrack, LUTGen, MultiStar, OptiSpot, PhotoWise, ProSlide, Python, QuickLink, SelectScan, SelectSet, Setprint, Star, Taipan and Viper are trademarks of Agfa Corporation.

AppleTalk, EtherTalk, ColorSync, ImageWriter, LaserWriter, Mac, Macintosh, Macintosh Quadra and QuickTime are trademarks of

Apple Computer, Inc. registered in the U.S. and other countries and AppleScript, Power Macintosh, PowerBook, QuickDraw, System 6, System 7 and TrueType are trademarks of Apple Computer, Inc.

Ethernet is a registered trademark of Xerox Corp.

Freehand is a trademark of Macromedia Corp.

HP, LaserJet and PCL are registered trademarks of Hewlett-Packard Company.

IBM and OS/2 are registered trademarks of International Business Machines Corporation.

Kodak is a registered trademark of Eastman Kodak.

Linotype, Hell, Delta, Prinergy, Optima, Helvetica, Palatino, Times, and Univers are registered trademarks and HQS Screening, RT Screening, are trademarks of Linotype-Hell AG, Heidelberg Druckmachinen and/or its subsidiaries.

Microsoft and MS-DOS are registered trademarks and Windows, Windows 95, 98, and 2000, and Windows NT are trademarks of Microsoft.

Novell and NetWare are registered trademarks of Novell, Inc.

OpenWindows, Sun, SunOS, are trademarks of Sun Microsystems.

Post-It is a registered trademark of 3M.

Scitex and Scitex Brisque are registered trademarks of Scitex Corp.

Solaris is a registered trademark of Sun Microsystems, Inc. SPARCstation is a registered trademark of SPARC International, Inc., licensed exclusively to Sun Microsystems, Inc and is based upon an architecture developed by Sun Microsystems.

UNIX is a registered trademark licensed exclusively through X/Open Company, Ltd.

QuarkXPress and QuarkXTension are registered trademarks of Quark, Inc.

All other company and brand and product names are trademarks, registered trademarks or service marks of their respective holders. If we inadvertently missed anyone, any word with a capital letter is probably a trademark of somebody's so please respect their intellectual property.

1

Digital Workflow

Unlike other manufacturing assembly lines, graphic art workflows do not follow a general model for the production process. Every printing plant is different. Every workflow is different. Every job is a surprise.

With conventional workflow, the production process used to start with printers or prepress houses. They received different kinds of artwork or raw text, and their job was to set type, scan images, build pages, make film and plates, and finally print the job. They knew how to scan the images, whether transparency or reflective, positive or negative. They knew what colors were "reproducible," what the variability of the process was, and what file formats to use. The printer and/or the prepress service had almost everything under control.

Today we see the integration of the job creator with the production process itself. Most jobs arrive in digital form because designers and graphic artists are using computers in their work. Content creators are doing tasks that used to be done by printers or prepress services, so printers and prepress services are losing control over file preparation for printing. And that file preparation controls the entire process.

Yet, although everything seems to be a lot easier to artists as they apply computers, and every image looks very good on the computer monitor, there may be a problem. Chances are that those beautiful images will not print correctly. Let's get basic.

Digital workflow for printing often comes down to two basic approaches: raster and vector. There are almost twenty different raster-based file formats available in the Macintosh version of Photoshop 5 alone, many with configurable subsets—plus vector formats.

BITMAP files contain both screening and dot gain compensation information, and reside as a 1-bit, pixel-by-pixel description of "laser on, laser off" commands. They reside with the dot gain compensation and screening "threshold array" already mapped out for final imaging. These files are typically referred to as being "locked" because you cannot alter the screening or dot gain compensation information without reprocessing the pre-bitmap data.

All of these formats come together in a container of sorts, which holds all page elements and combines them. The container application may vary throughout the workflow, which results in two distinct types of job control—component files, which are created by the designer or creative professional in the initial preparation, and consolidated files, which are used for various steps in the final production process.

Component Files

Component files for high-end printing can be assembled using QuarkXPress, Adobe InDesign, PageMaker, Illustrator, or FreeHand (the latter two for packaging) or FrameMaker or Corel Ventura Publisher for object-oriented, text-intensive documents. The components are raster and vector files. Each component is a separate element—a picture, a line art graphic, etc.—and the assembly program lets you position them on the page and in the document.

Consolidated Files

Consolidated files are used to convert all of the component files, both raster and vector, into a single format—a container—that is accepted by an output processing system—a RIP. The consolidated format has usually been PostScript, but TIFF and PDF are now alternatives. PDF and PostScript come from the same roots. Font handling, color handling, resolution, target output device, and compression must be set up in advance in order to achieve an acceptable consolidated file.

In PostScript, altering the consolidated file after creation requires re-creation from the original component files. PDF started the same way, but now there are many tools for editing PDFs.

When PDF lacked these tools, CT and LW formats, either in CEPS native formats, or as TIFF/IT files, found a reason to remain in production. These formats stayed in use because of the requirements of specific high-end output devices. However, raster files are uneditable and voluminous, and this can affect network performance. CEPS raster-based CT and LW files have a limited set of editing tools, usually based on proprietary systems. TIFF/IT has no editing tools. PostScript never really lent itself to interactive editing, although there were some attempts by third-party developers. PDF is moving rapidly via plug-ins to provide high levels of editability.

CT = Continuous Tone
LW = Line Work

Raster files have resolution (same as bitmap files do), but now the individual picture elements (pixels) have color depth, that is, levels of gray. These levels of gray will eventually be mapped into some type of "threshold array" as part of the screening process prior to (or during) exposure. Raster formats as they stand do not contain screening and/or dot gain compensation information. These parameters are defined as part of the exposure dialog. When you take a raster file, superimpose screening and dot gain compensation, and then store the mapping of the individual laser-on, laser-off commands, you create a bitmap file format. Raster files are not "locked" in that you may adjust (manipulate, edit, etc.) individual gray-level components for each and every pixel. You may also apply screening and/or dot gain compensation at will, based on whatever circumstances are required.

Embedded Elements   Vector files are usually saved in EPS; raster files have loads of options, with production efficiencies such as image replacement, data compression, and color management. It is almost impossible to control the file formats from clients; it is useful to try to control those used in internal operations.

Editability   The need to make changes to a job (sometimes after it has been shipped) is not really funny. Author's alterations, printer's errors, or Murphy's law make editability an issue at every stage in the process. With automated production processes, it is vital that we get the job right as far up front as possible and then have the ability to make changes at each step if necessary.

While vector files are usually saved in EPS, raster files have many options, not only changing the specific format, but also enhancing production with items like image replacement, data compression, and color-managed files. Now that we are moving to digital photography and scanning very early in the process, we must rethink the way in which we capture and apply our files. It is almost impossible to control the file formats from clients; it would be useful, at least, to try to control them in our internal operations. If technology helps us work faster, better, and more efficiently, why is it that it not always works, particularly in graphic arts? Because we have too many variables.

In the printing industry, there are many variables that affect the production process. Although it is important to notice the amazing technological developments that are helping printers and service bureaus to serve better and faster their clients, it is also very important to point out that this is a developing industry, which lacks a great deal of standardization. Every user is king.

Technological Pitfalls   Because there is a lack of standardization, especially on digital file preparation, the window for mistakes is enormous. Many of these mistakes come from the ignorance of the file creator about workflow issues and file preparation. In other words, the content creators should have enough knowledge about prepress basics and production workflow to avoid mistakes downstream in the process. Some do; many don't.

On the printer side, new technologies become outdated as fast as they emerge. Keeping up with these changes is one of the biggest challenges that services in this industry face. For example, digital workflow is becoming more common. However, production in a digital environment is dependent not only on the equipment but also on the ability of the people running that equipment.

This means that the productivity of a printing company is directly proportional to the level of employees' knowledge of digital technologies and to their commitment to productivity. It is crucial that both, printers and content creators, receive enough training in these issues to achieve high performance and improve throughput. There is no advantage in having progressed in technology if it is not accompanied by progress with people.

Islands of Automation   The ultimate and ideal workflow is a totally digital workflow. Unfortunately in this industry, in only a few instances is this the case. Traditional print publishing is plagued by incompatible equipment and disconnected islands of automation that electronic publishing has created, unintentionally, as entirely new forms of digital bottlenecks. This last sentence contains two key terms, "islands of automation" and "bottleneck." Islands of automation refer to those highly automated processes inside the workflow that do not have continuity with the other steps or processes that follow. It is like having computer-to-plate technologies and not having reliable digital proofing. The benefits of having a filmless and time-effective platemaking process are diminished by the fact that some customers require a film-based proof.

The second term, bottleneck, is any process or workstation with capacity less than or equal to the demands placed on it. Capacity is the measure of the system output. For example, on a printing press, it is the number of impressions that it can produce in a time frame, usually an hour.

Every system is composed of many steps. Every step or production operation has a certain capacity. The capacity of each of these operations is not the same. Some stations work faster than others, meaning that at some point some workstations will be idle while others will be overloaded.

In the case of islands of automation, we may have very fast, highly automated processes linked with slower processes that will constitute system bottlenecks. The problem with bottlenecks is that they determine the capacity of the entire system. If in my system I have very fast workstations linked to others that are not so fast, the capacity of my system equals the capacity of the slowest workstation, not the fastest. To be effective, workflows should be entirely automated. In the printing industry, we talk about automation, digital file transfers, etc., but the "full benefits" of the technology will not be seen if fully digital workflow is not in place.

Why Workflow Automation?

Automation permits the combination of complex and simple tasks that do not need manual intervention. Automation results in lower costs and faster deliveries. However, in graphic arts, there are probably as many exceptions as rules. Exceptions are those jobs that do not run easily through the workflow. Managing exceptions is more difficult and more expensive than managing regular standardized processes because exceptions require operator expertise and intervention. This concept applies not only for the production process alone, but also for customers, since they now have to archive, retrieve, manipulate, and reuse digital information. They must also deal with exceptions and nonstandardization.

Workflow Design   We can have as many workflow models as we wish. The bottom line is that when designing a workflow, it is necessary to analyze the different steps that are encountered most commonly. Then, identify the processes to produce the desired results, and finally design a workflow, or a group of workflows, which can handle those steps in an efficient way. The idea of workflow design is not to streamline each task in order to save time in each step of the process, but rather to automate the entire process. The whole is the sum of its parts. Here are the parts:

Typical Tasks in a Print Production Environment

Preflighting   To preflight a job is nothing more than checking that the digital file has all the elements necessary to perform well in the production workflow. Many software programs are designed for this task. Among other elements, these programs check that the fonts are embedded and that all images are present with the right format (RGB or CMYK color), etc. The idea of preflighting is to avoid mistakes before the job reaches the first output production steps. Preflighting attempts to avoid problems by fixing them upfront so these problems do not impair workflow later on.

Color Management   Color management has been a controversial issue. It has became more prevalent recently due to the fact that digital printing and digital proofing are becoming more popular. As it is described in this book, color management is an effort to match color as it is output from different output devices in a given system. It is important to maintain the consistency of the same color image across different media and output devices. Today, color management is based on profiles for encoding color.

PostScript File Creation   Most jobs are created in some sort of page-layout application like QuarkXPress or PageMaker. Most RIPs (Raster Image Processors) do not understand applications—they "speak" another language, PostScript. Therefore, at some point, it will be necessary to transform those application files into Post-Script code. When you click Print, the application program builds a PostScript file from your screen image, the underlying data, and some information from the operating system. In graphic arts, when you print, you are sending PostScript code.

PDF File Creation   PDF is an excellent file format for file exchange. As we will discuss later in this chapter, it is one of the most versatile file formats due to its portability and cross-platform charac-teristics. Trapping: When you have adjoining elements of different colors, registration is critical. The problem is that press registration is not 100 percent perfect; therefore, it is necessary to overlap these colors to compensate for misregistration, and we call this image trap-ping. Today trapping is accomplished using different software pack-ages. Some are more sophisticated than others, but the question is When in the workflow is trapping done? Some do trapping before RIPing, some do it while RIPing, and others after. Approaches depend on the configuration of the workflow, but for the most part, it will depend on the kind of applications and products service providers offer.

Imposition   Imposition is the arrangement of individual pages on a press sheet, so that when it is folded and trimmed, the pages are in correct orientation and order. To impose is a responsibility that should not be taken lightly. As in the case of trapping, there are advanced imposition software packages that do this automatically. However, this task can be done manually in the application software, depending on the type of operation.

RIP   The RIP (Raster Image Processor) takes in high-level page-description files and outputs low-level data streams that can be fed directly to a digital printer, imagesetter, or platesetter for image rendering, or to a video display to be viewed. The RIP has three main functions: Interpretation, Creation of the Display List, and Rasterization.

Interpretation: In this stage the RIP interprets the PostScript code that has been sent. It decodes PostScript and prepares the information to the following step, the display list.

Creation of the display list is an intermediate list of objects and instructions before rasterizing. It is a list of objects in a page description file that have a determined order. The order the page elements have in this display list is the same order in which they will be displayed or imaged.

Rasterization is the conversion of graphic elements into bitmaps for rendering on a monitor, digital printer, or imagesetter. In other words the RIP takes the display list and converts it into pixels. This stage is necessary because every output device needs pixels.

Proofing   A proof is an output of the job before it gets printed. There are different kinds of proofs available, ranging from conventional, which is film-based, soft proof, which uses a calibrated monitor, and digital proof, from a digital proofing printer.

Remote Proofing   Sometimes, the person who OK's the proof is in a remote location. To avoid mail delays some firms use remote proofers in their customers' sites. Files need to be transmitted over a digital telecommunications network. Once clients receive the files then they can output them on paper, using a digital printing device, or simply display them on a monitor (soft proof). The file that is sent can be an application file, a PostScript file, or a PDF file. This file can either have just the resolution necessary to output on the proofing device or the full resolution of the final reproduction device. File size is an important issue for file transmission over digital networks; therefore it makes more sense to have just the resolution needed to output on the proofing device. In any case, the most important consideration is to have the proofing devices accurately calibrated to the printing conditions of the press or digital printing device on which the job will ultimately be produced.

Corrections   The aim of a proof is to detect any error or mistake in the file prior to printing the job. When corrections need to be done, decisions must be made quickly. It is necessary to have excellent communication between customer and producer. Remote proofing, and digital proofing in general, is helping to speed up the process of correction and re-proofing. Therefore, it is important to have corrections as a task in the workflow with a clearly defined methodology.

Film Output   If film is still used, it is output by an imagesetter, after the RIP stage. Film can be output either on single spreads or on full-size imposed pages. The film is then used for plate exposure, or for making analog proofs.

Plate Output   Today there are two methods for producing a plate: the conventional way, using film, and the digital way, using a computer to plate device, also known as platesetter. With a totally digital workflow, the second way is more suitable; however, many printers still use film due to the capital investment required. With computer-to-plate technology, film is eliminated from the production workflow, which represents many advantages for printers and eliminates one level of variability in the system.

Another issue with computer-to-plate is proofing. Proofing must be done digitally; however, digital proofing, although it has improved in the past couple of years, is still not completely accepted as a contract proof by some critical customers. They demand a halftone dot-based proof.

Blueline Proof   The purpose of a blueline is to check final imposition and determine whether there is any element missing or misplaced. The blueline can be printed in many paper formats: It can be a single page or a big print of the entire press sheet imposition. These proofs are not intended to judge color or print quality in any aspect but to verify the position of the different elements in the page or the imposition (page order). Some print buyers are viewing "digital bluelines"—pages on a monitor.

Printing   Printing is the major task in a print production environment. Today we output using not only conventional printing methods, like offset lithography, flexography, or gravure, but also from a
variety of optional digital printing devices. Digital printers and presses use different technologies, and instead of ink, they use toner or
inkjet ink.

Storage   Storage refers to the warehousing of electronic files
from jobs already output. Files can be stored on central computerized systems, CD-ROMs, tapes, or magnetic diskettes. Many storage
technologies have been developed in the last few years; however,
graphic arts files are known for huge sizes, and therefore storage can
still be a problem more in the finding and retrieval than in the actual storage.

These are the most typical tasks in a print production workflow.
Some others are omitted here, but they probably are a subcategory
of the ones we just mentioned. As you see, each one of the tasks has
its own requirements. Workflows can be very different from one
print shop to another; they may combine tasks that are highly automated with conventional or manual methods, or they can have a fully
digital workflow. Therefore, the content creator must be aware of
these issues before creating the file for printing.

One of the promises of PDF does lie with the originators. If they
convert their layout program pages into PDF properly—and properly is the operative word—then workflow can be truly automatic. We
must assume that some originators will not make good PDFs (and
they probably did not make good application files either), so PDF
may begin when a job is accepted by the prepress or printing service.

Variable Data Printing   Print will no longer have to be simply
a long-run, broadcast-oriented information distribution medium.
Print will have to deliver a specific, targeted message to a specific,
targeted audience.

At the front end, master pages must be formatted, with provisions
for entering information that will vary from printed unit to printed
unit. Information must be imported from a database to fill the vari-

able areas of the layout. Most of the programs for variable-data printing provide some way to define portions of QuarkXPress or PageMaker layouts as subject to variation.

Personalization is an outgrowth of the mail merge features dating back to word processors of the 1970s (and to "player-piano" typewriters of the '40s and '50s), which made it possible to merge a standard letter with a list of names, addresses, and personalized salutations. Personalization on today's digital color presses mostly takes the form of supplementing name and address data with other text in specific areas of a static page layout. The source of the variable information is a database or delimited, sequential list of fields. A more advanced approach to personalization is adding not just text but also other content objects to the page, such as photos, graphics, scanned signatures, etc. They are retrieved from a database for placement in the layout.

A different aspect of variable printing is sometimes described as custom document assembly, or versioning. This has been done in the office for years. Word processors in the 1970s assembled individual paragraphs into reports, customized insurance policies, and other materials.

Short runs of specific layouts can incorporate variable data with some of the data varying from page to page, while other content is common to a series of pages. Many programs define the variable objects on the master page as a variable content box. Data areas on the page must be predefined (they usually must be rectangles of a predefined size). The database data is then linked by a variable data program and the master layout and the variable data are combined, either in the page (which then needs to be rasterized for each impression) or in the RIP.

Soon pages and layouts will be generated on the fly according to the defined content. The static master page must be rasterized and each of the variable-page components must also be rasterized, fast enough to keep up with the print engine.

The RIP task becomes more complex as graphics and color-separated photos are included as components that vary from unit to unit. Print server configurations such as Barco's and new multiprocessor

RIP configurations such as Adobe's Extreme are working in this area. For now, most pages to be printed are prerasterized, assembled on the fly, and input to the print engine.

The ability to pass these huge amounts of raster data through the pipeline to the print engine in such a way as to ensure that the device can run at its rated speed is the other major challenge. This task is complicated by the size of the pipeline to the print engine, i.e., the maximum speed of data transfer to the engine, which at this stage of technological evolution of engines is generally much slower than is required for true productivity.

The suppliers of digital color printers and presses have chosen a slightly different method for handling variable data and outputting custom documents. They all face other technical considerations that contribute to the complexity of the overall variable-printing work-flow, including the ability to handle input from a variety of database formats and mechanisms for ensuring and verifying job integrity.

Digital workflow is evolving rapidly to meet the demands of auto-mated press, printers, and systems. The printing industry must be competitive with mass media. It must be able to handle long and short runs, static and variable data, now not later.

From CEPS to DTP   When we think of digital technology in printing, we usually think of Desktop Publishing (DTP) using per-sonal computers. Digital technology in printing goes back to the 1970s when the first digital scanners had analog controls but were connected to film recorders similar to the imagesetters of today. Light passing through a sensitive Photomultiplier Tube (PMT) in a scanner was converted into electronic data and passed on to the recorder where it was then imaged onto film by a laser.

In 1979, Scitex introduced the first Color Electronic Prepress System (CEPS, pronounced "seps"). Costing nearly a million dollars, this was the first system that allowed images to be sized, color cor-rected, and placed on a page. Though the placement of text was not supported very well, the advantages in time of producing at size and in register multiple pages of color separations pushed many of the largest printers and prepress services to adopt CEPS technology. In

1985, three releases began the era of Desktop Publishing. The Macintosh computer was released, which featured an easy-to-use Graphic User Interface (GUI). Aldus Corporation released the first version of Pagemaker, software that could be used to lay out fully composed pages of text and graphics. Most importantly, Apple released the first version of its Laserwriter printer, which used Adobe PostScript as its page description language.

PostScript   The effect of the PostScript language on the printing industry was profound. PostScript allowed pages of graphics and text to be described using mathematics. A PostScript file is device-independent, which means that the specific parameters of the printer, resolution for example, are kept separate from the actual description of the page. A PostScript file contains all of the fonts and image information required to reproduce a page. The result is a file format uniquely suited to the graphic arts, which can be generated once but interpreted in different ways for different output devices. The same PostScript file can be used to print to a 300-dpi laser printer and a 2400-dpi imagesetter, taking advantage of whatever features are offered for a respective printer.

RIP   The development of Raster Image Processors (RIP) was another important development. The RIP processes a PostScript file and applies the attributes for the output device after it interprets the file. A RIP works by performing three separate operations on a PostScript file. First the RIP interprets the file and creates a list of all of the elements on the page, called the display or object list. The display list is then converted, or rasterized, to a single file using the parameters of the destination printer. A display list destined for a 300-dpi laser printer is rasterized at 300-dpi. A display list destined for a 2400-dpi imagesetter is rasterized at 2400-dpi. Finally, the RIP sends the data to the printer in a language that that printer can understand, and the page is imaged by the device.

Development of Imagesetters   Recognizing the potential for using PostScript in the graphic arts, Linotype added a RIP to two of its laser typesetting devices, the Linotronic 100 and 300, thus creating the first imagesetters. An imagesetter is a two-part device: a RIP to process incoming files, and a marking engine to image film or specialized photographic paper. Imagesetters come in two types, capstan and drum. In capstan imagesetters, the film is drawn through a set of rollers in front of a stationary laser that images the film. In drum imagesetters, the film is secured around either the inside or outside of a drum. The laser then moves across the film. The advantage to drum imagesetters is their ability to provide the level of registration needed for multicolor work.

With the combination of personal computer, software, RIP, and imagesetter, desktop publishing began making inroads to high-end printing. Despite the fact that at the time front-end systems for color were capable of producing superior quality, and desktop publishing had difficulty with process color, the price differences justified the adoption of DTP systems both by designers to produce work, and by printers to process it.

Color and Multiple-Page Imagesetters In 1987, QuarkXPress was capable of creating PostScript output for color separations. Soon after, the first desktop scanners capable of scanning reasonable quality color appeared on the market with an image editing software program from Adobe called Photoshop. With these tools a designer could now completely create and edit four-color process work without the need for the expensive Color Electronic Prepress Systems (CEPS).

At the same time there had been rapid advancements both in RIPs and in imagesetters. Adobe had announced the impending release of a new version of PostScript that was more reliable, faster, and better able to handle multicolor work. New imagesetters were also released that could image two-page spreads of four-color process on a sheet of film. The focus in printing companies began to move away from manual page assembly and toward electronic page assembly. If two-page spreads could be imaged, then the logical next step was to image an entire printing form at one time. Oversized imagesetters came on the market that were capable of running sheets of film up to 28 x 40 inches—large enough to accommodate the maximum sheet sizes of most presses. These imagesetters were called imposetters because of their ability to image an entire imposition at one time. New software was also released that could take in single PostScript pages, arrange them, and add any other marks or color-control bars that the printer might need. The use of imposetters with imposition software resulted in the first all-digital workflows from designer to film.

Computer-to-Plate (CTP)   Polyester plate material with a light sensitive coating had already been in use with imposetters to provide direct-to-plate solutions. The gravure industry had been using direct imaging engravers to create cylinders since the mid-1980s. Although the technology was in place to digitally create impositions, the task of digitally imaging aluminum plates for lithography posed a new set of challenges. The first CTP devices, or platesetters, that could image aluminum lithographic plates were flatbed machines. Individual plates were hand-loaded and imaged with visible light lasers. The problem was that the size of the plates was limited because as the laser imaged farther from the center of the plate, the beam of light would become more distorted. The next generation of platesetters were internal drum devices. Much like imposetters, the plate was mounted inside a drum, and the laser moved across the drum to image the plate.

Though internal drum machines proved successful with visible light lasers, the development of thermal laser/plate technology caused problems with this design. Thermal imaging uses heat energy to activate the polymerization of the image area on the plate. The advantage of thermal imaging is a much harder dot on the plate. The solution was to mount the plate around the outside of the drum, and then rotate the plate across the laser. This has proven to be an enormously succesful solution. Currently, the state of the art in platesetters is the thermal-imaging internal and external configurations.

Digital Printing and Direct-to-Press   The first digital printers were offshoots of digital color copiers. A color copier is essentially a scanner and a printer. By bypassing the scanner section and sending data directly from a RIP, a color copier/printer can be transformed into a digital press. A digital press, like Xerox's Docucolor, Xeikon's DCP, and Indigo's E-Print, is toner based. Thus it uses an image carrier that is re-imaged for each impression. In contrast, a direct imaging press uses a plate that is imaged directly on the press but does not change from impression to impression.

The Heidelberg Quickmaster DI is the most successful and well known of the direct imaging presses. It gives the quality advantage of ink on paper, while still maintaining the advantages of direct digital workflow. It cannot, however, be used for highly personalized and variable-data printing. The success of digital presses comes from the reduction of prepress costs and makeready time and the ability to print short runs affordably. Digital presses are used for personalized or on-demand printing—essentially a run of only one piece. Digital printing technology continues to advance. Xeikon's family of digital color presses provided the first high-speed Web-based solutions for digital printing.

2

It Started
with PostScript

It was not apparent that fateful day in 1985 that PostScript would be what it has become. It was spring when Apple Computer introduced us to desktop publishing, a combination of the Macintosh, Page-Maker, and PostScript. PostScript gave us a laser printer that thought it was a typesetting machine and linked to film imagesetting.

It was not apparent that PostScript would do what it has done because there were many competitors in the page-description language arena in 1985. But PostScript had one thing going for it: the high end. From that vantage point, it could control the emerging film imagesetters and then work down to laser printers on the desktop.

After a decade of competitive typesetting machines, each with a different encoding system, and an equal number of front-end systems, each with a different user-coding system, the industry was ripe for some standards. That got us to PostScript, and once there we started to pick at it, and push it and extend it. And that's what the PDF does. With Acrobat 3.0/3.01 it extends its franchise into high-end printing while maintaining its lead in document transmission and viewing. It is now a tool for both print and nonprint communication. Cave drawings, hieroglyphics, Gutenberg Bibles, and glossy magazines are all information containers. Although the form of each container is radically different, the end purpose is the same—to carry, share, and distribute information and ideas to some audience.

Today, we call these information containers, documents. To have value, these documents and the information contained within them must be easily shared and distributed. The printing industry converts that information into paper.

The printing industry looks inward in that it looks for a method for getting information from those who create the documents in order to replicate that information on paper for distribution. There is another—and competing—world that wants to distribute the document in electronic form. The ability to share documents with a large number of people is a goal.

From movable type to phototypesetting and imagesetting to 16-page computer-to-plate signatures, to digital printing, the publishing/printing industry strives for faster and more effective ways of mass-producing documents across all media and all platforms.

In the Beginning (No, Not that Beginning)   As document creation evolved into computerized forms, document composition was primarily limited to proprietary Color Electronic Prepress Systems (CEPS). These systems, produced by companies such as Crosfield, Linotype-Hell, and Scitex were not only expensive but also difficult to use. Another drawback to these proprietary systems was the difficulty or impossibility of cross-platform file transfer. Each had a unique file system that precluded any compatibility.

The Revolution (No, Not that Revolution)   March 21, 1985 marked the date when easy, economical, digital publishing became a reality. On this day Apple, Aldus, Adobe, and Linotype unveiled a working typesetting system with an open architecture. It was based on the Macintosh Plus computer, which was one of the first personal computers with a Graphical User Interface (GUI). The output was made with either a laser printer, the Apple LaserWriter,

It is ironic that PDF started out as a tool to eliminate paper. Now it is seen as a tool for the salvation of paper.

Phototypesetters
Character-based typesetters on film or photo paper.

CRT phototypesetters
Character, line art, and some photo using cathode ray tubes for higher speeds.

Laser phototypesetters
Character, line art, and photo output via lasers.

Laser imagesetters
Character, line art, and photo in color primarily to film—capstan or drum based.

Laser imposetters
Character, line art, and photo in color for imposed flats of 4-up, 8-up and more pages.

Laser platesetters
Character, line art, and photo in color for imposed polyester and aluminum plates.

Laser imaged on-press plates
Character, line art, and photo in color for imposed plates in registration on press.

or a high-resolution laser imagesetter, the Linotronic 300, from Linotype. Both output devices operated with a new Page Description Language (PDL), called PostScript, from Adobe. The typesetting front end utilized software from Aldus PageMaker, which was a graphic-oriented page-layout program operating on the Apple Macintosh.

The strength and importance of this prepress system was that several graphic arts industry vendors worked together on an open-architecture system that would be available to everyone at a fraction of the price of a CEPS system. During the years after the introduction of the new system based on the PostScript page-imaging model, more and more printer and imagesetter manufacturers implemented PostScript into their output systems.

Further developments in the prepress industry have produced devices and systems for scanning, page assembly, and output that are compatible with the prepress system based on PostScript. As a result of these combined efforts, digital workflows have been able to significantly speed up prepress production and related turnaround times.

Today, anyone with a computer can be a publisher. The publisher can choose from a wide range of applications, typefaces, and output devices, all speaking the same tongue, PostScript.

A Little about PostScript

The idea for PostScript began in 1976 as a Computer Assisted Design (CAD) language, and a language later called Interpress at Xerox's Palo Alto Research Center for driving early laser printers. When Xerox abandoned the project, John Warnock and Chuck Geschke left PARC and formed Adobe in 1981.

Their first product was PostScript. PostScript's power lies in the fact that it is a device-independent programming language. This means that the same PostScript file can be output on virtually any printing device regardless of its resolution, on film or plate or paper. As a programming language, PostScript can support almost any level of graphic complexity. Looping routines can be set to define

PostScript Interpreter
Parses and interprets PostScript codes and operators.

Display List
A list of all of the objects on a page.

Rasterizer
Builds the page from the list of objects in the Display List and creates a page bitmap for the output device.

For a vast oversimplification we give you this 1-minute lecture.

Most imaging recorders today use a laser. The laser creates a SPOT whose size is based on the resolution of the recorder. This is the basic laser SPOT, and its width is measured in microns—thousandths of an inch. A SPOT is an addressable element and is either there or not there, zero or one, if you will. We say dots when we mean SPOTS, and resolution, the number of SPOTS in an inch is expressed as DPI (dots per inch) instead of the more accurate SPI (spots per inch).

DOTS should refer to halftone dots. There is no gray ink in a printing press or laser printer. About eight to ten of the spots are clustered to form a shape that gives the eye the illusion of gray. Halftones are measured in lines per inch, e.g., 133 line screen.

extremely complex patterns and objects for pages and documents. While looping capabilities are a boon, they can also be a bane. PostScript files could contain loops that take two hours to process without ever placing a single mark on a page. Another boon/bane is PostScript's flexibility. Aside from syntax rules, the format of PostScript is very unstructured. There are an infinite number of ways to write code to perform the same task. Some of these ways are extremely efficient, and others are not.

This relationship is best seen in the way some software applications generate "good, RIPable" PostScript data and other software generates "poor, problematic" PostScript data.

Due its unstructured nature, PostScript is an extremely page-dependent page-description language. Page-dependence means that the entire file must be interpreted prior to imaging a single page. As a result, the individual pages described within a PostScript file cannot be easily extracted from that file. In other words, an object, like a circle, placed on the first page of a document, may not be described by the PostScript code until the end of the file. The unstructured nature of PostScript and its page dependence lead to a very unpredictable file format.

The RIP

In a sense, the RIP, or raster image processor, is really the PostScript programming language compiler. It interprets the file and "executes" its commands which are to draw objects on a page. A RIP is the essential element in any form of raster-based imaging that includes computer-to-: paper, film, plate, cloth, plastic, metal, and perhaps epidermis. The end result of ripping is a bitmap for the entire image that tells the output engine where to place spots. The RIP performs three functions:

1. Interpretation of the page-description language from the application program
2. Display list generation
3. Rasterizing (screening, color transforms, and making the page bitmap)

Almost every imaging device available today is a raster imager—using spots to build text, lines, pictures, and other visual elements. Thus, every imager must, out of necessity, have a RIP, whether it is a lowly desktop printer or a giant computer-to-plate (CTP) system. And every RIP is just a little bit different. Many are based on Adobe's design, with some additional features, and some are legally derived from public information on the PostScript language. These have been called PostScript clones. Most of the small or home-office market is dominated by Hewlett-Packard's PCL printer language, a PostScript "wanna be" that has never been used for high-resolution printing and publishing.

When you send a document to a printer, the RIP does its job and out come the pages. But today's digital workflow is much more complex, and multiple rippings are often the norm. In a CTP workflow, the document might be ripped to a color printer for color proofing, ripped to an imposition proofer to verify layout, ripped to a remote proofer for color checking, and finally ripped to the platesetter. In most cases this involves four different RIPs and four different imaging engines. And four chances for variation. Over time, two paths to RIP development took place by:

- Adobe licensees
- Adobe clones

In both cases, the RIP includes a core set of functions based on the PostScript interpreter. From there developers have added increasing functionality. Here are some of them:

- More efficient graphics handling
- More efficient picture handling
- Halftone screening with different dot structures, angles, and algorithms
- Stochastic screening
- Trapping
- Imposition
- Statistics and other reports
- Color management functions
- Other workflow features

PIXELS are spots with gray levels. On a monitor the intensity of the beam controls the amount of light energy to create a level of gray. Thus red, green, and blue pixels are combined at varying levels to display a picture. On color laser printers the intensity of the laser does the same thing for yellow, magenta, cyan, and black. A pixel is 100% dark or some percentage of gray. Some laser printers have both spi (spots per inch) and bit depth for gray levels. These are composite printers, as are all toner-based color printers. Film and plate printers output bi-level—zero or one—spots, which form type and lines and, through halftone dots, pictures.

RIP—Raster Image Processor

The RIP, or raster image processor, is really the PostScript program-ming-language compil-er. It interprets the file and "executes" its com-mands, which are to draw objects on a page. A RIP is the essential step in any form of raster-based imaging, which includes comput-er-to-: paper, film, plate, cloth, plastic, metal, or whatever. The end result of ripping is a rasterized bitmap for the entire page image that tells the output engine where to place spots. The RIP performs three func-tions:

1. Interpretation of the page description lan-guage code from the application program
2. Display-list genera-tion
3. Rasterizing (screen-ing, color transforms, and making the bitmap)

Almost every imaging device available today is a raster imager—using spots to build text, lines, photos, etc. Thus, every imager must, out of necessity, have a RIP, whether it is a lowly desktop printer or a

RIP Evolution

The PostScript page-description language was developed to commu-nicate the appearance of text, graphical shapes, and images to raster-based output devices equipped with a PostScript interpreter. Post-Script has become predominant in the computer-printing world be-cause of its device-independence. Device-independence means that the image (the page to print or display) is defined without any refer-ence to specific device features (printer resolution, page size, etc.). A single page description can be used on any PostScript-compatible printer from a 300-dpi laser printer to a $3,000^+$-dpi imagesetter or platesetter. In our opinion, another reason for its success is that it supports high-end printing. Computer-to-plate and digital printing as we know them could not have developed without a standardized page-description language.

Most applications that can print to a PostScript printer also let you "print" to a file. Printing to a file means that the application (or the computer running the application, with the help of a PostScript dri-ver) converts the job data into PostScript commands and saves the data as a file instead of transmitting the code over a cable to a print-er. You can then download the file to any PostScript printer to print it out. Downloading is different from printing in that no data con-version (from job data to PostScript) takes place; the file is merely sent to the printer. This allows you to directly send PostScript streams to printers, without opening any application program. The PostScript file contains all font and image data and can be stored on a disk and sent to a graphic-arts service. Most computer platforms have a variety of PostScript downloaders available.

PostScript Printer Description Files　Each application usu-ally creates and stores files in its own internal format, not PostScript. When you print a job, the application uses a PostScript driver to translate its data into PostScript. Depending on what computer or application you use, the printer driver could be installed as part of the application, or more commonly, the printer driver is installed in the System folder for any application to use.

PostScript is device independent…to a point. When you print, you print to a specific printer that has very specific features—such as certain resolutions, page sizes, minimum margins, choice of paper trays, etc. Although the PostScript driver can send the PostScript job to any printer, it can't specify a tabloid page for a printer that does not have a tabloid tray, for example. To access features specific to the printer, PostScript uses PPDs (PostScript Printer Description files), which are stored in the System folder. Some printer-specific information that a PPD might include:

- Input paper trays
- Page size definitions
- Print areas for each page size
- Output paper trays
- Duplexing (double-sided printing)
- Default resolution
- Resolutions available
- Black-and-white or color output
- Halftone screening functions
- Default screen angles
- Screen frequency combinations
- Custom screening definition
- Default transfer functions
- Default font

QuarkXPress also uses another file to relate printer-specific information: a Printer Description File (PDF), which is not to be confused with the subject of this book, the Portable Document Format, also a PDF. (Confusing, isn't it?) QuarkXPress uses data from both the PPD and PDF to generate PostScript for output.

At print time, you select the PostScript output device and select a PPD (or a PDF in QuarkXPress). If you later want to print the same job to a different printer, all you need to do is select a different printer with a different PPD.

PostScript Interpreters and RIPs   When the RIP receives the PostScript file for processing, it needs to convert that file to

giant computer-to-plate (CTP) system. And every RIP is just a little bit different. Many are based on Adobe's design, with some additional features, and some are legally derived from public information on the PostScript language. These have been called PostScript clones.

The small or home office market is dominated by Hewlett-Packard's PCL printer language which has almost never been used for high-end printing.

A RIP includes a core set of functions based on a PostScript interpreter. From there, developers have added increasing functionality. Here are some of them:
- *Efficient graphics handling*
- *Better picture handling*
- *Halftone screening with different dot structures, angles, and algorithms*
- *Stochastic screening*
- *Color transforms*
- *Trapping*
- *Imposition*
- *Statistics and other reports*

Today, many workflows use the Display List as the format of choice. In every case, it provides a flatter, more efficient file that can be handled automatically.

The Acrobat PDF is actually the Display List, which is why new workflows are evolving to apply it.

Bitmaps
A bitmap image is an image that is defined digitally by a number of pixels in a rectangular array. Because computers are binary entities, they must break up images into a map of small pieces, called picture elements, or pixels. All images that are scanned into a computer are bitmap images— whether black-and-white line drawings, or black-and-white or color photographs.

Monochrome bitmap images are the simplest and the smallest in file size. Scanned black-and-white line drawings are monochrome bitmaps. Each pixel of the bitmap can be either black or white (on or off), so only two bits of computer information are required to define these bitmaps.

bitmap data. PostScript printers, whether 300-dpi laser printers or $3,000^+$-dpi platesetters, need a PostScript interpreter to translate the PostScript code into the bitmap data needed to print or image the page. Raster data prints a page as a pattern of tiny printer spots. To place these spots, the RIP maps out the page as a grid of spot locations—this is called a bitmap. Any specific spot can be defined or located by its address based on x, y coordinates. To image a page, the output engine either images a spot or does not—zero or one, on or off. Data of this type is called binary because only two values are used. The term bilevel bitmap means spots. Composite data means pixels—spots with levels of gray.

Bitmap data is what the output engine or recorder needs. But PostScript really describes pages not as a table of spots but as a series of mathematically described shapes or objects. It takes a lot less data to describe a page by its shape, size, and location than by listing the state (on or off) of each individual pixel in the image. The PostScript interpreter converts the PostScript code to a list of objects. Then it rasterizes the objects to create the bitmap for actual outputting. The resolution of the output device determines how many spots are needed to image a page.

PostScript Level 2   Since the introduction of the PostScript language in 1985, Adobe and other developers have created improvements and extensions to it. Color extensions were added in 1988 to better support printing color images. PostScript Level 2 was announced in 1990. It integrated the original PostScript with all previous language extensions and added new features. Included in PostScript Level 2:

- Color Separation: Lets a user send a full-color job, not already separated, to the PostScript Level 2 interpreter, which converts the one-page color job into four files: one for each process color (cyan, magenta, yellow, and black).
- Composite fonts: Type 1 PostScript fonts can encode 256 distinct characters, but a typical Japanese font has over 7,000 characters. The composite font technology included in PostScript Level 2 supports these larger fonts.

- Data compression: Network transmission is a large percentage of the actual processing time for a job. PostScript Level 2 supports several data-compression schemes, such as LZW, JPEG, and RLE. Jobs sent over the network are sent in a compressed format, then decompressed by the PostScript interpreter. The amount of data transmitted is reduced, speeding up the network transmission portion of the job.

For this reason, they are also called bilevel bitmaps.

Hardware and Software RIPs

There are so-called hardware RIPs and software RIPs. The distinction is not always clear. Initially, all RIPs were proprietary, with a CPU, disk, RIP software, and related hardware enclosed in a cabinet and attached to an imaging recorder. There was no monitor and no keyboard, although a keypad and LCD panel on the recorder did allow some level of interface. You connected your network to the RIP and away you went. Then someone decided that they could sell you the RIP software and you could install it in your own computer. Usually, a special computer board and cable to connect to the imager were supplied. The latter approach was called a software RIP. Technically, however, all RIPs are software RIPs. No matter what hardware is used, there is usually some proprietary element, if only the interface board that connects the computer to the imager.

Configurable PostScript Interpreter (CPSI) CPSI (Configurable PostScript Interpreter) from Adobe is the basis for many RIPs from many vendors. It is guaranteed to be fully PostScript Level 2-compatible since it comes from Adobe. Developers can set it up to generate output for specific output devices, such as imagesetters, color proofers, laser printers, high-speed printers, large-format imagesetters, plotters, and computer-to-plate devices. CPSI can be modified to drive a complete range of PostScript devices. CPSI uses the host workstation's operating system and can be used in RIPs for Macintosh, Power Macintosh, SPARCstations, and Windows NT as well as others. Although the core of the RIP is CPSI,

What is Adobe's CPSI? Adobe CPSI (Configurable PostScript Software Interpreter) is the core software RIP Adobe sells to OEMs, and which OEMs can include in a deliverable product. How do Harlequin ScriptWorks 5.0 and Adobe CPSI differ? Both are aimed at OEMs and both include a PostScript language interpreter and a renderer. But the similarity ends there. CPSI does not include a user interface or a throughput controller or any form of media management. It has no drivers for specific devices, no color management options, no TIFF/IT-P1 support, etc. Adobe CPSI is a software kernel that requires development as a complete product by an OEM.

each RIP vendor has its own user interface and device drivers. The user interface lets you tell the RIP how jobs output: You want to use 2,400 dpi, produce a negative image, have pages automatically color-separated, and have the imagesetter punch each page (if it can). The user interface provides status information: Job 1 took 4 minutes 10 seconds to RIP and contained no PostScript errors, as an example.

In 1991, Adobe introduced PixelBurst, a NuBus-based card co-processor with an application-specific integrated circuit (ASIC) that speeds PostScript processing by freeing up the main CPU more quickly, accelerating halftone screening and generation of text and line art—particularly at high resolutions or when outputting large images. It is the basis for many RIPs.

Since its introduction in 1985 when Adobe PostScript software helped spawn the desktop publishing revolution, Adobe has continued to drive the industry forward with powerful printing solutions. The current version of the PostScript page description language developed by Adobe is publicly available to software and RIP developers. This has led to its adoption and recognition as a virtual industry standard. Although Adobe created the original specification for PostScript and then Level 2, other RIP vendors were the first to ship PostScript Level 2 language-compatible RIPs capable of both high and low resolutions running on all major platforms and operating systems. Some non-Adobe RIPs already have features that have not been announced as part of PostScript 3, such as support for symmetrical multiprocessing (SMP), TIFF/IT-P1 input format processing, integrated color management, and PostScript display-list access and editing. Adobe's typical upgrade cycle is about eighteen months.

PostScript 3

In September 1996, Adobe Systems Incorporated announced its newest printing-systems solution, which includes the next generation of Adobe PostScript called PostScript 3 (the word "level" has been dropped). Adobe's integrated printing system solution focuses on changing the printing experience by allowing OEM customers to build best-in-class printing solutions and providing users the ability to print complex graphics and Web content, when and where they need it. Adobe has gone beyond offering a page-description language to providing a total systems solution for delivering and printing digital documents.

Adobe has developed an advanced level of functionality in Adobe PostScript 3 to accommodate the new digital document creation process, which includes varying sources, complex composition, and virtually unlimited destinations. Users are now accessing content for use in digital documents from varying sources including electronic mail, Web pages, Intranets, on-line services, content providers, and digital cameras. Document composition now includes not only text but also complex graphics, clip art, corporate logos, Internet content, multiple fonts, scanned images, and color. Finally, the digital document's destination can be to printing systems anywhere in the world, such as personal printers, network printers, service bureaus, pay-for-print providers, or data warehouses for electronic archival.

Enhanced Image Technology ensures that documents print faster, easier, and with optimal quality. A key benefit to the user is that Enhanced Image Technology recognizes image objects and automatically optimizes processing to deliver the highest possible quality, and at the same time speed return to application. Adobe PostScript 3 will include new imaging features that support the increasingly complex documents available via the Internet, support for three-dimensional images, photo-quality grayscaling, smooth gradients in graphic objects, image compositing, and full-color spectrums.

Adobe PostScript 3 with Advanced Page Processing increases the performance of an imaging system. As components in a document become more complex, the printing system will process each component as a separate object in order to optimize imaging throughput. PostScript 3 will support direct processing of Web content, including HTML and PDF. Advanced Page Processing will also extend the resident font set to provide compatibility with the resident fonts of all leading operating systems, enhancing performance by reducing font downloading. PostScript 3 provides users with a more robust ability to manage individual pages within a document, thereby improving control over the printing process.

RIPs today

On early imagesetters and on most color copiers with RIPs, you will find a box with a set of plugs in the back and a small liquid crystal display on the front. Inside is a CPU, a disk, on which the RIP software was loaded, with special hardware in some cases for faster processing, and a special interface board to move data to the imaging engine very quickly.

However, most of these "boxes" have been replaced by an entire computer system, with monitor, mouse, and keyboard. Most of the other "stuff" is pretty much the same as the "box." Software upgrades are easier and the software itself is protected with a "lock" or "dongle" that has an encoded serial number.

Thus, the difference between a hardware RIP (the "box") and a software RIP (the whole computer) is pretty academic today.

What is new about PostScript 3 and high-end printing?
- *Smooth shading renders gradient fills at the resolution of the printing system.*
- *Selectable separations enable color separations to be printed, even from low-end monochrome printing systems.*
- *More gray levels provide monochrome desktop printing systems with the ability to print photoquality grayscales (up to 256 levels of gray).*
- *For high-resolution printing, delivers photoquality grayscales and 4,096 levels of each colorant.*
- *In-RIP trapping.*
- *HiFi color for more vibrant hues and richer colors.*
- *Improved color control provides greater control with respect to overprint between color components.*
- *Idiom recognition converts less efficient legacy constructs into higher quality, faster Language 3 constructs.*
- *Fast image printing enables fast draft mode and near-final quality raster-image printing.*
- *Improved font technology and extended font set*

Adobe's NetWorks System improves ease of use, ease of connection, and ease of printer management all in one environment through Adobe PostScript 3. A printer with NetWorks functionality will include a printer-based Web page, Web-based printer management, printing directly from the printer's Web page, support for all industry standard remote-management technologies, and a single-step CD-ROM installer for all drivers, fonts, and value-added software. Adobe's NetWorks System ultimately allows users to leverage the power and benefits of the Internet.

Adobe PostScript 3 also offers what Adobe calls "Planet Ready Printing" to allow local language needs of users anywhere in the world. Users will easily display and print any language with any PostScript 3 printer. OEMs will develop complete imaging systems that are savvy to localized demands of language and usage. Specific features include drivers that are tightly integrated into the operating system, be it Microsoft Windows 3.1, Microsoft Windows 95 or 98, Microsoft Windows 2000, or Apple Macintosh, and full support of international font requirements.

Adobe has completed Adobe PostScript 3 language-feature development and is now beginning its system-integration process. The product schedule included two internal quality assurance cycles before system delivery to OEM-printing system manufacturers and third-party development partners in December 1996. In the second half of 1997 Adobe disclosed the Adobe PostScript 3 operators and language-specific features. They were published in a large document that appeared on the Adobe Web site (in PDF form of course.)

Extreme and the Future of RIPs   The high-speed data requirements of automated digital presses, large-format film imposetters, and computer-to-plate systems demand radical changes in RIP and workflow architectures. Developers are also trying to eliminate PostScript-processing bottlenecks and accelerate deadline-production times. RIP suppliers have been converting PostScript into contone (CT) and linework (LW) files via proprietary methods or converting PostScript into some editable internal format in an attempt to make the RIPing process more efficient.

There are lots of alternatives out there. Covalent Systems' Job Monitor Protocol is a standard framework for collecting data from jobs as they pass through a series of steps and for transferring the data to business systems. Prepress production environments could collect critical information, such as how much time was spent on image-editing at one workstation and color correction at another, and to transfer it to a business system for analysis and billing. All of this is available now if you stick with the selection of proprietary systems and custom interfaces between them. Another proposed standard, CIP3, covers the interaction among processes at the front-end prepress operation, the press itself, and the back-end finishing operation. CIP3 is being promoted by Heidelberg, with the support of other press and finishing-equipment suppliers, in addition to front-end system vendors such as Agfa.

Adobe's contribution to an ideal digital workflow is a printing architecture known as Extreme, which was formerly named Supra, which uses PDF as its backbone. Demands for last-minute changes in pages fosters a concept known as "late binding." RIP developers are working toward a format that allows data to be changed after it has been interpreted by the RIP but before it becomes the bitmap. These changes take account of different printing or proofing requirements, or nonprint delivery.

Adobe's Extreme RIP architecture is a major step in RIP evolution. It is built around the 1.3 version of Adobe's Portable Document Format. PostScript is an interpretive programming language; PDF is a compact, noninterpretive format designed for fast imaging to a screen. PDF has lacked the ability to handle high-resolution images easily and to handle screening for print—both of these are included within Extreme. Extreme also connects Web and print publishing, as both will use the new version of PDF used as the plug-in to Web browsers.

The PostScript of the Red Book is fading away. Extreme ensures that PostScript document files can be processed as separate but complete pages. Multipage jobs can be processed by several RIPs simultaneously. Extreme is aimed primarily at high-volume applications, and many firms are supporting Extreme.

Extreme architecture
A PostScript Extreme printing system can take in PostScript or PDF files. When it takes in a file, the "Co-ordinator" evaluates the file to see what format it's in. If it's a PDF file, the Coordinator sends it to a "PDF Page Store" device (a disk or file system). If it's a PostScript file, the Coordinator sends it to a "Normalizer" component that converts it to PDF, and then sends it to the "PDF Page Store" device. Thus, all files are in PDF form.

From there, Adobe PostScript Extreme feeds individual pages to as many as ten PostScript RIPs (which contain converters that quickly convert the PDF pages back to PostScript to rasterize them), staggering them in special ways if necessary to accommodate duplexing and other needs. Once they're rasterized into bitmaps, Adobe PostScript Extreme sends the pages to an Assembler and then to the print engine. Because PDF files create pages as individual elements, they can be handled very efficiently.

Agfa, Autologic, Creo-Heidelberg, and Monotype have already delivered the capability for allocating whole jobs among multiple RIPs and ripped work among multiple imagesetters. The industry is getting excited because of Extreme's front-end processing.

Working with PostScript

Not all PostScript is equal; code generated by Photoshop conforms to Document Structuring Conventions (DSC), some from Quark-XPress does not. Page structure can't be easily determined. Extreme converts such files automatically into PDF format, allowing separate processing. Extreme incorporates both Adobe PostScript language and Adobe Portable Document Format (PDF) for production printers, and Adobe PrintMill, an Intranet-based printing and printer management solution.

When you create a page in QuarkXPress or PageMaker, you are interfacing with the program as displayed on the screen. The GUI describes the page on screen for the user. However, when you click Print, it is PostScript code that defines that page as it is sent to the printer or imagesetter. You can even save the PostScript file to disk and read it (if you can decipher it). However, a page described in PostScript is nearly uneditable without an understanding of the programming language itself. Admittedly, there are unique people out there who can edit PostScript.

PostScript is a voluminous file format. Placing a single "a" on a Quark XPress page and "printing" the page to an ASCII file produces at least sixteen pages of 10/10 type. Not very digestible for humans, unless you speak geek.

Outputting PostScript   There are four choices for outputting a file from an application:

1. Click Print and send the file to a printer on your in-house network. This is a great option if you're publishing a single copy for yourself. Or even a couple of dozen copies for the staff.

2. Send the application file to an outside service, but make

sure you send the image files and all of the screen and printer fonts. This file can be changed by the service bureau, making its integrity questionable.

Actually most of us don't need the job "yesterday." We need it "two weeks ago."

This second approach not only opens the door for further unpredictability but it also raises some tricky legal issues. Due to font licensing, the service bureau must install the fonts you use and/or supply, print your job, and immediately remove those fonts from their system. This must be done for each job and each time the file is printed.

What if the service bureau has purchased a license to the same font? For instance, suppose that you supply a document which uses Garamond. Whose version of Garamond is it—Adobe's, ITC's, Monotype's, or some overnight type house's? If you don't specify and/or the service bureau doesn't have the correct version of your typeface, a font substitution will occur. Possible repercussions of an improper font substitution could be the reflowing of text, sometimes destroying the original design. Or maybe you like Courier, the ultimate font substitution. Service bureaus deal with application files because they can open them, preflight them, and make changes.

3. Save the file to disk as PostScript code, which incorporates the images and fonts, and send it to an output service. This is a viable option if you have a very large external storage device to save all of that PostScript information. (Remember, a single "a" generates sixteen plus pages of PostScript text. Well, that's not really fair, because the sixteen pages of code could support many text pages. But, PostScript code is voluminous, never the less.)

A drawback to this method is the lack of "correctability." If the correct page-setup options were not chosen at the time of PostScript generation, the page may not reproduce as desired. Often, designers don't know the specifications of the imagesetter or output device of the service bureau. Without this information, specifications regarding page size, crop marks, line-screen ruling, and many other vari-

PDF, PPD, and PDF: What is what?

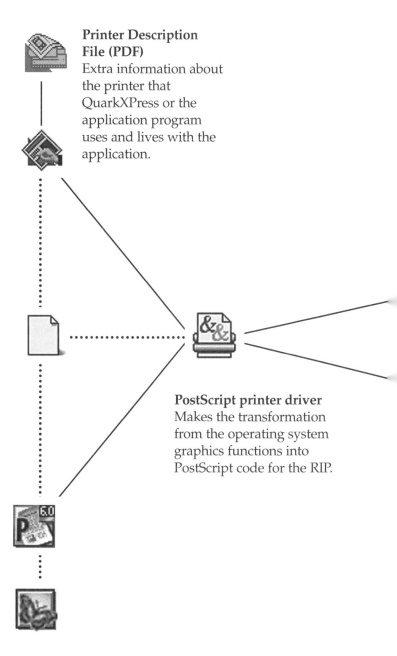

Printer Description File (PDF)
Extra information about the printer that QuarkXPress or the application program uses and lives with the application.

Printer Description File (PPD)
Information about the printer that any application can use because it lives at the System level.

PostScript printer driver
Makes the transformation from the operating system graphics functions into PostScript code for the RIP.

PostScript File
Includes the same information that would be sent to a PostScript printer but saved to disk.

Acrobat Distiller
Application that interprets PostScript data and builds a Portable Document Format file; like a RIP but not a RIP.

Portable Document Format (PDF)
A device-independent document format.

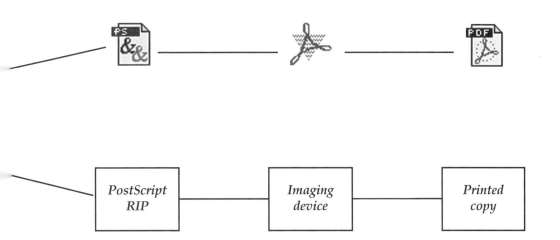

Figure 2-1
Relationship between PDF, PPD, and the other PDF.

ables can't be set. Once the PostScript file for that document is generated, it's too late.

What if only a part of a page or a graphic created in a drawing program needs to be placed into a page-layout application like QuarkXPress, InDesign, or PageMaker? Thus was born the Encapsulated PostScript (EPS) file—a file representing one page with (or in the early days without) a preview image. This allows you to save a graphic in a standardized form and place it into a composite document where it can be scaled and manipulated to fit. However, the EPS file does not save font data and many artists have seen their beautiful graphics output with Courier because the original font was not available at the RIP. The EPS was portable only to a point. Adobe Illustrator now saves EPS with the font data as does Acrobat 4, and the new Placed PDF could replace EPS.

PostScript Conclusions   As a platform-independent-page description language, PostScript has emerged as a de facto standard. Today, PostScript accounts for 95 percent or more of the final output of all commercial publications. On the downside, PostScript is extremely variable and page dependent.

There's no doubt that PostScript has brought on revolutionary advances, but with every revolution comes the need for further refinement. Even Adobe admits that PostScript has many deficiencies for the role it is currently playing. The use of PostScript has far surpassed Adobe's original intention, and thus, they are in the midst of solving problems and advancing their core technology in order to fulfill the expectations of today's digital workflow demands. The wide variety of applications, platforms, and typefaces has caused many headaches for the publishing industry. There are just too many places for things to go wrong.

While you can easily move documents around by e-mail, network, or disk, you can't assume that everybody has the right fonts on their system or that they have the right program to open your document or even (in a cross-platform environment) the right setup to receive the document. You could spend a lot of time and money installing the same software and fonts, plus the requisite extra hard-disk space and

RAM, on every system to allow document portability—and then train people on each program used to create the documents in the first place. Of course, this setup is inefficient and you don't have the capital to implement it, and neither does anyone else.

PostScript serves its purpose as a way to describe document pages in a design-rich fashion; however, in today's world of ever-increasing efficiency, the need for speed, and the customer's insistence on jobs being printed "yesterday," research and development into document handling is a never-ending process. Files need to be transferred from place to place, quickly, predictably, and efficiently. With the increasing use of digital presses, CTP technology, and completely digital workflows, the need for a platform-independent digital file transfer standards is becoming more and more necessary.

That brings us to the fourth alternative for communicating with graphic service providers and the outside world, the Portable Document Format.

> 4. Create a PDF of your file.

First, let us look into PostScript a little more. See the boxes on the next two pages for a little more information on PostScript than you may wish to know.

We were asked once when the digital age began for the printing industry. Our reply: March 21, 1985, when PostScript was introduced.

More about PostScript than you may wish to know:

When you create a page in QuarkXPress or PageMaker, you are interfacing with the program as displayed on the screen. Underlying what you see is what you get, and that is PostScript code. When you click Print, it is the PostScript code that is sent to the printer or imagesetter. You can even save the PostScript file to disk and read it. Here is some PostScript code. First, header information is output:

```
%!PS-Adobe-2.0
%%Title: PDF intro
%%Creator: QuarkXPress 3.33
%%CreationDate: Tuesday, November 27, 2000
%%Pages: (atend)
%%BoundingBox: ? ? ? ?
%%PageBoundingBox: 30 31 582 761
%%For: Onamor Knarf
%%DocumentProcSets: "(AppleDict md)" 71 0
%% © Copyright Apple Computer, Inc. 1989-92 All Rights Reserved.
%%EndComments
%%BeginProcSet: "(AppleDict md)" 71 0
```

In this case, the system sets up some shortcuts to reduce the verbose PostScript program commands to shorter versions, e.g., the command "moveto" becomes "/m".

```
/z/setmatrix load def      /m/moveto load def
/t/translate load def      /rm/rmoveto load def
/S/scale load def          /l/lineto load def
/g/gsave load def          /rl/rlineto load def
/G/grestore load def       /np/newpath load def
/H/setgray load def        /cp/closepath load def
```

Then, font data is loaded (this is just a snippet):

373A767D4B7FD94FE5903B7014B1B8D3BED02632C855D56F458B118ACF3AF73FC4EF5E81F5749
042B5F9CF1016D093B75F250B7D8280B2EACE05A37037F7BDF6E12226D7D4E2DF2C52FAFD5F
D40FE72A0D3AC4BD485D8369D4C87636E920D1DAF222D92155A9CB1667E715F0B82799B37CC8
F5B32B74B39CF494536DC39C7EF04A7BCB29E2CEC79073CADCCFB23B4AA1363F8

Every character in the fonts is defined:

```
/Adieresis/Aring/Ccedilla/Eacute/Ntilde/Odieresis/Udieresis/aacute/agrave/acircumflex/adieresis/atilde/aring
/ccedilla/eacute/egrave/ecircumflex/edieresis/iacute/igrave/icircumflex/idieresis/ntilde/oacute/ograve/ocir-
cumflex/odieresis/otilde/uacute/ugrave/ucircumflex/udieresis/dagger/degree/cent/sterling/section/bullet/par
agraph/germandbls/registered/copyright
```

Both PostScript and PDF use a notation known as "postfix." That is where the name PostScript came from. Postfix is an old mathematical notation, sometimes called reverse "Polish" notation. The "action" indicator, usually called the "operator," comes at the right-hand end of the expression (that is, after the variables) and complex expressions can be written without the use of parentheses. There is also a notation known as "pre-fix" notation, where the operator comes first. Normal notation (e.g., a + b) is called "infix" notation because the operator is between or within the expression.

Then the position and copy are set:

43 533.53 m 3.02 -.18 2 19.3 (RIP)d
67.39 h 3.02 -.18 23 101.5 (is just a little bit dif)d
179.48 h 3.02 -.18 2 14.48 (fer)d
193.2 h 3.02 -.18 11 67.38 (ent. Many ar)d
264.25 h (e)M
43 548.16 m 1.55 -.18 8 50.33 (based on)d
266.01 h (-)M
43 562.79 m 0 -.18 12 65.04 (tional featur)d
105.49 h 0 -.18 14 81.86 (es, and some ar)d
184.43 h 0 -.18 16 88.46 (e legally derived)d
43 577.42 m 2.59 -.18 1 8.73 (fr)d

The default measurement system in both PostScript and PDF is in units of 1/72 of an inch. The starting point is in the lower-left corner of the page or drawing area. An 8.5x11" inch page is 612 units horizontally and 792 units vertically— just like graph paper.

PDF objects are a construct that the PostScript Language does not have. The ability to randomly access portions of a PDF document and the page independence of PDF pages are based on the object structuring of PDF.

Color space resources are often called color "profiles." This terminology has been promoted by the International Color Consortium or ICC. The color-space resources in PDF and PostScript serve the same function and are roughly equivalent to ICC profiles. They aren't literally the same but contain the same or equivalent information. It is easy to convert from a PDF color space resource to an ICC profile and the other way as well. Most color management systems consider color spaces as being derived from and belonging to color devices. The material in this PDF file is associated with two devices, one L°a°b° and one an RGB device. Most color-management discussion and color-management software consider a whole job to be in one color space. This is a mistake that Adobe PostScript and PDF do not make. Any material in either language can be specified with respect to any color space.

The objects can refer or point to one another to form complex relationships and data structures. Streams of arbitrary unstructured data can be defined. The cross-reference table that occurs at the end of the PDF file allows programs to read selected objects out of the file at arbitrary positions. The objects don't have be in any particular order or place within the file. The cross-reference table determines where each object has ended up in the file. This notation is powerful enough to represent many other kinds of structured data beside a PDF document. In fact, Adobe has begun to use the notation for at least two other purposes: one for FDF files to hold the field name, field value pairs that result from filling in an Acrobat Form, and the second which is the PJTF or Portable Job Ticket Format used to control the workflow and post-processing.

Structured Data Format (SDF)

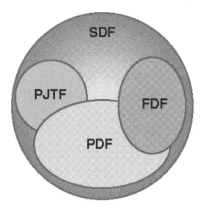

PDF files require that they have a /Root that points to a /Catalog that points to a /Pages object that points to the documents pages. Not all uses of this notation should have to follow those document rules. In fact, both the FDF and the PJTF do not. So to be perfectly logical, each of PDF, FDF, and PJTF are using a notation and specializing it for their particular needs. Dr. Jim King has coined the term SDF or Structured Data Format for the general use of this notation and reserve PDF for the specialization having to do with representing documents in this particular way. Thus, this diagram.

Box 2-1

From PostScript to Workflow

The Adobe imaging model is a way to represent text, graphics, and images in a coherent and consistent manner. It was originally implemented in the PostScript printing language and is now at the core of Adobe's printing and publishing technologies, including PostScript, Adobe's Portable Document Format (PDF), and application products such as Adobe InDesign. Adobe PostScript is both the page-description language that describes the format of a printed page and the system that understands that language and converts it into the pixels that are imaged onto output media. As a general-purpose programming language, PostScript contains procedures, variables, and control constructs that must be interpreted to render its page description. This processing is required to be in sequential order such that PostScript files are streamed into an output device from the first byte to the last. This also means that PostScript files are not inherently page independent, since imaging operations performed on the last page of a document may depend on the "graphics state" settings that have accumulated since the first page.

The Adobe PostScript language has become the standard printing technology for producing high-quality output. It is a completely device-independent page-description language. This means that the same file can be printed on desktop laser printers that cost a few hundred dollars or on high-end printing systems that cost hundreds of thousands of dollars, and the document will always print with the highest quality achievable by the particular output device.

The biggest issues facing prepress shops are predictability, reliability, and consistency of workflow. Most documents are delivered to prepress or print shops today in the authoring-application format. Once received, the file enters a workflow process based on the Adobe PostScript language or proprietary formats. Adobe PostScript technology was initially developed as a language for describing pages and controlling printers, but its flexibility enabled it to become the data format for carrying all prepress and production information. With PostScript technology's flexibility can come unpredictability, in part because so many different applications generate PostScript in so many different ways, and PostScript page descriptions can be arbitrarily complex. A typical imposition application may have to understand 200 or more different application versions of PostScript output. It is not uncommon for prepress application developers to spend half of their development time just keeping up with the latest application output streams.

Each prepress application must read in the entire PostScript file to understand its contents before being able to act on that file. Once any changes/updates are made, a new PostScript file is streamed out of the application. This is a very memory-intensive and storage-intensive operation. Production workflows built around PostScript technology have to deal with both the complexity of the desired product and the arbitrariness of the data stream.

PDF Is Different   PDF files are highly structured, and general programming constructs are not permitted. As a result, the imaging operations are usually much simpler. A PDF file can be thought of as a database of objects with direct access to each object, and each page of a PDF document is independent of the others. If a prepress application uses PDF files instead of the PostScript language as its input and output, it is able to directly access only the information needed and incrementally update the file. The prepress application also has just one format to understand—PDF. The apparent arbitrariness of PostScript technology is eliminated, so PDF provides the foundation for a print production system that delivers consistent, predictable results. That is why new workflows are going PDF.

One way in which many professional graphics service bureaus are using PDF is to build predictable PostScript language files to either print directly or put through a prepress workflow. They use the authoring application to output it to the PostScript language, convert it to PDF using the Acrobat Distiller, view it as a soft proof, and then output to the PostScript language using Acrobat. What results is a reliable PostScript file ready to be RIPed or processed by a prepress application. This process is particularly helpful when PostScript files are received for printing and the driver used in the creation of the file does not match the device configuration of the final output device. The process of going to PDF and then back to PostScript technology enables the service bureau to better control the creation of the PostScript language file.

As more users become familiar with the benefits of Acrobat and more applications support Acrobat, production printers will standardize on PDF as the delivery mechanism for documents headed for print. There is really no other alternative for the standardized transfer of documents for viewing and printing that incorporates all aspects of predictability, editability, and compactness. PDF is the present and future of workflow.

Acrobat and PDF   PDF 1.0 and 1.1 documents (Acrobat 1.0 and 2.1) should not be considered to be prepress documents. If they behave in your prepress environment, then you should consider yourself lucky.

Distiller 3.01 (PDF 1.2) documents behave consistently. You know what you are getting. Most people would say that its biggest problem area is fonts. Contrary to industry myth, the bulk of prepress functionality was added in PDF 1.2 and Acrobat 3. Many production applications were and continue to be served by this version. One must remember that Distiller 3.x is essentially a PostScript Level 2 interpreter. If you are dealing in PostScript 3 constructs, such as smooth shading, spot color blends, or duotones (DeviceN), then you really have no choice but to work with Distiller 4.

Distiller 4 supports new capabilities, but it messed up in some areas. It did not support the prepress application as expected. It still produced real PDF documents. Some of the issues can be correct with PitStop. Acrobat 4.05 will produce better quality PDFs. Distiller 4.05 should also win due to its treatment of the infamous "font embed" flag.

If you are looking to use ICC profiles, then you definitely want Distiller 4.05 documents (PDF 1.3). If you are trying to avoid ICC profiles, then you probably want PDF 1.2 documents, unless you are looking for PostScript 3-like features. Then, you want PDF 1.3. In our opinion, stay with the latest version—Adobe Acrobat 4.05 which is PDF 1.3.

PostScript Errors

These are specific errors detected by a PostScript printer that make it stop printing. This won't help you if the results are complete but not what you expect. PostScript errors are reported in various ways. Before you can get anywhere with a problem you need to know the error name and offending command.

Accurate information is the first step in solving any problem. Sometimes, the information appears on a printed sheet, and this often has supplementary information. If a problem is not exactly repeatable, you probably have a problem where files are being corrupted. This could be on your disk, as a result of cabling, or, if the printer is connected by serial rather than parallel cable, the serial port setup could be wrong. Corruption can occur even before the file is printed—as it is read from a network. Sometimes, switching a printer off and on will make a difference.

Checking for Corrupt Graphics   Check the error descriptions below to see whether corruption is listed as a possible cause. If so, and you are composing pages on screen, check for corrupt graphics (especially EPS graphics).

1. Make a copy of your file (important!)
2. Remove all of the graphics. If the file prints up to a particular page, concentrate on that page. It doesn't matter how small a graphic is.
3. If you find that removing all the graphics from a particular page means it now prints (albeit incomplete), add the graphics one at a time. If there are a great many, try to isolate them by making a fresh copy of the original and removing half of them. If the file still fails, remove half of the remainder, and so forth.
4. If the file apparently works with either half of the graphics removed, first check very carefully that you have not been overlooking a particular graphic. If you are sure, you are probably running out of printer memory.

Common Errors

Error -8133: Sometimes reported by Macintosh users. This just means "a printing problem occurred." It is no help.

configurationerror: Occurs when a device request cannot be satisified. For instance, A4 page size, but there is no A4 paper.

dictfull: A dictionary (used to store PostScript variables) is full. Some printers allow the size of userdict to be increased. Should not occur with PostScript level 2.

dictstackoverflow: Too many dictionaries used simultaneously. Usually caused by nested graphics (one graphic placed inside another, inside another). Simplify.

dictstackunderflow: The program used an end instruction at the wrong time. Corruption.

execstackoverflow: Too many active subroutines. Rarely seen; unlikely to occur in PostScript Level 2.

invalidaccess: Program tried to access data that is not allowed, like the inside of a font. Rarely seen.

invalidexit: Program used exit where it is not allowed. Rare.

invalidfileaccess: Tried to access a file in a way not allowed (e.g., write a read-only file; create a file in a read-only directory).

invalidfont: Something wrong with a font. Try using different fonts to identify which one is at fault.

ioerror: A real I/O error may have occured (e.g., a disk fault, or a problem controlling a printer). In Level 2 PostScript this can also be bad information for a filter, so this could mean corruption of some kind.

limitcheck: The printer has reached an internal limit. Some limits are fixed, some depend on memory. Most common cause is a path too complicated: for instance a cutout, or a drawn outline; also outlined text. Using the "magic wand" in Adobe Photoshop it is possible to get a very complicated clip path. The limitcheck error can also mean that there is not enough memory to do the page size and resolution requested.

nocurrentpoint: A program tried to do something relative

to the current point, but it wasn't set to anything yet. For instance, attempting to write text, without saying where on the page it is to go. This is also corruption of some kind.

rangecheck: A value was outside the acceptable range for the printer, or just wrong (like an attempt to get the fifth character from a four-character string). Could be a file tested on one printer but not suitable for yours. Also, look for very large values or objects well off the page. Possibly, corruption. The offending command may be a clue to what sort of value is out of range. If offending command is getinterval, the PostScript is produced by Adobe Acrobat, and the interpreter is not made by Adobe, you have found a bug in Acrobat. You can patch the file by adding:

% Patch for Acrobat bug—add after initial %% lines /version (888.000) def. Can be caused by sending a Level 2 file to a Level 1 printer, especially if offending command is one of "colorimage image imagemask."

stackoverflow: Too many items on the operand stack. In PostScript Level 1, there is a fixed limit; in Level 2 the limit is much higher. Can be caused by a program tested only with Level 2. If the error occurs only once and documents get past a certain level of complexity, there might be subtle errors that gradually fill up the operand stack—try printing fewer pages, if you can.

stackunderflow: Attempt to remove something from the PostScript stack when it isn't there. Can be caused by corruption or when PostScript has been modified in an attempt to fix a problem.

syntaxerror: The PostScript is not understood. Few situations cause this error, and they almost all indicate corruption. The only likely alternatives are using the Level 2 << symbol in a Level 1 printer, or mismatched { } brackets in a file, possibly caused by attempting to fix it.

timeout: The printer is waiting for something to happen, but it didn't happen. A printer has three different timeouts, and it could be any one: Job timeout is not usually set but means a job is taking too long. Manual feed timeout: Could this job be asking for manual paper feed? Wait timeout. A job hasn't finished, but nothing has arrived in the printer for some time. Can be caused by the computer giving up, or being asked to do something else for too long. Also, some printers need a Ctrl+D character at the end of each job: the printer driver should put it there. If adding Ctrl+D yourself, make sure that it is not followed by a new line—it must be that very last character in the file.

typecheck: An operator was expecting objects of one type, but got a different type. Like finding a name instead of a number.

undefined: The printer found something it did not understand. The offending command should tell you what that is, and it may be gobbledygook. Is this an EPS file that you are copying to the printer?

undefinedresource: Looking for a built-in resource that isn't there. Unlikely to occur, unless sending a file to the wrong device, or a badly configured one.

undefinedresult: Things like division by zero or the square root of –1. Less obviously, if a program scales everything down to a point, this error will occur.

unmatchedmark: Missing an open bracket in a program. Corruption.

VMerror: Printer out of memory. Fonts use printer memory: use fewer fonts, or use the fonts built in to the printer. Use a lower resolution, if available. Use a smaller page size, if applicable. If a printer, switch off and on. Don't download fonts you aren't using. If your printer driver offers a place to fill in the amount of memory, make sure it is accurate—and not the RAM size.

This is why we are moving to PDF. Distiller is actually a mini-RIP and these files that distill will usually print. PDF removes some, not all, of the problems with PostScript. Thanks to Andy Inston of Quite for these PostScript error insights.

Box 2-2

3

PDF Introduction

Paper is the culprit, we are told. The publishing industry's search for an ideal digital document had several software companies claiming they had the answer to paper documents needlessly killing trees, piling up unused in warehouses or filing cabinets, and causing frustration among business people lost in the sea of paper. With the increasing attention being given to the Internet, the idea of a paperless world seems tangible although we have said that there'll be a paperless office when there's a paperless bathroom. Our vision is that the ideal document must handle paper and pixels.

Yes, it's true: PDF prints three to four times faster than PostScript direct.

What Is a Portable Document? The underlying concept of document portability is that of printing to a file and distributing that file. As an analogy, take a sheet of paper with text and graphics on it and fax it. The sending fax converts the page images to dots, and the receiving fax prints them out. If you have fax capability from your computer, a program takes the page image, converts it to dots, and sends it to the printer. Now, save the last file we created—a repre-

Portable documents are self-reliant files that remain intact regardless of the platform they were created on. In other words, they can be moved electronically from computer to computer, for viewing or printing, and retain their content and format integrity.

Acrobat Distiller
Acrobat Distiller is used to convert any PostScript file into the Portable Document Format (PDF). Distilling a file is the best option when dealing with complex information such as high resolution images, gradients, and other artwork. The result is a page independent, highly structured, small file size format ready for delivery. Acrobat Reader allows for viewing, navigating, and printing a distilled document.

Acrobat Reader
Reader's role is primarily for viewing as well as third-party proofing and approving. The client can retrieve a PDF via the Internet, view it, and approve it without having the original application program. Adobe has made the Reader free and downloadable at www.adobe.com

Acrobat Exchange
Acrobat Exchange is also for viewing, however; editing features are included. Hyperlinking, bookmarking, deletion and insertion of pages, and password protection are all possible. Version 3.0 has also

sentation of the page as dots—and instead of printing it to paper, put it on the screen. This document can be sent, viewed, and digested on screen by a large audience without any hint or mention of paper.

However, there is something missing. Like any fax image, there is no underlying intelligence for the text. You could not search through it because it does not know an *a* from a hole in the paper. Searchability is something you want. You could use the application file, but then the receiver must have the same fonts you used, the images must be provided, and the applications must be at the same revision level.

Some portable document approaches save a bitmap of the page as it appeared on the screen, the underlying ASCII text, and the font data. By having the text in ASCII format, you can search for words and phrases. This is a major advantage over print. After all, the material in a book or catalog is not really information until you find what you want. Even with compression, some early portable documents were six to ten times bigger than the original application file.

By creating an electronic document that carries all the needed components—fonts, graphics, and even a program to view and print the document—portable document software can eliminate the cost and time of printing, distributing, and storing paper copies, while adding the ability to find text and link multiple documents so that information is more accessible and more dynamic.

The Portable Document Enters the Market In 1990, developers introduced portable-document software. First came No Hands Software's Common Ground. Adobe later shipped Acrobat, and Farallon Computing followed with Replica. Other companies also had portable document formats.

Adobe's Portable Document Adobe Systems dove into the competition in 1993 defining their Portable Document Format as a file format used to represent a document independent of the application software, fonts, hardware, and operating system used to create it. The software used to create this PDF was called Acrobat (actually, its original name was "Carousel").

Adobe's PDF was a third version of a PostScript file format. It took the PostScript file of the document and RIPed it (called distilling) to a new format that saved every page as an individual item, compressed the type and images, and cut out almost all the variability of the programming language. What remained was a portable document file that could be viewed on almost any platform, Mac or PC, running DOS, Windows, MacOS, or Unix. The first version of Adobe Acrobat did not fully support high-end printing for color separations. The PostScript code needed for production printing was not included. This did not hinder the use of PDFs to view on monitors or to print to monochrome and color printers, but it was not able to output a composite CMYK file as four monochrome PostScript streams to be sent to an imagesetter or a platesetter.

The Ultimate Portability   The printing and publishing industry saw more potential in the PDF than just looking at pages on a screen. Like the success of PostScript itself, the success of the PDF was based on capturing the high end of the printing world. Competitors to Acrobat saw viewing as the only problem to be solved. They forgot that paper was and always will be the only form of communicating to everyone in the world regardless of their lifestyle or location. Paper is the only democratic form of communication, because it does not restrict access because of technology.

Adobe acknowledged the need to meet the demands of the high-end printing market. As a result of their working relationships with organizations such as the PDF Group and DDAP, Acrobat is emerging as the software capable of creating the near-ideal digital document. The printing and publishing market expressed their needs, and Adobe listened. Acrobat 3.0 was released in November 1996 with added functions necessary for the high-end market. Acrobat 3.0 incorporated extended graphics-state functions so that color separation can occur more effectively and OPI image comments can now be preserved. The PDF pages can be exported as an EPS for insertion in a page makeup program, like QuarkXPress or PageMaker—only this time the font data is saved. In late 1997, Acrobat 3.01 was released, which fixed a few glitches and added a few new features.

PDF Components
PDF files contain a view file that displays the page as you created it, embedded type (Type 1 and TrueType), graphic objects (bitmaps and vector images), links for variable forms data, and links to sound and QuickTime or AVI movies—plus Job Ticket information.

PDF Group
A professional group of representatives from leading production and printing companies who have joined in support of the PDF in the areas of electronic delivery and prepress workflow. The group members are working directly with Adobe to solve problems as well as provide input for necessary additions.

DDAP
Stands for The Digital Distribution of Advertising for Publications. Started in 1991 as an ad hoc industry committee to implement various industry standards. Today DDAP is an active association in the role of digital standards.

The Ideal Digital Document   Imagine an ideal digital document. How many headaches would be avoided if there was a portable, page-independent, platform-independent file format that could not only preserve design richness but also allow for repurposability, searchability, predictability, and even some editability? This ideal digital document describes the Portable Document Format. PDF documents:

- Preserve design richness
- Create predictability
- Maintain some editability
- Create searchability
- Allow repurposability
- Allow high-end printing

Design Richness   Preserving design richness entails maintaining the look and feel from creation to final output by properly reproducing all content information within the document, such as bitmap, vectored line art, and text.

Bitmap (Scanned) Line Art

Grayscale Contone

Vector-based Line Art

Bitmap or Raster Images   A bitmap image is an image defined digitally by a number of pixels in a rectangular array. Because computers are binary entities, they must break up images into a map of small pieces, spots, or picture elements, or pixels. All images that are scanned into a computer are bitmap images, whether black-and-white line drawings, or black-and-white or color photos.

Monochrome bitmap images are the simplest and the smallest in file size. Scanned black-and-white line drawings are monochrome bitmaps. Each pixel of the bitmap can be either black or white (on or off), so only two bits of computer information are required to define these bitmaps. For this reason, they are also called bilevel bitmaps.

Grayscale bitmaps are a step above monochrome bitmaps because, instead of 2 bits per pixel, they contain 8 bits per pixel. Eight-bit images can then yield 256 levels of gray. Because more bits are used for each pixel, grayscale images are larger in file size than monochrome images.

Color bitmap images can be either 24 bit (RGB) or 32 bit (CMYK), yielding millions of possible color combinations for each pixel. Thus, color bitmap file sizes tend to be very large, humongous even. Because the human eye cannot discern the individual pixels, we perceive the images to be smooth lines (monochrome bitmaps) or continuous tone (grayscale and color bitmaps). These digital images can accurately describe an original image, but tend to be very large files.

Line Art   Line art is described as a combination of lines, curves, tints, and fills in vector form to allow it to be scaled, rotated, etc. and converted to a very compact version of the data that is independent of the final size of the image.

Unlike bitmap images, which are defined in terms of pixels, vector images are defined by the curves used to create the shape. Think of it as lots of little electronic rubber bands which are anchored at some points and pulled apart at others.

Text   Text is carried as character symbols with placement information, which can be converted to the final image through use of font drawing information. This allows the size of the text and the font used to be varied during the creative process.

PostScript allows users to design and create pages containing bitmaps, line art, and text without concern for a particular platform or output device. Acrobat Distiller transforms PostScript files from PC, Macintosh, and UNIX systems into all-inclusive bundles retaining all formatting, graphics, and photographic images that the original documents contain.

Portability   Computer users have suffered from a lack of formatted text, loss of graphics, and lack of proper fonts installed on particular computers that are used to view and print documents. Documents have been somewhat portable through the use of ASCII and Rich Text Format (RTF) files, but content alone does not always convey the true message without formatting or design richness.

PDFing a file makes it "portable" across computer platforms. A PDF file is a 7-bit ASCII file and may use only the printable subset of the ASCII character set to describe documents—even those with

ASCII
The American Standard Code for Information Interchange is the most basic coding system for text and serves as the foundation for virtually every system that encodes information. Almost every document can be saved as ASCII, which can then be imported to any other document.

Rich Text Format (RTF)
Microsoft format used to go across platforms, with fonts, style sheets, and graphics to some extent. Once thought to be a portable document format, it was not robust (rich?) enough.

About Adobe Acrobat
- *View documents with guaranteed page fidelity. It is not necessary for the user to buy the application. The Reader is free.*
- *Time is saved by sending information and files over e-mail.*
- *Collateral and technical documentation can be stored electronically and accessed instantly; this is helpful with sales and customer service groups.*

The PDF provides a solution to three information needs:
- *An interchange format for viewing richly formatted documents.*
- *A data format for archiving documents.*
- *A format for transmitting documents for remote printing.*

images and special characters. As a result, PDF files are extremely portable and compact even across diverse hardware and operating-system environments.

PDF makes a document independent of the fonts used to create it. Fonts can be either embedded or descriptors can be used. Embedding the fonts in the PostScript stage includes the actual font outlines in the file. Distilling this file will ensure that pages are displayed with type characters in exact position. The font descriptor includes the font name, character metrics, and style information. This is the information needed to simulate missing fonts and is typically only 1–2K per font. If a font used in a document is available on the computer where the document is viewed, it is used. If it is not available, two Adobe Multiple Master fonts are used to simulate on a character-by-character basis the weight and width of the original font, to maintain the overall formatting of the original document.

Font embedding does add some size to the document; however, it provides an all-important aspect of document portability—cross-platform font fidelity and the ability to print out at any resolution. This means that the receiver of the digital page can have a high-resolution color printer and print out pages as needed at a remote location. Pages can be created in one part of the world and then sent to a printer in the opposite hemisphere that uses the data to make high-resolution films for printing. Plus, embedding all fonts assures text editability.

Editability   Last-minute changes to a PDF can be made via a new plug-in for Acrobat Exchange called Text Touchup. Since the PDF is vector-based and includes the font name, character metrics, and style information, small type changes are possible. Full paragraphs cannot be edited due to the lack of reflow capabilities, but those small yet sometimes crucial changes such as misspelled words or incorrect phone numbers or prices can be made on a last-minute basis within Acrobat Exchange or with other plug-ins, such as Pitstop.

Predictability   Acrobat PDF eliminates the variability of Post-Script and provides a foundation for effective digital print-production workflow. A RIP interprets PostScript, converts it into a display list of page objects, and then rasterizes the page into a map of on/off spots that drive the marking engine. When you distill a document into a PDF, you are essentially doing the interpretation and display-list functions as in the RIP process.

The resulting PDF is a database of objects that appear on a page and how they relate to each other—a print-specific file with extensions for OPI, image screening information, and more. The variability of PostScript is squeezed out and only the essence remains, which can be output back into the PostScript stream again for printout—just open the PDF and Print it. If your document can be distilled to a PDF, the odds are that it will output reliably on most PostScript RIPs.

Searchability   With Acrobat software, it is possible to find information instantly. There is a full-text search tool, which allows the user to retrieve exactly what they need. Hypertext links can be used to simplify browsing and navigation features such as bookmarks, and cross-documentation links are also included to help the user move through numerous documents faster.

Repurposability   Adobe's PDF for some time has been marketed as a Web tool offering greater design richness over the HTML language constraints. PDFs can be downloaded to the World Wide Web and accessed through the free Acrobat Reader plug-in for the two popular browsers. A document created for print output and distilled into a PDF can now, with virtually no changes, be used on a Web site. Sites can now be created with all the design richness available in page layout applications such as QuarkXPress.

PDF and PostScript   Although PDF files require PostScript information to be created, the resulting PDF files are different from their PostScript counterpart. A PDF file is not a PostScript language program and cannot be directly interpreted by a PostScript interpreter. However, the page descriptions in a PDF file can be converted into a PostScript file.

PDF is not your father's PostScript.
PDF defines basic types of objects, such as numbers, names, arrays, dictionaries and streams. Page descriptions, outlines, annotations, and thumbnails are built from these objects, as in PostScript. Objects have an object number and a generation number, allowing multiple versions of an object to exist within a document. The object can be referenced indirectly by its object number.

PDF operators are mostly one letter, unlike the verbose PostScript operators. Several operators combine more than one PostScript operation. The "b" operator in PDF does the work of PostScript's closepath, fill, and stroke verbs, as an example.

PDF does not have programming constructions for branching (if… else) or looping. The PDF interpreter runs straight through the code when it displays or prints.

The pages of a file may not follow each other in sequence and are accessed through a catalog/balanced-tree data structure, analogous to a disk directory system. When versions of a file are saved, a new table is appended to the end of the file and contains a pointer to the previous cross-reference table to trace back through earlier versions.

A PDF file contains a cross-reference table of objects, which can be used to quickly find the data needed to display a page. The table allows different pages to share data. As annotations are created and erased, the table is updated.

Differences between PostScript and PDF
- *A PDF file may contain objects such as hypertext links that are useful only for interactive viewing. Sorry, PostScript.*
- *To simplify the processing of page descriptions, PDF provides no programming language constructs. It is a list of objects.*
- *PDF enforces a strictly defined file structure that allows an application to access parts of a document randomly.*
- *PDF files contain information such as font metrics, to ensure viewing fidelity.*
- *PDF requires files to be represented in ASCII, to enhance document portability.*

Predictable in file

How PDF Files Work

The PDF file format is not a programming language like PostScript. You cannot send a PDF file to a laser printer directly because the file format contains information that a current PostScript RIP would not understand. The PDF does contain PostScript code, but the extra PDF data would inhibit the RIP from processing the document. A PDF file must be sent to a RIP through the Acrobat Reader or Acrobat (formerly Exchange) application. When output by Reader, the PDF is converted into a PostScript file and sent to the RIP just like any other PostScript file. In the future, PDF could become the basic file format, and the very concept of RIPs would change. PDF and PostScript are highly interrelated.

Creating a PDF File   The three methods for creating PDF are
- PDFWriter
- Acrobat Distiller
- Directly from some applications

The PDFWriter, available on both Apple Macintosh computers and computers running the Microsoft Windows environment, acts as a printer driver. PDFWriter shows up as a printer in the Macintosh Chooser window. The user needs to choose that "printer" to create a PDF file. The user then "prints" the file to the PDFWriter, and an electronic file is produced. This is similar to "print to disk."

For more complex documents that involve special fonts, high-resolution images, and detailed illustrations, the PDF file must be created differently because of limitations of PDFWriter. Acrobat Distiller was developed. Distiller produces PDF files from PostScript files that have been "printed to disk." The Distiller application accepts any PostScript file, whether created by an application program or hand-coded. Distiller produces more efficient PDF files than PDFWriter for various reasons, and it is recommended if you are going to print to film or plate or on high-end digital printers.

Acrobat is a program that does everything the Reader does and more. It is an application that adds value to existing pages. You can add value to PDF files by using several of the built-in tools or third-party plug-ins. The main feature that puts Acrobat in front of Reader is the ability to make and save changes to a PDF file. Couple this saving ability with the use of specialized tools, and a powerful link is created. You should use the Acrobat program over Reader when you have to edit a file or want to add to it. For strict viewing needs, the Reader is a better choice because it not only loads faster (bcause of less plug-ins), but you eliminate the chance of unintentionally altering the file (besides the Reader is free).

What Is New in Acrobat 4.0 and 4.05   Acrobat software offers integration of other Adobe applications, as well as enhanced capabilities.

Major Features in Acrobat 4.0

- New fresh and updated interface. Easy access to all tools and options is a mouse click away.
- Enhanced Drag-and-Drop capabilities for converting single images to PDF without creating PostScript first.
- Completely revolutionary support for image editing with integration of Photoshop and Illustrator.
- Tremendous integration with the Microsoft applications which allows for easier integration of office documents to PDF.
- A Web Capture tool, which allows users to create a PDF rendition of a Web site for off-line browsing.
- Digital signatures, which can be included for peer document review and approval.
- Complete document markup tools, included in Acrobat's base tool set.
- Exciting new Forms capabilities.
- "Stamps" to create watermarks on pages.
- A Compare feature to automatically check differences between two documents side by side.

integrity.
Missing fonts or PostScript resources used to mean long coffee breaks. In "high-end" PDF, all the font information is included in the file. No more need to have all the fonts available by all the players in the production process.

Predictable in processing time.
In a modern workflow, you want to predict the time it will take to process a file. When your digital platemaker has to supply printing plates for a press, you should know how long it will take to produce your plates. Press downtime costs a small fortune. In a busy service bureau, you need to know how long a file will RIP so that you can deliver it yesterday.

Creating, Using, and Distributing PDF

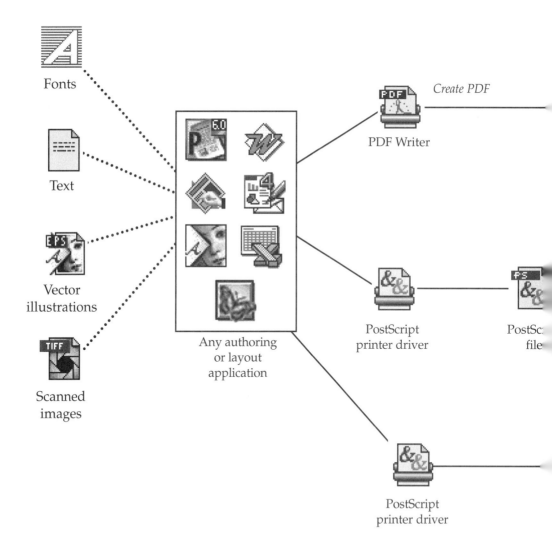

Fonts

Text

Vector
illustrations

Scanned
images

Any authoring
or layout
application

Create PDF

PDF Writer

PostScript
printer driver

PostScr
file

PostScript
printer driver

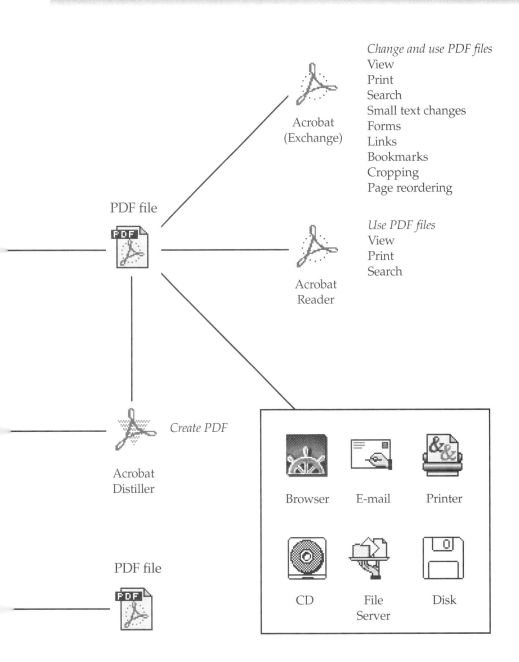

Figure 3-1
General PDF workflow.

- Further support of table formatting when using copy and paste operations.
- Support of Chinese, Japanese, and Korean languages for a truly worldwide audience.

Acrobat 4.05 Features and Revisions

Acrobat with Web Buy   Web Buy enables you to download encrypted content from the Web, such as eBooks and electronic documents in PDF, and unlock it. Find out more about Web Buy at www.adobe.com/products/acrobat/webbuy/main.html. A major trend involves e-commerce and e-business models for purchasing over the World Wide Web.

Integration with Microsoft Office 2000 (Windows Only)   Integration problems that caused PDFMaker 4.0 (the macro that automates PDF creation within Office applications) to hang have been corrected. Acrobat 4.05 is properly integrated with Office 2000 and enables you to automate the conversion of native Word, Excel, and PowerPoint documents to PDF files.

Proper JPEG Compression in PDF Files Created by Distiller   In Acrobat 4, Distiller's JPEG compression results are the same for High, Medium, and Low. Acrobat 4.05 corrects this problem so that in most cases the JPEG compression of images in PDF files is better than that achieved in Acrobat 3.

Less Restrictive TrueType Font Embedding   To stay within the industry specification for TrueType fonts, Acrobat Distiller 4.05 no longer interprets out-of-specification flags as meaning non-embeddable. Distiller 4.05 continues to read font-embedding flags and honors properly specified restrictions on font embedding.

Improved Web Browser Integration   Problems that prevented PDF files from being displayed properly in Netscape

Navigator and Internet Explorer browser windows have been corrected. In addition, Acrobat no longer crashes when you view PDF files embedded in HTML files.

Improved Printing   Several problems with PostScript and PCL (non-PostScript) printing in which the printout was incorrect, no output was produced, or Acrobat crashed have been corrected.

PDFMaker Support for all Windows NT User Privileges (Windows Only)   PDFMaker now functions properly regardless of the user's Windows NT privileges. You no longer need to be logged in with Administrator privileges.

Distiller Crashes and Color Management Fixed   Several problems that caused Distiller to crash have been corrected, as were problems that caused Distiller to embed incorrect ICC color profiles in PDF files.

Printer Driver Updates   The newest Adobe PostScript printer drivers (Adobe PS 8.6 for Macintosh, Adobe PS 5.1.1 for Windows NT, and Adobe PS 4.3.1 for Windows 95/98) are integrated. You may already have Acrobat 4.05, even if your product box lists version 4.0: The version of your copy of Acrobat is located only in the upper-left corner of the startup screen and About dialog box. To locate the version, choose About Adobe Acrobat from the Apple menu (Macintosh) or choose Help > About Adobe Acrobat (Windows). If you have not registered your copy of Acrobat, register at adobe.com.

Downloading Plug-ins for Acrobat 4.0 for Mac OS   If you already own Acrobat 4 for Mac OS, you can download free plug-ins for it at www.adobe.com/products/acrobat/acr4diff.html. These plug-ins provide Web Capture, digital signatures, and other features previously available only in Acrobat 4 for Windows. You can also purchase the plug-ins on CD, along with the Acrobat 4.05 Update for Mac OS, for $24.95 U.S. plus shipping. To order, call Adobe Customer Services at 800-272-3623.

A. The Acrobat work-space. There are now more tools and more functions, some of which are hidden under new side-pop-out menus.

B. *Menu Bar:* A list of primary functions that allow you to in-teract with the pro-gram to perform actions and tasks.

C. *Top Tool Bar:* Icons that provide rapid access to specif-ic tools and functions, selected because of their frequent use.

D. *Side Tool Bar:* Allows access to spe-cific Acrobat tools and features, espe-cially markup func-tions.

E. *Thumbnails:* Small versions of pages in a document, used for page naviga-tion and document management.

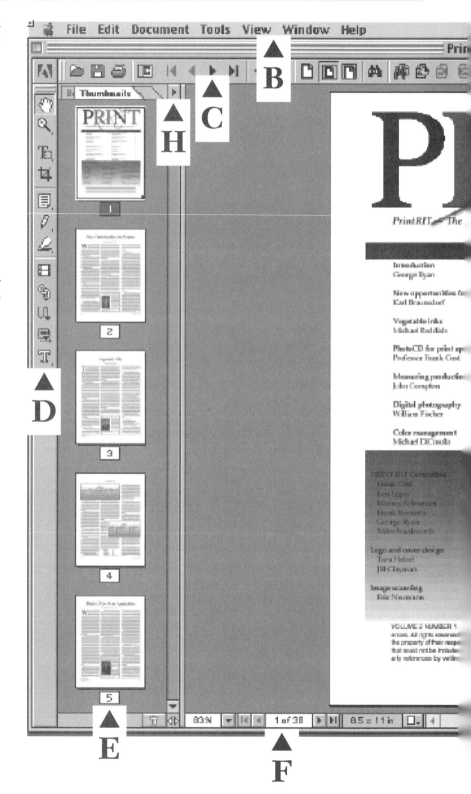

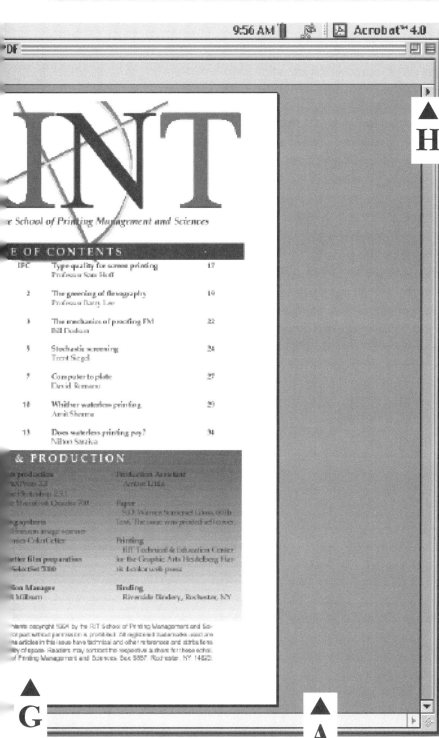

F. *Bottom Tool Bar:* Direct access to document navigation items, including zoom factors, current page number, and page-display layout.

G. *Current Document:* Defined as the document currently being viewed.

H. *Side Pop-out menus.*

Figure 3-2
Acrobat environment.

Acrobat 4 Menu Bar

Each option in the Acrobat menu bar contains a set of tools or controls, even for third-party plug-ins. Menu items from left to right are

- File
- Edit
- Document
- Tools
- View
- Window
- Help

File This menu contains tools for import and export functions, opening and closing documents, printing, and a tracking history of the most recent files that have been used. Additional functions are

- Reverting to previously saved files
- Batch processing
- Importing
- Exporting
- Document information
- Preference settings

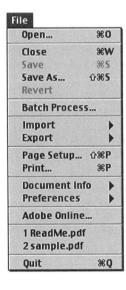

Figure 3-3
Acrobat File menu.

Edit This menu contains cut and paste tools, plus the ability to:
- Select all items in a document
- Use the Find text tool
- Use the Search Plug-in
- Access to properties of document parts

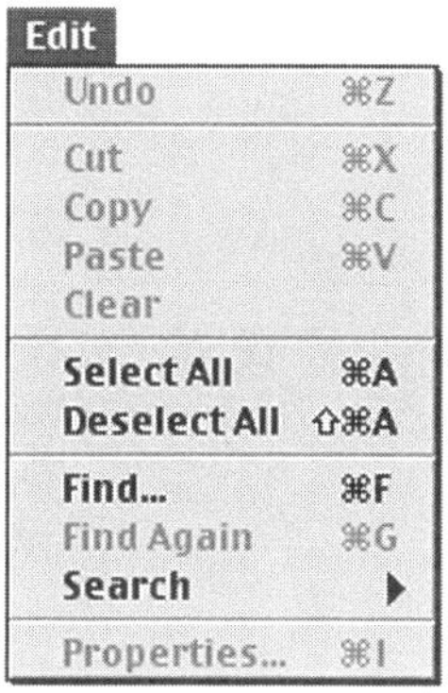

Edit	
Undo	⌘Z
Cut	⌘X
Copy	⌘C
Paste	⌘V
Clear	
Select All	**⌘A**
Deselect All	**⇧⌘A**
Find...	**⌘F**
Find Again	⌘G
Search	▶
Properties...	⌘I

Figure 3-4
Acrobat Edit menu.

Document The Document Item gives you control over document-page navigation, page-swapping control, and page actions, especially inserting and replacing pages.

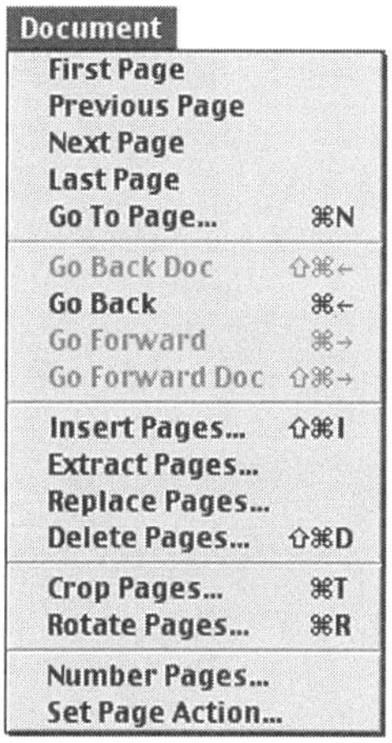

Document	
First Page	
Previous Page	
Next Page	
Last Page	
Go To Page...	**⌘N**
Go Back Doc	⇧⌘←
Go Back	**⌘←**
Go Forward	⌘→
Go Forward Doc	⇧⌘→
Insert Pages...	**⇧⌘I**
Extract Pages...	
Replace Pages...	
Delete Pages...	**⇧⌘D**
Crop Pages...	**⌘T**
Rotate Pages...	**⌘R**
Number Pages...	
Set Page Action...	

Figure 3-5
Acrobat Document menu.

And these tools are really everywhere. There are at least six areas where tools live. See Figure 3-2 and find them. It's like a high tech version of "Where's Waldo."

Tools There are tools everywhere—commonly used tools on the toolbar and additional Acrobat tools in the Tools menu, which include

- Text Touch tools
- Scanning Options
- Annotation Controls
- Forms Creation Controls
- Web Link controls

Figure 3-6
Acrobat Tools menu.

View View controls the way in which you see the pages on your screen. You have the ability to set the following options:

- Zoom options
- Page-display options
- Page-scrolling options
- Local font access
- Forms-alignment tools

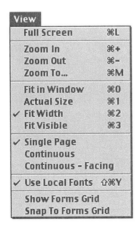

Figure 3-7
Acrobat View menu.

Window This item provides control over the characteristics of the configuration of the Acrobat interface. Options include

- "Window" (viewing) management
- Hiding or revealing the Tool bar and Menu bar
- Hiding or revealing Bookmarks and Thumbnails
- Hiding or revealing Articles
- Hiding or revealing Destinations
- Hiding or revealing Annotations
- Guide to currently open PDF files

Figure 3-8
Acrobat Window menu.

Help Gives direct links to on-line help files. Look for all programs to link over the Web to extensive Help capability. In addition, these features are available:

- Control over Balloon Help items
- Direct link on-line help files
- Information on how to purchase the Full Acrobat Suite

Help

| About Balloon Help... |
| Show Balloons |
| Acrobat Guide |
| Acrobat Tour |
| Forms JavaScript Guide |

Figure 3-9
Acrobat Help menu.

Apple Menu Provides information about the Acrobat application and any plug-ins loaded:
- About Acrobat Reader 4.05
- About installed Reader Plug-ins

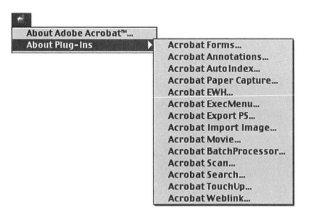

Figure 3-10
Apple menu.

Acrobat Toolbar

The Acrobat toolbar is split into two locations, a top bar and a side bar. Both allow efficient navigation through the document. The speed and functionality that are achieved with the use and understanding of these tools is great. Although you cannot preform all of the functions that Acrobat is capable of via the toolbar, you do have good control at your fingertips.

The items on the side toolbar that have subitems are indicated with a small arrow in the bottom-right corner of the tool. Click and hold on the toolbar item with the arrow and they will expand to display the options.

Top Menu Bar The tools on the bar are broken logically into several sections. Each section is grouped according to the operation that it executes. By grouping icons, you know approximately where to look for your shortcut icon.

Acrobat Tools

The tool set includes:
- Hand Tool
- Zoom Tool
- Selection Tool
- Crop Tool
- Annotation Tool
- Drawing Tool
- Markup Tool
- Movie Tool
- Link Tool
- Article Tool
- Forms Tool
- TouchUp Tool

Hand Tool   The hand tool is for pointing and navigating around a screen. Depending on function, page attributes, and scroll settings (single page or continuous), the hand tool will perform and appear differently.

Default Hand Tool

Hand Tool in Double-Click Mode

Hand Tool on a Link

Hand Tool on an Article

Hand Tool on a Web Link

Hand Tool on a Form Button

Hand Tool on a Form (info field)

I

Hand Tool on a Movie

When the default Hand Tool is active, click and hold the mouse button to grab the page and move it around the screen. If a zoom percentage is set, you can go left or right—otherwise, you are limited to up and down movement. In the continuous-scroll environment, the hand tool will follow the pages up or down. If you set for "single page," you will not be able to grab a page and jump to the next one. Click the up (or down) arrow to get to the next or previous page, or use the Thumbnail icons, or click and move the scroll bar on the right side of the window. It sounds more complicated than it is.

Zoom Tool   You can zoom into a specific region of the document:
   • Key shortcut (Command + + for Zooming In)
   • Key shortcut (Command + - for Zooming Out)
   • Toolbar (the magnifying glass tool)
   • Use Thumbnails to resize view window
   • Use the menu bar at the bottom of the Acrobat window

In the Thumbnail view, you have the ability to define the zoom area by resizing the little square in the Thumbnail icon to actively define the page area displayed in the main window.

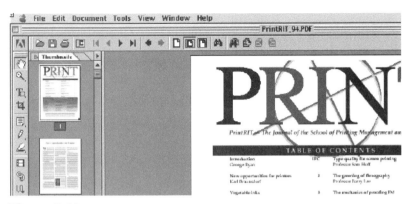

Figure 3-11
The little square in the Thumbnail icon
lets you define the page area viewed.

The Magnifying Glass is great for quickly zooming in and out. When you choose the Magnifying Glass in the Tools menu or on the Tool bar, the cursor will change to a magnifying glass with a plus sign (+) on it. Wherever you click on the screen, you will enlarge the image. If you hold the Option key down when the magnifying glass is selected, you change the plus (+) to a minus sign (–) to zoom out of an image and thus reduce the zoom percentage. A very useful feature of the zoom "in" and "out" tool is the ability to click and drag a box around a defined area to be magnified. You will be zooming constantly to read what is on the screen comfortably or viewing the entire page for navigation purposes so develop good zoom habits.

Selection Tool   You can use the Select Text tool to highlight and copy text in a document. The Select Text tool can be accessed by either the shortcut (Command + V), or you can use the toolbar and select the Text Selector icon. You then have the ability to click and drag to select text in the document. With the Text Selector chosen, your pointer will look like an I-beam or a capital "I."

When you have selected an area of text, you can choose Copy, in the Edit menu (Command + C). This will copy the text to the clipboard. You can paste the text to any other file or application (except another PDF file—sorry). When you copy text, it is line for line with a Return at the end of each line.

Another option for selecting text is to use the Column Select tool. This tool gives you the ability to pull defined (marqueed) zones for text selection. If a particular word is only partially selected with this method, the entire word will be automatically selected.

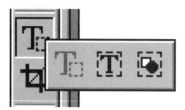

Figure 3-12
The first tool takes all text line by line. The second tool lets you define the text to be selected. The last tool is for graphics selection.

If you want to select a specific area of text (like a line or a paragraph), hold the Option key when you are selecting the text (note the cursor changes). You can then define a rectangular box and select only the text inside that shape, which is then highlighted. After you have selected the area of text and copied it to the clipboard, the Show Clipboard option will show exactly what is currently active.

Selecting Graphics   Just like selecting text, the Select Graphics Tool selects defined images in the document for copying. You can access the the graphics selector by choosing the selection tool, or by using the keyboard combination of Shift + V + V. Your cursor will change to a cross-hair target and you can click and drag across any image area on the PDF page.

When you release the mouse button, you will have a dotted-line frame around the area selected. Do not click the mouse button again (or you will lose the selection marquee), and then copy the item. A bitmap image of the screen will be placed on the clipboard. Do not try to use this image for high-resolution printing. It is only at screen resolution.

File Management

Click this magic icon and you will be linked directly to Adobe On-line via the Web browser of your choice.

Click and go directly to the File Open Dialog box to open any PDF file. Do not pass Go.

This button will perform a standard Save function. This will over-write the existing document, so be sure you want to do a Save and not a Save As, which creates a new file and leaves the old one alone.

This icon will link you directly to the Print command dialog box. If the document has printer security enabled by the author, you will not be able to print it

Document Layout

This icon will split the screen so that you can view both the page and thumbnails on your monitor. This will restrict the maximum size of the page that can be displayed.

Page Navigation

This button will take you directly to the first page in the document from any location in the document.

This button will take you to the the previous page of your document.

This button will take you to the next page of your document.

This button will take you directly to the last page in the document.

This button will show you the previous view. This button has multiple levels—it remembers more than one action and will cycle back through them.

This button will show you the next view of a document and is only activated after you have used the Previous View button.

Page View Modes

This button will automatically show the document at its actual size—in other words at 100 percent.

This icon will fit the page in the viewable area of the window. It will be smaller with Thumbnails or Bookmarks selected.

This icon will choose to fit the width of the document across the viewable window.

Web Link Tool

This button will launch the Web browser of your choice. It has its own set of Preferences. Look for continuing expansion of Web link functions.

Location Tools

The Find command is accessed via this button.

The Search plug-in is automatically activated with this button.

This button will display the hit list from the most recent Search.

Used after a search has been completed, this button automatically displays the previous document on the list.

This button automatically takes you to the next document on the list after a search has been completed.

Side Menu Items

New to Acrobat 4 is the Side Menu Bar. The tools in this area perform most of the editing and production features of Acrobat and most have submenus that can be accessed by clicking and holding the mouse.

The Hand tool will allow you to move around the page and navigate your way through a document. It will activate the Links and Form fields.

The Magnifying glass lets you zoom in or out of the page. To zoom out, hold the Option/Control key and then click.

The Select tool lets you click and drag over an area to select text or graphics. You can then cut and paste the text or graphics to any other application.

Many tools have submenus or subsets. Click on the tool and hold the mouse button for the submenu to appear. Then, drag on over to the desired tool.

The Crop tool lets you define the area for a page crop. After you define the area, the Crop Pages dialog box will appear and the marqueed area will be within the page-crop margins.

The Annotations tool is what you use to create notes, attach sounds (especially voice), attach text, attach files, or stamp PDF files.

The pencil tool will allow you to draw freehand lines onto the PDF page. Submenu tools include a rectangle tool, an ellipse tool, and a line tool. Great for annotation.

The Highlight Text tool lets you highlight text with a color. Submenu tools include underscoring text and strike-through text.

This tool lets you insert a movie in the PDF document. Don't try to print it.

The Link Tool lets you create Web- or cross-document links. These buttons add interactivity to PDF files.

The Article Tool also lets you add interactivity. It lets you string defined views and links.

The Form Tool lets you create interactive form fields in PDF files. Forms can even incorporate JavaScripts.

You can selectively edit text, images, and alter page layers with this tool.

Other Toolbars

Figure 3-12
Bottom toolbar.

In addition to tools and buttons at the top, bottom, and sides of the Acrobat window, there are shortcut buttons at the bottom of the window too. These buttons at the bottom link you to dialog boxes to perform a specific task. After a while, it does look like the cockpit of a Boeing 777.

With the Bookmark window active, these slider buttons scroll the Bookmarks left to right so that you can read long lines of text.

Click this button to go directly to the first bookmark on the current page. Do not go directly to jail.

This button will create a new bookmark. Have the page view and page position set before clicking this icon or you will bookmark the wrong page.

Use this Trash Can to delete a selected bookmark, a selected page via the thumbnail menu, or an annotation.

When using the Annotation palette, this button will mysteriously appear. When selected, it will start a scan of the document for annotations and produce a report, which you can view.

Click and hold this button and drag it left or right to resize the thumbnail or bookmark window. The bigger you make one side, the smaller the other side, and the other side is your document.

The magnification percentage indicator also serves as a button. Click on it and you are in the Zoom dialog box.

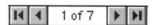

This dialog box tells you where you are in the current document and when clicked lets you input a specific page number to jump to.

The dialog box tells you the current page size, and when it is clicked you can choose the mode of the view; either continuous, single page, or continuous facing page.

The PDF File

The PDF file icon is cross-platform and will appear the same on Windows, on a Macintosh, or on a Unix-based system. Double-click on the PDF file icon and Acrobat is opened. The PDF icon has the signature red swash as well as the PDF letters on it. It is one of the most recognized logos in the world.

If you are operating in a cross-platform environment with PDF files created with Acrobat 3, PDF icon issues are raised. Due to the structure of those files, when a PDF file created on a PC is brought to a Mac, the PDF icon for that document is not seen by the system. To work around this, open the file using the File and Open method. Your other choice is to download a free utility from Adobe that puts a utility icon on the computer desktop—the Acrobat PDF Type Utility. This drag-and-drop applet is essential in a cross-platform environment. It has been improved in Acrobat 4. Drag the PDF file over it and the PDF icon is created. Double-click to open.

PDF File Icon   PDF File Icon

Figure 3-13
The Adobe PDF icon.

When you click on a PDF file icon and you do not have Acrobat running when you click, you will automatically launch the Acrobat program and the file will open. If you have Acrobat running, the file will open immediately in Acrobat.

The second option for opening a PDF file is using the Open command in the File menu. You must have Acrobat running. In order to start the application, find the icon on your system, and launch it as you would any other application. An alias is a good idea.

With Acrobat started, go into the File menu and then to the Open command. With Open highlighted, click the mouse, and you will be brought to the Open File dialog box.

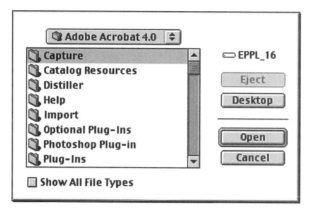

Figure 3-14
The Adobe Acrobat Open dialog box.

The last step in opening the PDF file is to find it and highlight it. You can either double-click on the file name, or you can highlight it and click on the Open button in this dialog box. If you still have Acrobat 3 on you computer, Acrobat 4 will open. (The question is why you still have Acrobat 3?)

Drag and Drop   Acrobat fully supports operation in a drag-and-drop environment. You can take any PDF file icon and drag it on the Acrobat application icon to automatically open the PDF file in Acrobat.

File Management   After opening a PDF file, you may want to get additional information about the file. Go to the File menu, then to the Document Info submenu. When you get to the Document Information choice, you will have several subchoices;

- General information
- Open
- Fonts
- Security
- Prepress
- Index
- Base URL

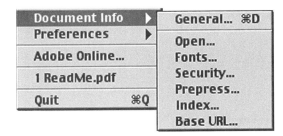

Figure 3-15
The Acrobat Document Info submenu.

The General Information dialog box (Command + D) provides information about the file, such as author, creation date, subject, and other file-related information. The main fields are filled in by the Acrobat user when they save the file. The creation date, size, path, and modified date fields are automatically inserted. The General Information dialog box includes

- File Name and Path
- File Subject
- File Keywords
- File Creator
- PDF File Version
- File Modification Date
- File Byte Size
- File Title
- File Author
- File Binding Style
- File Producer (converter)
- File Creation Date
- Optimized State

The Document Information fields are also used in an index created in Acrobat Catalog. The Document Information fields are a source for searching. Save often in order to keep the changes with the file.

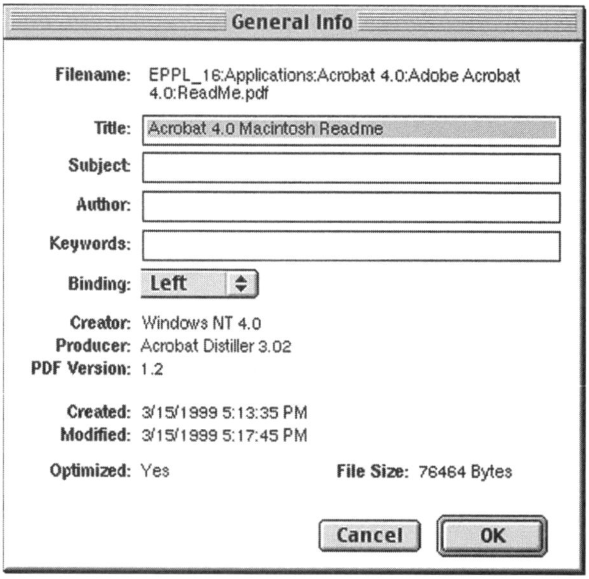

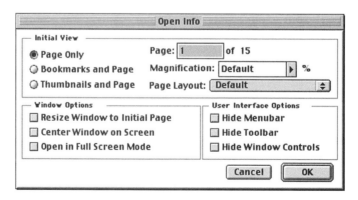

Figure 3-16
The Acrobat General Info dialog box.

Open Document Settings Acrobat allows you to set how and where a document will open. You do not always have to open at the first page, or at a specific magnification. In the File menu under Document Info, choose Open, click on it, and you will activate the Open Info dialog box.

Figure 3-17
The Acrobat Open Info dialog box.

This dialog box allows you to set just how the document will open in either Reader or Acrobat. The settings are broken down into:

- Initial View
- Window Options
- User Interface Options

By setting the checkboxes and radio buttons, you can customize the way that each individual PDF file is opened. Remember to save the PDF file in Acrobat when you make any change to the settings.

Font Information   To find out what fonts are used in a file, and to see if they are embedded either in whole or in part, go to the Fonts item in the Document Info choice in the File menu.

All fonts used in the PDF file are listed in this box. The information contained in this box will give the exact status of the fonts. Examine the first font in the list; the six-character string in front of the Original font name indicates that the font has been subset. You can be assured that this subset is used in the display and printing of the document by looking in the Used Font catergory, for this first font the entry is subset.

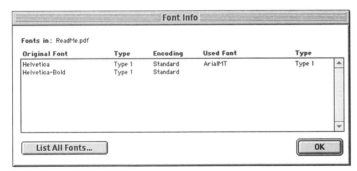

Figure 3-18
The Acrobat Font Info dialog box.

The Fonts area can be misleading. This view box will report only fonts on the pages already processed. If you have a 20-page document and only view the first 19, run the fonts usage function, and you will get a report on pages 1 through 19. If a new font is used on page 20, you will not see it in this box. You have to either click on List all fonts, or process the twentieth page. This way, Reader has to look at every page in the document.

Be aware that Acrobat will look first on your system for an instance of a font used in the document. The system font will take precedence. This means that if Warnock Pro is used and fully embedded in your PDF document, the embedded font will be used only if Warnock Pro is not available on the host system. If it is, it may cause problems if extensive kerning or tracking has been applied to the font. A way around this is to make every font in the document a subset. With a font subset, Acrobat will always use the subset over any installed system font of the same name. There are features discussed in the fonts chapter to overcome this situation.

Security Options   Security features can be built into the file in much the same way as the Document Information is added to the file. There are several levels of security. They range from opening the document to limiting the printing of the document. If you come across a document that has a security password on the document, you must key in the password when you are prompted.

Figure 3-19
The Password dialog box.

As you key in the case-sensitive password in this field, the characters will be represented by dots. This occurs so that you do not know what you are typing, to protect the password even from yourself. Okay, we're kidding. After keying the password, click OK, or hit the Enter key. After you get pass this stage, you are right in the file, and it is standard operating procedure. Other security options that can be imposed on a file include printing and modifications to the file. To check the security settings, go to the File menu to the Document Info submenu, then to Security.

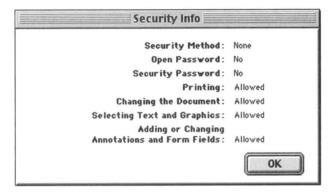

Figure 3-20
The Acrobat Security Info dialog box with all security allowed.

Prepress Information   In Acrobat's attempt to provide some level of information for prepress-specific items, a dialog box is available that contains choices for the file's trapping requirements, as well as control over output of ICC profiles attached to four-color images for color management.

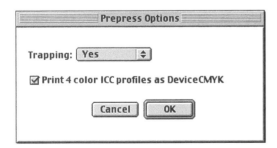

Figure 3-21
The Acrobat Prepress Options Info dialog box.

Index Information   The last alternative in the Document Info submenu is a choice to select an Index file (with Acrobat Catalog) to be mounted when the file is opened. This feature will set an index to automatically mount.

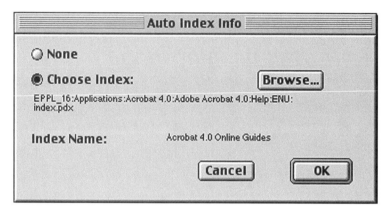

Figure 3-22
The Acrobat Auto Indent Info dialog box.

Base URL   In the Document Info submenu, you can set a Base URL for that document. A Universal Resource Locator (URL or Web address) can be assigned to a document for setting Web Links in that document. An example of a base URL is http://www.rit.edu.

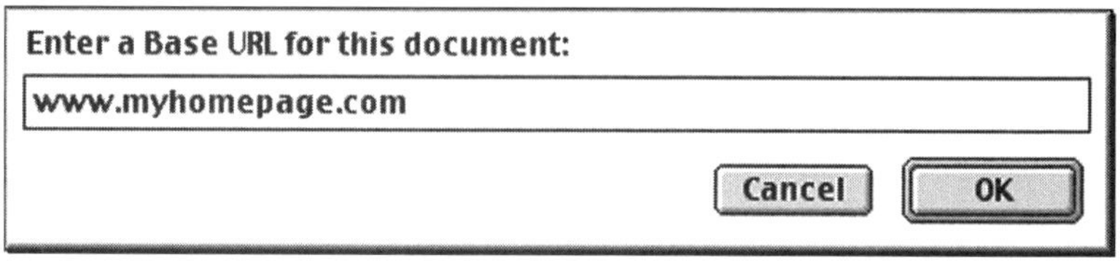

Figure 3-23
The Acrobat Base URL Info dialog box.

When the Base URL is used, you only have to list the directory or HTML file reference when creating links in the document. You can then click on the URL to connect to it.

Acrobat Preferences   Acrobat has several categories of preference settings. Third-party plug-ins will also have specific preference
settings. Refer to the original manufacturer of the software for
specifics on that product. Acrobat's preferences can be found in the
File menu under the Preferences submenu. Within this menu are
several choices for specific application settings, and we are going to
go through them in agonizing detail.

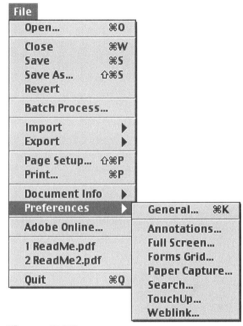

Figure 3-24
The Acrobat Preferences submenu.

General Preferences   Most of the preference settings for the
Acrobat application are made within Acrobat's General Preferences
dialog box. You can go through the menu items, or go to the File
menu and select Preferences. Within Preferences choose General.
The shortcut for this dialog box is Command + K.

    If you set a preference when no document is open, it will apply to
all documents that you open after that. When you set a preference
with a document open, it applies only to that current document.

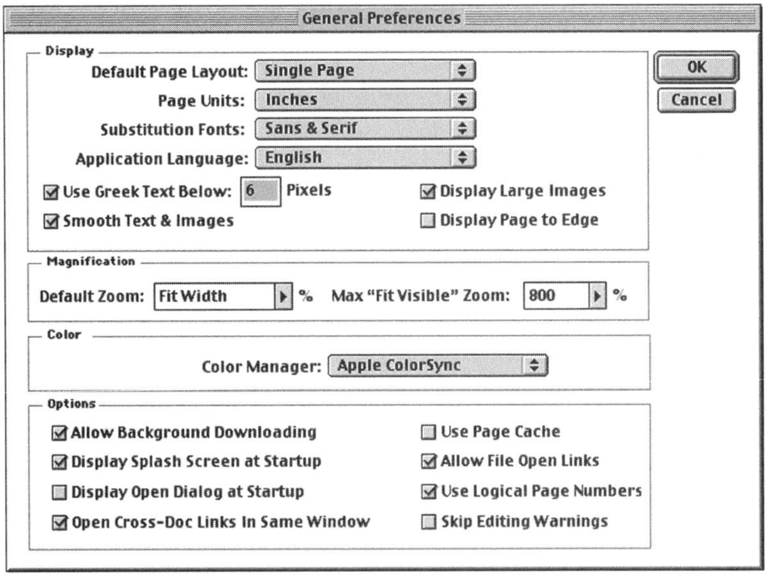

Figure 3-25
The Acrobat General Preferences dialog box.

Here are the specific areas of preferences for Acrobat:

Display

- Page Layout—sets the page display for page scrolling as: Single page, Continuous, and Continuous-Facing.
- Page Units—sets the default measuring units for page size display as: Points, Inches, or Millimeters.
- Substitution Fonts—selects the Multiple Master fonts Acrobat Reader will use in font substitution situations with Type 1 and TrueType fonts. Settings will take place only after Reader is restarted.
- Text Greeking Threshold—specifies the point at which text will display as lines of gray. This will aid in the speed of document display.
- Smooth Text and Images—will smooth the edges of text and monochrome images on the screen by using an anti-aliasing approach.

- Application Language—sets the language used for the Adobe Reader application, reflecting what is installed with Reader. All changes will take place after Reader is restarted.
- Display Large Images—will allow all images to display to the screen as "high-res" images. Deselecting will gray out any images that are over 128K in size.
- Display Page to Edge—allows PDF files to print to the edges of the sheet. If this is not selected, some printers may produce a white border around the sheet.

Magnification

- Default Zoom—will set the magnification level of a PDF document when opened unless the author of the PDF has specified otherwise. The choices are Specific zoom percent, Fit in Window, Actual Size, Fit Width, and Fit Visible.
- Max "Fit Visible" Zoom— sets the maximum zoom level for the Fit Visible view option and for article viewing.

Color

- Color Manager—will select the color management methodology for color display. The default value is for the Built-in Color Management System.

Options

- Allow Background Downloading—used in Web down-loading situations. This will allow simultaneous download of other document pages of a multipage document while viewing a current page. If this option is not turned on, pages will be downloaded on a per page basis. Addition-ally, the Go Back command may not operate properly in a partially downloaded file when this option is not enabled.
- Display Splash Screen at Startup—will enable or disable the Acrobat Reader startup screen when the application is launched.

- Open Cross-Document Links in Same Window—will permit the viewing of linked PDF documents, and pages linked with the *Go To View* command, in the same Acrobat window. This will reduce the number of open windows that Reader has to manage. Regardless of the setting made here, users can override it by holding the Control key in Windows or the Option key on a Mac when choosing a document link.
- Confirm File Open Links—warns you of the possibility of security problems when linking to a file in another application. This will allow you to cancel the operation and avoid possible risks.
- Use Page Cache—used with multipage documents, this option will pre-cache the next page in the document. This will speed viewing and navigating documents.
- Use Logical Page Number—allows you to set the page numbering of a PDF file. This page numbering is used for the Go to page commands and page navigation.
- Skip Edit Warnings—disables any screen warnings that pop up when you delete annotations, pages, etc. from a file.

Usually, once these preferences are set, it is rare that users go back and change them. Most users rely on the Acrobat defaults instead of modifying these settings.

Preferences

Annotation Preferences   The annotation preferences in Acrobat gives control over how notes are summarized and viewed in a PDF file.

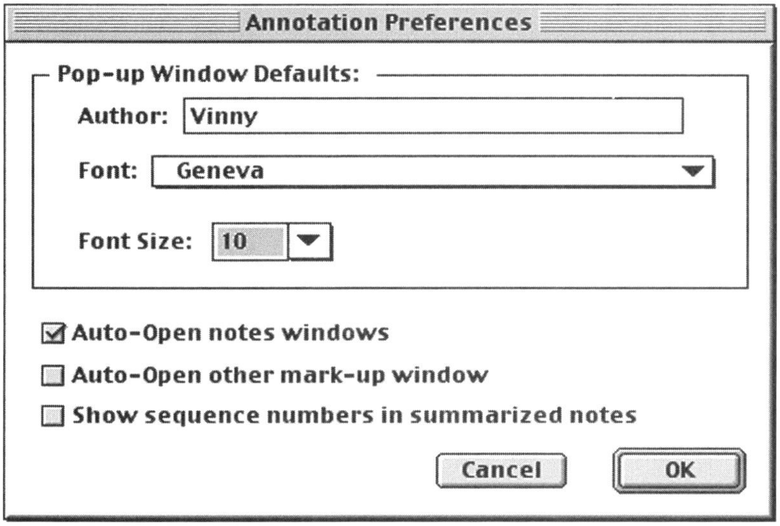

Figure 3-26
The Acrobat Annotation Preferences dialog box.

To access the Note preferences, go to the File menu to the Preferences submenu, to the Annotations selection. When adding or viewing notes in a PDF file, you have control over the fonts used in their display. You can choose from any font that is resident on your system. The default font is —ugh—Helvetica. You can also choose the point size of the text in the note itself. The name that is put on each note is the final interaction of Note appearance.

The checkboxes at the bottom of the dialog box are used to determine how you want to manage the annotations in a document. You can choose to have all notes and other annotations automatically opened for you or have the annotations numbered in a summarized report according to their sequence in the document.

Preferences for Full Screen   Choose File menu to Preferences submenu to Full Screen. Full Screen is great for presentations. Make all your pages and visuals in any application, and then make a PDF document. You can even make presentations with QuickTime movies, sound and graphic effects, like transitions. The settings are broken into Navigation and Appearance.

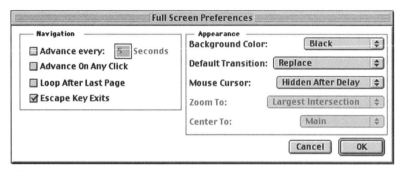

Figure 3-27
The Acrobat Full Screen Preferences dialog box.

Navigation Settings   When viewing a document in Full Screen mode, you must navigate around it. You can use the keyboard command keys if you know them, or any icons or links you have set in the file. Preferences can be changed at any time.

The most important setting to remember in a full-screen view presentation is to check on the Advance on Any Click option. By doing this you can merely click on the mouse button any time you want to advance forward in your pages.

Watch this setting on other full-screen applications. If you set up an interactive document with icons and links, you will not want this box to be checked because you will want the user to navigate through the document according to the icons. You can also advance through the document by using the up-and-down or left-and-right arrow keys.

Use the Command + L keyboard shortcut, or the Full Screen choice in the View menu, to enter full screen view.

View Appearance Settings   This group of settings has a significant effect on document viewing conditions. Background color and default transition (between pages) are the most important.

Your choices for setting a background color are virtually unlimited because of the ability to custom mix any color. You can create the custom color by choosing custom color in the background-color pull-down menu (or choose the very boring black or white). Click on the Define Custom Colors button and you will be brought to a color picker to choose your color. You can move the mouse over an area on the picker to choose a color, or you can key in the specific numerical values. You must click on Add to Custom Colors button to finalize the choice. Highlight the new color that appears in the Custom Colors field and click OK. You are then brought back to the Full Screen Preferences dialog window.

Forms Grid Preferences   A new feature in Acrobat 4 lets you overlay a grid for the alignment of forms. You can use this grid in a "snap to" fashion. The preferences for the size of the grid are found in the Forms Grid selection of the Preferences in the File menu.

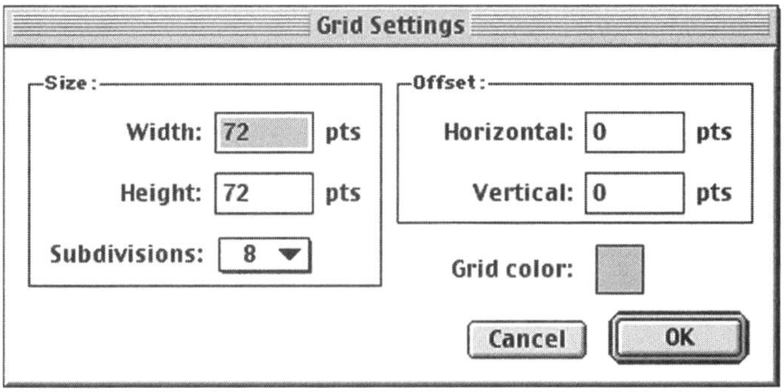

Figure 3-28
The Acrobat Forms Grid Settings dialog box.

The size of the grid setting will determine the size of the main grid, and subdivisions sets how many sections the main grid is divided into. The Offset settings will move the origin of the forms grid using the upper-right corner of the document page as a reference. Heaver lines indicate the grid settings, and lighter lines indicate the subdivisions.

Figure 3-29
The Grid lines have different weights.

Capture Preferences   The preferences settings for the Scan plug-in requires that you go to the Paper Capture settings in the Preferences submenu of the File menu. You need to select the dictionary you want to use when performing OCR (Optical Character Recognition) and what type of scan to perform.

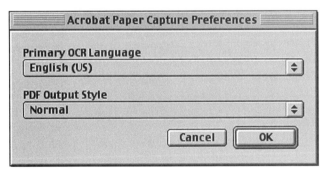

Figure 3-30
The Acrobat Capture dialog box.

The settings for PDF Output Style can be either Normal, or Original Image With Hidden Text. The Normal setting will retain only the original image (that was scanned), whereas the Original Image with Hidden Text will retain the text along with the scanned image—which is searchable.

Search Preferences   Acrobat Search is a plug-in, and it has its own set of preferences. The dialog box is found in the File Menu under Preferences in the Search selection and is divided into four major areas:

- Query
- Results
- Hilights
- Indexes

Figure 3-31
The Acrobat Search Preferences dialog box.

By unchecking the Hide Query Box in Search, you will always keep the Search query box open. This will make it easier for you to Refine the original search results. See the chapter on Search and Retrieval. Some Search settings require that an index be mounted in order to make changes.

TouchUp Preferences   Acrobat 4 provides the ability to perform extensive "TouchUps" to images as well as text. These touchups are actually performed in the newest versions of Adobe Photoshop and Adobe Illustrator which open automatically. The preference must be set to tell Acrobat where these programs are located on your system. To set these preferences, go to the TouchUp selection of the Preferences submenu in the File menu.

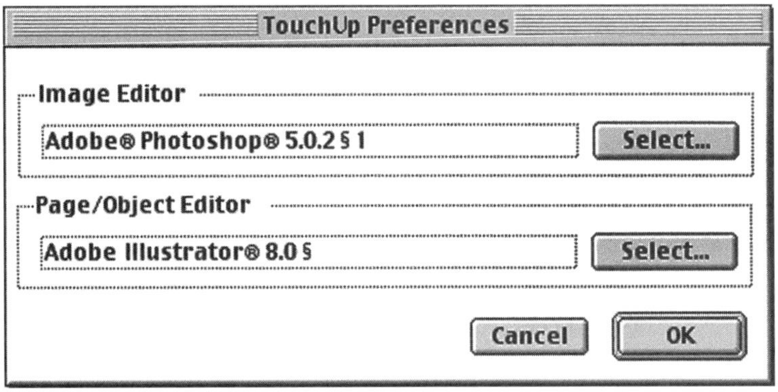

Figure 3-32
The Acrobat Touchup Preferences dialog box.

To make a selection for image TouchUp, choose the select button, and then go to your application. In this case, Adobe Photoshop 5.0.2 was selected. In order to use these features, you must have these versions of software:

> Adobe Photoshop 5 or better
> Adobe Illustrator 7 or 8 or better

Web Link Preferences   One of the important features of Acrobat and PDF files in general is the ability to provide users with hypertext links. A hypertext link allows you to jump around the World Wide Web with mouse clicks.

The Web is a network of networks of sites linked together by these hypertext links. These links are denoted usually by a difference in color of the text, or by an icon. If your document has a hypertext link in it, then it can link to the Web or jump from site to site.

When you come across a link in your PDF document on your desktop and you want to follow it, you must launch a browser and connect via your Internet Service Provider. The settings in this area tell Acrobat where to look to launch the browser.

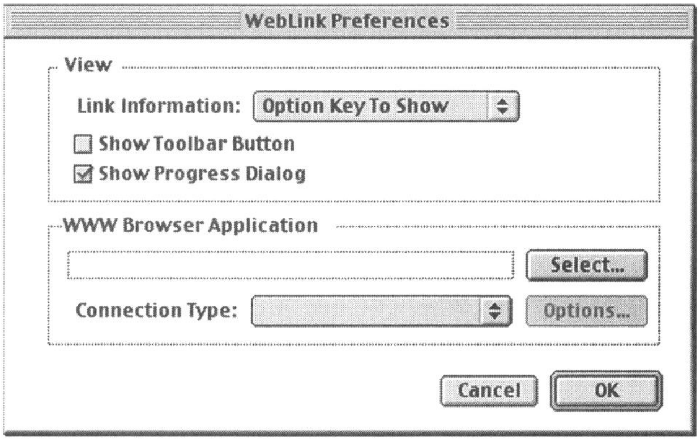

Figure 3-33
The Acrobat Web Link Preferences dialog box.

If you choose to show the toolbar button, an icon will appear in the toolbar. This icon will automatically launch your Web browser. The most important part of this dialog box is the selection of the location of your Web browser. To find your browser application, click on the Browse button and follow the prompts and navigate your way to your program.

When you have located the program file (Netscape, MS Explorer, etc.), click on the Open button. After this, select the type of connection you have. When you are satisfied with the other settings, click OK to verify and make these settings.

Saving a PDF file

Acrobat (formerly Acrobat Exchange) saves changes to a PDF file—Reader does not. Acrobat offers two ways to save a file; the Save command and the Save As command. The Save command should be used when you want to update a file. The Save command includes additions and changes to the original file.

With each Save you are increasing the file size. When you perform a Save As, you are rewriting the file, so the file size can be reduced (it can also increase if features are added, or the file size may stay the same). In addition, when you do a Save As, you will apply some editing features that may have been used in the document. Another advantage of doing a Save As is to optimize a file as well as to add security options. These two functions can now also be performed by Distiller. See that chapter for more information.

Save As   The Save As function will eliminate the "patches" or additional file size that is associated with the Save function. You can access the Save As function in the File menu under Save As (Command + Shift + S). When you enter the Save As dialog box, you will come to what appears to be a standard Save dialog box. But looks are deceiving. The Optimization and Security features are set within this dialog box.

Optimization is selected by clicking the Optimize checkbox. When you activate the Optimize feature, you are instructing Acrobat to:

- Reduce the file size by eliminating redundancy.
- Use the Byte-Serving feature of PDF files (which loads pages in progressive levels of visibility).

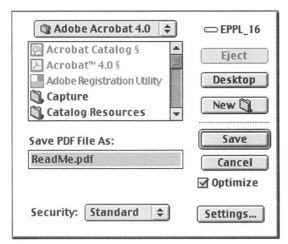

Figure 3-34
The Acrobat Save As dialog box.

Byte serving is the distinguishing feature of PDF files that allows "page at a time" downloading. When you select a PDF file on the Web and link to it, you do not download the entire file at once if it is optimized. You download only the first pages of the document. This will speed the use of PDF files on the Web. Some servers may need special CGI scripting in order to use Byte Serving.

Optimized files also apply font simulation for faster display. This refers to the ability of the PDF files to be displayed on your monitor by temporarily replacing the fonts with simulated Multiple Master fonts. After the entire page is rendered, the actual fonts are applied into the page.

An Optimized file reduces file size by eliminating repetitive images or fonts within a PDF file. The file format will support this because of the database-like structure of PDF. The primary application of an Optimized PDF file is displayed on a screen. It also takes into consideration the delivery method of the data since bandwidth is an issue in Web document delivery. We do not see a downside to optimization. It should have been a default setting that is always activated, and then de-activated if the user has a reason not to apply it.

Security Settings   To set the security attributes of a PDF file, click the Security button in the Save As dialog box. You will then be brought to the Security dialog box. The Security dialog box contains a series of checkboxes for user limitations of the PDF file, especially for setting passwords to restrict access and certain actions.

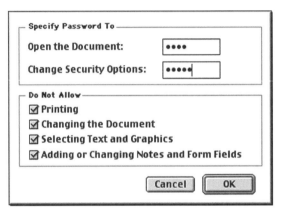

Figure 3-35
The Acrobat Password dialog box.

Within the Security dialog box, you can limit user actions by enabling or disabling the following options:

- Printing
- Modifying the Document
- Selecting Text and Graphics
- Adding or Changing Notes and Form Fields

Performing a Save As to a file will wipe out any security settings. You can set different passwords for opening the file and also for making changes to the security options. Passwords require confirmation before they are applied. When you open a PDF file that has security options set, you will know by observing that the secured or restricted areas are grayed out in certain menus. If printing a file is prohibited by a security setting, the Print choice in the File menu will be grayed out.

Batch Processing   If you have a folder of PDF files that you want optimized, secured, or thumbnailed, use Batch Processing.

Figure 3-36
The Acrobat Optimize dialog box.

Move all the applicable PDF files into a single folder, or a number of folders within a master folder. You then have the ability to set the automatic actions and functions for the following:

- Process all subfolders from the one selected
- Optimize the PDF files
- Creation or deletion of Thumbnails
- Use Passwords to open and override security settings
- Set security to new PDF files
- Apply certain Open information to new PDF files

The original files will be "saved as" in the same location and will not overwrite the original. You can specify what the Open file and Security passwords are by highlighting a file name and then clicking on the Password checkbox. Passwords are case sensitive.

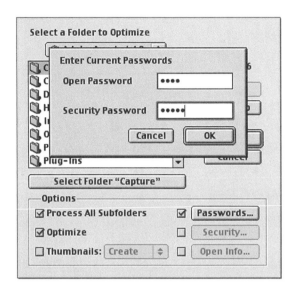

Figure 3-37
The Enter Password dialog box.

Click on the select button bar at the bottom of the file chooser and Acrobat activates all settings. A floating dialog box will appear and provide a status bar as processing procedes.

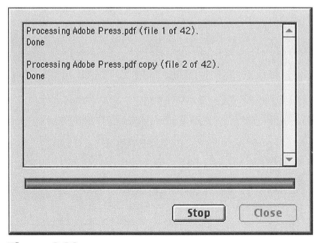

Figure 3-38
The security status bar.

Importing

There are a variety of methods used to enter documents and images into PDF files. The Import menu in the File menu of Acrobat will allow you to import certain items directly into the PDF file format. Supported menu options are:

- Scan
- Import Images
- Annotations
- Form Data

We think that the most interesting feature is the ability to scan a page directly into Acrobat. This allows users to perform OCR functions on files via the Acrobat Capture plug-in. It makes it very easy to convert a document for electronic mail applications. Advances in drag-and-drop capabilities make the Import Image feature one to consider in advanced PDF workflows.

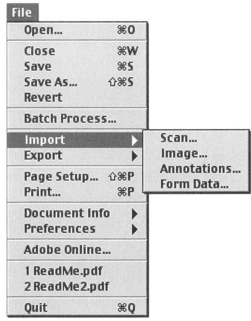

Figure 3-39
The Acrobat Import submenu

Importing Images   Acrobat 4 supports the automatic conversion of several bitmap image types directly into PDF. This will bypass Distiller. Using the new TouchUp tools, you can then move these images to any PDF file. The file types supported are

- GIF
- TIFF
- PNG
- JPEG
- BMP
- PCX

PDFs are now extensible. Images can be imported directly into Acrobat via the Import Image selection in the Import submenu of the File menu. This will bring you to the Import Image dialog box.

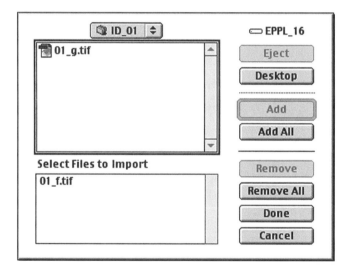

Figure 3-40
The Import Image dialog box.

To add image files to the import list, identify them using the top navigation box and either double-click on them, or highlight them and click the Add button. Then, click the Done button for a dialog box requesting for a destination of the new images. The choices will be to create a new page for each image in the currently open document, or to create a new PDF file that will contain only the images.

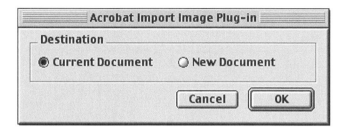

Figure 3-41
The Import Image Plug-in dialog box.

After you decide where the images will reside, there will be a status bar indicating the progress of the file as it is imported. As with all status bars, this one will provide feedback to insure that the process is actually doing something.

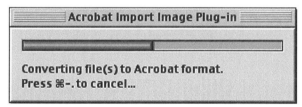

Figure 3-42
The Import Image Plug-in dialog box status bar.

After the image is imported, it will be scaled to 100 percent on the selected page. The page size will be the size of the image area. You then have complete cut and paste capabilities with these images.

Import Annotations   Annotations to files (attached notes, attached sound links, attached file links, attached text, and attached stamps) can be imported and exported from PDF file to PDF file. This comes in very handy in large documentation markup. If everyone in a group of reviewers has the base PDF file, the smaller file containing just the annotations can be imported and exported by users. This new exported FDF file (Forms Data Format to be discussed in Chapter 16) is very small (about 20K for an average document) and is ideal for attachment to an e-mail. Then, the receiver of this mail can import the notes back into the main PDF file, and all the placement and note information is intact.

To import a PDF file of Annotations only, open the main document that the Annotations came from (the base document), then to the File menu, then to the Import submenu, then to Annotations. You will be prompted by a selection dialog box and all you have to do is select the file that contains the annotations, and you will import them into the file.

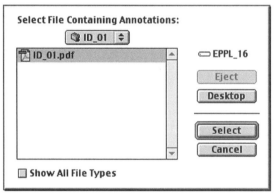

Figure 3-43
The Select Image dialog box status bar.

Importing Form Data　The process of importing forms data is similar to that of importing annotations. Both processes operate on the FDF file (Forms Data Format), a file that is uniquely structured to communicate data pertaining directly to any forms created in a PDF document. For this transfer to be seamless, or to work at all, the base PDF file must reside at both the originating site and at the receiver's site.

The Forms Data Format will be also discussed later in the Interactive Acrobat chapter.

Page Navigation

You have several options to navigate around a document, especially from page to page. The document menu offers the ability to move through a document. The toolbar also offers shortcut buttons to navigate the document. The basic navigation approaches are

- First Page
- Previous Page you were on
- Next Page in the Document
- Last Page in the Document
- Go back to Previous Document
- Go to Previous View
- Go to Next View
- Go Forward to Next Document

Go To Page   If you select the Go To Page option in the document menu, you will come to a dialog box prompting you to specify what page you want to go to. Key in the page number you want and either click the OK button or hit Enter.

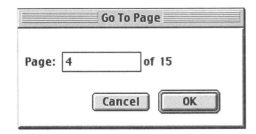

Figure 3-44
The Go To Page dialog box.

You can also use the bottom toolbar in the document window for page navigation. In the area that indicates the current page of the document, highlight the number (by double-clicking on it) and key the new page number. In the Full page view of a document (Single Page option), the arrow keys can be used to page through a document.

Forward and Backward   The Forward and Back commands in Acrobat are like forward and back icons in most Web browsers. The two ways to access the Forward or Back command is either to use the toolbar icons for the navigation or to go under the Document menu and select either Go Forward or Go Back. No matter how you approach the Forward and Back commands, they operate in the same manner as in a Web browser, and you must go Back to activate the Forward function.

Page and Document Management

You can manage PDF pages in one document or between documents. Almost all of these page-management functions are done with the use of Thumbnails:
- Insert Pages
- Replace Pages
- Crop Pages
- Number Pages
- Extract Pages
- Delete Pages
- Rotate Pages
- Set Page Actions

Inserting Pages   Use the Insert Pages command in the document menu (Command + Shift + I) to—you know—insert pages. You will be prompted by a dialog box to choose the PDF file with the pages you want to insert. Then, you will be brought to a dialog box to choose the location in the original file where you want the new pages to go.

You will have to insert every page in the file, but in many cases you want only one or two pages of a file to be transferred. When this is the case, you can use the Thumbnail features. Thumbnails allow you to select and drag pages from PDF to PDF.

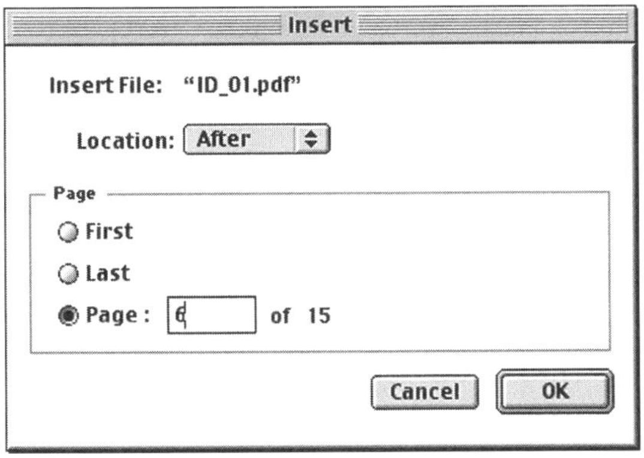

Figure 3-45
The Insert dialog box.

Thumbnail Pages   To insert pages that you want to move from another document, tile the windows vertically or horizontally, and view the documents in the Thumbnails mode. Scroll through both documents so that the pages you want to insert are visible on the screen. With the handtool selected, click the Thumbnails and drag the cursor across the Thumbnails of the pages you want to move.

As you do this, the Thumbnails are surrounded by a blue outline. Click and hold on a page (in Thumbnails) of the highlighted section. The cursor will change to a pointer with a rectangle (representing a page).

The Thumbnail palette can "tear" away from the main screen as a floating window. You can grab the divider bar between the page area and the thumbnails area, and drag it left and right. This will show more or less Thumbnails on the screen.

Hold the mouse button and drag the page or pages across the screen to the Thumbnail section of the destination file. You will see a black bar where the page or pages will be inserted. When you are over the required area, release the mouse and the pages are inserted. You can insert pages anywhere in the document. Hold down the Option key to delete the page from the original file if you want.

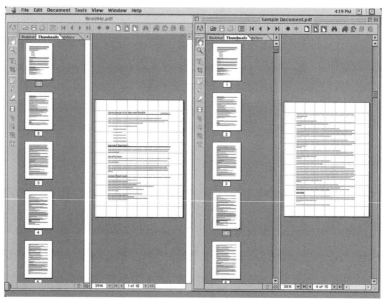

Figure 3-46
Two PDFs in Thumbnails mode.

Extracting Pages The Extract Pages lets you create an entirely new file from selected pages in a document. Go to the Document menu to Extract Pages. You can specify any set of continuous page numbers from the original document for extraction. You can also delete the pages from the document.

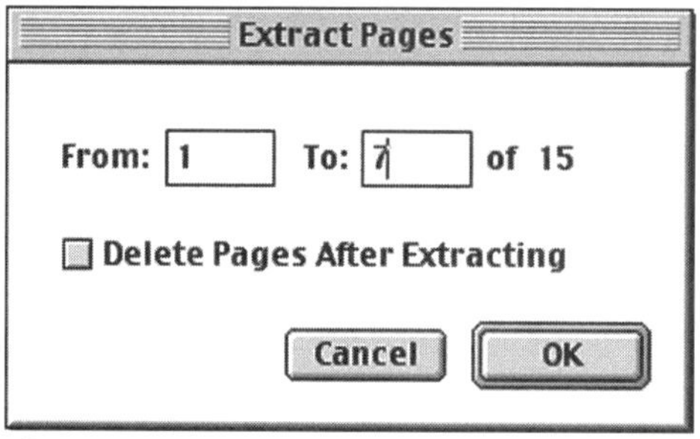

Figure 3-47
The Extract Pages dialog box.

Replacing Pages   In the Document menu, use Replace Pages to specify pages from a new file to replace the pages in your current file. This will let you update a document that may need a few pages to be inserted. Open the Destination file in Acrobat and select Replace Pages in the Document menu. You will have to select the new file, and the Replace Pages dialog box will come up. Choose the pages to be replaced, and click the ever-popular OK.

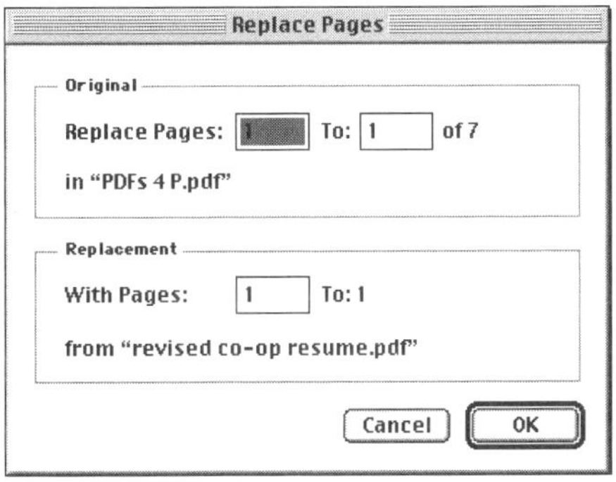

Figure 3-48
The Replace Pages dialog box.

You can replace pages using the Thumbnails approach in the same manner that pages were inserted using the Thumbnails approach. To replace pages from one document to another, open both documents and tile the windows vertically or horizontally on your screen. We like them side by side, although some people like top and bottom. Set the view to Thumbnails. We will assume that you did, in fact, create Thumbnails for the document. Scroll through both documents so that the pages you want to insert are visible on the screen. With the handtool selected, click and drag over the Thumbnails of the pages you want to move. The Thumbnails are then surrounded by a blue outline. Click and hold on a Thumbnail page of the highlighted section. The cursor will then turn to a pointer with a rectangle (representing a page).

The Thumbnail palette can then "tear" away from the main screen to become a floating window. You can grab the divider bar between the main page view and the Thumbnails, and drag it left and right. This will show you more or less of the Thumbnails on the screen. While still holding the mouse button down, drag the pages across the screen to the Thumbnail section of the destination file. Place the cursor on top of the page number that you want to replace. A black bar will appear where the page is going to be inserted. When you drag the mouse over the Thumbnail page, it will turn blue. At this point, release the mouse, and the page will be replaced.

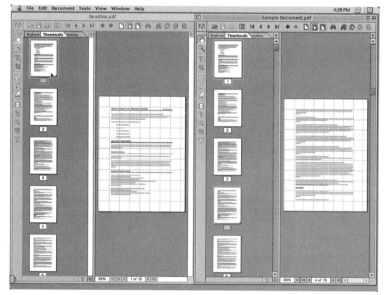

Figure 3-49
Highlighting a page in Thumbnails view.

Deleting Pages   Use the Delete Pages option in the Document menu (Command + Shift + D) to—this is too easy—delete pages. You will be prompted by a Delete Pages dialog box. Key in the page numbers. Insert the page numbers of the pages you want to delete and click OK. See Figure 3-49.

You can also delete pages using Thumbnails. Just highlight the pages to be deleted and hit the Delete key. This is a little too easy, so use it with care.

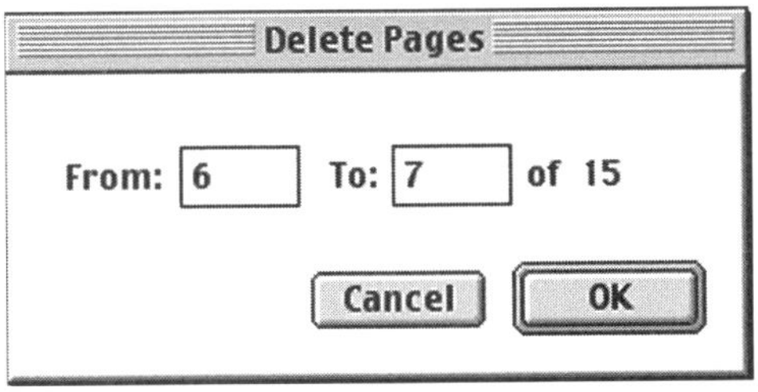

Figure 3-50
The Delete Pages dialog box.

Cropping Pages   Acrobat allows you to resize pages. You can independently crop the edges of each page. To do this go to the Document menu, then to the Crop Pages option (Command + T). The Crop Pages dialog box is the command center for page cropping.

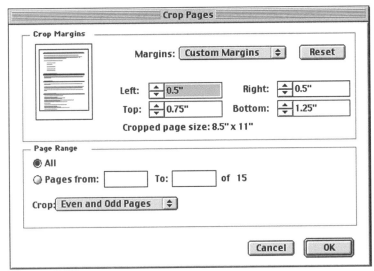

Figure 3-51
The Crop Pages dialog box.

The first choice to be made is in the Margins section at the top of the dialog box. This section has a pull-down menu with the choices for cropping to page margins, or to bounding box margins. In either case, the values entered will correspond to the thumbnail version in the upper-left corner of the dialog box.

Specifying the crop amount is handled in the center portion of the dialog box. You can either click on the arrow keys (they increment in ± 0.01) and set the crop values or enter the measurements directly. As you enter in the measurements, you will see dynamic rule lines come across the sheet to indicate where the crop will take place.

Your next step is to choose the pages to crop. You can choose a single page or a range of pages. New in Acrobat 4 is the ability to select cropping of only the even or odd pages.

After you have made the settings for the crop margins and the page ranges, click OK. The Acrobat page crop function works by applying a mask around the edges of the page. Elements that have been cropped out are not visible but still reside outside the crop area. You can see this for yourself. Using the object TouchUp tool, try to grab elements of pages that are "cropped."

Rotating Pages   From the Document menu go to Acrobat (Command + R). to rotate pages clockwise or counterclockwise. The rotation angle is set at 90°. You cannot adjust the page rotation angle. Choose the direction of the rotation in the top pull-down menu. Choose all pages, or a range of pages.

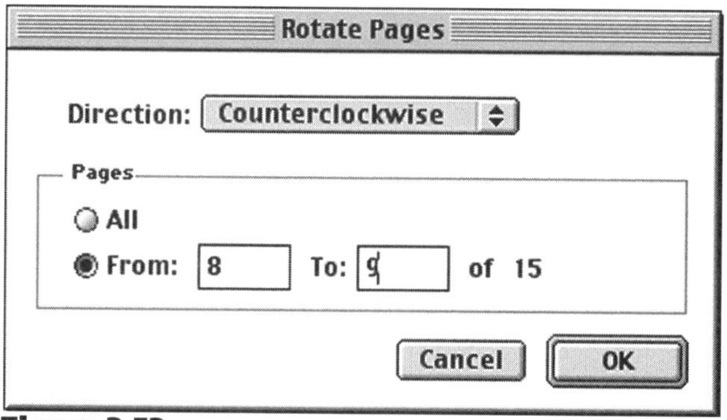

Figure 3-52
The Rotate dialog box.

Page Numbering A new feature in Acrobat 4 is the ability to renumber pages in a document. This function is enabled or disabled in the General Preferences panel using the selection for Use Logical Page Numbering. See the earlier section of this chapter on setting Acrobat's preferences.

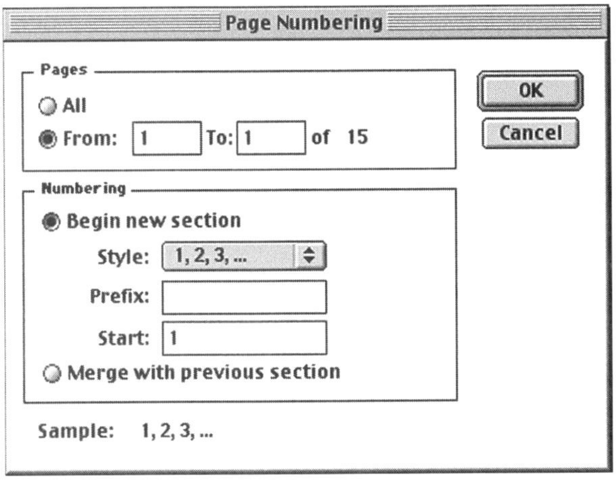

Figure 3-53
The Page Numbering dialog box.

When Logical Page Numbering is enabled, the Page Numbering feature in the Document menu will allow you to specify page numbers in sequence and style. The page numbering dialog box has two parts: pages and numbering. You can select a range of pages to apply the numbering sequence and set the numbering style.

After you have selected the page ranges, you set a number style by pulling down the Style menu in the numbering section. There are several styles, with the most common being arabic numerals. After you select of the numbering style, you can specify a prefix for the page numbers. A prefix is an alpha or numeric character which may precede the page number. The final setting is to choose a page number which will start a section. Use the dynamic sample of numbers and style at the foot of the dialog box to ensure the settings you are making are what you want.

Bookmark Multiple
PDF Files

Bookmarks

Bookmarks are created in Acrobat (what used to be called Exchange). A Bookmark is a navigation tool that you can create to go directly to certain pages, or set to zoom to certain places on the page.

Select the exact place in the document that you want tagged with a Bookmark. That is, go to a specific page and make sure that your zoom is set to the value you want. Then go to the Bookmark palette side pull down menu, and to the New Bookmark option (Command + B). You will automatically be in Bookmark view mode, and an Untitled Bookmark will be in the Bookmark list. Name the Bookmark and type it in.

To change the destination of the Bookmark you just created, move the page to a new view and position. Click once on the bookmark that you want to update—this will highlight the Bookmark. Hold down the Control key and click on the Bookmark a second time. This will show a pull-down menu specifically for this Bookmark. Select the Set Destination option to prompt a confirmation dialog box. Click OK to reset the Bookmark.

Bookmark Properties   If you want to check on the properties of a Bookmark, click once on the bookmark that you want to update; this will highlight the Bookmark. Hold down the Control key and click on the Bookmark a second time. This will open a pull-down menu specifically for the Bookmark selected. Go to the Properties selection in the pull-down menu for the Bookmark Properties dialog box. In the dialog box, you can set the properties of that Bookmark.

Moving Bookmarks   To embed Bookmarks and create an outline format, click and hold the Bookmark icon to the left of the Bookmark you want to move. Drag the icon on top of the text of an existing Bookmark to create the structure. You can create a series of subsets or subheads. A Bookmark can be moved to any other place on the Bookmark list by dragging the icon. To delete a Bookmark, just choose it in a similar manner to the way that they are selected; then, hit the delete key on your keyboard, or go to the Edit menu,

If you want to create bookmarks that point to pages in other PDF documents, you must open the target pages in the other documents to create the bookmark. There is no batch insertion of bookmarks. You could create a single-page, for-placement-only PDF file (blank) and place the file in the same directory as your actual PDFs. Open this placeholder PDF and create your bookmarks in the usual way, via the New Bookmark command in the Bookmarks palette pop-up menu. Name your bookmarks and use the Properties dialog (Edit menu) to specify type and location. Save changes. To append these bookmarks to the actual PDF documents: Open the real PDF and choose Document, Insert Pages, and double-click on your placeholder PDF file. Hit Return to accept the default setting (add the page to the end of the document). The placeholder's Bookmarks are added to the current Bookmarks list. Choose Document, Delete Pages. Hit Return twice: once to delete the last page (the one you just added), and again to confirm what you want to do. The newly added Bookmarks remain.

and then to Clear. You will be asked if you really want to delete the Bookmark. If you do, click OK.

Figure 3-54
The Bookmark Properties dialog box.

Thumbnails

Thumbnails are Lilliputian-like views of each page in a document, which are used for navigation. To create Thumbnails, choose the Create All Thumbnails option in the quick menu for the Thumbnail palette. You can also have Distiller create them automatically. Thumbnails are either all on or all off. Thumbnails will increase the file size by approximately 25 percent depending on page count.

Tearing Off Panes New in Acrobat 4, and similiar to Adobe InDesign, is the ability to "tear off" panes for the various palettes. Options in the Navigation window (Thumbnails, Bookmarks, Annotations) can be grabbed by the tab at the top of the pane and dragged to another part of the window. This will create a floating window that contains just the specific pane or tab of information in question. To re-attach the tab, grab the palette tab in the floating window, and drag it back into the Navigation pane. It's magic.

Showing Destinations Destinations are new features in Acrobat 4. A destination is a special type of a link that lets you set the link to a specific point on a page, rather than just to a page. Using a

destination when cross-linking documents is preferred because of
the fact that destinations are not affected by the adding or deleting
of pages in a document.

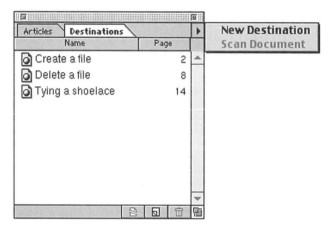

Figure 3-55
The New Destination side pop-out menu.

Switching Between Multiple Open PDF Files   When you
are working with several PDF documents at the same time, you may
want to be able to go directly to one of those files. With more than
one PDF document open, go to the Window menu. At the bottom of
the window the file names of the open documents appear. You can
mouse on down to any one of these documents to select and then
view them.

4

Print-Related Issues

Now that we have reviewed how PDF becomes a predictable, platform-independent, page-independent entity, which solves many of the limitations of PostScript, we must tackle other print-related workflow issues. PDF is the link for completely digital workflow for high-end printing and publishing. PDF alone is nice, but PDF in a digital workflow is nicer.

The very essence of digital workflow for printing and publishing involves the integration of many process steps. Workflow is a collection of functional processes. The most common processes include

- Preflighting
- Trapping
- OPI serving
- Imposition

Each of these steps has evolved from manual techniques to computer operation with manual intervention, and now to totally automated approaches. For a long time, each step often required a dif-

There is debate about placing device-dependent trapping within a PDF. If one wants to make a PDF that will be printed flexo, offset, and gravure, he or she would need three different trapping schemes or three different PDF files, instead of one PDF file that could have the trapping applied in RIP.

Agfa showed an IRT (In Rip Trapping) approach that keeps these device-dependent process control "elements" outside the PDF "digital master." Although one can represent traps within a PDF file, a better approach is to have these as comments that can be modified and applied for different printing requirements, keeping the PDF device independent. Agfa used the Adobe PJTF (Portable Job Ticket Format) to hold trapping and other device controlling information (such as imposition).

Anyone can convert a PDF to EPS and trap it and re-distill it. This is a valid workflow. One can even RIP a PDF (that is, output PDF from Reader or Exchange to a PostScript file and send it to a RIP) and into a raster file and trap it, and if he or she wishes, Save as EPS and distill this. Even TIFF/IT-P1 files can be sent through

ferent computer server to perform a function or functions. The trend today is toward more comprehensive and cohesive systems that are transparent to the user.

Trapping

Trapping can take place at the application program level, at a separate computer with dedicated trapping software, or at the RIP equipped with trapping functionality.

Trapping Approaches Automating the analysis process for a PostScript file has two approaches.

- The first approach parses the PostScript code to identify the logical objects on the page (text strings, tint blocks, contone images, line drawings, and other objects) and their relationships to each other. It works with geometric properties and is called the vector method.
- The second approach rasterizes the file and then analyzes the resulting raster image to determine where colors are adjacent—called the raster method.
- Hybrid systems use a combination of vector and raster technologies.

Each approach works. Vector-based trapping is a mathematical masterpiece and works well with PostScript, which is a geometric, vector-oriented method of describing a page. Analyzing the objects to be trapped should be simpler from a vector viewpoint. The output of a standalone trapping product (if it is also PostScript code) for most pages will be more compact if it is derived from an object description rather than a rasterized bitmap. That, in turn, reduces the transmission and processing time for the RIP that will receive the code.

Once the objects have been identified within the trapping program, sometimes relatively little mathematical manipulation is required to generate the chokes or spreads needed—just a matter of changing the width and depth of an object according to a set of formulas. (When objects cross over multiple colors, then a new

PostScript trap object is generated with its own width and depth. Here, more arithmetic is required.) With complex object outlines, such as serif type, vector trapping is more effective in generating the smaller trap outlines for type without losing its defining shape. Part of this is because sharp corners can be regenerated mathematically with precision, which is better than a raster approach that might round off corners.

One type of PostScript data that resists vector analysis is scanned images. These are truly raster data, so vector-oriented trapping programs must look at the pixel values to determine the color value of the trap. To trap to a vignette or a photographic image, there are two approaches:

- Determine an average value for the entire image.
- Figure the traps on a pixel-by-pixel basis (often known as sliding traps).

Using either approach requires some level of analysis of the raster data. Vector approaches can bog down when there are lots of tiny objects on the page because of the need to generate and process the many tiny objects needed to create the trap areas.

Raster-based trapping algorithms have been refined to the point that they can be executed very quickly. A raster file is the least common denominator for any page once separated into plates; it is very easily converted into screened bitmaps, the ultimate form for any page when it goes to a raster output device. Raster-based algorithms should not have to redo the rasterization process and should find it equally easy to work with any number or combination of objects on the page. Raster approaches generate gobs of binary data. The interim data structures tend to need lots of RAM and disk space, and the results can take a long time to output. This is not quite the problem it used to be, as disks and chips get cheaper by the hour, and data compression techniques improve. High-end prepress systems have always done trapping by analyzing raster data.

Hybrid trapping uses combinations of vector and raster analysis. Some approaches rasterize the file at relatively low resolution to locate object boundaries and color combinations. They use this

solutions by Total Integration or Shria and made into EPS and Distilled or one can represent pre-separated copydot scans of 4-color film in PDF, though it will be tough to trap the TIFF/It and copydot files when in this state.

knowledge to create new objects containing the trap colors, which are then output as a series of PostScript objects. These objects are then merged with the original EPS file and sent to be ripped. Hybrid approaches sometimes end up rasterizing the file at two different resolutions in two different machines, which could lead to noticeable trapping problems.

No mathematical program can anticipate all design situations and corrections, and some of these situations must be made at the source application, while others can be done in the trapping program. The more changes that can be made in an automatic trapping program, the more efficient the resulting workflow will be.

Some Trapping Functions:

- Trap color and placement based on components of adjacent colors
- Trapping of blends with sliding traps for smooth transitions
- On-screen preview of all trap locations and colors
- Unlimited trap zones to confine a trap area or apply different parameters
- Integrated batch-processing capability
- Trap-conforming EPS files or multipage PostScript files, from anywhere to anywhere
- Correctly spread light into dark colors and achieve optimal colors and placement
- Increase productivity by outputting files immediately after trapping is complete
- Maximum control trapping bitmap and continuous tone images against other objects
- Evaluate and adjust traps before committing to page or imposed film
- Trap only the areas that need it, or alter parameters based on custom requirements
- Set parameters for each file to be trapped; leave file unattended during processing

In-RIP Trapping A while back, Mitch Bogart, the technical genius at Rampage, emphasized that trapping functionality should be moved to the RIP. Some people have argued against such a move, claiming that, if the trapping took place in the RIP, you wouldn't be able to check the trapping before you have printed on the press. As long as a RIP takes input in a standard form (EPS files for example) and output is in standard form, a RIP should be considered open rather than closed and proprietary. Trapping may also be handled faster and better when integrated with the RIP. There are other functions such as screening that are also best left integrated. What about spot color separation, JPEG decompression, and OPI replacement? There is a technical synergy that comes from grouping functions together. It also removes the burden for many of these tasks from the originator.

Regarding proofing, the mistake lies in thinking of a RIP as an invisible black box that comes glued to each output device. Not only is this more expensive, since each output device, proofer, and printer must have its own RIP, but, as many have pointed out, the multiplicity of RIPs leads to inevitable visual fidelity problems. Different rippings produce different results. This is especially true when dealing with OPI replacement, fonts, spot colors, and other enhancements for high-quality, high-speed-production RIPs. Instead, one should view the RIP as a sort of central workstation, taking in files and outputting to the screen and multiple peripherals. Before, the RIP was part of a system; now, the RIP is the system. However, Extreme and PDF change the concept a tad. Visual fidelity is assured because the PDF captures the page with more data about the page and the same RIP architecture is used.

Adobe has a PostScript interpreter that incorporates built-in trapping of color pages with a patented, state-of-the-art in-RIP trapping technology. Trapping of color pages is the process of micro-adjusting images on multicolor output devices to compensate for physical limitations of printing presses and other reproduction systems. Adobe expects to license to OEM customers the Adobe PostScript interpreter software with built-in trapping capabilities.

OPI was born with Aldus and then became part of Adobe when the companies merged. Adobe eventually spun off all the prepress systems products as a separate company, called Luminous. Luminous was then acqiured by Imation. Now Imation has done away with the Luminous name and integrated the product line into Imation but some of the parts have been sold to Scenic Soft—got all that?

The concept of Automatic Picture Replacement was born with Scitex when they sold a product called Visionary, based on QuarkXPress. OPI was intitially developed for PageMaker by Aldus using single-file TIFF images. DCS was developed by Quark, Inc.and a prepress/catalog company. DCS is a sort of extension to the EPS format. It consists of as many plates as you have colors plus a preview (on top of the preview that you have on a Mac for EPS files in their resource fork—this other preview is used if you print to a composite device such as a color printer).

In DCS 1.0 you had only multifile DCS-EPS files, and you could handle only CMYK, so you always had files like _filename_.eps (the preview), _filename_.K (the black plate), _filename_.Y (the yellow plate), _filename_.M (the magenta plate), _filename_.C (the cyan plate).

In DCS 2.0 you can have the same thing as one single file, where internal indication of byte offsets lets a digesting software know where to find the respective pieces. And above that you can have any combination of plates,

Imposition

One area in the prepress industry that has developed rapidly in the past couple of years is electronic imposition. Due to the prevalence of large-format imagesetters and platesetters, many users are turning to imposition programs for workflow automation. Following are some imposition functions:

- Standard and custom imposition layouts for sheet or Web printing
- Enhanced shingling and bottling controls
- Form, file, and page-level positioning and rotation, with verso/recto page controls
- Customizable page, and sheet marks, with the option to use EPS art as a mark
- On-screen preview of press sheets, with all marks and pages in place and proportion
- Support for pin-registration systems with full control over form and sheet position
- Impose PostScript files from any application or platform, output them to any device
- Accommodate all standard binding methods, as well as irregular layouts
- Gain maximum control by applying parameters by the job, file, or page
- Achieve highest degree of accuracy when compensating for folding discrepancies
- Modify any printer's mark to meet particular production requirements
- Check the accuracy and placement of all parts of a form before output
- Accurate placement of imposition forms for plate-ready film or press-ready plates
- Send, impose, and return pre-trapped files for separation without intervention

OPI

Aldus' Open Prepress Interface (now under Imation) has become a generic term meaning automatic picture replacement. PageMaker users wanted a simple way to use high-res color photos that had been scanned on high-end scanners, without having the data burden that accompanies those images. Aldus decided it made more sense to use PageMaker to design the layout and compose the text, then add a few commands to tell the output system how to position the color files. They were right.

OPI is an extension of the PostScript language and was developed by Aldus Corporation. OPI workflows can improve prepress system performance by reducing the amount of data that workstations and networks must carry and process. An OPI Server keeps high-resolution graphics stored until imagesetter or printer or platemaker output time, and creates a low-resolution "View file" for applications to work with. The preview is sometimes called

- a proxy image
- an FPO (For Position Only)
- a view file
- a screen viewfile
- a placement file

An OPI Server adds the ability to "OPI-Publish" TIFF images from the Server database. For each high-resolution TIFF image that is "OPI- Published," a view file (a low resolution of the same image) is made available. When users of OPI-compatible applications need TIFF graphics, they can use these view files instead of the actual high-resolution graphics. Because the view files may contain fewer than 75 pixels per inch (compared with high-resolution TIFF contones with up to 300 samples per inch or line art with up to 1,000 samples per inch), much less data is transmitted and processed in the workstation.

The computer operates faster because these view files contain much less graphic data, but users can still see each graphic on the screen and can scale, crop, rotate, etc., as if it were an actual high-

e.g., spot colors. The PlateMaker plug-in for PhotoShop has been devloped by alap (www.alap.com) and should be available from any XTension/Plug-in distributor.

Image workflow with OPI

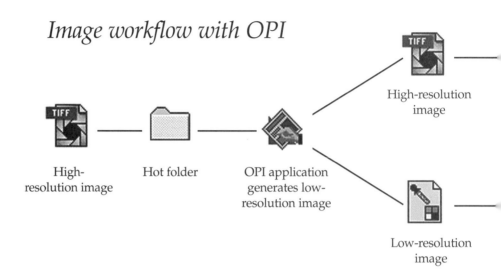

High-
resolution image

Hot folder

OPI application
generates low-
resolution image

High-resolution
image

Low-resolution
image

resolution graphic. These low-res "placement only" files contain information about where the high-resolution file is located, how the image has been scaled, cropped, and rotated. This information is in the form of OPI comments within the low-resolution file. At output time, the application creates a PostScript file with image-processing instructions (OPI Comments) substituted for each OPI view file. The OPI Server scales, crops, rotates, and merges the high-resolution images with the PostScript file according to these instructions.

Macintosh users can access OPI features only via OPI-compatible applications such as QuarkXPress, Adobe InDesign, or Adobe Page-Maker. OPI operation with these applications is identical to standard operation with two exceptions:

- Some functions are faster, due to the smaller quantity of graphic data that is being handled by the computer.
- To output an item containing OPI view files, or to place the item in the Server database, a Macintosh user "saves"

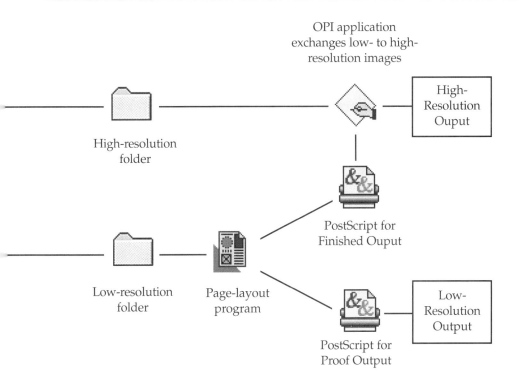

OPI application exchanges low- to high-resolution images

High-resolution folder

High-Resolution Ouput

PostScript for Finished Ouput

Low-resolution folder   Page-layout program

Low-Resolution Output

PostScript for Proof Output

it as an EPS file in a Server folder, with TIFF images omitted.

Sometimes two Server folders are set up for this purpose—one for direct output and one for storage in the Server database. QuarkXPress also offers an alternate method for OPI output in which the user can "save as EPS" with TIFF omitted.

For direct output, the OPI merging function (part of the OPI Server) receives the PostScript file, integrates the high-resolution image from the database, and performs scaling, cropping, and rotation as directed in the OPI comments before automatically outputting the entire job to the PostScript device. OPI resolves the problem of large image files and deals with the data burden that impedes productivity.

The OPI industry-standard convention defines how to embed instructions in a PostScript output file to tell the output device where and how to merge the various text and graphics components of a page. OPI enables users to work with low-res preview images in their page-makeup programs and keep the high-res graphic images close to the imagesetter. This maximizes workstation productivity and minimizes network traffic.

Working with OPI   Pre-1: Send your images to a service bureau or printing service and have them scan them and provide you with the low-res screen images while they maintain the high-res print images on their OPI Server.

1. Make up pages using any of a variety of desktop publishing applications. Compose and assemble the editorial content, line art, charts, ads, and other page elements.
2. Place low-res OPI images on the page using a preview image, which is a low-resolution TIFF image.
3. Send the job to the service bureau or printing service for output.
4. The OPI server reads the path name, fetches the high-res image from the Server, and merges the image in position with the text and other elements.

The high-resolution image resides at or near the RIP or RIP Server or the network Server, and its storage path and file name must match the storage path and file name on the Server. Many vendors offer OPI solutions that support TIFF, EPS, or DCS files. Most support all the cropping and sizing commands issued in the page makeup program. When the page-makeup program creates a PostScript output file of the job for the printer, it appends these commands, along with the path name and file name, as PostScript comments in the job stream. When the OPI-compliant output device reads these comments, it acts upon them by retrieving and merging the high-res image.

DCS and OPI   Many OPI solutions also support DCS (Desktop Color System or Separation), another standardized convention for handling color separations created with desktop publishing programs. DCS originated with Quark Inc. as a way to manage color separation files. In general, DCS is a subset of the EPS file format. In producing color separations, DCS-compliant programs such as Photoshop generate a set of five EPS files. These five files include a main, or "composite" file, as well as a file for each color separation: cyan, magenta, yellow, and black. The composite file contains

- the names of the cyan, magenta, yellow, and black EPS files
- the path name to their storage location
- PostScript commands to print a nonseparated version of the image
- a 72-dpi PICT version of the image for viewing on the screen.

DCS 2.0 offers easier maintenance by offering a single file format that contains all of this information.

In a typical DCS operation, the user places the composite image in the Quark file. When the user prints the job, Quark sends the color separations instead of the composite image. OPI systems that also support DCS enhance this operation by allowing the color separation files to be stored on the Server, so Quark does not have to transmit these large color files at print time. Quark sends only the callouts, containing the path name to the separation files, and the OPI Server fetches those files accordingly.

Encapsulated PostScript   PostScript was originally designed to describe typographic characters and to send files to a printer, but PostScript's ability to scale and translate (move the origin of) objects makes it possible to embed pieces of PostScript and place them anywhere on the page. These pieces are EPS files. EPS is considered a graphic file format.

The PostScript code in an EPS has to follow certain rules. For instance, it shouldn't erase the page since that would affect the whole page, not just its own part. It is forbidden to select a page size, because this would both change the size of and erase the whole page.

An EPS file includes a special header made up of PostScript comments (starting with %), which have no effect on a printer. The most

It might be said that somewhere in the mists of time it was thought that EPS could do what PDFs do. But EPS did not embed font data (which it now does with PDF).

EPS wanted to be what PDF is: a viewable, editable PostScript file.

In a nutshell:

Format   Images
View File
OPI   TIFF
Low-res TIFF
DCS   EPS
PICT

Proof
The contractual predic-
tion and verification,
through simulation, of
the expectation of even-
tual reproduction, that
is legally defensible

The time to attach an
output profile (a de-
scription of the behavior
of the imagesetter or
platesetter) is when
sending a job to the out-
put device. At that
point, it does not matter
whether the profile is an
ICC profile or a
PostScript CRD. The
real issues:

- *Tools to calibrate the*
  device and produce
  accurate profiles
- *Attaching profiles to*
  devices and/or jobs
  to honor calibration
- *Means to coordinate*
  rendering intent (a
  characteristic of each
  object in a job) with
  profiles for an out-
  put device

PostScript 2 already has
the mechanisms to pro-
vide the underlying data
model. PDF has equiva-
lents. Using Distiller to
clean up PostScript is
not possible, when ICC
information is embedded
in the file.

ICC profiles cannot be
embedded in a Post-
Script file. ICC profiles
can be attached to (or
embedded in) images (in
a TIFF file), and appro-
priate CSAs and CRDs
can be inserted into the

important comment is %%Bounding Box, which gives the location of the EPS picture if it is not scaled or translated. A program uses this information to place the picture accurately within a page. The PostScript part of an EPS file is "stripped in" to the PostScript generated as the document is printed, preceded by PostScript "scale" and "translate" instructions.

If you send an EPS file to the printer, it might print a copy of the graphic, or it might print nothing at all. Or a blank page. EPS files aren't designed for printing, but sometimes you get lucky. At the very least, EPS files always print on a default page size since they must not include a page size.

When a desktop publishing program uses an EPS graphic, it isn't smart enough to interpret the PostScript in the EPS to show a picture. Therefore, the EPS file is often accompanied by a preview. This is a low-resolution picture the application program does know how to show. There are several forms of preview. An EPS file without a preview is still usable but probably shows on screen as a gray box—people expect more than that!

There are three types of preview:
- Macintosh
- DOS
- System independent

The Macintosh preview is a PICT graphic in the EPS file's resource fork. This means the EPS file's data fork contains just PostScript. The DOS preview is embedded in the file, and there's a special header. A DOS EPS with preview cannot be printed until the header and preview are removed. In DOS, the preview is embedded as a TIFF or WMF graphic.

An EPS file with system-independent preview is called EPSI. This adds a monochrome bitmap as comments inside the file. It isn't really system independent since in Macintosh and DOS many applications don't support it. They can use the file but won't show the preview. Many Macintosh programs will read DOS format EPS files and handle them suitably if they contain a TIFF preview. DOS programs can read Macintosh EPS files, but they can never see the preview hidden in the resource fork.

Other variations of EPS that may make a file unusable are binary and Level 2. Binary EPS files work well on a Macintosh, but most PCs can't print them because any Control+D in the data will reset a typical PC PostScript printer. Most EPS files written on a Macintosh are binary and don't work on most PCs. Level 2 EPS files can only be printed on a Level 2 printer.

This little discussion on EPS and related forms was provided to help you understand that we, as an industry, have been struggling to find a universal, standardized format for moving files and documents around networks.

Placed PDF and Refined PDF Export You now have the ability to place any page from an Adobe PDF file into a PageMaker publication. The Placed PDF feature enables PageMaker users to reuse and repurpose the millions of PDF pages that have been created with Adobe Acrobat. For example, using the Import PDF Filter, a user can select an individual page from a catalog saved as PDF and place it into an ad or brochure being created in PageMaker. In addition, the PDF import filter allows users to control the resolution of the PDF on-screen preview for faster performance.

With the rapid adoption of PDF for digital printing workflows, Adobe has improved the Export PDF interface to streamline the process of preparing PDFs for print production. Customers and service providers will find the controls for an output color model (such as CMYK or CIE device-independent color), OPI comments, and font and file size optimizations easier to use.

PDF Import Filter The PDF Import Filter works with Windows 2000, Windows NT, and MacOS. The Placed PDF is similar to a placed EPS graphic. It appears in Adobe InDesign and PageMaker as an on-screen preview, using the preferences from the Filter Preferences dialog box, and cannot be edited. The PDF always prints at high resolution, but at the resolution of the screen preview when printed to a non-PostScript device. To import a PDF page:

PostScript file by the application or driver. When Distiller creates PDF, the CSAs are preserved and the CRDs are discarded. To "reattach" CRDs or otherwise honor output-specific ICC profiles in a PDF as part of the PDF language may be counter productive and device dependent. Preserving transformation profiles might be useful.

If you want to honor an output ICC profile, you probably want specific behavior in Exchange, Reader, or some other PDF interpreter or printer, not in Distiller, which only "produces" the PDF. This would probably be handled using an Exchange plug-in.

- In Pagemaker's layout view, choose File > Place. In Windows, Pagemaker lists PDF documents with a ".pdf" extension. To see a valid file without that extension, choose All Files for Files of Type. In MacOS, Pagemaker lists PDF files with file types of PDF<space> and TEXT.
- Double-click the file to place it, or select the file and click Open (Windows) or OK (MacOS). If prompted to select a file, type in Windows, choose Portable Document Format from the list, and then click OK.
- In the Filter Preferences dialog box, select options for importing specific pages, and for including PostScript printing information and display settings.
- . Position the graphic where you want and click.

You can also import a PDF directly from Netscape Navigator or Internet Explorer.

The PDF Import Filter dialog box provides options for PostScript printing and display settings. The dialog box includes Navigation arrows beneath the thumbnail image to advance through the PDF document page by page. Thumbnail images of each page appear in the dialog box. The number 1 is the default page number. Specify a page number, and then click to select.

Once documents have made the transition to electronic form and have made their way through a prepress or prepublishing system, one of the most important steps—and it occurs at various points—is proofing, or the verification of documents prior to printing.

Proofing   "Edging closer to dotlessness," as Seybold Publications describes it, may be the theme in the color proofing area. The contract proof (the verification proof that the client, service bureau, and printer agree will be the standard for color and quality) issue is moving toward an uneasy acceptance.

Most contract proofs have used film-based technology, but with the increasing move to all-digital workflows, and as computer-to-plate systems avoid film entirely, film-based proofing is being

replaced by proofs from digital data. A contract proof has traditionally shown the exact halftone dot structure so that potential printing
problems like moiré can be avoided. Some digital proofing systems
reproduce halftone dots, and some do not. Print buyers are accept-
ing contract proofs without halftone dots. Screening is now pretty
much a nonissue since print buyers seem prepared for moiré passé.
The contract proof market now appears to be a battle between
proofers with and/or without dots.

*Placed PDF may replace
EPS since it includes
fonts. But applications
must add code to accept
PPDF files.*

Most vendors of CTP systems also offer imposition proofers to
replicate blueline imposition proofs. These tend to be large-format
monochrome plotters, although there are some in color and some
that print on both sides of the sheet to show true imposition.
Imposition printers, used in conjunction with inkjet, dye sublimation, or other proofing engines, are looked at as the future course for
digital proofing within new workflows.

*Quark, Inc. has stated
that they will support
PDF export and import
capabilities in an even-
tual upgrade to
QuarkXPress 4.*

For people who still want traditional dot proofs (and are willing to
pay for them), digital dot proofers are available. Some users may
even keep an imagesetter around to produce film only for proofing
purposes in a CTP environment.

There are even some print buyers who accept a PDF for on-
screen viewing as a soft proof. They must really trust their printers.

Remote Proofing A major trend is that of remote proofing,
where an ink jet or dye sublimation or other color proofer is physically installed in a customer location. PDFs from the customer are
sent to the prepress or printing service and processed. The Server
system prepares a version of the PDF that calibrates to the eventual
reproduction device, and the files are returned to the customer for
proofing printout. Since the PDF files are compressed, they can be
sent via telecommunications lines to and from the customer.

New Servers and RIPs based on electronic job tickets will automatically direct PDFs to queues based on the customer's name, the
reproduction device (litho press, flexo press, digital color press, or
whatever), and convert or modify files as required for each step in
the workflow.

Fonts, What Are They?   In the good old days of printing with lead type, a font was one kind, one size, and one style of type. For example; Palatino Bold 48pt, was one font, and Palatino Bold 14pt was yet another font, but that was then and this is now. Today, we generalize and call a font just Palatino. What is more important is that the font itself has to be described in the digital file. There are many digital methods to describe the fonts and their characteristics.

Basically, digital fonts come in two major kinds: outline and bitmap. Both font types have different methods to describe the letter shapes. Outline fonts use mathematical models for descriptions, and bitmap fonts use a grid to place the letter boundaries. When used correctly, both will display and print as well as the other.

5

Workflow Environments

Face it—mechanicals are gone. Do you really feel bad about it? Workflow is digital. And discussions of digital workflow always seem to start with conventional workflows: scanning, assembly, film output, stripping, contacting exposure, duping, proofing, and plate exposure. Since most print-oriented organizations have moved into film image-setting and imposetting, there are now more users with partial digital workflows than those without them.

Partial digital workflow refers to the fact that most users still have little islands of automation that are not integrated into a comprehensive system. Using network or sneaker-net, they are moving files to specialized servers for specialized operations. Too often digital workflows have been constructed around people rather than machines and software processes. The trend today—and the PDF is in the forefront of that movement—is to move workflow to totally automated systems. We cannot continue analog thinking in a digital world.

The benefits of PDF printing and publishing are most evident in a systems environment. Today, our perception of a system is a bunch of

In the Macintosh environment, this software is included—AppleTalk. In the Windows environment, it is necessary to add additional software such as Microsoft Windows for Workgroups, Artisoft Lantastic, Novell Netware, or others. Microsoft Windows 95 and 98 network software is built in.

Macs and/or PCs cabled together to share various output devices. In reality, the network configuration and functionality are the most important issues in prepress and prepublishing productivity.

Before Networks When computers were first introduced, they were batch-processing oriented. All work was delivered to the computer for processing en masse. By the 1970s, typewriters, and then video terminals were attached to the computer to provide access to files and CPU processing. This gave users increasing amounts of interactivity. There were limitations to the number of terminals that could be connected, and users were limited in what they could do and when they could do it. Modems introduced long distance tele-computing. This led to the development of local area networks as an alternative method of connecting computers . . . and people.

Network Basics A network is everything that ties computers together and enables them to communicate, including hardware and cables (the physical things) and software (the stuff you can't see but does all the work). A network allows computers to be connected together so that they can share common software, data, or devices. A network is the sum of all its parts. Computers can be connected in a number of different ways. Apple Macintosh computers can be connected using either LocalTalk or Ethernet. Windows-based PC's, and compatible computers, are typically connected using Ethernet. LocalTalk and Ethernet describe the physical aspects of connecting computers, and additional software is needed for the system to operate.

Networking Macintosh Computers In the Macintosh environment, the simplest and least expensive networking approach is LocalTalk, which is built into every Macintosh.

You can construct a simple network of two Macintosh computers using LocalTalk with PhoneNet-compatible connectors—common telephone wire that connects computers and the same wire that is used to connect a telephone to the wall jack. You can also use the same connectors to connect computers to your printer and share it. Unfortunately, it is very slow.

A LocalTalk-based network can be as simple as two computers and a printer connected together. With LocalTalk, computers and printers may be over a thousand feet apart, depending on the quality of the cable used. Computers are strung together, or daisy chained, using the connectors. If additional computers or printers need to be added to the network, they can be daisy chained into the existing connections.

This type of connection is inexpensive, but not very fast. The speed of the communication between computers is 230,400 bits per second. This may seem fast when compared to the fastest modems available, but it may not be fast enough.

An alternative is to use Ethernet, a much faster networking technology—at least 43 times faster than LocalTalk. 10-Base-T Ethernet is at 10 million bits per second; 100-Base-T is at 100 million bits per second; and 1 billion bps Ethernet is not far away. Fiber optics connections are being applied by early adopters. With its high-speed data transfer rates that can outperform copper wire, optical fiber will clearly become the new method for transmitting data.

A Macintosh-based network using Ethernet does not connect computers and printers together by daisy chaining them—they are connected into a Hub. A device known as an Ethernet Transceiver is used to connect the cabling to the computer. For the Macintosh to use an Ethernet network, it must have an Ethernet card installed Most recent Macintosh computers are delivered with a built-in Ethernet connector, as well as USB and FireWire. Most computer stores or catalogs can supply the card and instructions for installing it. The Ethernet Transceiver connects the card in your computer to the cabling of the network. The maximum distance supported by Ethernet is 500 meters.

Once the Ethernet network is physically set up, the Network Control Panel in the Macintosh is used to select Ethernet rather than built-in LocalTalk. With Ethernet in place, the only difference the user will notice is improved performance. One of the computers on the network is designated as the Server, and the other computers are its Clients. Usually, the fastest computer should be the Server.

Bits per second
Kbps = kilo (thousands) of bits per second
Mbps = mega (millions) of bits per second

230,400 bps would be 230.4 Kbps.

Usually, if the number is thousand, or million we use kbps or mbps, but if it is not, the whole number is presented.

Computer modems are now about 56.6Kbps or 56,600 bps. They started out at 300 bps—honest!

Most printers for Apple computers are not directly compatible with Ethernet, so the use of a LocalTalk-to-Ethernet gateway is needed. The gateway converts the high-speed Ethernet communications to the lower-speed LocalTalk format so that existing printers can understand the information. Some high-end printers, imagesetters, and platemakers will directly support Ethernet without a gateway.

Two cabling types in use: 10-Base-T and 100-Base-T. The number comes from the speed of the network (10 or 100 megabits per second), "Base" refers to the communications technology (Baseband), and the "T" refers to Twisted Pair, the actual physical cabling type. Devices in a 10-Base-T network must be within 100 meters of another.

Bits galore
Bit = 0 or 1

Byte = 8 bits

Kilobyte ≈ 1,000 (thousand) bytes or 8,000 bits

Megabyte ≈ 1,000,000 (million) bytes or 8,000,000 bits

Gigabyte ≈ 1,000,000,000 (billion) bytes or 8,000,000,000 bits

Terabyte ≈ 1,000,000,000,000 (trillion) bytes or 8,000,000,000,000 bits

Humungabyte ≈ A Whopper with large fries. About seven bits.

Networking Windows Computers   The networking picture in the Windows environment is more complex. The physical aspects of networking are almost the same as those of the Macintosh environment, but LocalTalk is not used in the Windows environment. The networking method built into Windows for Workgroups or Windows 2000 is known as the Microsoft Windows Network. This method is similar to AppleTalk in appearance and operation. The printer is connected directly to a computer, rather than to the hub itself. In the PC environment, the computer allows its directly connected printer to be shared. Any computer on the network can then connect to the shared printer and print. Most Ethernet cards for PCs come with a connection on the card, so a transceiver is not needed. Certain newer Macintoshes are also configured this way.

AppleTalk and the Microsoft Windows Network are known as peer-to-peer networks: Any computer can be a Server, and any computer can be a Client. A computer can also be a Server to one computer and a Client to another at the same time.

Local Area Networks A local area network (LAN) is a collection of hardware, software, and users brought together so as to allow them to cooperate in a fully integrated environment. A LAN typically covers a limited geographical area, measured in meters rather than in kilometers. LANs can cover the linking of two to several hundred users spanning a single office, to one or more departments spanning several floors of a building or spanning an entire site. LANs usually complement Wide Area Networks (WANs) to extend this environment to interconnect or bridge LANs locally or across great distances to form larger networks. Local Area Networks encompass:

- Computers
- Workstations
- Peripherals, such as printers and fixed disks
- Cabling and associated components
- Software

Interconnection There are three techniques for interconnection of computers and related equipment:

- Centralized: The system is a self-contained entity capable of autonomous operation. The units of communication in such cases are Address and Data Blocks and work in a master-slave relationship. A standalone mainframe is a prime example.
- Decentralized: This is communication between systems. The units of communication in this case are Byte and Data Blocks and work in a master-slave relationship. A mainframe computer with Concentrator(s) attached to it falls in this category.
- Distributed: This is network communication among self-contained autonomous intelligent systems. Such a system works in a relationship of cooperation and not master-slave. A cluster of Macintoshes connected to a cluster of Sun workstations connected to a cluster of PCs is a good example of such a system. LANs fall in the category of Distributed Systems.

Sharing of Information and Resources   A distributed system should look transparent to the user. The whole system should appear as one large dedicated local system, and all the remote resources should appear as if they were local to the user. The interface to such a system should be user friendly. People usually work in groups and perform related tasks. Whatever information is presented on paper can also travel over a LAN in the form of data. This ability to transfer data throughout a department or an organization enables users to exchange messages, documents, forms, and graphic files. They also have access to common software packages on the LAN. Though information itself is a resource, the primary purpose of installing a LAN is to share system resources, like software and peripherals such as laser printers, optical disks, etc.

Disadvantages of a LAN   The disadvantages of a LAN are:

- General administration, backing up, adding new users, loading software, etc. have to be done by a competent person or staff, called the Network Administrator.

- If the file server fails in the middle of a session, sometimes it is not possible to salvage all user files, as some Servers do not provide for incremental backups.
- Security of Data: If the file server is not in a reasonably secure place, then unauthorized people may gain access. If user privileges and file protection mechanisms are not properly implemented, it becomes open to misuse.

In a properly administered network, data stored on the file server would be regularly backed up and this would take the pain out of backing up files from the user's point of view. Also, the file server itself can be kept in a physically secure room, which means better security, particularly for sensitive customer data.

LAN Concepts　　The first component of a LAN is the Communication Channel, also called the transmission or the LAN medium, and typically should have the following characteristics:

- High-speed bandwidth
- Flexibility and extendibility
- Reliability and maintainability

A LAN medium defines the nature of the physical path along which the data must travel and allows a great number and wide variety of hardware devices to exchange large amounts of information at high speed over limited distances. A Local Area Network is more than just the cables.

LAN Topologies　　The physical medium may be arranged in a number of ways. The overall geometric shape, or topology, is very important in a LAN design.

Star Networks　　This topology usually forms the basis of a wide area network. In this type of network, each station is connected to a central switch by a dedicated physical link. The switch provides a path between any two devices wishing to communicate either physically in a circuit switch or logically in a packet switch.

Ring Networks　　Stations are connected by a loop of cable and each connection point, called a Repeater, is responsible for passing on each fragment of the data. Access is not under central control, and the data is sent in packets. Within each station, there is a controller board which is responsible for:

- Recognizing packets addressed to that workstation
- Controlling access to the ring—deciding when it is clear to start transmitting

Bus Networks   Bus networks are the most common LANs. They do not need any switches, and in their simplest form, no repeaters. They share a common, linear communication medium, and each station requires a tap that must be capable of delivering the signal to all the stations on the bus. The data is sent in packets, and each station listens to all transmissions, picking up those addressed to it. Bus networks are passive, since all the active components are in the stations, and a failure affects only that one station. Stations on a bus network are limited in distance, and only one station at a time can transmit.

Choice of a Server   On a network, a Server is a computer with a large amount of disk storage that has shared software and information. Other computers on the network are Clients and access the software or information as needed on the Server. Choosing the right server and equipping it properly are the keys to the success of a LAN. A server is usually a computer that holds the bulk of the LAN Operating System and shares its resources with workstations. In most LANs, a single Server:

- Stores shared files
- Stores software
- Links to printers or other output devices
- Links to tape drives and storage media
- Links to modems
- Links to RIPs

These resources are shared by all connected users. As a LAN grows, these functions are spread over many servers, and separate data management and communication servers may be needed. One of the first decisions is whether to buy

- A standard PC or Macintosh as a dedicated server and tailor it with third-party add-ons

Transceiver
To connect your network cable to a computer, you need an adapter. The transceiver converts the network signal into one that the computer can deal with (and vice versa for data going out from the computer).

Repeater
Network cables can only carry a signal so far before resistance degrades it. A repeater takes the signal at some point, pumps it up, and lets it travel a greater distance.

Hub
A number of computers may be clustered into a section of a network. That section is connected to a hub, which connects to other sections.

As a rule of thumb, plan on 1 Tbyte of Server storage—or at least 500 Gbytes.

You can boost perfor-mance further by using a disk controller that also incorporates a dedi-cated cache of high-speed RAM.

Typically, a LAN out-grows a server at about 40 users, but the limit depends on the applica-tions in use. A server can be used either as a Dedicated Server or as a Concurrent Server. Using the server as a Concurrent Server degrades network per-formance and may even crash the network—so forget it.

- A PC or Mac designed as a proprietary server unit
- A Sun or Silicon Graphics workstation as a server
- An NT running on an Intel Pentium PC

Dedicated Server   Networking methodologies use a Dedicated Server. In this case, one computer (typically, a very fast one) is des-ignated as a Dedicated Server. All other computers that attach to it are Clients only. This technique is used for larger networks that demand higher performance than can be realized with peer-to-peer networks.

With a Dedicated Server, all shared files are on the Server, and the Client computers access it for their information. A Server will usual-ly have a network operating system installed on it (Novell, Lantastic, etc.), and the monitor and keyboard will be removed. The Server will automatically start its software on power-up, and service requests only from the network. Printing is shared as before, except that in very large networks, another computer is usually designated as a Print Server and will service only printing needs.

Proprietary Servers   Because proprietary Server options are designed for a particular LAN operating system, you avoid incom-patibilities that crop up with a standard PC. For example, some third-party backup systems and power supplies do not work reliably with certain LAN Operating Systems. Proprietary units are opti-mized for their specific LAN Operating System.

Storage   A fast hard disk and disk controller are vital to the Server's performance. A disk with 40 ms average seek time is too slow for most LANs. If you expect a lot of traffic, consider a 16 ms or less system. How much storage you will need depends on applications. If you want to store a lot of shared files and programs on the server, think big. Get a disk controller that can daisy-chain several drives together, so you can add storage as needed. You will certainly need more drives, especially if you plan to use the disk-mirroring options available with LAN operating systems as a backup approach.

Cache RAM   The more memory available for a server's hard disk, the faster the Server and LAN operating system will run. Think big again—say 256 Mb of RAM. Since fetching data from the cache is much quicker than getting it from disk, disk-caching can speed access to hard disk data. It stores the last data read from the drive plus the next few sectors in RAM, gambling that the software will request that data next.

ms= millisecond
A measure of disk-access time. For instance, the amount of time from when data is requested by the CPU to when the drive returns the data.

Network Adapter Cards   No matter how fast the Server, performance is limited by the speed of the Server's LAN-adapter card. Most vendors offer intelligent cards, equipped with RAM to speed throughput, but they are a bit more expensive.

CPU   Make sure the Server uses a CPU with the fewest wait states. Zero is the best, and two are too many. If the network is really busy, use a Server with a 400-MHz CPU or better.

Backup   A Server should preferably be equipped with a tape backup unit that can hold all the files you want to store. The backup software should be compatible with your LAN operating system and should be capable of backing up all system files. It should also be capable of running while the Server is on-line and perform while unattended.

Drivers   One adapter card will exchange packets over a shared cable with any other adapter, since they all conform to the same electrical signaling, physical connection, and media-access specifications. However, things are different on the software side of the card. Since each manufacturer designed and implemented its adapter using slightly different hardware components, each adapter needs a customized software in order to address them and to move data through the system. This piece of software is known as the driver software.

Print Servers   A Print Server receives jobs from a user on a network, stores that job in a queue, and then forwards the job to an output device on the network—most networks have multiple output devices, from low-res laser printers to high-res imagesetters and platemakers. Features such as queue management, statistics reporting, printer setup, and file storage for later printing are usually common. A typical scenario:

- Select Print from the application's menu.
- Your computer connects to the printer and asks if it is ready to accept a job.
- If the printer is busy with another job, the computer waits for the printer which may need only to finish somebody else's job or have seven others waiting.
- When the printer is ready, the computer sends the first packets of data, which the printer receives and processes (while your computer waits) until the job has been completely sent to the printer.

If you're the ninth person waiting to print, the wait could be enormous. (You might show your college ID when you enter the queue and get a senior citizen discount before your computer is free for use again.) OK, we exaggerate.

Most computers allow you to print in the background. Background printing means that when you select Print, the computer saves the job to a temporary file and a separate piece of software handles communicating that file to the printer, when the printer becomes available. You can continue working on the computer while the job prints. When the computer needs to send data to the printer, the application running in the foreground may have to pause, tying up your computer. Within a few years, true multitasking will be available on most systems. In addition to releasing your workstation faster, a print server should also be able to:

- Manage multiple print queues
- Set up the printer
- Produce status reports

Queue Management   A print queue is a series of jobs waiting to print. A Print Server usually manages multiple queues, either for the same printer or for different printers. When combined with the setup feature, a Print Server can have different queues for a single output, each with an individual setup. The Print Server usually has different types of queues:

- Active—jobs print when the output device is available
- Hold—jobs print when the administrator releases them
- Completed—printed jobs remain stored on disk for archiving or reprinting
- Error—jobs that could not print are stored for review

The active queue is used when you have a job to print and you want to print it now. You can use a hold queue, for example, if you want to print jobs overnight. That way, jobs that need to get out during the day get sent to the active queue, and jobs waiting in the hold queue get sent when network load is lower, or when higher-priority jobs have finished printing. A completed queue lets you hold onto jobs for future printing; and an error queue holds the jobs that could not print because of either a printer error, a PostScript error, or a network error. Then, you can fix the error and resend the job. The hold queue, in particular, lets you manage the printing services on your network. Jobs can be sent to the print server computer, but don't print until the system administrator directs them to the appropriate active queue. This type of queue works for jobs requiring special attention, such as special media (film or plate) or switch settings. They can be held until the system administrator has the output device set up properly.

The ability to support multiple print queues allows you to designate queues for specific print devices, so you automate job routing and eliminate manual switching. For instance, you can have a queue for a plain-paper device and one for a film device. During the proofing stages of the job you send it to the plain-paper queue; for the final pass you send it to the film device. To manage all these queues, the Print Server should be able to:

Queues are electronic "waiting lines" like the one at the checkout counter. Files are sent to a queue and then routed automatically to a particular device or function.

- Delete jobs in a queue
- Redirect jobs from one queue to another
- Change priority of jobs in an output queue
- View the status of jobs in the queue
- Enable or disable any of the queues

n addition to managing the jobs within the queues, the Print Server should let you tie specific printer options to a queue. If you have a hi-res imagesetter, you might want to have different queues for low, medium, and high resolutions, depending on the job's requirements. Then, you only need to select the queue that is called "2400 dpi film," for example, and the job automatically goes to the correct output device and prints at the correct resolution. For plain-paper laser printers, you could have different queues for the different paper trays. For digital color presses like the Agfa Chromapress or Xerox Docucolor, you could have multiple devices with certain types of paper in use.

By including a printer configuration in the print queue, jobs always print the way you want them to print. For an imagesetter, you can use printer setups to make sure all the RIP settings are set correctly. Settings such as page orientation, negative or mirror-image modes, resolution selection, and page grouping can be set by the Print Server before a job is sent to the imagesetter. A Print Server should be able to set any of the options available from the RIP's software.

The Print Server also maintains statistics about each job, providing the user with a report on printing times, number of pages printed, source workstation name, date, and time of job, and more. This report could be in a format that can be imported into IBM Lotus, Microsoft Excel, or other programs for billing or accounting. Prepress service bureaus charge by the minute for jobs that exceed expected runtimes, and a Print Server's job log provides the exact runtime for each job.

OPI Servers   High-resolution scanned images are the largest consumers of disk space, processing time, and transmission time in a printing and publishing network. While larger disks, data compression, faster computers, and faster networks help to carry the load, better management of graphics data is one of the best ways to improve any system's performance.

When the image requires color correction, retouching, or special effects, it belongs at the workstation. When the image has been approved for use, it belongs either on a Server or at the RIP. When the job is run, the system should be able to locate the image without tying up anybody's workstation. OPI lets you configure an efficient production cycle by performing tasks at appropriate locations on the network.

Color Separation Houses   Color separations are the largest files encountered in electronic prepress. When you add up all four separations, you could have files totalling 60 Mb or more. Files of this size can impair productivity unless they are managed correctly. In color separation houses, OPI

1. Scans images into a color workstation.
2. Touches up images on that workstation, or moves them to a workstation dedicated to image editing.
3. Makes color separations and transfers them to the OPI Server. For network efficiency, you can transfer the images to the server in a batch during periods of low network traffic or via "sneakernet" on appropriate media:

    - Tape cartridges
    - Zip or Jaz disks
    - Syquest disks (remember them?)
    - Magneto optical disks
    - CD-ROM disks

With the separations resident on the Server, the output device can be fed a continuous stream of image data. At the same time, the workstations are freed of data transmission burdens and used as intended: page design, image retouching, and separation. In this way, OPI allows color separation and outputting to run in parallel, with no time wasted for data transmission.

Prepress Service Bureaus   Service bureaus benefit from the same production flow as color separators. Service bureaus send not only color separations through their imagesetters, but also lots of monochrome pages or text pages that contain color images. The workstation operators making up the pages use only low-res EPS or TIFF callouts, so their layout files are easily managed. When they send the job to the imagesetter, their workstations release quickly and they can begin working on the next job.

Benefits of OPI
- *Higher prepress productivity.*
- *Fast workstation release lets you get back to work in seconds rather than minutes.*
- *High-speed fetches to the Server result in more efficient network usage.*
- *Efficient system management.*

After they have scanned and stored the high-res images, they can return only the preview file to customers. Customers can work with the preview file in their page-layout program, and crop, scale, rotate, or perform any other manipulations. The preview file is generally small enough to be sent on diskettes or e-mail.

Newspapers   Newspapers use different production systems to create different types of work with one system for editorial text, another for charts and illustrations, and another for display ads. A single newspaper page may contain elements from all these systems. At deadline time, when the last element required for a page is approved, the page must be printed as fast as possible. Printing complex broadsheet pages containing many images without an OPI solution ties up a page-layout station. OPI allows the storage of graphics in a central location on the network, so users can access them with low-res callouts.

Magazines   Magazines, like newspapers, use different production systems to create different types of work with systems for editorial text, charts and illustrations, and display ads. OPI enables the integration of these separate files at the output device. Magazine production operations accrue the same benefits as newspapers for display ad work, and many of the same benefits as a color house for color separations. For display ads, magazines have logos and clip art that are used repeatedly by advertisers. In addition, magazines use photos, graphics, and icons for section identifiers. Typical magazine color uses 133-line screen halftones. Higher line screens mean scanning at higher resolutions, resulting in larger file sizes. When a magazine brings its production work inhouse, it sets up a color production cycle similar to a color separator's.

Data management is now probably the biggest hurdle publications need to address. For a single publication produced direct to plate, there are huge volumes of data. Each full-page ad scanned on a copy dot scanner requires 180 Mb of storage (45 Mb for each single-color separation). The data management situation for ads is complicated by the requirement to handle scheduling, versioning, and sometimes split runs. There are composite editorial pages, which include low-resolution FPO view files and associated high-resolution scans of editorial images. Storage, both live and archival, becomes a major issue, as do management and tracking. In order to produce one hundred of its periodicals using computer-to-plate technology, there will be the need to store and manage 2–2.5 terabytes of information.

Publishers   Because PDF follows a page model, PDF files are appealing to traditional publishers. One area receiving much attention is the capability to put newsletters or other publications on-line in PDF form and then have subscribers download the files and read them. To the subscriber, there is the appeal of timely information. To the publisher, there is the appeal of being able to distribute without the overhead of printing. Printers are not thrilled with this idea. This distribution method amounts to a site license to customers to print and distribute copies. Restricting the number of times a customer can download a file does not prevent thousands of copies being sent via e-mail or printed and distributed conventionally by the subscriber, all from a single download.

Image Server   The terms Image Server and OPI Server are used interchangeably, but there is an important distinction evolving. Graphic arts firms are storing all images for repurposing, from print to Web or CD-ROM and back again. These images can be in separate files or part of PDF documents. Since an OPI Server serves only print, the term Image Server may now take on a broader connotation. An Image Server can be any computer on the network with one or more large disks to store image files, whether they are high resolution for print, or Web screen images or both. You can use one or several computers as Image Servers. The RIP computer must be able to access a disk used to store the high-res graphics.

An efficient way to configure an OPI system is to use the same workstation running the RIP as the Image or Network Server. The high-res image is then transferred to the Server once. At output time, the RIP reads the image from its own disk. No matter how many times the image is output, it needs to be transferred over the

Improvements in workflow and automation of the communication between production processes are crucial success factors. Until today the choice for prepress automation has been:

- *the closed system approach with proprietary "big file" data formats including a proprietary workflow approach*
- *the open PostScript system, based on separate components—each the very best available for specific functionality—but also with unpredictable production performance and an incremental step-by-step workflow approach.*

network only once. In the real world of production, an image is usually used more than once in the publishing process. This does call for very large disk capacity.

The high-resolution images placed on the Image Server will usually be final images with all color correction, retouching, and separation done. If users need to make changes to the high-res image or perform a color correction, they can do so if they replace the image on the Image Server with the new image. For such a change, the preview image does not need to be updated. But if a change is made that would affect the way the preview image interacts with the page makeup program, a resizing of the image, for example or the way the image is accessed on the Server, like a name or location change, then the preview image must also be regenerated.

If the RIP computer is used as the Image Server, this function only needs to retrieve the high-res image from its own disk. RIP software with OPI functionality is available for Macintosh, Power Macintosh, Sun Computer, and Silicon Graphics, and the growing prevalence of PC/NT computers.

OPI functions may be done at the RIP while some OPI solutions require a free-standing Server for integration. You can configure an OPI system to suit your production needs with:

- Each component on a separate workstation
- RIP and Image Server on the same workstation

When printing to a Print Server (a Server that spools jobs for an output device), the workstation program releases within seconds and the operator goes back to work. Without a spooling capability, the workstation is not released until the job is printed. When you send a job containing an OPI callout to the proper queue on the Print Server, it routes it to the appropriate OPI server for output.

Acrobat 4 now supports OPI more completely than Acrobat 3 did. OPI is an important capability so long as we use a CMYK workflow, where images are scanned and converted to CMYK and then carried throughout the workflow. When RGB workflows evolve, OPI may be less of a factor.

One Workflow Model

1. Workstations running OPI-capable application programs place images on the OPI or Image Server over the network.
2. Any workstation on the network sends the job to the appropriate Print Server queue.
3. The Print Server spools the job, releases the workstation, and transmits the job to the appropriate output device.

You can use the network or any file sharing utility, or transportable disk to transfer the high-resolution file to or from the Image Server. Once you make a callout to a high-res file, do not move it or change its name. If you do, the OPI function cannot locate it to include in a job.

Transmission time is quick because the job contains only a low-res callout of the image. The RIP with the OPI integrating function reads the callout in the job and connects to the Images Server as directed. Because the same workstation may be used as the Image Server and the RIP, the integrator needs only to retrieve the image from its disk. The integrator merges the high-res image into the job stream with the other page elements and the page is printed.

Once the publication is output, what happens to the images? In the old days, they were archived to tape. Today, publishers and service firms are interested in the future of their images. That means they want to store them in such a way that they can be found quickly, accessed rapidly, and converted (repurposed) to various file formats for print or presentation.

Prepress systems are also linking OPI Servers to image archives. An image database becomes important because users cannot find images based only on their file names. Some production pros can retrieve images on this basis, but designers may not. Without reliable image pattern-recognition technology, we have to rely on keywords, indexed fields, and full-text queries of captions or description files. These are typically stored in a database (relational or fixed-field) and searched by a full-text indexing engine.

Server Evolution and Integration   It all started with one PC connected to one printer. Add more PCs and more printers and you have a system. A prepress networked system usually consists of multiple workstations, a file server, and a printer or printers connected by network cables. But now we are thinking of workflows beyond prepress—to the press, finishing, and beyond.

Servers galore
*A Server is any device
with information shared
by Client workstations
on a network. Every
network must have a
Server and it is simply a
Network Server.*

*A Network Server stores
centralized files that are
shared by Clients. It can
also be called a File
Server.*

*A network could have
multiple Servers, one of
which could be used to
store large image files. It
would be called an
Image Server.*

*With large volumes of
image and data files,
some Servers could sup-
port a database capabili-
ty for searching and
retrieving the stored
data more efficiently.
This would make it a
Database Server.*

*Another Server common
to networks supports a
shared printer or other
output device. It has its
own disk so that jobs are
transferred to the disk
and the Client worksta-
tion does not have to
wait until the printer is
finished. It is called a
Print Server. The Print
Server retains files for
future runs or archiv-
ing.*

*All PostScript output
systems must have a
RIP, a raster image
processor. The RIP usu-*

Sometimes, a print spooler is added so that files destined for the printer are accepted by the spooler to release the workstation's application. The spooler then queues the job or jobs based on prioritization and sends them to the printer. The difference between a print spooler and a print server is based on the amount of time files remain on the disk. A spooler may delete files sooner than a server.

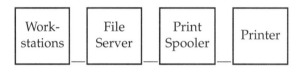

The printer on a prepress network is usually a PostScript-based printer and therefore has a RIP. Most desktop printers have the RIP inside the printer . . .

. . . while imagesetters and platesetters and proofers have the RIP as a separate unit, connected by a cable. Today, every raster-based output device must have a Raster Image Processor.

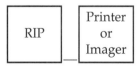

A server may be added to the output function to store ripped files for later printout of the entire file of one or more of the color separations. This may be called a print server or a print spooler. We are going to call it a RIP Server because it serves the RIP. At one time, there was a RIP for each and every output device. Today, the trend is to try to RIP-once and output-many-times. Or, another trend is to normalize once and rasterize many times. Thus, the RIP server functions as a print spooler/server, holding files for later printout or archiving.

The RIP server and the RIP may be integrated into one unit.

An OPI server could be added to the system for automatic picture replacement.

The OPI server and the RIP server could be integrated while the RIP is a separate unit . . .

. . . or the OPI server, RIP server, and RIP could be integrated into one unit.

ally has a large disk to store software and pre- and post-ripped files. It is called a RIP Server.

The RIP should be equipped with OPI functionality. The disk and system associated with the RIP is then also called an OPI Server.

The Server could encompass multiple functions, such as trapping, imposition, and ripping. It might be called a Super Server.

Lastly, the Server could fully support Adobe Acrobat with its superb collection of high-end printing functions. PDF files can be trapped, imposed, and color managed. That gives us a PDF Server.

Thus, a network could have all of the above functionality, or some combination, or like most, it could integrate the Server (for the network, image storage, OPI, and ripping) and the RIP into one Server. Or the Server into one RIP.

The RIPs and systems described in this section are only for illustration. It was not our goal to provide a comprehensive review of all available workflows, but rather to provide a sort of overview of some of the products and trends. Those trends that we have observed are:

- *Multivendor systems evolving to single-vendor systems.*
- *Totally automated workflows—the mouse is in charge.*
- *Industry-standard hardware platforms.*
- *Industry-standard networking.*
- *Integrating RIP functions at multiple stages in the process.*
- *The use of the Web as a business tool.*

At various levels there could be more than one printer, proofer, imagesetter, digital color press, platemaker, or other output alternatives.

When the functions of OPI, RIP, and print serve are integrated into one Server, we are going to call it a Super Server. It then is networked with the file server and the printer or imagers.

To the Super Server we add the final ingredient of PDF handling, trapping, and imposition. The final system now takes form as a PDF Server.

The Adobe PDF will change the very nature of networks and servers and systems and prepress. With scripts or plug-ins many routine tasks can be automated. For instance, a script might take a QuarkXPress file, open it, distill it, open Acrobat Exchange, perform a function, save it, and then server functions would trap the PDF, impose it based on the electronic work order, direct it to a proofer, and prioritize it to a print queue.

Server Schizophrenia   There are OPI Servers, Workflow Servers, and Database Servers, File Management and Image Servers. Servers are migrating to ripping and archiving, and archive image databases are expanding to handle work in process. Print Servers, once limited to spooling, now perform trapping and imposition and promise to automate workflow, as database-driven workflow software makes similar claims. RIPs once only ripped; now they serve. Servers only served; now they rip. The result is that almost every Server and almost every RIP system almost do the same thing.

Workflow is changing. Workflow software has migrated from text-based systems to prepress document production that helps route jobs to the required queue or invoke processes when work is dropped in a queue or hot folder. The Server is simply a central (network) function that can run background tasks like automatic trapping or rasterizing (ripping) a file for output to a printer, imagesetter, platemaker, etc. File Servers are based on Unix or Novell networks, with Macintosh, PC/NT, and Unix workstations handling processing. Workflow may simply mean setting up "hot folders" to perform prepress functions and letting the Super Server do the rest

The Server approach shifts the processing burden from individual workstations to a central Server for more efficient printing and job handling. Sending files to the Server takes seconds, even for pages with gigabytes of images. Software directs where and when each job is to print, inserts high-resolution scans precisely where they belong in the layout, monitors print progress, and maintains statistics. Queued jobs can be rearranged, placed on hold, deleted, or moved among queues with ease. Some Server functions are

- Unattended management of a number of printers through multiple queues
- Image substitution through OPI.
- User-definable printer setups
- Queuing controls
- Device-, application-, and platform-independence.

Job Tickets are just the ticket

Job Tickets handle the queueing and job management of all jobs in process. They have some extra features such as load balancing, preflight, filmsaving, and more. They can also automate trapping and imposition using standard desktop applications such as TrapWise and Presswise. They use the concept of "hot folders." This concept came from a need:
- *to define and indicate upfront the steps the job must go through*
- *to have the full "processing" information available at any moment by anyone involved in completing the process*
- *to control and "post calculate" a job*

- Control over a job from the server or a workstation
- Centralized image and print processing
- Security for printing resources
- Fast spooling to a central Server
- Storage and retrieval of images on the network
- Multiple projects moving and numerous devices working without intervention
- Accurate replacement and positioning of high-resolution scans before imaging
- Configuration of any output device to the resolution, line screen, and screen angle preferred
- Assignment of multiple queues to the same device, or multiple devices to the same queue
- Spooling of PostScript files from any source and outputting to any PostScript device
- Managment of files from anywhere on the network, and re-queueing without respooling
- Sharing of images and management of printers through one Server, even if computer types vary
- Network-based job management
- Enhanced queue monitoring
- Workflow optimization and job load balancing
- PostScript 2 or 3 resource management
- Preflight job verification
- Support for in-RIP separation
- Film optimization
- RIP and output device management
- Integrated RIP
- OPI image replacement
- Image File Conversion (for PhotoCD, TIFF/IT, CEPS data formats)

Workflow Solutions Aplenty   In 1995, Linotype-Hell (now Heidelberg) pioneered RIP operation, building on the early work done by Monotype with the Lasercomp in the late 1970s. In 1995 the company developed Delta Technology, which essentially splits the

RIP process into two steps: PostScript interpretation and the Delta list. PostScript processing takes place in the DeltaWorkstation; half-tone screening takes place in the DeltaTower. This whole process is controlled by DeltaSoftware, which includes capabilities such as print spooling and OPI. The DeltaWorkstation multiprocessing capabilities enable several processors to work in parallel, increasing throughput. It produces the DeltaList, a single-layer file identical to what will appear in the final output. The file is transferred to the DeltaTower for screening. The entire system concept allows functions to be handled by separate components: PostScript processing by the DeltaWorkstation, screening by the DeltaTower. All are controlled by DeltaSoftware, including DeltaImage manager and DeltaPrintmanager.

Delta workflow was as follows: Send single Quark pages to Delta1. RIP, trap, and scatter proof on Iris. Once proofs are checked, the Delta Lists are transferred to Delta2. The low-res bitmaps created with the Delta lists are then imposed on the Signastation. The Signature is then printed to Delta2; the Delta lists are picked up (similar to OPI). The print queue on Delta2 is set up to proof the signatures to the forms proofer first. If the proofs are okay, the same signature is forwarded to the CTP system. After plates are imaged, CIP3 files are automatically generated. In this workflow the pages are ripped only once. The created Delta Lists are used for exposure of plates, color proofs, formproofs, imposition, and CIP3 file generation.

Delta Technology allows pre-ripped files (Delta Lists) to be trapped, proofed (digital blueline or Iris), and imposed before committing to plate or film. As screening is done in a separate box attached to the output device, the operator has control of the output parameters. They are not locked in at RIP time. Delta runs on Windows NT and is configurable with off-line RIPs, trapping stations, etc. CIP3 files can be generated automatically from the Delta lists. Color management (ColorSync profiles) can also be applied to the Delta data.

In 1999, Heidelberg and Creo introduced the Prinery workflow, which is PDF-based and discussed later. It may replace Delta.

Scitex developments
Brisque is the Scitex line of digital front ends that integrate and auto-mate all prepress pro-duction output opera-tions.The Brisque DFE coordinates the essential prepress production tools and processes: pre-flight checking, auto-mated job tickets, image replacement schemes (Scitex APR, OPI), soft proofing, trapping, queuing and job man-agement, imposition, screening, and RIPping. The Brisque's architec-ture accommodates PDF in a comprehensive way, from RIPping to print. The company has inte-grated PDF into the Brisque infrastructure to allow Brisque DFEs to seamlessly accept both PostScript and PDF files in a single workflow. Implementing PDF RIPping involves the same drag-and-drop process as PostScript RIPping. When PDF is enabled, users choose which type of file they want to RIP, and using the icon-based Graphical User Interface, drag and drop the file onto the RIP icon, define RIP parameters as with PostScript files, then select PDF parameters, and define the page or pages to RIP. The selec-tive RIPping option is possible only in PDF because of the page-independent nature of the format.

The high-end PDF format is very flexible

The PDF format brings all the functionality needed in the next generation workflow. PDF is a self-contained format that includes job data and job ticket information. You can view and print or proof it whenever and wherever you want, from any major platform and operating system. It is really device independent.

In contrast with the bitmap or vector formats, the object-based PDF is slim and smart. "Slim" because, unlike the complex, continuous datastream in a PostScript file, it consists of a compact—or distilled—object-oriented database of imaging operations that can immediately represent the document, on a page-by-page level. "Smart" as in editable—long the dream of PostScript workflows—since you can find and change elements on the page and data level. Smart, too, because of the job ticket information, part of the PDF file, that lets you store and manage device-dependent information, independent from job content.

Scitex Solutions   The Scitex Brisque RIP system is an output controller for prepress production. Brisque automates production processes with "job ticket" templates. Each job ticket describes a workflow consisting of operations to be finished in a particular order according to specific parameters. It will not work with non-Scitex output devices, either for final output or proofs (except an HP printer). Brisque now supports OPI on a Scitex device, as well as DCS. It works with CT and New Linework formats, which handle 65,000 unique colors in linework and 32 color channels.

It rips data into the internal Scitex CT and linework formats. Both the CT and New Linework formats can be edited. CTs can be edited in Photoshop. Screening is done on the fly by the screening controller built into the Scitex imagesetters. For continuous-tone proofers, the Brisque combines CT and Linework files into a single high-resolution format and will trap CT to LW, LW to CT, and CT to CT. Scitex prefers to rasterize first and work on the rasterized file after. Brisque can drive three different types of output from one RIP.

Harlequin Solutions   Harlequin provides workflow management and a facility for editing the data in a "late-binding" fashion that includes trapping (Harlequin pioneered the concept of "late binding.") Harlequin has multitasking and multiprocessing but doesn't offer OPI within the RIP, but its OEM customer implementations provide this support. Harlequin also supports a PCI card-screening accelerator. Harlequin Display List Technology allows for editability of the PostScript display list, providing a hook for customization between interpretation and rendering.

This option lets OEMs and other third-party vendors write tailored applications that add customized features to ScriptWorks. Applications include PostScript verification and previewing; object editing; integration of trapping and/or imposition capabilities; conversion from PostScript into other languages or formats like TIFF/IT; the detection and rendering of vignettes using alternative processing; enhanced image-processing capabilities. Harlequin is taking advantage of this access to the display list for an integrated automatic RIP-based trapping solution, called EasyTrap.

When the PostScript job draws an object, instead of simply adding the object to the display list and continuing as usual, HDLT will first invoke a procedure. It can use PostScript to do any computation necessary. Harlequin Display List Technology is available as a layered option for ScriptWorks running on all industry-standard platforms.

ScriptWorks is a high-performance software RIP Management System configured with all the necessary features and functions to run in a wide variety of commercial printing and publishing environments. It is also a universal interpreter able to process a wide variety of file formats such as PostScript, EPS, PDF 1.3, TIFF 6, and TIFF/IT-P1. ScriptWorks was designed from the ground up to meet the varied and demanding needs of its OEM partners and their end users and to run on the OEM's choice of hardware platforms and operating systems. ScriptWorks includes a complete and functional user interface that provides extensive controls for page setup, output device calibration, media management, etc.

Harlequin ScriptWorks is a software RIP Management System that implements PostScript LanguageLevel 3 operators. It is a multi-language RIP Management System that lets users follow whatever workflow they prefer—a PDF workflow, PostScript 1, 2, and LanguageLevel 3 files, TIFF 6.0, TIFF/IT-P1, EPS, and more. ScriptWorks is a hardware-independent software RIP. It can process files produced by applications that are LanguageLevel 3 compatible and that contain the new extensions and changes to the PostScript language as specified in the recently published update to the PostScript Language Reference Manual, entitled "LanguageLevel 3 Specification." New LanguageLevel 3 features in ScriptWorks 5.0 include

- Hi-Fi Color—Harlequin's new N-Color capability allows an arbitrary number of colors to be correctly processed and printed from virtually any color system, including CMYK and spot color systems as well as Hi-Fi color systems such as Hexachrome. In addition, Harlequin N-Color is fully-integrated with screening, calibration, rendering, raster formats and page buffers, trapping, separations, and all Harlequin color management options.

Harlequin PDF developments
Harlequin is developing its own extensions to the PDF 1.2 specification. They see some issues and opportunities with the current PDF specification and feel the need to address these. Their "PDF+" plan includes:

Plate Colors—all PDF jobs are assumed to be composite (or gray). This extension would allow marking of plates as cyan, magenta, etc. for easy recognition by film or plate processors.
Vignettes—This extension quickly recognizes and optimizes in-line vignettes for circles and rectangles for improved performance and reduced file sizes.
Encapsulated Functions—This extension handles required procedures that are specified in PS definitions of colorspaces to provide more precise color representation.

Imation Corp. changed the name of its subsidiary, Luminous Technology Corporation, to Imation Publishing Software—a developer of software products, services, and technologies for the prepress, print production, and graphic arts industries, which was acquired by Imation in October 1996. Software solutions within the Imation Publishing Software business portfolio at that time included Color Central, Media Manager, OPEN, PressWise, Printers-Web, TrapWise, Virtual Network, and Virtual Network Pro.

Luminous Technology Corporation is now officially Imation Publishing Software. APX is now LPX. The name changed from APX to LPX when Luminous spun out of Adobe in early 1996. The goal of LPX from the beginning has been to support PressWise, TrapWise, Color Central, and PrePrint Pro workflows by allowing users to produce DSC 3.0-conformant PS directly from QuarkXPress. APX is a QuarkXTension that is designed to smooth the process of creating QuarkXPress Post-Script files for use with

- Smooth Shading—reduces printing time and improves output quality by rendering gradient fills at the resolution of the target device using a series of designated pattern libraries
- Masked Images—enables printing of composite images clipped to a raster mask
- PDF direct processing—ScriptWorks 5.0 continues to support native printing of PDF v1.2 (and earlier) files.
- Job Ticket Format (JTF)—Initially ScriptWorks 5.0 will be able to read an Adobe Job Ticket and use information contained therein to build page setups. Additional functionality will follow as the JTF becomes more widely implemented in the industry;
- Embedded ICC Profiles—ScriptWorks 5.0 recognizes an ICC format device profile embedded in the PS/PDF/TIFF input stream and uses it to remap file output to the target device;
- Remote RIP operation—Harlequin's new RIP Remote feature is a Java applet that allows the use of a standard Internet Web Browser to select, input, submit, and control job processing to ScriptWorks RIPs located in virtually any location in the world.
- Remote proofing of color-managed files
- The ability to handle Photoshop duotones
- The ability to control spot-color separations at any point in the process
- User-programmable screening extensions
- Symmetric multiprocessing (SMP) support
- "Extra Grays" (over 4,000 gray levels)
- "In-RIP" color management with Harlequin Color Production Solutions
- Full ICC 3 support, including "device-link" profiles.
- TIFF/IT-P1 processing
- Display list access with Harlequin Display List Technology (HDLT)
- "In-RIP" trapping with EasyTrap
- Native processing of TrueType fonts and storage in compressed formats

Platforms supported include Power Macintosh; all Intel-based Pentium PCs (supporting Windows 95 and Windows NT); Digital Alpha workstations and servers (supporting Windows NT), and UNIX platforms, including Sun Solaris and SGI IRIX. Symmetrical multiprocessing (SMP) systems and all popular network environments are supported.

What is "PostScript LanguageLevel 3" and how does it differ from "PostScript 3"? And, how does ScriptWorks 5.0 compare with Adobe PostScript 3 products? The terminology and distinctions between language and product are subtle and have been a source of substantial confusion in the marketplace. This confusion has tended to mask the fact that Adobe PostScript 3 products and Harlequin Script-Works are significantly different products developed for and suited to significantly different printing and publishing applications. LanguageLevel 3 is the name of the latest version of the PostScript page description language (PDL). It includes a series of extensions and/or changes to the language documented in the supplement issued on October 10, 1997 to the PostScript Language Reference Manual entitled "LanguageLevel 3 Specification."

Adobe prepress products. Using this XTension ensures that the resulting PostScript file conforms to the Adobe Document Structuring Conventions (DSC) so that they can be post-processed by Color Central, PrePrint, PressWise, TrapWise, and OPEN.

Helios PDF for OPI   Helios PDF Handshake allows PDF documents to be integrated into prepress workflows, including those incorporating OPI file and print servers. HELIOS Software PDF Handshake 2.0 provides a complete prepress workflow solution for Adobe portable document format files—from layout to output-including ColorSync/ICC-based integrated color management and flexible output options including Internet printing.

Using PDF Handshake, users of QuarkXPress and Adobe InDesign can work with PDF input as easily as they would with EPS or TIFF images, whether it be a single drawing, logo, or a fully designed advertisement or page layout. "With PDF Handshake 2.0, users have the most complete PDF workflow solution available today," noted Helmut Tschemernjak, president of HELIOS Software GmbH. "PDF Handshake is completely vendor independent and can be used with any output device." PDF Handshake 2.0 adds support for Adobe's PDF specification 1.3 and Acrobat 4.

New features include support for bleeding that is compatible with both existing applications using enlarged pages or registration marks, and new applications that include the bleeding parameters of the PDF 1.3. Other new features include support of preseparated PDF documents and "PDF Internet Printing" to support the remote delivery and printing of PDF documents over the Internet.

HELIOS has enhanced PDF Handshake's PDF printing and OPI capabilities by expanding its imposition support. An "Export for Imposition" Acrobat 3/4 plug-in enables users to place OPI-based low-res PostScript files into imposition applications including DK&A INposition, Heidelberger Signa, Imation PressWise 3.0.2, ScenicSoft Preps 3.5.2, Farrukh Inposition Publisher 3.0.7, STRIP IT∆, ULTI-MATE Impostrip 5.6, and other leading PostScript-compatible imposition programs. Imposed jobs can be sent to EtherShare OPI's print spooler to include the original PDF high-resolution data during printout. PDF Handshake works with any Level 1, 2, or PostScript 3 compatible RIP. HELIOS PDF Handshake 2.0 provides printing and OPI support to PDF documents that have already been separated, enabling either composite or separated input or output. In addition, HELIOS Print Preview supports a composite soft proof of the separated or composite PDF documents.

PDF Internet Printing   This is an innovative feature of Helios PDF Handshake 2.0. PDF Printing supports the remote delivery and printing of PDF documents over the Internet. HELIOS PDF Internet Printing requires no special file transfer or workflow solutions, allowing simple transfers and printing over the Internet in just four steps using any Web browser.

Many suppliers have provided RIP systems that maximize off-the-shelf workstations. Thus, Agfa, for example, has software RIPs for Sun, Mac, PC/NT, and other computer hardware platforms.

The real-world benefit of HELIOS PDF Internet Printing is that it combines all aspects of a typical print workflow via a simple Web interface that handles user authorization, PDF job delivery, customizable print parameters, PDF preflight, remote notification, plus printing/archiving of PDF print jobs that can be used by every Internet user.

With PDF Internet Printing, HELIOS PDF Handshake 2.0 gives users easier and faster access to reliable, professional output of PDF documents. With PDF Handshake's built-in ColorSync/ICC-based color management, font management, and transformation, users can benefit from professional printing of PDF documents whether they are separations, composites, or even proof simulations.

Print and copy shops can now expand their business, giving customers a no-hassle solution for remote delivery of their print jobs like color proofs, poster prints, forms, or copy jobs. Easy to set up and use, PDF Internet Printing provides e-mail notification that new documents have arrived. Based on a 4,000-line Perl script, the CGI program can be fully customizable enabling print houses and copy shops to brand the interface with banners, logos, advertisements as well as for custom order information, credit card, and legacy database connections. Cost of entry is low, as an inexpensive PC-based Linux server running Apache and a 5-user EtherShare license and PDF Handshake are all that are required for a turnkey system that maximizes ROI (IP connection purchased separately).

AII Solutions   Autologic Information International (AII) has streamlined its RIP capabilities by enabling some key functions to be performed after a job has been rasterized and before it is output to an imaging device. Among these functions are imposition, step-and-repeat processing, proofing, and outputting a job multiple times without having to rasterize the file again. This capability, which AII is marketing as Post-RIP Assembly among its commercial customers, is similar to the Bitmap Stitching feature offered to its newspaper customers. For label production and other applications involving step-and-repeat operation, Post-RIP Assembly requires only that an element be rasterized once, after which it can be repeated horizontally and vertically any number of times without re-rasterizing.

For color proofing, AII recombines the rasterized CMYK data and prints them on a color proofer. A software algorithm downsamples the resolution of the raster data for the 300-dpi printer, without having to rasterize again for the different resolution. It is possible also to replace part of a page by substituting one rasterized block for another one based on x, y coordinate positioning. Other post-RIP capabilities include rotating pages 180 degrees and replacing an

The phrase "PostScript 3" is used in different ways, which has led to much confusion. Adobe now uses PostScript 3 as its trademarked brand name, referring to its product implementations as in the phrase, "Adobe PostScript 3 Version 3010 Product Supplement." The PostScript 3 name or "brand" refers to Adobe-based products and not to the PostScript language-specification which Adobe now calls "LanguageLevel 3." What does "PostScript 3 compatibility" mean? PostScript 3 products can interpret files containing PostScript LanguageLevel3 operators that have been prepared by compliant applications. In addition, PostScript 3 products have other functionality that is new but not necessarily part of the PostScript PDL. For example, the ability to accept PDF files is widely accepted as a PostScript 3 product feature as is the ability to perform in-RIP trapping. Other PostScript 3 product features in various levels of availability include WebReady Printing, PlanetReady Printing, etc., yet none of these features are operators within the LanguageLevel 3 specification.

entire page within an imposed job. The program has facilities for tracking elements of a publication being output, including reporting where each element resides (with filters available to limit the display to items conforming to certain criteria), which publication and edition each one belongs to, the output device each was sent to, etc. It also provides an error queue for jobs that fail to output and an option to specify how long finished jobs are held before purging.

Rampage Solutions   The Rampage RIPping system is a comprehensive solution for film or plate output. It uses an open-architecture design and lets you connect multiple RIPs to one output device. The RIP runs on industry-standard hardware. Additional productivity features include automatic trapping, CEPS format support, OPI server functions, imposition, step and repeat, and Ramproof, a function that allows a ripped file to be output to a proofing device or monitor and then to an imagesetter (RIP once plot twice). Rampage's TrapIt1 rasterizes an incoming file at low resolution to do its analysis of what kinds of traps are needed, based on the relative luminance values of each pixel.

At the same time, it generates a display list of the objects on the page in drawing order, taking into account the order in which they are layered on top of each other. Traps are then computed for each object relative to the others that are below it in the display list and have intersecting boundaries. The output, new PostScript-like instructions, is generated from the trap decisions and combined with the original PostScript file. Object formats allow layering objects with transparency values, generally impossible in normal PostScript. Another is the ability to select and modify trap areas or other attributes easily because each object is its own element rather than a set of colored pixels. RIP enhancements include

- Automatic vignette detection, which treats all objects in a vignette as one object at high resolution; support for gravure output, with antialiasing from high resolution down to gravure resolution, eliminating the need to output film and scan it to accommodate gravure printing
- Facilities for adjusting press compensation, replacing one set of values with another when switching from a sheetfed press to a Web press

- "Smart shadows," which puts shadows over areas outside a clip path, regardless of what is underneath them
- "Automatic touchplates" to replace one to four inks, each with a different transfer curve of that ink plus add a special spot color with its transfer curve. This works like a duotone to change the curve of one or more of the CMYK inks and add a spot color based on the same data.
- Expansion of blends to 256 elements, regardless of the original input

Agfa PDF Workflow   In 1997, Agfa advanced RIP and Server architecture to a higher level by establishing the Acrobat 3.0 PDF as the standard for moving document files around a prepress network. Agfa designed a digital workflow that re-engineers preflight checking, automated job tickets, automatic picture replacement, soft proofing, trapping, queuing, imposition, screening, and rasterization.

Agfa "Apogee" is a PDF-based Publishing Production System including the "PDF Pilot" Production Manager, the PDF RIP, and the "PrintDrive" Output Manager. Agfa has been developing new workflows based on the high-end PDF file format standard from Adobe Systems. PDF is a flexible, editable, predictable, compact file format that works on a page-independent level and is device independent. Agfa's new Apogee system will use PDF to allow highly automated and efficient connection of prepress functionality such as creation, trapping, imposition, RIPping, OPI, job tracking, color management, etc. Apogee is based on the use of PDF as a "digital master" and consists of the PDF Pilot Production Manager, the PDF RIP, and the PrintDrive Output Manager.

The PDF Pilot Production Manager combines PDF-based workflow automation technology for preflighting, imposition, OPI, etc. with systemwide implementation of PDF-based job tickets. The PDF format allows viewing, editing, and processing from any workstation on the network, local or over the Internet. The PDF RIP rasterizes PDF, as well as PostScript Level 2 and PostScript 3 files. The PrintDrive Output Manager automatically stores, manages, and

What is the relationship between PostScript 3 and LanguageLevel 3? Adobe PostScript 3 product implementations include the ability to interpret the extensions to the PostScript language known as LanguageLevel 3 plus selected additional features that have been described in peripheral documentation. However, not all PostScript 3 products include the same feature set, other than the fact they conform (or will conform) to the new PostScript LanguageLevel3 specification.

queues the rasterized jobs for imagesetter, proofer, and platesetter output.

It allows immediate plate remakes and intelligent backups for digital platemaking, as well as a Preview feature. You can disconnect the RIPping process from the imaging process by grouping similar jobs together. To the RIP, the Apogee PrintDrive acts as a fast "writing engine," allowing you to process more jobs. Preview software allows you to preview single and multiple pages of the same job by connecting to the RIP and view the RIPped pages from any Macintosh or PC on your network.

You can zoom, pan, and request any combination of color separations, as well as view spot colors, screen angles, and ink coverage. Taipan and Taipan AX RIPs directly connect to the PrintDrive through TCP/IP. The output of the RIPs is automatically compressed and sent to the PrintDrive.

A graphical user interface allows you to view the status of the RIPped jobs, as well as manipulate and control the timing and priorities of the output. You can control the PrintDrive from any Macintosh or PC in your network and determine a preferred set of parameters, selectable at print time. Previewing of raster files, as with Agfa's Taipan or Taipan AX RIPs, is also possible on the Apogee PrintDrive, regardless of the number of connected RIPs. Apogee PrintDrive acts as a file buffer in digital workflows, offering digital imposition proofing capabilities—in black and white and in color—for a large format proofer, and directly from the bitmaps stored for final output.

Adobe Solutions   Extreme is a RIP technology that can process both PostScript and PDF streams. Files first enter the "Coordinator," which determines whether the file is PS or PDF by its inherent page independence. The PS files go to the "Normalizer" and the PDF files go to the "Page Store." The "Normalizer" acts as Acrobat's Distiller and converts the PS file to a PDF. These distilled files then continue on to the "Page Store" where all documents are stored as PDFs. Pages are processed through the RIP and finally passed on to the "Assembler," which dictates the flow of information to the marking engine. In addition to digital presses, Extreme's technology is applicable to large-format imagesetters, proofers, and platemakers, as well as digital printers. Below is a schematic of the internal flow of data from PostScript file to processed pages stored for output to the imaging engine.

Inside Adobe PostScript Extreme   Since Adobe PostScript Extreme is all about high-speed printing, the key to understanding it is knowing what determines printing speed. The two main factors that determine this are rasterization speed (how fast a printing system can turn a document into a series of dots) and the printer's engine speed (how quickly it can pass paper through its system and transfer a rasterized image onto the paper).

The new class of high-speed production printers have extremely fast engine speeds, so the only thing that tends to slow them down is the rasterization process. Most professional printing systems today use PostScript RIPs (raster-image processors) to rasterize documents. While PostScript RIPs can be very fast, they're not as fast as the engine speeds of high-end production printers.

The initial idea behind Adobe PostScript Extreme was to design a system that could quickly "feed" rasterized pages to a high-speed printing engine by using several RIPs, each simultaneously rasterizing various pages of a document. That design, however, wouldn't have worked with PostScript print jobs because they usually can't be split into separate pages before they're rasterized. (A PostScript file is typically a single, complex program that describes an entire document. What it takes to rasterize a certain page can depend on information or a graphic state that was defined within the description of an earlier page.) The Adobe PostScript Extreme architecture needed to be able to process page-independent print files—print files that consist of discrete page units that can be processed separately.

PostScript print files can be page-independent if they conform to a standard set of document-structuring conventions (DSC), but few applications create PostScript files that are DSC-compliant, so this wasn't a very practical way to provide the page-independent files required by Adobe PostScript Extreme. That's where PDF comes in.

Adobe's portable document format is by definition page independent and far more standardized than PostScript. Adobe enhanced PDF so that it could include certain types of information required for high-end printing—OPI comments, halftone settings, and the like. PDF files created by Acrobat can include this high-end information.

Prepress files inevitably have problems: missing components (fonts or graphics), missed deliveries (problems with modem or other electronic delivery methods), accidental changes, unpredictable PostScript language files (created from native applications), and enormous file sizes. Service providers have to maintain different versions of many applications to support customers. The solution is based on two Adobe core technologies: Adobe Acrobat 4 software with its version 1.3 Portable Document Format (PDF) files and Adobe PostScript 3 printing technology. The result is a portable, device-independent solution. Here's how it works:

1. You develop your illustrations and/or publications using application software.

2. Before handing the final document to a commercial printer or service provider, use Adobe Acrobat Distiller 4 to create a composite color or black and white PDF file. This PDF file contains all of the fonts, graphics, and other layout information necessary to print a high-resolution version of the document.

3. Deliver a single-file PDF to your service provider electronically or use traditional delivery methods.

PDF files streamline the printing process because they are

• Complete: They contain all of the fonts, graphics, and page-layout information necessary to display and print the file exactly as you laid it out.

• Compact: The PDF standard supports a variety of lossy and lossless compression methods, creating smaller files that are easier to transmit and faster to print than native application files.

- Portable: One of the key benefits of a PDF file is its page, platform, application, and device independence. You can print high-resolution PDF files on any Adobe PostScript Level 2 or PostScript 3 output device with the same high-quality results from each.
- Reliable: Acrobat Distiller interprets a PostScript or EPS file, creating cleaner, more reliable PostScript for final output.
- Editable: If you create composite PDF files, you maintain editing control over the final file. You or your service provider can do simple, late-stage text and image editing in Acrobat software using the improved TouchUp tool or a third-party plug-in. PDF files are page independent— allowing you to sort, extract, or insert pages without returning to the native application file.
- Extensible: You can add third-party plug-ins to your Acrobat toolkit to perform a number of supplementary tasks. (Adobe Web site at: http://www.pluginsource.com/.)
- Adobe PostScript 3: The latest version of PostScript provides in-RIP technologies (e.g., separations, trapping, and late-stage binding) enabling a more efficient composite PostScript workflow. This new approach replaces the less efficient "host-based" (multifile) color-separated workflow.
- Direct PDF Printing: Some PostScript 3 printing devices support Direct PDF Printing, which means that a prepress operator can print PDF files without selecting the print command in the native application file. This capability increases productivity and decreases operator errors because it uses drop or hot folders defined with specific printing parameters and job specifications. Check with your service provider or printer manufacturer for details about whether they support direct PDF printing.

New PDF Workflows

Heidelberg and Creo Products created Prinergy, a new PDF work-flow management solution. The Prinergy solution is based on Adobe Extreme technology and the Portable Document Format (PDF). Prinergy is a new addition to the existing Heidelberg Delta Tech-nology and Creo iMPAct families of workflow products. It is an exceptional prepress management solution for commercial, publica-tion, and catalog printers. Prinergy is an integrated, state-of-the-art workflow management solution that organizes and automates the individual tasks in prepress and in the production of film and plates. By increasing workflow speed and efficiency to match the exception-al performance of Heidelberg/Creo output devices, Prinergy unlocks the true profit potential of computer-to-plate (CTP) and computer-to-film (CTF). As a result, businesses in the printing industry can benefit from a marked increase in productivity. The Prinergy system architecture was designed with four major objectives:

- To help printers and prepress professionals achieve reli-able process control and maximum productivity
- To bring visibility to job progress at all stages of prepress
- To focus on strengthening teamwork by removing bottle-necks in prepress and making it easy to share information in real-time
- To make Prinergy an open, accessible tool based on industry-standard file formats

Prinergy leverages Adobe Extreme technology and Portable Job Tickets, which control and perform the prepress tasks initiated by users. Prinergy accepts PDF, PostScript, copydot, TIFF/IT, and CT/LW files. In Prinergy, all incoming data is optimized into individ-ual PDF pages. The PDF file format used throughout Prinergy min-imizes file sizes, network transfer time, and processing time. It also minimizes required archival and storage space. Because all layout program files can be optimized to PDF, designers and prepress experts have access to a greater selection of affordable desktop tools than with proprietary file formats.

People are skeptical about RGB workflow. It's based on scanning and editing images in RGB, only saving to the measured color space of an output device as a last step. For many, RGB is for Web pages, not for page printing. We print in CMYK, so why would we want to work in RGB and then convert to CMYK?

Case history: An RGB to CMYK conver-sion was already taking place on a drum scan-ner. The scanner was making appropriate cal-culations based on the color program, white point, black point, and other settings, produc-ing a CMYK image "on the fly." When we had good originals, the method of conversion made little difference. But when we had a poor original, automatic cal-culations meant we could end up scanning an image two or three times to get a file worth retouching. Apple ColorSync would allow for scanning and work-ing with an image inter-actively before the CMYK conversion.

For People *maga-zine's 25th Anniversary issue there were nearly 400 pages and a 7 mil-lion impression press run. Over 600 images would need to be sepa-rated, many of them old and faded. The plan was to scan in raw RGB,*

Prinergy uses predefined automation sequences called "Process Plans" to expertly manage tasks such as "Refining" (which includes normalizing to PDF), preflight check, OPI, file optimization, trapping, color management, and thumbnail generation. It also automates imposition, proofing, film production, platemaking, and archiving. To perform trapping, Prinergy integrates the advanced algorithms of the Heidelberg DaVinci software. The result is the first PDF-to-PDF trapper on the market meaning that the trapper takes in PDF files and applies traps as vector layers to the PDF pages. The traps in the PDF file can be checked in Acrobat 4.0 prior to output. Traps can also be edited interactively on an object basis using the optional PDF Trap Editor, an Acrobat plug-in tool.

The Color Matching Method from Heidelberg has been integrated in Prinergy for color management. In addition to this color-matching facility, transferred data can be converted immediately to the press color space for output on page and form proofers. Prinergy also handles spot colors. Prinergy tracks and documents each step in the prepress process using an integrated Oracle database. This can be used to quickly identify errors and isolate potential bottlenecks before they happen. Tracking the progression of jobs and tasks gives prepress managers more control and information, increasing the production planning and efficiency.

Prinergy stores all prepress data in job context application files. Imposition layouts, process plans, job history, and error messages are all organized by job or customer name, making it easy to find and retrieve both live and archived files. System resources can be assigned on the basis of job priority.

Prinergy is designed to be a groupware solution. As a multiuser system that provides up-to-the-second job status information to all users in real-time, Prinergy builds a stronger, more cohesive team—on Mac and PC. Consequently, operators can work on the same job simultaneously from their own desktop. Prinergy is device independent. Changes can be made to page content or imposition layout right up until the second before output. Prinergy adds greater efficiency to printing presses and can react quickly to changes in press scheduling. It also supports output on numerous proofing devices,

and then use ColorBlind edit to work with the images and finally convert them to CMYK. They created an RGB scanning program on the Heidelberg drum scanner which would override the internal conversion process, giving the maximum image data possible. Time spent at the scanner decreases because you need only to mount, focus, scale, and crop. No highlight and shadow points are chosen; no color decisions are made.

They then scanned a color target transparency in order to profile the scanner in Color Blind Professional. This process was relatively painless. The software compared the scanned target to the known information about the original, and a scanner profile was produced for the drum scanner. They did the same for a desktop CCD scanner. The output device also had to be profiled. They printed a color swatch proof on their contract proofer, which was measured using a spectrophotometer. Color Blind edit compared the spectrophotometer readings to the known values and gave them an output profile.

At this point they had the input and the output device profiled and were ready to go. With a ColorSync-calibrated and profiled monitor, the scanner operator was able to make visual decisions about how to convert the file rather than by choosing points through an eyepiece at the scanner and making color decisions based on sampled points. With ColorSync and an RGB workflow, they had 700, not 1,200, image versions and zero rescans. They judged success on how many versions of color corrections had to go through for each image before it was approved by the art department.Their normal rates under the old CMYK workflow for special issues was about 20-35 percent passed on the first version, 40-60 percent on the second version, and then 15-25 percent needed three or more versions.

For 600 images, they expected to rework 370-450 of them at least once; for another 120, they estimated two or more approval rounds. The count of image versions climbed to 1,200 or more. Out of those, 2 to 3 percent would require rescans due to unworkable color. So they estimated they might have as many as 20 or so rescans out of 600 original scans.

With Colorsync and an RGB workflow, they had 700, not 1,200, image versions and zero rescans. They reduced

filmsetters, and plate recorders. Prinergy is scalable to a multiserver, multiuser environment. Its distributed architecture allows the system to grow with the pace of business. Software and hardware components are independent and can be added or upgraded individually as required. The use of parallel processing and load sharing across servers maximizes performance and productivity.

PDF Plug-in　　A new plug-in for the Adobe Acrobat Distiller that enhances and streamlines the Portable Document Format (PDF) was developed by Heidelberg and Creo, and is user-installable and available for download free of charge at www.prinergy.com. Distiller is an Adobe product that reads PostScript data and produces PDF pages as output. It is available off the shelf to any consumer wanting the ability to make PDF. The new Distiller plug-in optimizes the benefits of digital workflow systems based on PDF v 1.3.

The Distiller plug-in enhances current PDF capabilities in a number of ways, adjusting for inconsistencies and improving the image quality of the finished product: correcting flatness, so curves appear curved on high-resolution output devices; correcting hairline width, adjusting for minimum line-width to make sure that output from a high-resolution device can be held on press; enhancing the ability to maintain image separation; removing the influence of some PostScript printer control characters, which can be responsible for application failure; creating an automatic trim box that saves prepress time by reducing the effort required to set offsets and margins manually; offering FrameMaker corrections by declining FrameMaker's directive to map all objects to an RGB color space; maintaining font and resolution integrity throughout the file creation process.

It also works with Illustrator by allowing for downstream font detection or replacement, and selecting smooth shades inherent with more gray levels for Illustrator gradients, as well as maintaining spot color integrity when used in conjunction with QuarkXPress. This plug-in was developed by the Prinergy teams of Creo and Heidelberg as a widely accessible, efficient mechanism for creating high-quality PDF.

Agfa Apogee2   ApogeeSeries2 is an enhanced version of the Agfa PDF production system, with new versions of the Apogee Pilot, Apogee PDF RIP, and PrintDrive system components and adds a fourth component—Apogee Create—that makes reliable PDF digital masters, enabling content creators to collaborate more efficiently with production shops. The new system also introduces a page-based workflow specially designed for the needs of magazine and catalog production and uses the latest Extreme technology from Adobe. Apogee features:

- Apogee was the industry's first PDF-based workflow system, and with Apogee Series2, Agfa takes this leadership role one step further, incorporating refinements and new features that keep you one step ahead.

- The Apogee Workflow Suite is the industry's only truly open System, creating "workflow optimized" PDFs and digital masters that are not restricted to any specific output conditions—seamlessly integrating with new and/or legacy systems. This modular architecture ensures forward and backward compatibility, with easy upgrade paths.

- All Apogee Series2 components support Adobe's Acrobat PDF 1.3 format and optimize the latest Adobe Extreme technology, offering greater speed and functionality.

- Apogee Create, the fourth and newest component of the Apogee Series2 system, is a desktop tool that empowers content creators to integrate directly into the Apogee workflow at a printer or trade shop production partner.

- In the new Apogee Series2 Pilot module, Agfa has added sophisticated PDF processing to the Extreme Normalizer to facilitate working with Pantone special and spot colors, vignettes, and colorized TIFF images from most any new and legacy desktop applications. The Apogee Pilot Job Ticket processor imposes pages that can be sent to an Agfa PDF RIP, or any PSL2 or PSL3 RIP. Automatic preflighting and controls and correction capabilities are also enhanced in Apogee Series2 Pilot through an Enfocus PitStop plug-in.

version count almost by half. The art department approved 82% of the version one images. Of the 18% that needed second rounds, all but one passed. These corrections were nearly all very minor color tweaks. These are results from scans produced for one special issue working consistently with an experienced art director. The version counts will probably vary as they incorporate this new way of scanning into our other titles, but the figures above are still extraordinary.

1. Under CMYK, your scanner operator must make image color judgment calls prior to spinning the drum or during a flatbed's prescan. This holds up the scanning station by about one or two minutes per image. Multiply that by the 40-80 scans per shift, and you gain a couple of hours to scan more.

2. The only training a new scanner operator needs is mechanical skills—oil mounting, crop, focus, scale, and naming. They no longer have to decide if they should apply a T1 or a T2 table to the magenta midtones or make it a "long" or a "short" black.

3. If your scanner is color calibrated and profiled, you will never have to rescan again for color. While mechanical defects like bad crops, scaling, or focus will still require spinning the drum, rescans for color will not be necessary because you've captured the absolute maximum amount of image data the scanner can give.

4. Instead of scanning an image several times at different settings, use the original raw scan and separate it two or three times. You can take this even further and separate for foreground and then do another separation for background, compositing the two together seamlessly in Adobe Photoshop. The layers are really the exact same image with two different profiles.

5. Accurate softproofing built enough confidence in the color specialist that visual and intuitive enhancement of the color was possible without resorting to "going by the numbers." Keeping on top of calibrations and profiles is essential. If a bulb on the scanner is changed, its profile should be recreated. Check the output device periodically to make sure it is still calibrated. Monitors need calibration from time to time. The results are well worth this effort.

- A more powerful Apogee Series2 RIP boosts the rendering speed and overall throughput, while also offering the faster in-RIP trapping. This new RIP offers remote viewing, as well as support for Agfa Balanced Screening, Agfa CristalRaster, and ICC Color Profiles.
- Further supporting Agfa's open-workflow philosophy, Apogee Series2 PrintDrive will feature OpenConnect for the import of third-party RIP data, enabling Apogee to integrate with non-Agfa workflows and output systems. PrintDrive 2.1 will also support multiple output engines with load balancing and last minute re-direction. The popular QuickFix feature has also been expanded to enable last minute page placement or correction from the Apogee Pilot. These page-oriented workflow features offer productivity advantages for magazine and catalog production.

Using Apogee Series2, each partner in the production chain gains the competitive advantage of streamlined workflow, cost savings, and expanded product offerings. Files generated using Apogee Create will integrate seamlessly with prepress and printing partners' Apogee RIP, Pilot, and PrintDrive systems—and their multivendor production environment. It has a modular, open architecture and is the operational center in the Agfa Apogee PDF-based workflow production process. It uses a three-step approach to organize the workflow: normalize the files into PDF Digital Masters, edit the job tickets, and process the PDF file as instructed in the job ticket. All incoming files are normalized into Digital Masters in PDF format. This happens only once and is similar to the interpretation phase of a RIP. It makes the resulting Digital Master efficient, regularly structured, and compact.

Job information, workflow routing, and page and formatting settings for the production processes are specified with the Job Ticket Editor and stored separately in Adobe's Portable Job Tickets Format (PJTF). To output films or plates, the job ticket instructions are processed, and pages are retrieved from the PageStore and imposed. If needed, high-resolution images are exchanged with OPI. Using

Acrobat Exchange, or any other PDF editing tool, changes can be implemented on an object, page, or flat level until the last minute. The Apogee Pilot takes advantage of all PDF benefits:

- Agfa's unique normalizer generates fully predictable PDF files, using them as Digital Masters
- Agfa's normalizer includes specific solutions to handle bleeds, in-RIP trapping, Duotone, and Tritone settings.
- The PDF format guarantees compact, fully viewable, editable, searchable, and portable documents
- Job tickets automatically instruct the system components to perform specific actions.
- Apogee's job tickets are compatible with Adobe's Portable Job Ticket Format specification standard
- It allows for integrated imposition, OPI, trapping, production, and a short learning curve.
- Every step uses PDF-based, nonproprietary tools.
- The Apogee Pilot directly processes PDF and PostScript jobs for flexibility when working with customers.
- CEPS data formats can be converted into PDF files to support input from proprietary systems.
- It handles both PDF or PostScript Level 2 files for RIP flexibility.
- It handles imposed "flats" or a continuous stream of pages.
- With extra compression or downsampling for proofing or CD-ROM/Internet/Intranet publishing.
- Changes made at the last minute are done in PDF so your Digital Master remains up-to-date for repurposing.
- It handles automatic extracting and cataloging of job data.
- Simple queries allow for extensive process and information management.
- Uses Normalize Once, Render Many—a flexible, reliable approach based on the use of the open standard PDF Digital Master files.

Screen Trueflow A Web browser-operated PDF workflow—Trueflow—has been developed in cooperation with Screen (USA) and Adobe Systems. Although the system architecture and prepress functions were developed by Screen, Trueflow uses the latest Adobe PostScript 3 interpreter handling Adobe PDF 1.3, as well as preflight module. Two versions of the workflow software will be available. Both Truflow and Trueflow Pro run with Windows NT on Intel Pentium platforms.

One of the key features of this new PDF workflow solution is its ability to be accessed and managed via a Web browser interface, meaning that production and scheduling can be managed and controlled from any place (with Internet or Intranet connection), at any time. It also allows a large number of front-end workstations to be connected to the system with a minimum level of investment.

In addition to the Web browser interface, Trueflow's standard features include automatic job processing using a Job Ticket workflow and direct interpretation and RIPping of PDF 1.3. Other features are Adobe PostScript3 and other industry-standard formats, preflight checking, automatic trapping, imposition, and RIPped PDF files output. Trueflow Pro includes all of those features plus plate layout and editing, and page-independent RIPping and swapping of individual pages. Trueflow is upgradable to the functionality of Trueflow Pro.

A number of options are available for use with both versions of Trueflow. The Trap-Editor option, which runs on a separate Windows NT platform, provides additional control of detailed trap settings and supports object-based trapping by [Image] width and color. The Flat-Worker option is a useful tool to layout multiple files on a single flat or plate, and can adjust dot gain and xy position for each color. Other Trueflow options include output for-mats in CIP3, and presetting the ink keys on the printing press as well as TIFF/IT-P1, and RIP'ed PS/EPS.

As the Portable Document Format (PDF) continues to become the new standard in the graphic arts industry, and the Web continues to impact the communications industry, Screen has harnessed the advantages of both to provide an exemplary solution for computer-to-film (CTF) and computer-to-plate (CTP) users.

Screen was the first company to develop and introduce a late-binding workflow solution (TaigaSPACE). There are more than 2,600 Taiga workstations installed worldwide.

New Screen RIP   Screen (USA) and Adobe Systems have a new Adobe PostScript 3 RIP called the AD-710NT, a new generation of software RIPs based on Adobe's PostScript 3, and the result of a joint development. It runs on a Windows NT-based Intel platform, and employs the latest Adobe Printing System Delivery (APSD) PostScript 3 technology with PDF 1.3 capability. In addition to the use of the newest Adobe PostScript 3 technology deliverable, called APSD, the AD-710NT has several other new features to enhance quality and productivity. New features include the ability to control all settings by other host computers connected to the network, and parallel processing of jobs. Moreover, the utilization of a new 12-bit Alphalogic screening technology renders much smoother halftones and gradations on the final separations.

The system lets users control the RIP from the front-end workstations, together with the ease of transferring jobs over the network by the use of hot folders. Other features of the AD-710NT include in-RIP separation, in-RIP OPI, Adobe in-RIP trapping, as well as TIFF file output and previewing.

The Race for Standards

Adobe, Agfa, Heidelberg, and MAN Roland jointly announced the creation of the Job Definition Format (JDF), a new electronic job ticket specification designed to bring new levels of process automation, collaborative workflow, and asset management to both print and cross-media publishing markets. JDF is being positioned as an open, scalable, Web-compatible job ticket standard that is built on the success of market proven standards like the CIP3 PPF (Print Production Format) and upward compatible to de facto standards like PDF and PJTF (Portable Job Ticket Format) from Adobe.

The graphic arts professional is faced with production systems from myriad vendors, each with its own unique messaging, file management, job tracking, and workflow formats. Few if any of these systems today sufficiently link the content authoring, editorial, or project review process with the back-end production and output systems required to create film, plates, or direct printed output. None of the systems available today are able to cover the complete workflow from content creation and prepress through the printshop up to the post-processing area of media production, including possibilities to exchange all the relevant job description data between the resources, planning, and business support systems. JDF has been designed to fill this gap and is being launched as an open, object-oriented XML framework for passing information or metadata about a job and its unique characteristics from one set of processes or systems to another set of processes or systems.

Combining the core competencies of four industry leaders covers the full spectrum of the publishing process—Adobe with its Internet, print authoring, PDF, and RIP businesses; Agfa with its knowledge of PDF workflow systems; Heidelberg with its prepress, pressroom, and finishing control systems; and Man Roland with its electronic pressroom management architecture—and gives us a unique perspective from which to quickly and efficiently derive this important XML-based language specification.

With over 1,000 Apogee sites using PDF and PJTF job tickets to manage their production workflow, the Job Definition Format is a way to incorporate additional data from other sources in the Job Ticket, thus providing more flexibility and automation. By incorporating XML data from the broader enterprise and ensuring that PDF and PJTF systems are forward-compatible with the JDF job ticket, we are able to bring our customers the benefits of XML while protecting their investment in systems and training.

Five years after the introduction of the CIP3 PPF, the industry has to make the next important step by integrating production and business support systems into the existing technical workflow. The future of the graphic arts industry will be influenced by both faster equipment and optimized processes. The JDF initiative supports open interfaces, which will help integrate flexible solutions on a standardized platform.

The JDF specification will be published by the four companies and made widely available to all interested OEMs, third parties, and end users via its Web site www.job-definition-format.org.

Inter-workflow Connectivity   Agfa Corporation, Creo Products Inc., and Heidelberg have announced open system connectivity that will enable the Agfa Apogee and Heidelberg/Creo Prinergy workflow management solutions to support Agfa, Creo, and Heidelberg/Creo imaging engines. This announcement underscores the companies' commitment to open, PDF-based digital workflows for the printing industry.

This type of intersystem connectivity reinforces the growing role of Adobe Systems' reliable, editable PDF file format as the core of the industry's most open and accessible workflow systems. PDF-based workflows maximize all of the production-enhancing benefits of PDF, including easy late-stage editing, output predictability, and device and page independence.

Prinergy currently supports a connection to the Avantra imagesetters, using raster-screened DCS2 files via the Apogee PDF RIP (formerly Taipan RIP). This new level of connectivity will enable Prinergy to support Agfa proofers, imagesetters, and platesetters through an interface with the Apogee PrintDrive module.

A screened, 1-bit TIFF file will be sent from Prinergy to PrintDrive, which will then output the file to an Agfa imagesetter or platesetter. Special features of the Apogee PrintDrive, including proofing, multiple RIP input, and multiple engine output, will still be available.

Similarly, the Agfa Apogee workflow solution will be able to support output to Creo and Heidelberg/Creo imaging devices through the Creo Recorder Interface (CRI). The Apogee system will send 1-bit TIFF files with Agfa Balanced Screens to the CRI—the same interface used by Prinergy and other third-party front ends—which will image the files on Creo or Heidelberg/Creo output devices.

We envision approaches that will allow files to move between competitive workflows for multinational print buyers who must deal with a number of production organizations.

PDF in Production with Enfocus PitStop Server

In this age of collaborative workflow, where the functions of layout and final production are often separately housed, there is a need for efficiency, consistency, reliability, quality, and the possible modification or correction of pages or their subelements. Adobe Acrobat software, whose Distiller is the progenitor of the PDF format, succeeds well at maintaining consistent viewing and printing conditions across various platforms. With its controls for type and image handling, Distiller assimilates PostScript output into a highly ordered display list, thereby simplifying the internal construction of the original document and laying the groundwork for reliable rendering. Provided that the Distiller Job Options have been set correctly for the intended output or display path, the quality of the processed page is not only preserved, but optimized for its targeted use.

The Acrobat suite does not provide a mechanism for the users to determine the true fitness of their files for off-site print or Internet production. Obviously, it makes sense to fix any problems as early as possible, which would indicate the need for an advanced preflight solution capable of isolating these errors. Furthermore, if the person forwarding the PDF on to production is not in possession of the original document, or the application(s) that generated it, some recourse for correcting these problems must be available. Acrobat provides only for minimal editing of PDF content and many, particularly within prepress production environments, have bemoaned this lack of editing support. This is a little ironic, in that editability and safe exchange are contradictory notions; traditionally, one often had to be traded to get the other.

Preflight (Profiles and Reports)   With user-definable preflight Job Profiles, users can inspect incoming (or outgoing) files for a wide range of format, page, font, text, color, image, and line art options. These profiles can also be exported for use with PitStop on other stations, even at client sites. A chief complaint from service bureau operators is that many of the preflighted files they receive are no good because the client didn't have the expertise to properly configure the software for a particular output condition. PitStop compiles its Preflight Reports in a logical fashion as a standard PDF file. The report is separated into six sections, each of which occupies a separate page within the report:

1. Errors and warnings
2. General file information
3. Font information
4. Color information
5. Image information
6. OPI information

These reports are produced in Acrobat PDF, and the interactive inspection of the files is accomplished by means of hyperlinks placed within the file. The hyperlinks will still work at other workstations even if the report is being viewed using the free Acrobat Reader software (even if PitStop is not available), but without the enhanced interactivity of PitStop's floating Navigator palette. Minimally, at least one version of Acrobat 4 and one version of PitStop 4 must be purchased since they are necessary for creating the preflight Job Profiles and Action Lists, as well as for basic or interactive editing purposes.

It is probably a good idea to have both Acrobat and the PitStop plug-in available on all primary production workstations that are involved in PDF workflows.

Editing the PDF   It's one thing to do preflighting and quite another to do editing inside the Acrobat application. Enfocus has equipped its software with a tool set that compares favorably with many graphics applications. In doing so, PitStop has raised the standard for PDF editing. Users can move, scale, and rotate objects, change their color (fill and/or stroke), alter type by face, size, character and word spacing, embed or unembed fonts, or strip the file of prespecified halftone, separation, or OPI data. Changes can be performed by item selection, by page, or throughout the entire document. One can even re-associate text lines into logical lines or reflowing paragraphs.

Perhaps too many spot colors were created during the layout of a five-color print job. The intended mix was for process inks, plus Pantone 200 CV. Instead, after various designers had a hand in the development of the piece, there are now three extra spot colors named: Red, Pantone 200, and Pantone 200 CVC. This type of error is easily remedied within PitStop and, before you know it, you've got the anticipated five-color job.

PitStop's ability to forge a link between problem detection and correction represents a powerful advantage over other solutions. Similar to the Go To Problem option in Markzware's FlightCheck or the Pilot in Extensis Preflight Pro, alterations can be made interactively with the PitStop floating Navigator palette. It takes the user to each trouble spot in the PDF file that has been flagged by the preflight report in accordance with the active Job Profile. The user simply makes the necessary repairs right in Acrobat.

The Action List function allows the scripting of specific corrections that are required to bring the document into compliance with the preflight Job Profile. Individual Actions can be grouped together under the banner of a single Actor for easy execution and can be canceled with a single Undo. A user can create an Action that globally changes all Adobe Garamond text, 8-point or smaller, to 9-point Helvetica, or all black text can be set to overprint.

With a simple mouse-click, the changes are implemented. While not all editing functions can be tapped from within the Action Lists (you wouldn't want to rewrap text without operator guidance), this nevertheless represents a formidable weapon in the war against bad files. Recognizing the range and versatility of this application, Agfa and Scitex have licensed the PitStop engine for use in their Apogee and Brisque workflows (respectively).

Driving a Workflow through PitStop Server   While PitStop is a tool for the manipulation of PDF files on an individual basis, there is also a tangible need to process these files in a more direct and forceful manner. Enter PitStop Server. Running on Windows

95/98, Windows NT 4.0 on x86, and MacOS 8.x on PowerPC, PitStop Server is a standalone application that can assign preflight Job Profiles and Action Lists to Hot Folders. These folders can be made available on a local area network (LAN). Associated with each unique hot folder, PitStop Server creates five directories: a Keep Original folder, a Success folder, a Failure folder, a Log Success folder, and a Log Failure folder. Dropping files into a hot folder (providing that it is enabled) leads to a chain reaction of events:

1. Original PDF files are deposited in the Keep Original folder for safe keeping.

2. New PDF files (whether or not changes are made to the originals) are placed in the Success folder if they pass all tests without error. Otherwise, files that contravene the guidelines of the Job Profile are sent to the Failure folder for operator attention.

3. Preflight reports are created in the Log Success folder (pass) or the Log Fail folder (fail).

While it's not necessary to have Adobe Acrobat 4 and PitStop 4 available on the server host machine, it's advisable to do so if the user intends to manually process files from that station. The PitStop plug-in, which can only operate from within Acrobat, is required for inspecting the Preflight Reports with the Navigator palette.

The creation and management of Hot Folders is conducted within the PitStop Server software and doesn't require Acrobat or the PitStop plug-in. This includes the assignment of preflight Job Profiles and Action Lists to any Hot Folder, as well as the enabling, disabling, deletion, and prioritization (high-priority folders are processed first) of these folders. The Hot Folders dialog provides the user with the ability to select the location of all associated folders mentioned above.

The name of the Preflight Report (log file) is derived from the name of the original PDF (e.g., the report for bobsyouruncle.pdfwill be named bobsyouruncle_log.pdf). The Macintosh character limit for a filename is 31 characters, which includes the suffix. This requires that your original input PDF have a name (prior to suffix) of no more than 23 characters; otherwise, concatenation (shortening) of the name will occur. Because the subfolders within each of the Hot Folders tend to collect numerous files, it's advisable to keep your naming procedures as straightforward as possible to cut down on confusion. You might consider an efficient naming strategy or the use of a job numbering system to keep things in order. Files may also be purged from these folders based upon the number of files, folder size, or the number of days that a file has resided in the folder.

Font Handling   After all the improvements we've experienced in digital workflow in the past ten years, it is odd to consider that the incorrect display or printing of fonts still accounts for about half of all imaging problems. Thus, it's appropriate that Enfocus has paid particular attention to this aspect of PDF file wrangling. Additional font directories may be set for each Hot Folder. These fonts will be used in the processing of any PDF files dropped into the Input folder in addition to those font resources made available by the system and from globally specified font directories.

The Server can even use fonts from the current platform regardless of whether the PDF was created on the same hardware. Although the software is able to handle cross-platform fonts already embedded in a PDF file, font resources that are to be supplied by the PitStop Server must be compatible with the server platform. Users should also bear in mind that the software does not support bitmapped fonts.

Workflow Security and Centralized Control   One of the benefits of coordinating functions through a server-based solution (besides the obvious throughput issues) is the ability to maintain a great degree of compliance with established workflow routines. Left to their own devices, most operators will deviate to some extent from any prescribed workflow. This can make it very difficult for production managers to isolate the cause of trouble within the architecture. Likewise, when these routines change, server-driven processes ensure that all operators are in-step with one another. Additionally, security issues can be addressed on a network-, machine- and software-basis, providing an extra layer of comfort for the production environment. From a disaster-recovery perspective, backup and archiving can be performed on all vital workflow components at the same time.

PitStop accommodates password protection of Job Profiles and Action Lists to forbid unauthorized editing. Metadata (CIP3, etc.), which has been incorporated into the PDF file, is not affected by the saving or resaving actions of PitStop or PitStop Server. This keeps intact any specialized notations or process flags that are part of your overall workflow.

Every production system has intrinsic requirements for the formatting of files if they are to result in high quality, high-efficiency output. PitStop Server is equally effective across a range of processesfrom offset printing to the Web.

Typical Examples   Sample Workflow (Prepress—Simple): In a rather mundane prepress workflow surrounding the production of a single-color directory, there is a need to ascertain that all text is in the correct font, that foreign embedded fonts are removed, that local versions of fonts are embedded instead, and that all line weights are of a consistent thickness.

Sample Workflow (Prepress—Complex): With more complicated prepress requirements, PitStop Server may be called upon to delete all halftone-related specifications so that they may be defined directly at the RIP. All overprinting functions may have to be removed due to the fact that in-RIP trapping will be used later. Images will be checked for CMYK separation and to make sure that they possess relative resolutions of at least 200 dpi. Tapping into the new PDF 1.3 specification for the measurements of the Crop Box, Media Box, and Bleed Box, all of the measurements are checked to ensure clean processing through the downstream automated imposition process. No indexed color images. No RGB images. All OPI comments must be OPI 1.3.

Sample Workflow (Internet): All files should be optimized for byte-serving (page-by-page Web viewing). Modern compression methods must be used. No CMYK images allowed. All fonts must be embedded.

The inherent flexibility of the PitStop Server application, its future extensibility through the addition of features, along with opportunities for enhanced networking awareness, indicate strong possibilities for the inclusion of this software in custom-designed workflows, especially within the prepress market segment. PitStop Server offers many trade shops the foothold that they've been seeking in their attempts to develop independent PDF workflow solutions for themselves and their clients. This is the first time that a product has been able to satisfy many of the needs of professional image processors with respect to PDF troubleshooting and correction cycles.

6

Creating PDF Files

The first step in any information distribution system involves how the document will be used and who will use it. An end-use evaluation for the PDF focuses on distribution and usage concerns. How will the PDF be distributed and used? If the intended distribution is Web-based and on-screen viewing, then portability and small file size are more important than quality. However, if the end use is high-end output to an imagesetter or platesetter, then image integrity becomes the overriding factor. An analogy is that of a scale. On one side of the scale is image integrity and on the other side is file compression.

Currently there are two ways (actually 2.5 ways) to create PDF files—PDFWriter and Acrobat Distiller. Depending on end-use, one or the other will best suit your needs. The choice is actually very sim-

*There are two version
numbers to be aware of:
the PDF specification
version and the Acrobat
Software version.*
- *PDF version 1.0
  was introduced
  with Acrobat 1.*
- *PDF version 1.1
  was introduced
  with Acrobat 2.*
- *PDF version 1.2
  was introduced
  with Acrobat 3.*
- *PDF version 1.3
  was introduced
  with Acrobat 4.*

*All Acrobat software
can handle PDF ver-
sions at the same and at
the lower version num-
ber than what came
introduced with them.*

*Acrobat (formerly
known as Exchange)
sets the version number
to its own version num-
ber when it writes a
document back, even if
the original document
was on a lower version
number and has not
been changed.*

*Acrobat can read doc-
uments with a higher
version number correct-
ly if the document does
not use any new fea-
tures of the higher ver-
sion number. When it
encounters an unknown
feature, it either ignores
that particular object, or
it creates an error condition. This is per se not
predictable; it all
depends on the docu-
ment.*

ple. When producing text documents with small amounts of graphics that are not intended to be printed for professional production purposes, PDFWriter is a good choice. If high-end production is the goal and proper reproduction of graphics is essential, then use Distiller. The growing repurposability of documents and intense needs of high-end printing require the use of Distiller.

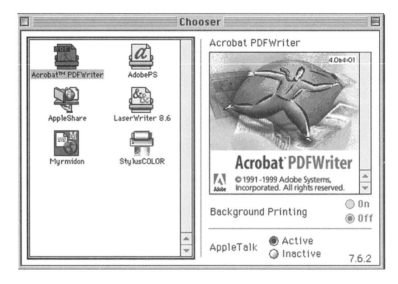

Figure 6-1
Chooser shows PDFWriter as a choice for Distilling.

Acrobat PDFWriter   The PDFWriter appears as a printer choice in the Chooser. PDF files are created by accessing the Page Setup and Print dialog boxes of the document-creating application. Compared to regular printer drivers, there are two buttons in the Page Setup dialog box that are special for PDFWriter, Compression, and Fonts. With these functions the user can control how the PDF file will be created. Only use the PDFWriter for simple text or Web projects.

Compatibility   There are different base compression schemes used by Acrobat 2.1, 3, and 4. Acrobat 2.1 base compression is LZW and Acrobat 3 uses a ZIP-like base compression. ZIP compression is approximately 20 percent more effective than LZW. Acrobat 3 compatibility also preserves halftone information, which was discarded by Acrobat 2.1.

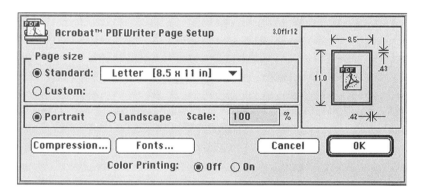

Figure 6-2
PDFWriter Page Setup.

To ensure that your PDF document can be read by everyone, Acrobat 3 compatibility is a safe choice. However, if you'd like the added benefits of better compression, use Acrobat 4 compatibility. This also makes sense because the Acrobat 4 Reader is available for free download at www.adobe.com.

ASCII Format vs. Binary Format   PDFWriter's default setting is binary, which makes the PDF files approximately 20% smaller than saving them in ASCII format. As a general rule of thumb, as the resolution of an image increases, the effectiveness (compression ratio) of JPEG will also increase. This is because the color transitions are smoother, and therefore, there are more compressible areas.

In the world outside continuous tone images, JPEG compression technique should never be used. Images such as black and white line art (1 bit per pixel, on or off) reveal increasing artifacts or unwanted noise in the image with higher levels of JPEG compression. Images such as line art or cartoons are not suited for JPEG compression.

PDF Creation   Once options for font embedding and compression have been chosen, creating a PDF is as simple as hitting the Print button.

 1. Select Print from the File Menu.
 2. Name the resulting PDF file.
 3. Determine where the file is to be saved.
 4. PDFWriter handles the rest.

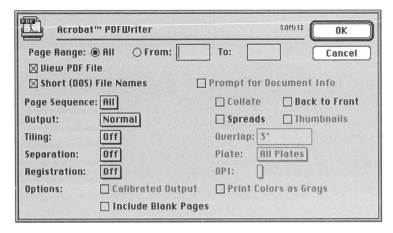

Figure 6-3
Choose shows PDFWriter as a choice for Distilling.

Even though PDFWriter is extremely convenient and is the easiest way to prepare PDF files, it is not without drawbacks. First, applications do not "see" the PDFWriter as a PostScript printer, which means Encapsulated PostScript (EPS) images will be sent to PDF-Writer as low-resolution rough-screen versions. Also, PDFWriter cannot be used with Apple's old page display and description format, QuickDraw GX. If QuickDraw GX is installed, PDFWriter will not be displayed in the Chooser.

As a general rule, if your document contains EPS images or you would like more control over the compression and font embedding options, Acrobat Distiller should be used to create the PDF.

PDFWriter does not support all controls that are supported in a PDF file. And as mentioned above, PDFWriter is a non-PostScript printer driver, and the information will not be treated the same way as if the file were printed to a PostScript printer. To solve this problem, Acrobat Distiller must be used.

Acrobat Distiller   What Distiller lacks in ease of use is more than made up in its reliability and extended capabilities over PDFWriter. Distiller can be seen as a software RIP, where the Post-Script codes are interpreted and an object list is generated. But instead of generating a raster representation of the page, it is formatted into a PDF document. In version 3.0/3.0x of Distiller, version 1.2 of PDF is used. The major difference from the previous PDF versions, 1.0 and 1.1, is that PostScript commands for professional print production are included. Some of these features are accessed in Acrobat Distiller, and for other functions, third-party plug-ins must be developed to take full advantage of the possibilities of PDF 1.2. PDF version 1.3 extends many of the PDF features.

Creating a PDF with Distiller requires first "saving" the document to a PostScript file (the data that would have been sent to a printer is instead saved in a file) and then opening that file in Distiller. The advantage of creating a PDF this way is that all of the data necessary to render the page is described in the PostScript file. As a result, Distiller can also act as a preflight tool to ensure that jobs are "RIP-able." Chances are that if it distills, it will print. Another advantage of Distiller is that it offers more control over compression and font opts than PDFWriter. High-end printing controls are also available through Distiller.

Why Use Distiller vs. PDFWriter?

1. You have more control over compression and font embedding options.
2. Your document contains EPS images.
3. You can distill PostScript files from another platform.
4. You encounter problems using PDFWriter.
5. You do not want to go on medication to deal with stress.

Distiller can create PDF documents from both EPS and Post-Script files. The first step in creating PDF documents with Distiller is to produce a PostScript file. Because the PostScript file is going to be used to generate the PDF document, the correct page-setup options must be set here. If the page orientation is not correct at this point, it cannot be corrected in Distiller.

When using QuarkXPress, it is also important to use the Acrobat Distiller printer description in the Page Setup menu. If a black and white printer description (most laser printers) is selected, the result-ing PDF will be in black and white. This is also helpful if you choose to use a Custom Page size not supported by the selected printer description.

After the correct Page Setup options have been chosen, select Print under the File menu.

1. Choose the radio button File in the Destination box.
2. With this selected, the Print button will change to Save.
3. Click on Save.
4. Name the PostScript file and designate the location where it will be saved.

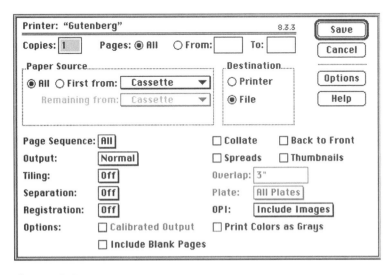

Figure 6-4
Choose shows PDFWriter as a choice for Distilling.

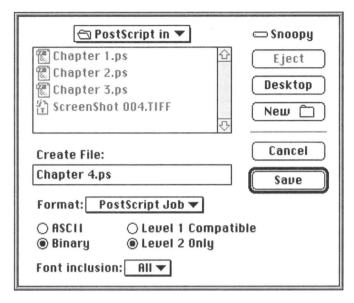

Figure 6-5
Choose shows PDFWriter as a choice for Distilling.

5. Select either PostScript Level 1 or Level 2. Since Distiller is a Level 2 RIP, it's best to select Level 2. If you have problems distilling the file, try using Level 1.
6. Determine the font inclusion—None, All, All but the standard thirteen, All but those in the PPD file.

All: All typefaces that are used in the file will be embedded in the PostScript file.

All but Standard 13: There are thirteen fonts that always are included in a PostScript printer (Courier, Courier bold, Courier italic, Courier bold italic, Helvetica, Helvetica bold, Helvetica italic, Helvetica bold italic, Times, Times bold, Times italic, Times bold italic, and Zapf Dingbats).

All but Fonts in PPD File: This will send all fonts not included in the PostScript Printer Description (PPD). The PPD file contains information about the fonts installed on the output device. If the Distiller PPD is being used, there should be no problem. However, if you are using a PPD for a printer with installed fonts not available to Distiller, you could get Courier in your PDF file.

The best advice is to include All fonts in the PostScript file. It is possible to *not* include the fonts, but you must then make sure that Distiller knows where to find them for PDF creation. However, the foolproof method is to include them in PostScript.

Remember, you need a PostScript file for Distiller, and that PostScript file can either have all fonts, embedded or Distiller knows where to look to find them on the local computer (the one where the job was created usually). Since the latter approach is fraught with peril, embed the fonts when you save the PostScript file to disk. Then, there is no question that they are available. You must also set Distiller job options to embed all fonts.

Why would Distiller come up with a blank list when doing "Font Locations" on a TrueType directory, yet come up just fine with the PSFonts directory?

Because Distiller can only see PostScript fonts in its font locations. This is normal and not a problem—make sure all TrueType fonts are embedded in the PostScript file. (Don't distill Quark EPS files, they won't embed fonts). The reason is very simple. Acrobat Distiller only embeds TrueType Type 42 fonts that appear in the PostScript job stream being processed. It does not have the capability of embedding TrueType fonts from outside the job stream, such as from the Windows or Mac system fonts folders. The font locations are only for Type 1 fonts. After all options for the PostScript file have been chosen, click on the Save button and the PostScript file will be generated.

Distilling PostScript Files   Creating PDF files from Post-Script is as simple as opening Distiller, selecting Open from the File menu, and naming the resulting PDF document. Although the actual process is easy, setting up how the PostScript file will be distilled into a PDF document requires a little preparation.

This chapter is not the definitive source of information on how to make a PDF. You should read the chapters on compression, fonts, advanced options, and high-end printing. Actually, you should read the entire book.

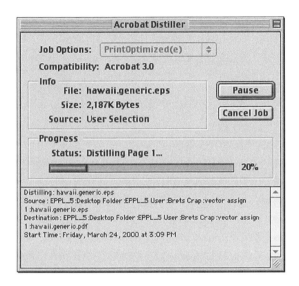

Figure 6-6
Acrobat Distiller status bar.

You really don't want to ever create PDF files with "bitmaps." These are device resolution dependent causing problems for display and also for printing at any device other than that for which the PDF file was originally created. For creation of PDF, ALWAYS use "Send Fonts as Type42" (AdobePS 4.x) or "Send Fonts as Native" (AdobePS 5.x). At print time, Acrobat properly sends either Type42 (native TrueType support for PostScript) or unhinted Type 1 (for printers without native TrueType support) fonts, depending upon the printer's capabilities.

General   Most of the General settings resemble those available within PDFWriter. However, there are added controls for Default resolution and Default page size. If the page size is not specified within the PostScript file, the page size will be set by the value placed here. This is useful for distilling EPS files, which do not contain any page size information. If the page size is specified within the PostScript file, Distiller will use the specified size, not Distiller's default.

Distiller Job Options   This is the heart of customizing PDF documents within Distiller and is available in the Distiller menu. There are four sections to Job Options:

      1. General

      2. Compression

      3. Font embedding

      4. Advanced

Create Adobe PDF

*The Easy Install instal-
lation option requires a
minimum of 9 Mb of
disk space to install
Create Adobe PDF com-
ponents and documen-
tation. Installing Create
Adobe PDF will over-
write the components
from any previous ver-
sion. The Installer
installs the following
items:
- DistillerLib (installed
in the selected folder)
- DistillerLib Helper (in
  the selected folder)
- DistillerLib Helper
alias file (installed in
Preferences folder)
- Create Adobe PDF
  Read Me file (installed
  at root of the volume
  with System Folder)
- Distiller License
Agreement (same loca-
tion as Read Me file)
- Folder called Printer
  Descriptions contain-
  ing a PostScript
  Printer Descriptions
  file called Acrobat
  Distiller
- Folder called Printing
  Plug-ins containing a
  plug-in for AdobePS
  8.6.0 and later called
  DistillerHose (in the
  Extensions folder)*

*Previous versions of
AdobePS may have
installed a "PDF
Plugin" file into the
Printer Descriptions
folder. This plug-in pro-
vided PDF functionali-
ty when used in con-
junction with Acrobat*

QuarkXPress PDF Filter 1.3

PDF Filter 1.3 for QuarkXPress and QuarkXPress Passport is QuarkXTensions software that allows you to save a page or range of pages from a QuarkXPress document as a PDF file. The filter saves the pages in PostScript format and employs the Adobe Acrobat Distiller to create the PDF file. The filter also allows you to import a page of a PDF file into a QuarkXPress picture box.

Confirm that Acrobat Distiller PPD is in the list of PPDs shown in the PPD Manager (Utilities & PPD Manager). This PPD is available on the Adobe Acrobat CD-ROM, and must be installed either in the PPD folder (if you have one) within your QuarkXPress or Quark-XPress Passport application folder, or in the system folder on your computer's hard drive. Adobe Acrobat Distiller must be installed to create a PDF file.

For Windows: The PDF Filter is installed automatically by the install.exe program in the Freebies folder. Click Continue and then click Customize. Make sure a check mark is placed next to the name of each QuarkXTensions module you want to install. Double-click each file name to add or remove a check mark. Click OK and then click Continue. Launch QuarkXPress or QuarkXPress Passport to access the features of the PDF Filter. The PDF Filter will not load on Windows NT versions earlier than 4.

Confirm that Acrobat Distiller PPD is in the list of PPDs shown in the PPD Manager (Utilities & PPD Manager). This PPD must be installed either in the PPD folder (if you have one) within your QuarkXPress or QuarkXPress Passport application folder, or in the System folder on your computer's hard drive.

For the PDF Filter to export correctly, you must map a PostScript printer to print to file. To do this, add a PostScript printer (Start & Settings & Printers & Add Printer). Then, set the properties of the printer to print to file (Start & Settings & Printer (select printer) & Properties & Details & Print to the following port & FILE).

Using the PDF Filter   To import a PDF file as a graphic element: While in a QuarkXPress or QuarkXPress Passport document, select a picture box. Choose File & Get Picture. Navigate to the PDF you want to import. If the PDF contains multiple pages, you will need to select a single page using the PDF Page field at the bottom of the Get Picture dialog box. To display the preview of a different page of a PDF in the Get Picture dialog box, check the Preview check box. Then, enter the page number in the PDF Page field. On Mac OS, press Tab to exit the PDF Page field. Click Open.

The preview for the PDF page imported into a QuarkXPress picture box will display at the color depth specified in the Color TIFFs pop-up menu in the Application Preferences dialog box Display tab (Edit menu) when the PDF page is imported. If you are importing a PDF into a QuarkXPress picture box, choose 16-bit or 32-bit (Mac OS) or 24-bit (Windows) in the Color TIFFs pop-up menu to import a preview with a higher color depth. Confirm the settings in the PDF Export Preferences dialog box (Edit menu).

- Choose Utilities & Export as PDF to display the Export as PDF dialog box.
- Enter a name for the PDF file, or use the default file name.
- Enter the page numbers or page ranges to export in the Pages field.
- To export one spread per page, check the Spreads check-box.
- Click Preferences to change or confirm settings in the PDF Export Preferences dialog box, if you haven't done so already. Modify settings as necessary and then click OK.

To avoid Courier substitution for fonts, make sure your print driver is set to include or send necessary fonts when saving to a PostScript file. For information about how to check this setting, see the documentation for your print driver. Click Save.

Setting PDF Filter Preferences   The PDF Export Preferences dialog box lets you specify preferences for exported PDF files. If you specify these preferences while a document is open, the new

Distiller 3. In AdobePS 8.6, this plug-in will continue to work if the user has version 8.5.1 or 8.5.2J of PDFPlugin installed. However, if the user is upgrading or has upgraded to Acrobat Distiller 4.05, there are two scenarios. First, if the user continues to use AdobePS 8.5.1, make sure to do the "easy install" for Acrobat 4 (or select the "AdobePS" package in custom install) to get the new PDFPlugin 8.5.3. Second, if the user is using AdobePS 8.6, we recommend that PDFPlugin be removed altogether (from the Printer Descriptions folder). AdobePS 8.6 has the new "Create Adobe PDF" feature for use with Distiller 4.05.

Problem: DistillerLib and DistillerLib Helper files not installed. The DistillerLib and DistillerLib Helper files must be installed in the same folder as a copy of the Acrobat Distiller application, version 4 or later, in order for them to operate properly. If a folder is selected for installation that does not contain Distiller, the Installer will not install DistillerLib, DistillerLib Helper, or any of the other Create Adobe PDF components, but it will install this Read Me file.

Problem: the "Create Adobe PDF" printer does not appear as a printer to use. One or more of the files necessary for Create Adobe PDF to work has been moved or deleted. Please re-install the Create Adobe PDF package. If that does not fix your problem, you should also re-install Acrobat Distiller (some files used by Distiller may have been inadvertently removed).

settings apply only to the active document. If you specify preferences in the Default PDF Export Preferences dialog box when no documents are open, the new settings apply to all new documents.

You can set preferences for general information about exported PDF files in the Document Info tab of the PDF Export Preferences dialog box. Choose Edit & Preferences & PDF Export to display the PDF Export Preferences dialog box Document Info tab. Use the Document Info tab of the PDF Export Preferences dialog box to enter general information about PDF files.

Choose Edit & Preferences & PDF Export to display the PDF Export Preferences dialog box, and then click the Hyperlinks tab. Use the Hyperlinks tab of the PDF Export Preferences dialog box to create hyperlinks for QuarkXPress lists and indexes. To change QuarkXPress indexes to hyperlinks, check Indexes become hyperlinks. You must have the Index 1.1 QuarkXTensions software in order to have index links. To change QuarkXPress lists to hyperlinks, check Lists become hyperlinks. To change QuarkXPress lists to PDF bookmarks, check Lists become bookmarks. Clicking a bookmark in the resulting PDF file will take the reader directly to the list item's text in the main body of the PDF.

- Choose Use All Lists to change all QuarkXPress lists in the document to PDF bookmarks.
- Choose Use List to change only one QuarkXPress list in the document to PDF bookmarks. Then, use the menu to the right of Use List to choose the list that will change to bookmarks.

For the PDF Filter to convert lists to hyperlinks or bookmarks, the lists must be created and built using the QuarkXPress List feature before exporting to PDF (Edit and View menus). Click OK. Use the Job Options tab of the PDF Export Preferences dialog box to specify compression and font embedding options. Choose Edit & Preferences & PDF Export to display the PDF Export Preferences dialog box and then click the Job Options tab. Check Override Distiller's Job Options. To embed all TrueType and Type 1 fonts in the PDF file, check Embed all fonts.

To embed only the font characters that are used in the document, check Subset fonts below and enter the character threshold percentage in the edit field to the right. The character threshold is the point beyond which Acrobat Distiller embeds the entire font. For example, the default character threshold is 35 percent. If fewer than 35 percent of the characters in a font are used in the PDF file, Acrobat Distiller will subset those characters; however, if more than 35 percent of the characters are used in the file, Acrobat Distiller will embed the entire font. Use the Color Images, Grayscale Images, and Monochrome Images areas to choose compression settings for color, grayscale, and black and white images.

Quark has released an update to their PDF Filter (1.3 Beta 2); however, despite the new version number, you still cannot import Acrobat 4 PDFs.

- In the Color Images area, choose the item in the Compression pop-up menu that suits the way you want Acrobat Distiller to compress color bitmap images. If you choose an automatic compression option, Acrobat Distiller applies the compression method that best suits each individual image. If you choose a manual compression option, you determine whether ZIP or JPEG compression will be applied to color bitmap images. When choosing a JPEG compression option, choose the amount of compression Acrobat Distiller should apply (High, Medium High, Medium, Medium Low, or Low).

- In the Grayscale Images area, choose the item in the Compression pop-up menu that suits the way you want Acrobat Distiller to compress grayscale bitmap images. If you choose an automatic compression option, Acrobat Distiller applies the compression method that best suits each individual image. If you choose a manual compression option, you determine whether ZIP or JPEG compression will be applied to grayscale bitmap images. When choosing a JPEG compression option, choose the amount of compression Distiller should apply (High, Medium High, Medium, Medium Low, or Low).

- In the Monochrome Images area, choose None, CCITT Group 3, CCITT Group 4, ZIP, or Run Length in the Compression pop-up menu to specify the type of compression Acrobat Distiller should apply to monochrome (black and white) images.

- Use the Resolution pop-up menu in each area to choose whether to maintain the resolution of the images or to downsample or subsample them to reduce file size. If you choose Downsample, Acrobat Distiller determines the average pixel color in an area and replaces the area with a larger single pixel containing the average color. If you choose Subsample, Acrobat Distiller selects the center pixel in an area and enlarges it to replace the area with a single pixel.
- If you choose Downsample or Subsample, enter the final resolution of the image in the dpi field in each area. Click OK.

Use the Output tab of the PDF Export Preferences dialog box to specify settings for PDF files that will be printed to output devices. Choose Edit & Preferences & PDF Export to display the PDF Export Preferences dialog box, and then click the Output tab. Choose the appropriate PPD in the Printer Description pop-up menu. To create device-independent PDF files, choose an Acrobat Distiller PPD. To create PDF files with device-specific information (for example, device halftoning), choose the appropriate PPD for that device. To create separations for exported PDF files, check Separations, and then use the Separations area to specify separation settings.

- From the Plates pop-up menu, choose Process & Spot or Convert to Process. Process & Spot produces all process and spot color plates. Convert to Process converts all colors in the file to process colors and produces process plates.
- To produce plates for all document colors, regardless of whether the colors are applied to items, check Produce blank plates.

To include Open Prepress Interface (OPI) comments in exported PDF files, check Use OPI, and then choose an option from the Images pop-up menu.

- Use the default setting, Include Images, when you are not using an OPI server. Include Images does not embed OPI comments for EPS pictures, and if a high-resolution file cannot be found for printing, the screen preview is substituted.
- Choose Omit TIFF when you are outputting to an OPI prepress system that replaces TIFF pictures only. (Most OPI systems use this method.) Omit TIFF replaces TIFF pictures with OPI comments in the file. EPS pictures are included; OPI comments for the EPS pictures are not included.
- Choose Omit TIFF & EPS when you are outputting to an OPI prepress system that replaces both TIFF and EPS pictures. Omit TIFF & EPS replaces both TIFF and EPS pictures with OPI comments in the file.

OPI is a technology that lets you import a low-resolution version of a picture, called a proxy file, into a QuarkXPress document during the layout and proofing stage. By using a particular set of PostScript comments, QuarkXPress and the PDF Filter can then create a PDF file that tells a prepress system or OPI server to automatically exchange the proxy file with a high-resolution version of the picture when outputting the PDF file to film. For detailed information about OPI, consult the Adobe OPI documentation or your OPI software documentation, or consult with your service bureau.

To use OPI technology, final output of the PDF file must be made to a prepress system or server that can interpret OPI comments and that has access to the high-resolution versions of pictures targeted for OPI. To specify that crop marks and registration marks should print on every page of exported PDF files, choose Centered or Off Center from the Registration pop-up menu. To specify the distance between the edge of the page and the beginning of the crop marks, enter a value in the Offset field.

Choose the type of bleed for exported PDF files in the Bleed area. Choose Page Items Only to create a bleed by extending items from the document page onto the pasteboard. An item that extends off the document page (left) prints in its entirety (right), while pasteboard items that do not extend from the page do not print. To automatically create a bleed by defining how far the bleed extends from the document page edges, choose Symmetric or Asymmetric in the Bleed pop-up menu.

A symmetric bleed extends the same distance from each page edge. If you choose Symmetric, enter a value in the Amount field to specify the bleed amount from the page edge. When you are working in a facing pages document, the Left and Right fields for an asymmetric bleed become the Inside and Outside fields. The Inside bleed affects the side nearest to the document's spine, and the Outside bleed affects the side of the page farthest from the spine. When creating a symmetric or an asymmetric bleed, QuarkXPress uses the bleed values to clip items.

For example, if the bleed is set to 2 picas, any item on the pasteboard that is within 2 picas of the page edges will print, but any portion of the item that extends beyond 2 picas will be clipped by the bleed rectangle. If Clip to bleed limits is unchecked, QuarkXPress prints all document page items and pasteboard items that are at least partially within the bleed rectangle. These items will not be clipped, unless they extend beyond the limits of the printing device's imageable area. Pasteboard items that are not in the bleed rectangle will not print. Click OK.

Setting Preferences for Distilling the File   The PDF tab of the Application Preferences dialog box (Edit menu) lets you set preferences for the action Acrobat Distiller will take when you export a QuarkXPress document as a PDF file. Use the PDF tab of the Application Preferences dialog box to set preferences for the action Acrobat Distiller will take when you export a QuarkXPress document. If the Acrobat Distiller area does not display the correct path to the Acrobat Distiller application on your computer, click Browse and use the controls in the Locate Acrobat Distiller dialog box to choose the application. Choose Edit & Preferences & Application to display the Application Preferences dialog box, and then click the PDF tab. The Workflow area settings control whether Acrobat Distiller will distill the PDF file after QuarkXPress exports it. Choose Distill immediately to automatically launch Acrobat Distiller after export and create a PDF from the exported PostScript file.

Choosing Distill immediately will cause Acrobat Distiller to launch if it is not already running, and to distill the PostScript file. After the PostScript file has been distilled, it is deleted from the computer and Acrobat Distiller quits. Acrobat Distiller does not quit if it was already running at the time of the export.

Creating PDF Files in Excel

Before you create an Excel spreadsheet, set up Acrobat Distiller as the default printer. If you receive Excel spreadsheets from another source, you should ask the documents' creator to set the default printer to Acrobat Distiller before creating the documents. To specify Acrobat Distiller as the default printer, choose Start to Settings to Printers. Right-click Acrobat Distiller, and then choose Set As Default from the pop-up menu.

Adobe recommends that you use Acrobat Distiller with the Adobe PostScript (AdobePS) printer driver, and that you configure AdobePS to send TrueType fonts as Type 42 fonts. Type 42 fonts preserve the appearance of the TrueType fonts and prevent them from being substituted with Type 1 fonts.

Acrobat 4 automatically sets up Acrobat Distiller to use AdobePS. If you're using Acrobat 4 in Windows 95 or Windows 98, you should set up AdobePS to send TrueType fonts as Type 42 as follows: Choose Start to Settings to Printers. Right-click Acrobat Distiller, and then choose Properties from the pop-up menu. Click the Font tab, and then click Send Fonts As. Choose Type 42 from the Send TrueType Fonts As pop-up menu. Click OK to close the Properties dialog box.

If you're using Acrobat 4 in Windows NT, you should set up AdobePS to send TrueType fonts as Type 42 as follows: Choose Start to Settings to Printers. Right-click Acrobat Distiller, and then choose Document Defaults from the pop-up menu. Click the plus sign next to Document Options. Click the plus sign next to PostScript Options. Select TrueType Font Download Option. Select Native TrueType in the Change TrueType Font Download Option Setting section. (Type 42 is called "Native" in Windows NT.)

Previewing Your Excel Spreadsheet   After you've set up a default printer, you should preview how your Excel spreadsheet will print to see whether the PDF file will appear the way you want it to. If your spreadsheet previews with cropped or blank pages, the resulting PDF file will have blank or cropped pages as well. To preview how an Excel spreadsheet will print, choose File to Print Preview. Navigate through the preview to see whether there are any cropped or blank pages. If there are, modify the spreadsheet by selecting the Setup button in the Print Preview area. In the Page Setup window, you can adjust the orientation, scaling, and margins. You may also need to modify the spreadsheet itself to get the desired printing results.

Creating a PDF File   In Excel, choose File > Print. Make sure that you've chosen Acrobat Distiller from the Printer Name pop-up menu. If another printer is set as the default printer, your document may be reformatted when it's converted to PDF. Select Entire Workbook in the Print dialog box. Click OK and specify a filename and location for your PDF file. When Excel sends a print job to the print queue, it sends multiple jobs (one job for each sheet). Because Excel sends multiple jobs, Acrobat Distiller may interpret these jobs as separate files and create separate PDF files. If this is the case, you can combine the separate PDF files in Acrobat Exchange 3 or Acrobat 4.

Capturing a Web Page   New to Acrobat 4.5 is the ability to capture a Web URL as a PDF. You must select Adobe PS and then Create Adobe PDF. You can specify how many levels deep you want to capture.

Creating PDF Files in Word

Before you create a Word document, you first need to set up Acrobat PDFWriter or Acrobat Distiller as the default printer. If you receive Word documents from another source, you should ask the documents' creator to set the default printer to either Acrobat PDFWriter or Acrobat Distiller before creating the documents.

To specify Acrobat PDFWriter or Acrobat Distiller as the default printer, choose Start > Settings > Printers. Right-click either Acrobat PDFWriter or Acrobat Distiller, and then choose Set As Default from the pop-up menu. When should you use Acrobat PDFWriter or Acrobat Distiller? Use Acrobat PDFWriter for documents that contain text formatted with TrueType fonts.

Use Acrobat Distiller for documents that contain images or text formatted with Type 1 fonts and for documents that contain both images and TrueType fonts, and configure AdobePS to send TrueType fonts as Type 42 fonts. If you'll be using Acrobat Distiller, Adobe recommends that you use it with the Adobe PostScript printer driver (AdobePS), and configure AdobePS to send TrueType fonts as Type 42 fonts. Type 42 fonts will preserve the appearance of the TrueType fonts and prevent them from being substituted with Type 1 fonts.

Acrobat 4 automatically sets up Acrobat Distiller to use AdobePS. If you're using Acrobat 4 in Windows 95 or Windows 98, you should set up AdobePS to send TrueType fonts as Type 42 as follows: Choose Start to Settings to Printers. Right-click Acrobat Distiller, and then choose Properties from the pop-up menu. Click the Font tab, then click Send Fonts As. Choose Type 42 from the Send TrueType Fonts As pop-up menu.

If you're using Acrobat 4 in Windows NT, you should set up AdobePS to send TrueType fonts as Type 42 as follows:

1. Choose Start to Settings to Printers.
2. Right-click Acrobat Distiller, and then choose Document Defaults from the pop-up menu.
3. Click the plus sign next to Document Options.
4. Click the plus sign next to PostScript Options.

5. Select TrueType Font Download Option.

6. Select Native TrueType in the Change TrueType Font Download Option Setting section. (Type 42 is called Native in Windows NT.)

7. Acrobat 3 does not automatically set up Acrobat Distiller to use AdobePS.

Specifying Word's Printing Options After you've set up a default printer, you can specify printing options in Word's Options or Print dialog box. Acrobat PDFWriter and Acrobat Distiller will use the printing options you specify. To specify printing options for all your Word documents, choose Tools > Options, and then click the Print tab. You can then select options in the Print pane. Make sure to select Drawing Objects if your documents contain line drawings (arrows, flow charts) or graphics. Make sure to deselect the Reverse Print Order option to ensure that pages appear in the correct order in PDF files. Other options in the Options dialog box can affect how your documents look after they're converted to PDF. Make sure you select only those options you want to apply to the resulting PDF file.

Creating a PDF File After you've specified Word-specific printing options, you can create a PDF file from your Word document. In Word, choose File to Print. Make sure that you've chosen either Acrobat PDFWriter or Acrobat Distiller from the Printer Name pop-up menu. If another printer is set as the default printer, your document may be reformatted when it's converted to PDF. In the Print dialog box, select any printing options you want to use. Acrobat PDFWriter or Acrobat Distiller will ask you for a filename and location for your PDF file.

7

Annotation and Remote Proofing

New in Acrobat 4 is increased functionality for annotations. A specific menu item has been established in the Tools menu under Annotations.

Figure 7-1
Tools for annotation: menu options (left), tool palette (right).

Summarizing Annotations This menu will give you the ability to work with the annotations that may be present in a file. The first option in the menu is to Summarize the Annotations in a File (Command + Shift + T). This command will scan the current document and create a new PDF file that is a summary report of just the annotations present in the original PDF file. The information in the summary is:

- Page of the annotation
- Annotation number on that page
- The annotation's label
- The date the annotation was created
- The time the annotation was created
- Annotation contents

Annotations Filter Manager You can control which annotations are viewable and which are not viewable. The interface to control the annotation viewing is the Filter Manager. This option is located in the Tools menu, under the annotations submenu, in the Filter Manager option.

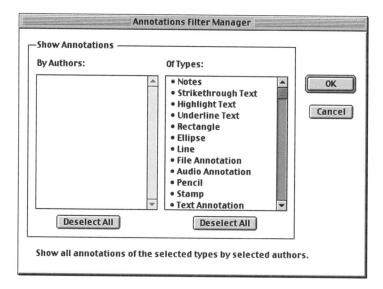

Figure 7-2
Tools for annotation: menu options (left), tool palette (right).

The command center for the display of annotations in a PDF has a deceptively simple interface. To ensure that a specific type of annotation is being displayed, make sure that there is a bullet point in front of that type of annotation. Simply clicking on a specific annotation type will turn it on or off.

The left side of the window is the control for the selection of various authors of annotations in a particular document. Selecting or deselecting specific authors will show or hide their contributions to the annotations in a PDF file. Turning the authors on and off is performed with a single mouse click on the author's name.

Deleting All Annotations The last option in the Annotations submenu of the Tools menu is the option to delete all annotations from a particular document. This action is irreversible, and cannot be undone. Be sure that you really want to delete all the annotations from the document before proceeding. A dialog box will prompt you to confirm your decision to delete the annotations.

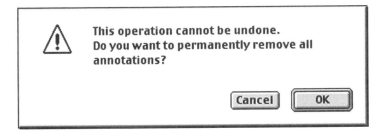

Figure 7-3
Tools for annotation: menu options (left), tool palette (right).

Annotations Palette On the left side of the main Acrobat window is a palette dedicated to annotations. This palette will allow you to list all annotations and provide rapid access to specific listings. This palette can be torn away from the main window and float anywhere on your screen. In the upper-right corner of the annotations palette is a pull-down menu. This menu is accessed by clicking on the arrow in the corner of the palette. This pull-down menu will allow you to choose how the list of annotations is displayed in the palette. In this case the choice is to display the annotations according to the Author.

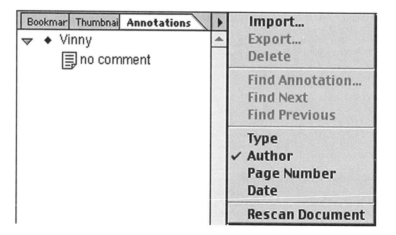

Figure 7-4
Options for display of annotations.

This pull-down menu will also allow you to perform all the other annotation functions, especially Find Annotation. New in Acrobat 4 is the ability to search for annotations according to the first several characters of the comments inserted when the annotation was created. To use the feature, select the Find Annotation option in the pull-down menu. At the dialog box key in your search query.

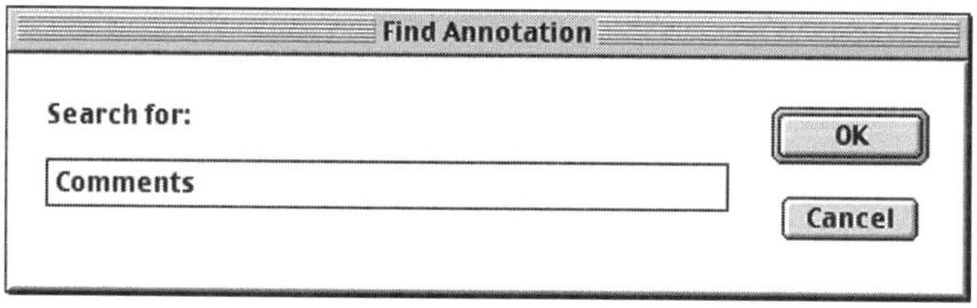

Figure 7-5
Find Annotation dialog box.

This is a great feature and we hope it will be expanded to search for anything in the annotation boxes.

Annotation Tools   New in Acrobat 4 is the provision for more powerful built-in communication tools. Each of these markup tools can be used to question, inform, alert, or just get extra attention for something. When the PDF file is opened in Acrobat, you have the ability to attach the following annotation types:

- Sound files
- Stamps
- Notes
- Attached files

Sound Files   Creators of PDF files can record and embed a sound file to a PDF. This sound file is denoted in the PDF file by a small icon that looks like a speaker. Doubleclick on it to hear it. This can be a verbal query or comment. You better have lots of disk storage if you use voice annotation.

Attached Files   You can attach a file of virtually any format to the existing PDF file. This allows for the possibility of supporting documentation to accompany the PDF file. The attachment of a file is only a reference to automatically open the other document; it is not part of the PDF file. An attached document is denoted by one of these icons:

📎   — Attach

📖   — Tag

📥   — Graph

📌   — Paper clip

When you attempt to follow the link to the attached document, Reader will prompt you to ensure that you really want to take the action. This is a safety measure that you can disable by clicking the "Do not ask this question again" checkbox.

Figure 7-6
The Launch dialog box warning.

Keep in mind that this type of annotation is only a reference to another application file. People receiving these types of annotation references need both the referenced file and the application program to open that file. Always be very careful that users of a referenced file have the tools necessary to open the file.

Stamps   One of the Notes choices lets you place an approved stamp on a page. There will be other stamps with other messages. Since PDFs are used for remote soft proofing, the "Approved" stamp is a natural choice.

Notes   Notes are the wonderful ability to communicate with others about the PDF document. Notes are viewable on screen but do not print. When you encounter a note in a document, the icon will look like the one below. Preferences can be set to change its color.

Click on the closed-note icon and open the note for reading. You can quickly see whom the note came from by looking in the title bar at the top of the note window. The note's content can be in any font you want; just go the Notes Preferences. When you are finished reading a note, click on the square in the upper-left-hand corner to close the note. The note icon will remain.

Figure 7-7
A note from Vinny. Not very interesting.

Drawing Tool

New in Acrobat 4 are enhanced notes and annotation features. The Drawing tool located in the side menu bar allows you to create defined shapes and freehand drawings as indicators for annotations. When you use the drawing tools, you will attach a note to the markings.

The drawing tools in the side menu bar are accessed either by using the shortcut keys Shift + N, or by clicking on the pencil tool in the side menu bar. The shapes that you can make with the various tools are:

Pencil Tool

Rectangle Tool (hold down Shift to get a perfect square)

Ellipse Tool (hold down Shift to get a perfect circle)

Line Tool (hold down Shift to get angles at 45 degrees)

Drawing Properties   Before you use the drawing tool, hold the Control key, and click the mouse. A pull-down window will appear and the final choice in the list is Pencil Properties.

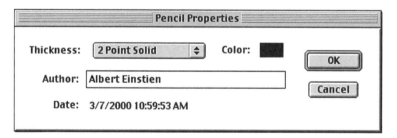

Figure 7-8
The Pencil Properties dialog box.

This dialog box will specify the attributes that you want applied to the pencil for the drawing you want. You have the ability to choose settings for the line colors and for the thickness of the lines in the drawing.

MarkUp Tool

Included in Acrobat 4 are more interactive group-oriented MarkUp tools. The tools located in the side tool bar for Highlighting text, Striking through text, and Underlining text are examples of this effort. These tools can be accessed through the side menu bar or using the shortcut keys Shift + U.

Highlighted Text

To install Acrobat 4.0, follow these steps:

Strike Through Text

~~To install Acrobat 4.0, follow these steps:~~

Underlined Text

To install Acrobat 4.0, follow these steps:

Figure 7-9
Three approaches to attention-getting text are shown above.

To select any of these styles, select the tool in the side tool bar, and then drag the cursor over a defined amount of text.

Article Tool

Articles are special links that create a thread for a sequence of screen views. A great use of the Article tool is similar to that of a newspaper article which is broken up and placed in several different places in the newspaper. An Article thread in Acrobat would be placed over the article segments and the user could follow the article threads by clicking to jump to the various segmnents.

Article threads are created by going to the side menu bar and choosing the Article tool, or using the keyboard shortcut key "a." Your cursor will change to a an article icon. You can then click and drag over the area containing the first part of the Article. When you release the mouse, you will have the ability to click and drag over any other parts of the Article thread.

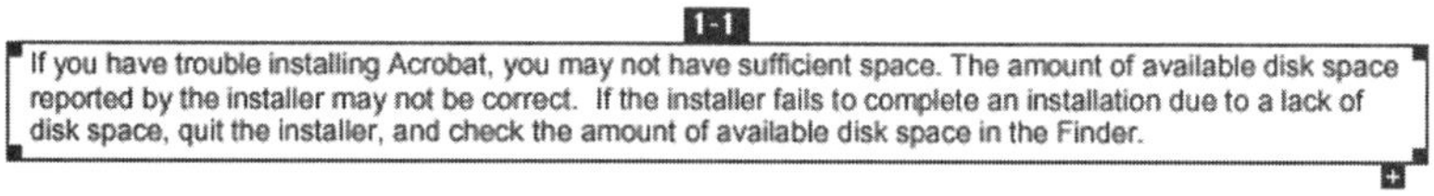

1-1

If you have trouble installing Acrobat, you may not have sufficient space. The amount of available disk space reported by the installer may not be correct. If the installer fails to complete an installation due to a lack of disk space, quit the installer, and check the amount of available disk space in the Finder.

Figure 7-10
You define articles with the article tool and then dragging over the text.

When you are finished with all article segments, hit Enter. After you do this, you will be prompted by a dialog box that requires the specification of Article properties, such as a Name and other information. This name is used in many functions such as setting a Form Field to read an article. To view an Article, you can go to the Window menu to the Show Articles option. You will be given a list of the current document's available articles.

Article Properties   The properties that you gave the article when creating it can be viewed by using the Properties choice in the Edit menu (Command + I). The Article properties include:

- Title
- Subject
- Author
- Keywords

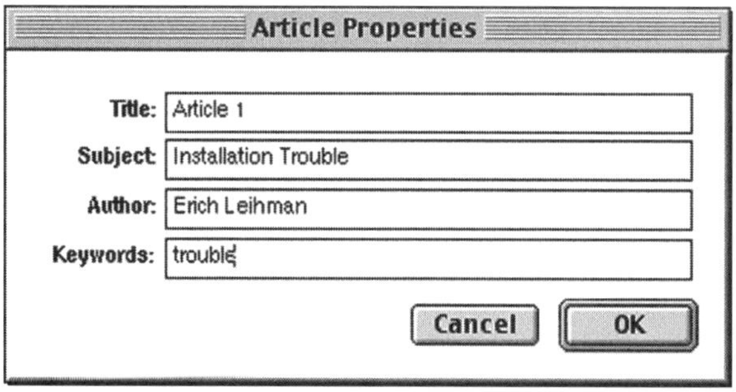

Article Properties	
Title:	Article 1
Subject:	Installation Trouble
Author:	Erich Leihman
Keywords:	trouble

Cancel   OK

Figure 7-11
Article Properties dialog box.

Designer/Printer Relationship   In order to create a seamless production environment and to best use the benefits of new reproduction technologies, there must be an efficient exchange of files throughout the entire life of the document. Partial digital workflows have dominated the exchange of files from designer to printer for quite some time, but the results are often far from seamless.

Whether you are the designer or the printer, you have most likely witnessed some very, let's just say, less than perfect situations. For instance, how many times have you opened a file, and that horrible window appeared saying, Fonts Missing? How many times have you begun to preflight when you realized pictures were missing? How many times did these problems occur when the job needed to be output no later than yesterday? PDF provides the solution to these nightmares.

Currently, the majority of jobs are laid out and paginated in an application such as QuarkXPress or PageMaker. The scans are either done in-house or are sent out and placed in as FPOs. Once the designer has completed the job, the client must then approve the job. From there, the job is sent to a printer where it is trapped, imposed, proofed, approved, and printed. Since the file changes hands so many times, it is essential that the file be all-inclusive and consistent. PDF may not decrease the change in hands, but it becomes the common denominator making the process easier, quicker, and more trustworthy.

Let's create a specific scenario. Imagine that you are a designer producing a menu for a restaurant chain. You have received the photographs via FedEx, have sent them to the printer to be scanned, who in turn has supplied you with the low-res images to work with for your page layout. The menu has been designed in QuarkXPress and is ready to go to your client for approval.

How do you send the job to your client? At this stage in the game, we are past the usage of faxes. A fax requires retyping, fax quality is yukky, fax is yesterday. Since this job is four colors, the client needs a more accurate representation of the design richness. Traditionally, you would send the file together with any digital artwork and illustrations back to the printer who then opens the file, and makes sure that images are correctly linked in the OPI system. Fonts, which are (hopefully) from the same supplier and have the same set of kerning information, are loaded into the system. The prepress operator then sends the file to film, makes a proof, and charges you $100 for labor and material. Even if the proof is mailed directly to your client, the entire process still takes two to three days.

Not only is this a tremendous hassle, but you have already added a decent chunk of money to your client's bill. After the job gets revised, and even more proofs, it becomes obvious that there must be a faster, cheaper solution. How about PDF as a soft proof? As a designer, your job will be easier, and more important, you can provide a better price for your client. Thus, instead of sending the original application file together with pictures and illustrations to the printer for hard proofs, make a PDF file and send it to your client, who can then view the job with detail and accuracy on screen.

Generating the Soft Proof   The generation of a soft proof (an on-screen proof, not hard copy) is not difficult but very crucial. PDF will be your best friend if and only if you distill your file correctly. For a soft proof, there are several things you should play close attention to:

- Preferences in Distiller
- Font Embedding
- Compression

Client Approval   Once the client receives the PDF file, it can be opened in Acrobat Reader. Acrobat uses anti-aliasing to represent the text on screen, so the overall appearance will be more realistic than a faxed copy. Images on screen are not high resolution. After the client reviews and approves the design, it's time to send the file to the printer. However, if the client has the full Acrobat (what used to be called Exchange) they can then annotate the PDF as we have discussed in this chapter. It opens a whole new world of possibilities for remote proofing and collaboration.

8

Editing

The TouchUp Text tool allows you to perform minor text editing in a document. Now read that again and say the word "minor" in a loud voice. You can alter individual letters and lines, but you still do not have the ability to reflow text in the document. You can access the TouchUp tool in the side menu bar. When you do this, your cursor will turn into a straight bar.

You are now ready to select some text. Click once anywhere on the line of text that you want to edit. A box will surround the line. When you are using the TouchUp tool, you have the ability to act on only one line at a time.

Once the line of text is selected, you can highlight individual letters or words in a way similar to other programs. At this point you can change characters in the line, their typeface, their size, their position, and their spacing. If the line is justified and you need to replace more than one character and the line exceeds its measure, you will need patience and care to get the line where you want it to be. It was called Text TouchUp for a reason.

Attributes Menu   After you select the text, you should launch the Text Attributes floating tool bar. To do this, go to the Tools menu, then to the TouchUp menu, and then to the Text Attributes option. You will see a three-tabbed folder with tabs for:

- Font
- Character
- Line

Figure 8-1
There are three tabs in the Text TouchUpAttributes dialog box.

The Font Tab   The font tab indicates the font being used for the highlighted selection. You can change the point size of the highlighted text, the fill color, and the outline color. You will notice that the top of the list will include the fonts that are embedded in the file.

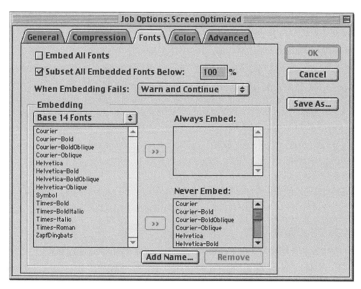

Figure 8-2
The Font tab is the most important in the Attributes dialog box.

It is important to note that you can only modify a font that has been fully embedded in the PDF. You have limited ability to use the TouchUp tool on a font that has only been subsetted. This decision was made at the point of PDF creation.

If you decide to change a font, from either a fully embedded font or a system font, you should know that the font encodings may differ, resulting in unacceptable font display and printout. You will be alerted by the program if you encounter such a situation.

Figure 8-3
Alert informs you of possible font problems.

Editing text in a PDF file should be reserved to situations where there is no other alternative. By editing text at this stage, you will be faced with a layout application file that does not match the PDF. Be sure to always go back and update the original files.

The Character Tab   The next tab in the folder set is the Character tab. This tab allows control over the character attributes of the the selected text. The controls that you have include:

- **T** Character width (in percentage units)

- A³ꜛ Baseline Shift (in points)

- AV Letterspacing (in 1,000ths of an EM)

- AV AV Word Spacing (in 1,000ths of an EM)

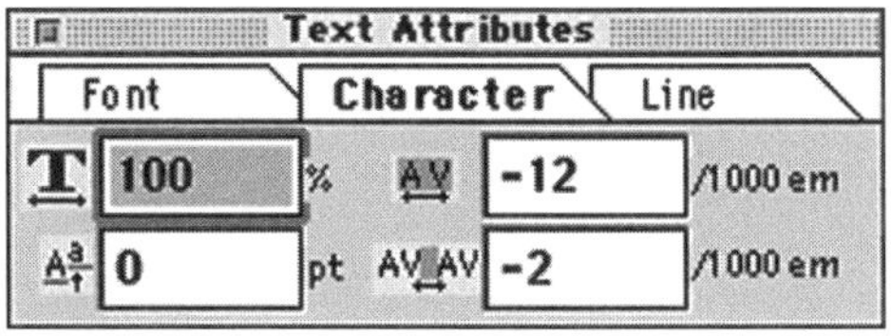

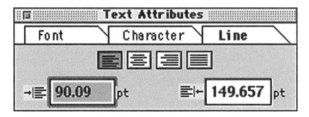

Figure 8-4
Text Attributes dialog box for Character attributes.

The Line Tab The Line tab of the folder is unlike the other tabs in that it controls the attributes of the entire line of text that you have selected, rather than the individual letters or words. You have the ability to choose the justification of the line. Your choices are:

- Ragged Right
- Centered
- Ragged Left
- Force Justified
- Left indent (in points)
- Right indent (in points)

Figure 8-5
Text Attributes dialog box for Line attributes.

Each line setting will give you pull bars to indicate the setting. Only the Force Justify setting allows you to resize the line length.

Text TouchUp Drop Menu New in Acrobat 4 is the availability of a quick drop-down menu when text is selected with the TouchUp Text tool. First, select some text. Then, hold the Control key on the Macintosh and click the mouse. The menu will pop down from the pointer. It is a contextual menu.

Figure 8-6
Text TouchUp drop-down menu.

There is no such thing as a "text box" in a PDF file, as there was in the page layout program. This is "lost in the interpretation" to PDF. There is such a thing as a Marked Content operator defined in PDF, which may be used to preserve structure. Export PDF directly from Illustrator 8.x and reopen it with Illustrator, for example and text frames are retained, text reflows, even layers are preserved. PDF 1.3 adds to this capability with more explicit structural syntax.

When you add or remove text from a line in a PDF file (using the built-in editing tools), it immediately oversets or undersets the line off the page or into the next column, graphic, whatever. There's no such thing as column and depth boundaries, let alone H&J (Hyphenation & Justification) information.

Specifically, the H&J information used for line breaks in the authoring application (Quark, PageMaker, InDesign, MS Publisher 2000, etc.) each use very different and sophisticated routines (InDesign's prowess appears to be the new leader) and are not preserved. Although Acrobat does have a few advanced "preserve" buttons, this mission-critical link is missing.

There's a difference between the content stream that is being run into columns and the technical details on how it is broken into lines. It is practically impossible to impart the algorithm used to break text in such a way that it could be used by other programs, but it is rather simple to preserve the intent of the content (this is a real hyphen, this is a paragraph, this story continues on the next page, etc). The PDF 1.3 format is rich enough to do this now.

Preserving H&J characteristics of MS Publisher would be a dubious achievement in any event. This becomes more of a legal and

How do you convert text inside a PDF file to curves? Select the text with the Object Edit Tool, and Control/Alt Click and select Edit—Illustrator should open. Convert the text you want to curves, then save. The PDF should be as desired. This will increase file size.

political issue since companies like Quark and Adobe consider such code "the family jewels" and are unlikely to release it into public domain or companies like Enfocus. Porting such information into PDF files is no small technical feat either from many standpoints.

Acrobat 4 includes modifying and replacing images contained in PDF documents. A new "PDFFormat" plug-in for Photoshop 5.x is installed with Acrobat 4, and provides the link between the two Adobe applications. The PDFFormat plug-in must be properly located within the Photoshop plug-ins folder to be able to access it. If not placed there during installation, move it into the Adobe Photoshop > Plug-ins > File Formats' folder/directory. (Restart Photoshop if it was open.)

After using Acrobat 4 to open a PDF file that allows changes, select the "TouchUp Object Tool" from the vertical row of tool icons on the left frame of the PDF. It may be hidden from view initially; it's located behind the TouchUp Text Tool. Click and hold the cursor on the Text Tool icon until the Object Tool's icon is visible, then select it to make it active. Position the TouchUp Object Tool's icon on the image you wish to edit and then click once to select the image and drag it from the PDF file. Or, while holding down either the Option key/Mac or the Control key/Win, double-click on the image in a PDF to automatically launch Photoshop, directly opening the selected image for editing.

After making the desired changes in Photoshop, save the image to have those changes applied to the version of the image in the PDF. Or use Save As to save a copy of the selected image as a separate image file, choosing from the list of Photoshop's supported file formats—including saving the image as its own PDF file.

Photoshop 5.x may not open some PDFs created with Acrobat 4, which uses the 1.3 PDF technical specification. (Photoshop 5.5 will handle the newer PDFs as well as those created with earlier specs.) Photoshop can also be set to open a batch of PDF pages into a folder or directory, then used to automatically create "contact sheet" pages of thumbnail images from the PDF pages.

9

Search and Retrieval

Acrobat Catalog builds full-text indexes of PDF document collections. A full-text index is a searchable database of all text in a document or set of documents. The Acrobat Search plug-in allows you to search them. Index building has three phases:

1. Preparing documents for indexing
2. Building the index for the documents
3. Maintaining the index

Preparing Documents for Indexing   Create a separate PDF for each chapter or section of each long document. This aids searching and assures better results in interpreting relevance rankings (part of the search results).

- Always put a descriptive title in the Title field.
- Always use the same field for category information. Don't use the Subject field for some documents and the Keywords field for others.
- Use the same word for the same category. Be consistent.

Building the Index for the Documents   Provide useful information about the index (up to 250 characters) in the Index Description text box. For each folder that contains the documents to be indexed, click Add in the Include Directories box and use the Select dialog box to locate and select the folder. If an included folder contains a subfolder with PDF files that you do not want to index, click Add in the Exclude Directories box and select the folder.

Maintaining the Index   Acrobat Catalog updates to indexes are incremental to minimize updating time. This technique causes indexes to grow with each update, which requires periodic purging to rebuild the index. This will reclaim disk space and speed up searches.

Acrobat Search   Acrobat Search is a plug-in supplied with Acrobat and Reader. Search preferences must be set before you do your first search. It is a relatively easy task to change and redefine the preferences. Settings for queries, results, highlighting, and indexes can be applied.

Setting Search Preferences   The Acrobat Search Preferences dialog box can be found under the file menu, preferences, search. The checkboxes found give the flexibility to customize the way the search reports hits. Results can be organized by a host of categories.

1. Go to the Search preferences dialog box.
2. Select how much of the query box you want users to see:
   - Show Fields: will choose whether or not to show document information fields
   - Show Date: shows or hides with date information box
   - Show Options: enables options set in Catalog such as sounds like, word stemming, etc.
3. The Hide on Search checkbox refers to keeping the Acrobat Search window open or closed after the search is done. Checking this box will hide the window when the search reports back.

4. The order in which results of a search are displayed can be set in the results option field. Several options are available for sorting returned hits. Choose the one that best suits your needs. You can further limit the number of returned documents at this point. Also, you can click on the Hide on View box to hide the results box when you view a document.
5. Highlighting the hits on a page can be set in the highlight box. Highlighting by page, word, or no highlights at all can be chosen. Page highlighting is the default value.
6. Automounting servers in the indexes area will automatically mount all available indexes available when starting a search. This function is available only on a Macintosh platform.

Figure 9-1
Acrobat Search Preferences dialog box.

Performing the Search   Once all of the preferences have been set, it is finally time to perform the search. To get to the Search dialog box, go to the Tools menu and Search.

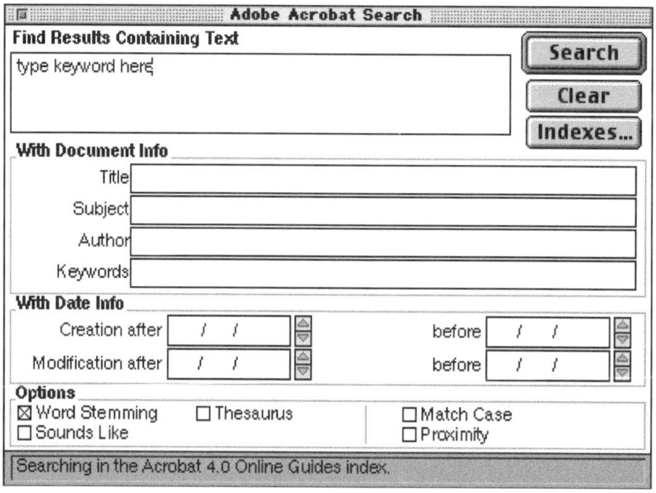

Adobe Acrobat Search

Find Results Containing Text

type keyword here

Search

Clear

Indexes...

With Document Info

Title

Subject

Author

Keywords

With Date Info

Creation after　/　/　　　　before　/　/

Modification after　/　/　　　　before　/　/

Options

☒ Word Stemming　　☐ Thesaurus　　　　☐ Match Case
☐ Sounds Like　　　　　　　　　　　　　　☐ Proximity

Searching in the Acrobat 4.0 Online Guides index.

Figure 9-2
Acrobat Search Query dialog box.

Using the Search Box　Use the search box to choose where and what you want to search. The search engine does the real work and reports back to you with a hit list dialog box.

This icon can also be used to access the search query box.

1. The first step is to decide where you want to search. Click on the Indexes button. You will be brought to a box, where you can select or deselect indexes. The sensible division and subdivision of created indexes becomes important at this point. If an index you want to search does not appear in the box, deselect any index currently in the box and click on the add button. This will bring you to a box which allows you to find your index. When you find it, click on the open button. After all indexes appear in the Index Selection box, click OK.

2. Now that you have decided where to search, you must decide what to search. There are several ways to drive the search engine. First, determine what options you want to include in the search, such as:
   - Word stemming
   - Sounds like
   - Thesaurus
   - Match case
   - Proximity

3. Searching for files created on, between, before, or after specific dates is the next set of options to be set. This is a useful feature because date information is automatically included with all documents and is searchable.

4. Performing searches in the "With Document Info" area is where the document information box becomes vital. The fields in this area consist of the information provided in the planning stages of the index. Each of these fields can be used to perform a search within that particular field across the selected indexes. Proper and consistent information provided in these fields is invaluable.

5. The final method for searching documents is the straight text calls made in the Find Results Containing Text field. Several methods and options exist for narrowing or expanding these specific searches. Wildcard, boolean, phrase, and comparison searching can be performed. This type of search uses typical protocols for the usage of these operators.

6. The last step in the search process is to click on the Search button. Acrobat Search will then access each index called for and search its text list. When it is done, it will return the list of "hits" in the order in which you set in the preferences menu.

If Automount Servers is not selected in the preferences box, then either click on this button, or mount them by going into the Tools search, Index menu item.

Explanation of Search Options

- Word Stemming: returns words with the same stem or root as the query word
- Sounds Like: returns words that may be spelled differently (incorrect spelling) but are pronounced the same as the query word (these words are called homographs)
- Thesaurus: returns words with the same meaning as the query word
- Match Case: returns words which match the letters of query word in both majuscule and miniscule letters—upper and lowercase to nontypographic folks
- Proximity: returns words with the boolean AND restriction to be within three pages of each other
- Boolean operators are typed in all capital letters:

  AND: both words

  OR: either or both words

  NOT: does not contain word

Search Results   Each document on this list contains the information called for in the search box. To view a file from this list, either double-click on it or highlight it and click on view. See Figure 9-3.

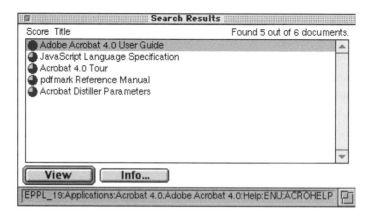

Figure 9-3
Acrobat Search Results dialog box.

Refining a Search   An option to refine a set of returned search files can be done by reopening the search dialog box, keying in the limiting parameters, and holding down the Option key (Macintosh) or the Control key (Windows), which will change the Search button to Refine. Click on Refine and the new requirements will be applied only to the original search results.

Word Assist   This option can be thought of as a preflight for search with the Stemming, Sounds Like, and Thesaurus help functions. By using this function you can perform a mock search and see what words will be returned as hits.

To access this box, go under Tools, Search, Word Assist. Here is what the Word Assistant Dialog box looks like:

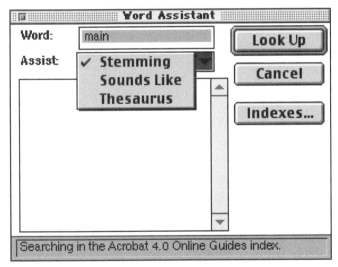

Figure 9-4
Acrobat Word Assistant dialog box.

1. Select the indexes you want to search across by clicking on the Indexes box. The process is now just the same as previously explained for search.
2. Choose what type of search you want to perform: Stemming, Sounds like, or Thesaurus.

3. Type in a word in the Word box.

4. Then, click on Search. A list will appear in the lower box. This list consists of words that are in the indexes chosen to search. You can then use the information from this box as a guide in your searching.

The use of catalog and search features in Acrobat seems to be relatively insignificant on the surface, but in reality these features are the backbone of a powerful archival system. These functions are the basis for a necessary structured system to store and retrieve data. You should plan ahead when preparing PDFs so as to facilitate search and retrieval.

Digital storage methods have consistently changed, as we have sought an ideal structure and format for archiving. The PDF file offers tremendous advantages and solutions over previous approaches. The efficiency and reliability that the Acrobat suite offers for archiving may very well be the answer to many concerns and problems.

It is important to realize that the construction of any storage system utilizing PDF files as the base needs to be extremely structured and well thought out. It is the planning aspects that will ultimately determine the success or failure of a system.

The Search command relies on an index of PDF document or documents created in Acrobat Catalog. The Find command operates on only the current file. It works from a base point in the document (the top of the active page) and "reads" the text from that point. If you start on page 1 and you are looking for a word that appears for the first time on page 50, the Find tool reads every word to page 50 and then it returns you a hit on page 50. As your document becomes larger, the Find tool becomes slower and slower.

Find Tool   The Find Tool can be launched in one of three ways. The one thing to keep in mind when you actually go to launch the Find Tool is to make sure that you are at the beginning of the document. Even though the Find Tool will loop the entire way through the document ending where it began, most times it is more orderly for you to find a series of occurrences for your search word.

- Go to the Edit Menu, and click on the Find command.
- Use the keyboard shortcut: Command + F.
- Click on the tool bar icon with the binoculars on it.

Find Dialog Box   Whatever the method you use to launch the Find Tool, you are brought to the Find dialog box. This box consists of a query line and some limiting parameters. The function of the box is to offer an interface to looking for words or word combinations in a single document. It is important to note that you have only straight word association capability on searches. This means that boolean operators are not recognized. When searching for words in a document, spelling does count.

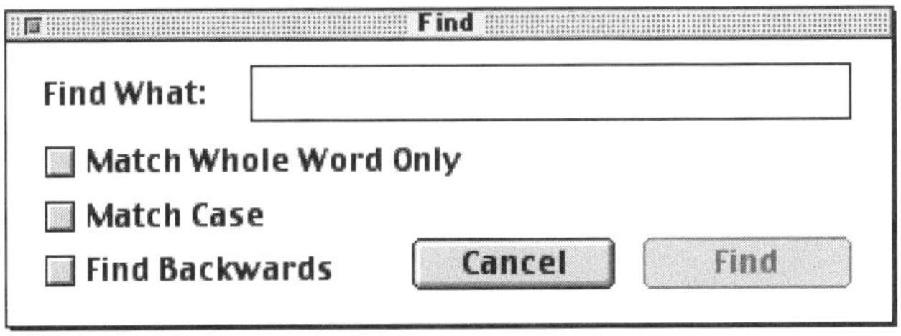

Figure 9-5
The Acrobat Find tool dialog box.

Using the Find Tool   When you launch the Find Tool, you will notice its almost boring appearance. What it lacks in aesthetics, it makes up for in usability. In fact one of the advantages of the Find command is its straightforward design.

You start, of course, by determining what word or string of words you want to search for. The maximum amount of characters that you can search for is 64. After you key in the information, you have to select the restrictions you want to put on the search. Your options are
- Match Whole Word Only
- Match Case
- Find Backwards

All of these options are self-explanatory, except for the Find Backwards choice. Contrary to what one might think is meant by this command, palindromes (words spelled the same both forwards and backwards) are not the target of this command. The Find command takes the start point of the document and travels to the next page in the document. If you want the find command to work backwards in the document from the start point, then choose the Find Backwards command in the Find dialog box.

Find Again   This function repeats the Find command. You can find the next occurrence of a word you were searching for with the Find tool. When using the Find tool, you will notice that once your word is found, the Find dialog box closes automatically. To find the next occurrence of the word you are looking for, you do not have to restart and rekey the word. Just use the keyboard combination Command + G. Or you can go to the Edit menu and the Find Again selection. This will save you time and grief in searching for all occurrences of the word in a document.

Search Plug-in   One of the standard plug-ins that is packaged with Acrobat is the Search plug-in. Many times it is grouped in the same category as Acrobat Catalog. It is in fact a separate entity in the Acrobat suite; it is a search engine that uses the result of Acrobat Catalog. You should know how it works and how to use it to your advantage.

Setting Search Preferences   You have already been taken through the preferences setting procedures. You can always go back to the settings by going under the File menu to Preferences, to the Search. You will most likely want to go back and set the preferences again after learning more about Acrobat's search function.

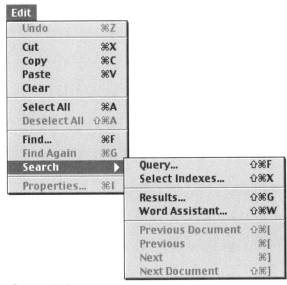

Figure 9-6
The Acrobat Search submenu.

To find the word or phrases you want, Search uses an index of the text from several PDF documents. This index is the product of Acrobat Catalog. The unique result of the Acrobat Catalog is a PDX file. This PDX file must be mounted by Acrobat Reader or Acrobat when you use the Search plug-in.

Search Query   At this point you are ready to use the omnipotent Search feature. When you launch the search engine, you are engaging a powerful tool in today's digital workflow. A document is just a document until you extract exactly what you are looking for. When you find what you are looking for, this is now considered information. In the Information Age, getting to what you are looking for needs to be as effortless and as fast as possible. The team of the Acrobat Catalog and the Search plug-in provides such an avenue to rapid retrieval of data, and consequently, information.

The first step in attaining the information you need is to set the Search Preferences. This has been covered in a previous chapter, but you may want to rethink some of the settings after reading this section. With the preferences set, you have to choose the Query item in the Search subdirectory in the Edit menu. This is the most straight-forward approach to launching the Search plug-in, but you can also click on the search icon on the toolbar, or you can use the shortcut key combination Command + Shift + F.

The Adobe Acrobat Search dialog box serves as home base for your searches. What you see at this point is determined by the settings you made in the preferences.

As you can see, the dialog box is systematically broken down into four main parts:

- Query Box
- Document Information
- Date
- Options

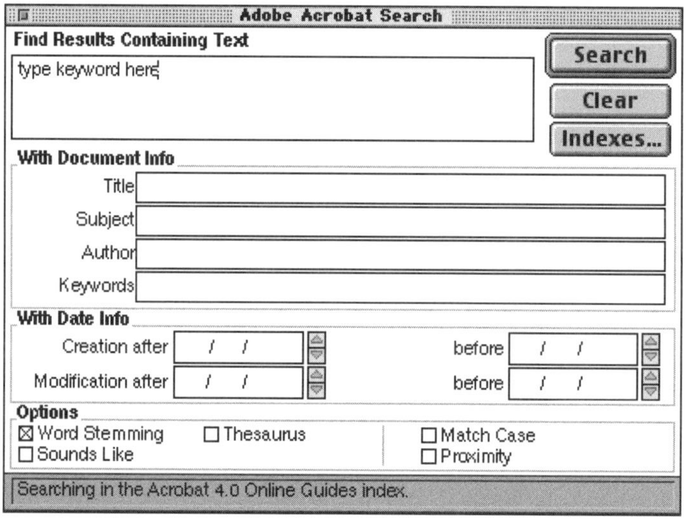

Figure 9-7
The Acrobat Search dialog box.

In your Preferences settings, you can turn every area off (it will not show up in the Search dialog box when Search is launched) except for the query section. It is recommended that you choose to leave every section open in the preferences because this will give you the most flexibility in the searching process. With this understanding of the main areas of the dialog box, you can move on to the actual functions of each section.

Indexes   After you launch Search, you are ready to mount your index. The index file you want was created in Acrobat Catalog and has a PDX extension. The index that everyone should have is the Acrobat Online Help Files. This particular index should automatically mount when you start Search, but if it does not, you need to mount it manually. Go to the Query area of the Search dialog box. There is a button named Index. Click on it and you will be brought to the Index.

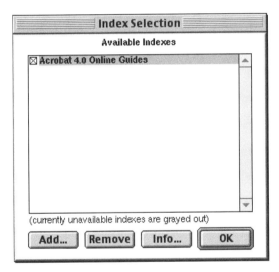

Figure 9-8
Index Selection dialog box.

You will notice that an active index will be in black text, whereas an inactive index is grayed out. If an index you want to search is not mounted and present in this dialog box, you have to click on the Add button. When you do this, you will come to a selection box where you must locate the volume that you want to mount. The Acrobat Online Help file is located in the Acrobat 4 folder in the Help folder in the ENU folder.

As you go through the folders, make sure that the Show All Files setting in the lower portion of the window is not checked. This is the default setting, but make sure it is set properly; it will make locating the files much simpler. Once inside the Acrobat folder, go to the Help folder; inside this help folder resides the file index.PDX; highlight it and click Open.

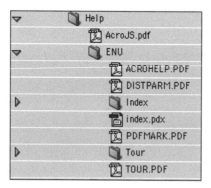

Figure 9-9
The Acrobat Help folder.

As you click Open, you will mount the Index, for Search to use. You can mount several indices at a time, but this does not mean that you have to search through all of them. If you notice on the Index Selection dialog box, there is a checkbox in front of every index. By checking this box, you will either activate or deactivate the index. By turning off the indexes you are not using, you will reduce the time it takes to perform a search.

Removing an Index   Going back to the Index Selection window again, you will see a button to remove an index from the list. Removing an index is simple: Just highlight the index, and click the Remove button. You need at least one index available in this section to perform a search. If you attempt to remove all the indices from this list, you will be prompted and warned. You can, however, remove all listings; just be sure to mount a new index before you proceed.

Index Information   To find out the origins of the index and get
a description, you go to the Index Selection dialog box. By highlighting an index in the Index Selection dialog box and clicking on the
Info button, you are at the Index Information report box. The information provided will depend on the creator of the index file—title
and description of the index. The rest of the information is automatically inserted (date, path, and time).

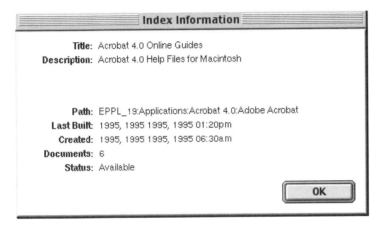

Figure 9-10
Index Information report box.

    When you are satisfied with the information, click OK and you will
be brought back to the Index Selection dialog box. Click OK in this
box to be returned to the main Search dialog box.

Setting Options   You have some options that you must set
before you make the search of the index that you just mounted. If
you look at the bottom of the Search dialog box, you will see that you
have the following options available:

- Word Stemming
- Proximity
- Thesaurus
- Match Case
- Sounds Like

These settings are intended to aid you in the narrowing or broadening of the criteria for the words you are searching for.

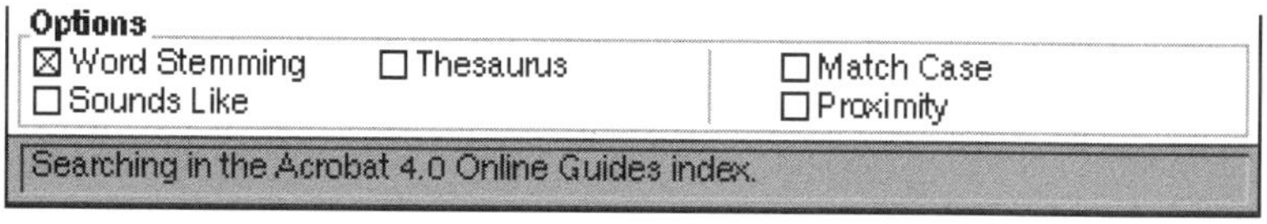

Figure 9-11
Options dialog box for Searching.

> *Word Stemming* This will broaden your search to return all words with the same stem or root word as the search word. A good example is the word *book*. Hits will be instances of *book* (all forms) and *booklet, bookmaker,* or *bookie* and the words must be in the index that you are searching.
>
> *Sounds Like* This will return words that sound similar to the search word. This function may be useful if you do not know the exact spelling of a search word. With the Sounds Like feature you may be able to approximate, and your desired word may be returned. Using the word *book* as an example, words returned might be *book* (all forms), *bookish, broke,* or *broom.*

Thesaurus   This option will activate a Thesaurus feature in the search engine to return words with a similar meaning as the search word. Using the word *Book* may show *book* (all forms), *tome, volume, arrest,* or *accept.*

Match Case   This option will limit a search, where the previous options broaden the search. Match Case allows hits for words that match in the upper- and lowercase instances only. Match Case would only allow the return of *book*, and not the proper noun for someone's name: *Book*. Notice the upper- and lowercase of the initial 'M.' When you use this limiting feature, you are disengaging all of the broadening options. In other words, the Word Stemming, Sounds

Like, and Thesaurus features are turned off when the Match Case option is turned on.

Proximity   This is a narrow option. Proximity is used in conjunction with the boolean operator AND. This feature will limit the AND operator to three pages of the words in question. When you choose the Proximity option, you will not have use of the Thesaurus feature.

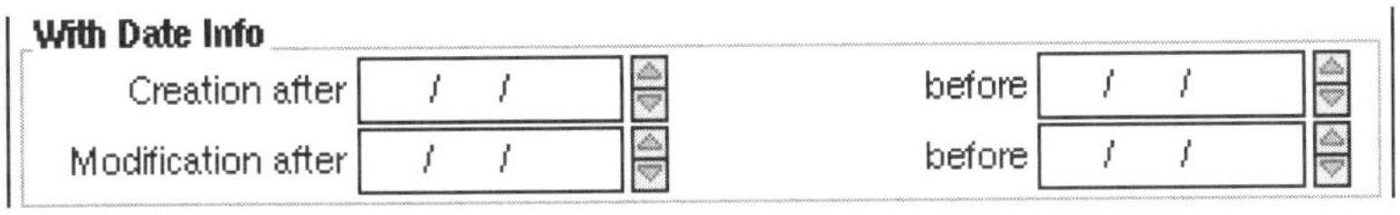

Figure 9-12
Proximity ranking dialog box.

Date Searching   Date searching is a limiting feature of Search where you can set thresholds for the creation or modification of files. This feature is only somewhat reliable because the date of creation and modification are always put into the PDF file when they are created or modified and the system clock could be wrong. Upon creation Acrobat looks at the date and time information from the user's computer; the disadvantage to this is if you have set your clock or date back on the computer, you may not find that file you want.

Assuming everything is correct, you can tell Search to return only the files between the thresholds set. Thus, if you are in a situation that you want just the most recent file, set the date accordingly. Of course this means that you have to know the date of creation, but you can make settings to return files in an index that were created or modified after or before a certain date.

Document Information Fields   Searching for documents based on criteria in the Document Information field is a great way to narrow any search. The one dependency you have is that the creator of the PDF file included the information in the original file. Since this is an extra step in the PDFWriter or in Acrobat, you may not want to rely solely on these fields. However, if you do decide to use these fields for searching, they become a powerful tool for pinpointing a search.

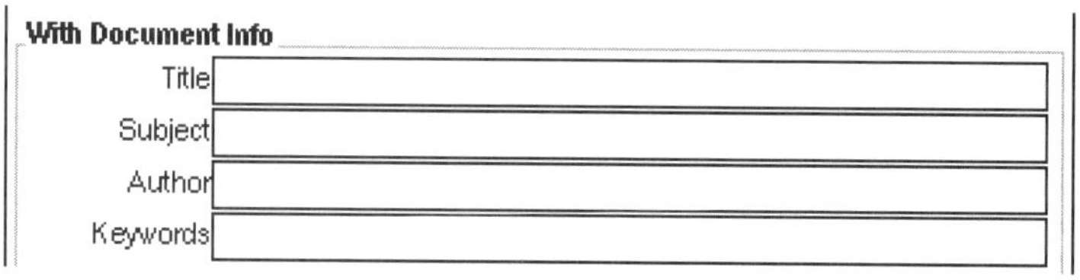

Figure 9-13
Search Document Information fields.

There are four Document Information fields available:
- Title
- Subject
- Author
- Keywords

Document Information fields can be used in conjunction with the Date fields to pinpoint a search. Watch your typing.

Searching for Words   In the Find Results Containing the Text field, you can type in a word search to find occurrences of the word or words in the index. You can also perform wildcard, boolean, and phrase searches. The top part of the Acrobat Search dialog box is devoted to these word-searching functions.

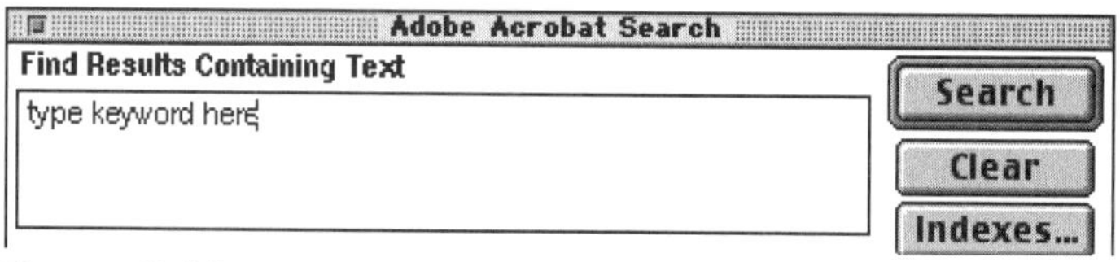

Figure 9-14
Acrobat Find Results Containing the Text dialog box.

Declaring a Search   With the index mounted and other limiting or broadening search parameters set, you declare a search. Point your mouse to the Find Results Containing Text dialog box. Key in the words for your search.

Simple Boolean Searches   Boolean searches will help to group more than one word.

- AND will return hits that contain both words.
    An example: song AND dance.
- OR will return either the first word or the second.
    An example: song OR dance.
- NOT will return documents that do not contain the word.
    An example: NOT chickens.

Complex Boolean Searches   Boolean operators can become complex when combined to form compound operands. The word order of the query is important:

- If the operator NOT is used with either or both the AND and OR operators, it is considered before either the AND operator or the OR operator.
    song AND NOT dance
This statement will return all documents that have the word *song* but not the word *dance*.

- If the operator AND and the operator OR are used in the same expression, then the operator AND is evaluated before the OR Operator.
    song OR dance AND snappy patter
This statement finds all documents that have *dance* or that have both the words *song* and *snappy patter*.

- Using parentheses will change the order in which the boolean operands are considered. Take for example:
    (song OR dance) AND snappy patter
This will return all documents that have either *song* and *snappy patter* or that have *dance* and *snappy patter*. The parentheses will nest the boolean operator and change the order around.

Wildcard Options   Wildcard options are symbols that are used in the query to represent characters that you are not sure about. If you know that the word you want to locate starts with the three letters "ABC," but you don't know the rest of the word, you can declare a wildcard query. Your options for wildcard characters are:

- An asterisk (*) to represent zero or one or more missing characters. An example

     fr*

  This will return all words that start with the letters "fr"
- A question mark (?) to represent one missing character. An example

     fr???

  The return will be on all words that start with "fr" and are followed by three characters.

You can combine a wildcard and boolean search together.

Search   After you are finished with setting the parameters for the search, all the limiters and broadeners, you are ready to Search. When you click this button, you will enact a powerful chain of events. The first thing that will happen is that the mounted index (or indices) will be accessed and Acrobat Search will look through them for words or word combinations that match your query. When it finds a document that contains your words, it will return the title of that document in a hit list. This list (according to your preferences settings for Acrobat Search) will be ordered in a confidence-level hierarchy (the default setting). You can then open the actual document where the hit occurred and view the document itself.

Hit List   The interface for returned documents is relatively straightforward. The titles of the documents are returned to the list according to your preference settings. If you notice large pie-shaped graphics before the titles, this is the symbol for confidence ranking.

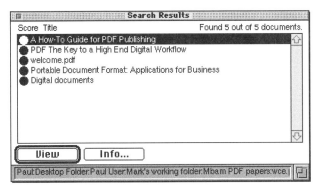

Figure 9-15
Acrobat search results, better known as the hit list.

The View button takes you directly to the document that contains the hit. Make sure you have the original PDF file. The path and file name to the document appear at the bottom of the dialog box. The other button found on the screen is the Info button. This button will access the Document Information dialog box of the highlighted document. The Document Information box must be filled in prior to the creation of the index (in Acrobat Catalog).

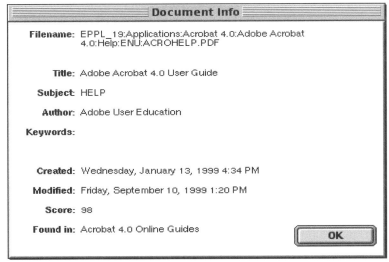

Figure 9-16
Document Info dialog box of highlighted document.

Relevance Ranking   There is a relevance or confidence ranking of the returned files. You can make certain decisions about the file based on these rankings. The system consists of five icons ranging from a full circle to an empty one. The full circle indicates the most likelihood of the search parameters being matched exactly. The empty one means the opposite.

Highest   *Lowest*

Figure 9-17
Relevance ranking symbols.

An additional factor is the amount of occurrences when the words are matched. As the fullness of the circles drops off, the likelihood of the match is less. There are many factors that influence the ranking. Proximity is one of them. When this option is on, the ranking of a document with the two words closer together will receive a higher ranking than with the words farther apart.

A second influence is with the use of the OR operator. A document that contains both search words in the document will receive a higher ranking than documents with only one of the words.

Refining a Search   Once you perform a search and you review the hit list, you may or may not have the result that you wanted, or you got more than you thought. In such an instance, you can refine a search. In order to use the refine function, you have to go back to the original Search query box.

You can do this by either relaunching Search (the most recent query will still be in the box), or if you set the correct preferences, the Search box will not go away on a search.

When you are inside the box, make your adjustments to the search parameters and then hold down the Option key. You will notice that the Search button turns to a Refine button. While holding the Option key, click on the Refine button. You will then perform a refined search on only the documents that were returned in the original search. This makes the already fast search even more efficient.

Hit Navigating   When you are satisfied with the list of returned documents, you can move through them. In the hit list, you can view a document by double-clicking on it, or highlighting it, and hitting the View button. In either case, you will be brought to the actual document, and depending on how you set the Search preferences, the search words will be highlighted.

After the document is opened, you have the ability to jump to the next hit in the current document, or you can jump to the next document. You can do this in one of three ways:

- The shortcut keystrokes
    Previous document: Command + Shift + [
    Previous hit: Command + [
    Next document: Command + Shift +]
    Next hit: Command +]
- The menu bar
    Go to the Edit menu, then to Search, then to the appropriate choice
- The tool bar
    Previous highlight
    Next highlight

Word Assistant   This feature allows you to perform a test run of the words you are looking for with the Search tool. The main purpose of this tool is to allow you to see what words will be returned to you when you apply some of the available limiting or broadening features. You can access the Word Search feature by either going to the Edit menu, to Search, then to the Word Assistant item, or using the shortcut keys Command + Shift + W.

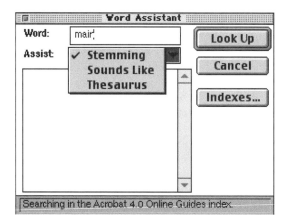

Figure 9-18
Word Assistant dialog box showing pull-down menu.

With the Word Assistant feature enabled, you are at a basic interface dialog box. This dialog box consists of three buttons and a pull-down menu. The pull-down menu allows you to set one of the three limiting or broadening options to the search. In order to run the Word Assistant, you must have an index or indices mounted. The process is the same here as in the Search function. For instructions on mounting an index, see the Search section.

With the index mounted, you can key in the word or word combination using both wildcard and boolean operators. By doing a test on the actual index, you will get the results you want and need for a speedy retrieval of information on the real search. Refer to the Search section of this chapter for more detailed information on Boolean searches and wildcards.

10

Exporting and Importing PDF

No, we did not get it backwards. Exporting from Acrobat is more important and extensive than importing. Thus, we are covering exporting first.

Acrobat makes it easy to export data from a PDF file. In addition, the software has created an easy interface for extracting full pages into PostScript or to an Encapsulated PostScript format. These functions can be performed in the Export menu of the File menu.

Exporting Annotations When your document is full of annotations, you may choose to simply export just the annotations to an "FDF" file and have the next user execute the Import Annotations function. This reduction in file transfer will result in a faster, more efficient, handoff. To export data, go to the File menu, then the Export submenu, then to the Annotations option. You will be asked to choose a file name and destination for the new file. Be sure to actually have file Annotations, or you will be reminded that there are none.

247

Let us say that in Acrobat 4, you have applied a security password to a PDF file for opening the document and changing the document. You also enabled "Do Not Allow" the following: Printing, Changing the Document, Selecting the Text and Graphics. You needed to do so in order to send PDF proofs to Authors. When they received the file with the supplied password, they can do a Save As and bypass the security. They are free to change the document and print the document. Is there a way to create a more secure PDF that cannot be altered by a Save As?

There are two passwords: the owner password and the user password. Confusingly these are presented in the Acrobat GUI as the "security" and "open" passwords, respectively. When saving the PDF, set your security options and your security password as you wish, and either set the "open" password to something else or simply leave it blank. If you set an "open" password, so no one can read the PDF without that password, then you need to send that to the authors. If you leave it blank, they need no password at all to open the PDF, and can't change any of the security options you

Exporting PostScript or EPS

Once you have entered into a PDF workflow, how do you get out of it? The answer is the PostScript or EPS export tool. It will allow you to write PostScript or EPS page descriptions of the PDF pages. This exported PostScript is written in a "headless" fashion, that is to say that there are no device dependencies built into the code.

To start the export process, go to the File menu, then to the Export submenu, then to the PostScript or EPS choice. The Export dialog box will appear on the screen.

Exporting Forms Data

Forms data export is handled in a similar fashion to the exporting of Annotations. Both rely on the FDF (Forms Data Format) file. We think that Forms is one of the most important parts of Acrobat. Eventually, it will be one of the foundations of e-commerce.

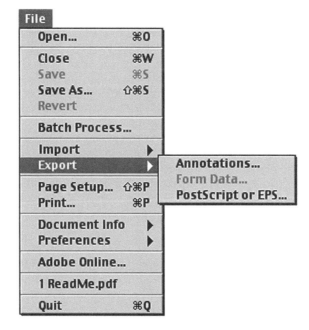

Figure 10-1
File submenu for export as PostScript or EPS.

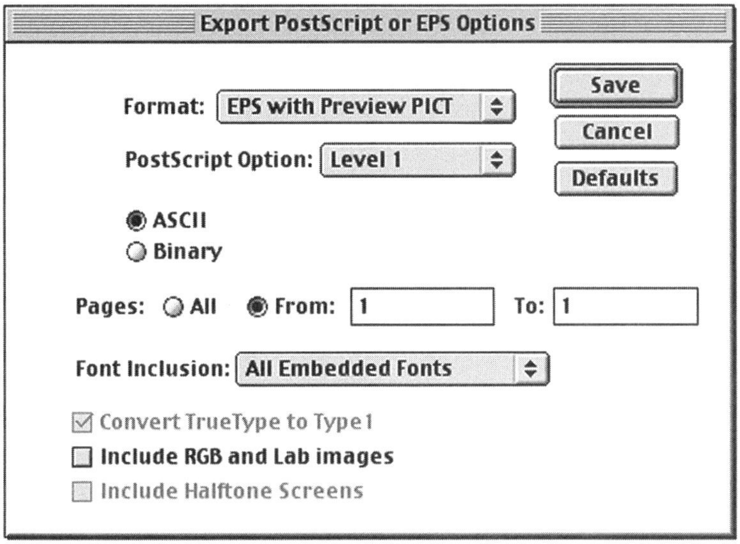

Figure 10-2
Expoting PostScript from Export PostScript and EPS File dialog box.

PostScript Level Options   You can export PostScript or EPS files as Level 1, 2, or 3 code. Whatever comes into the PDF will go out of the PDF. If you start with Level 2, for instance, you can save as Level 3, but some Level 3 functions will not be possible because they were not possible with the Level 2 code.

Exporting an EPS   Few other programs actually let you embed fonts into an EPS file. A unique feature of this export function is the ability to exclude RGB images and include all fonts in the EPS file. TrueType fonts can be converted to Type 1 fonts. The exported EPS can then be placed into most page-layout applications.

Exporting PostScript   Make the selections for font embedding and converting fonts for the resulting stream of PostScript code. Over time, PostScript will be used less and less as PDF truly comes into its own.

select. Either way you keep your security (owner) password for yourself, and only you can change the security options on the files.

You have set an open password but not a control password. Without a control password, a document is not the least bit secure. This is a common mistake.

Is there a "generic" PPD file that an artist can use to generate PDF files for output to an Imagesetter?

The Distiller PPD is always a good starting point for making PDFs. The final imagesetter is rarely a better choice, and occasionally prevents the PDF from working at all. Make sure that the Distiller PPD uses a CMYK color model. If you don't do this, then some applications/drivers will output images and other objects as RGB.

Some imagesetter PPDs are okay because they use a CMYK color model. Others are not. These use a DeviceGray color model, which might force Distiller to create gray objects when you wanted color. To check or change the color model, just open the PPD file with a text editor. Just search for DefaultColorSpace.

While you are there you can also check your DefaultResolution. Today's Distiller PPDs use 600 dpi. You could change this to one of the other resolutions called out in the file. This parameter can affect quality and file size, in particular, for smoothness of curves and blend transitions (especially pre-PDF 1.3 smooth shading operators).

AdobePS 4.3 PostScript Driver for Windows9X

The English language version of the AdobePS 4.3 PostScript Driver for Windows'9X is now available for download from Adobe Systems at the following address: http://www.adobe.com/supportservice/custsupport/LIBRARY/5712.htm

It is this version of the driver that fixes the infamous text layout and dropped-characters problems when printing to printers with PPDs indicating a PostScript version less than 2015 with AdobePS 4.2.4 through 4.2.6. In other words, "hacked" PPD files should no longer be required (finally!). However, you need not undo those PPD changes for AdobePS 4.3 to work correctly.

In conjunction with the use of Acrobat 4.0, this driver version also finally fully fixes the problem of Acrobat text searchability when text is formatted using TrueType (Type 42) fonts.

AdobePS 4.3 provides full support for Windows 98—including Windows 98 Image Color Management 2.0, full sRGB color support with Office97, and conversion of sRGB input profiles into CRDs (Color Rendering Dictionaries) for Windows 98. It allows users to override application settings for Image Color Management processing; provides a new, easy-to-use, InstallShield-based installer; provides support for printing the Euro character currency symbol for printers that support it; and supports remote printing to WebReady printers connected to the Internet.

Some very critical issues about installing this driver:

1. To simply upgrade your existing AdobePS 4.1.x or 4.2.x drivers, run the installation program and select the "upgrade driver only" option. You should delete any previous AdobePS 4.x setup programs (and shortcuts) thereto from your system.

2. Contrary to any readme files, the installer allows only one printer to be set up at a time. Rerun the installer as many times as necessary to add additional printer/driver instances.

3. When simply updating the driver from AdobePS 4.1.x or 4.2.x, be sure to examine all your standard printer settings and record them for later use. The AdobePS 4.3 upgrade process resets many of the device settings to "default" values that are very likely NOT what you want and/or need. For example, information about available memory, optional trays, duplexors, etc. may all get reset to default values. Image color management may be enabled although you don't necessarily want it on. The advanced PostScript options for data transmission may be reset to ASCII with CTRL-D instead of TBCP or pure binary. That is why it is so important that you manually record all these settings BEFORE you do the upgrade and reset those values after the upgrade. Failure to reset the values could cause total job failure, print job performance degradation, and/or unexpected colors (or lack thereof) in output.

4. The number of copies to be printed has been removed as a global property of a particular printer/driver instance. Most applications allow you to set this value, though, for the current job, via their print menu.

5. The ability to set particular image-screening frequencies and angles has been totally removed from the printer properties. This functionality was removed for a number of reasons, including the fact that a large number of PostScript printers ignore these settings and substitute their own screening algorithms and that for critical applications that generate their own PostScript (PageMaker, Quark XPress, Illustrator, Photoshop, Freehand, CorelDraw, etc.), these settings were totally ignored. Depending upon the target printer, screen settings in EPS files generated by Photoshop, Illustrator, Freehand, CorelDraw, Acrobat, etc. may be honored but that is not and hasn't been a function of the driver.

Acrobat Exchange 3 Windows has a command that lets you copy and paste the entire contents of a PDF as RTF to Word: Ctrl-Shft-K— Acrobat Exchange 3 Mac has no such command, and no way to select more than two pages simultaneously. In Acrobat 4 Mac you can select the entire contents of your PDF and copy and paste that to Word. However, you must set scrolling to "Continuous," and the result is unsatisfactory: hard returns at line endings.

6. When setting up an HP LaserJet 8500 with this driver, the available memory setting will indicate an error when you set it to high values, but it will "take" anyway.

As with previous versions of AdobePS, the license for this driver, to which your acceptance is required during the installation process for each printer instance, limits its use with printers with Adobe PostScript software (i.e., no clones) or with Adobe application programs with which it is explicitly bundled (i.e., AdobePS 4.3.x will be explicitly required by and will be bundled with InDesign 1.0 for Windows 98).

PostScript Printer Driver and Related Issues with Windows 2000

The following section relates to support for PostScript printing and related issues under Microsoft's recently released Windows 2000:

There are no current plans for an AdobePS PostScript printer driver version for Windows 2000. The AdobePS 5.x drivers do not install under Windows 2000. The PostScript printer driver that ships with Windows 2000 is the result of a joint project of Adobe and Microsoft. It is functionally equivalent to AdobePS 5.1.1+.

There is an updated PostScript printer driver already posted on Microsoft's Windows 2000 update site. This update resolves a severe incompatibility problem between FrameMaker 5.5.x and the PostScript printer driver for generating Acrobat data and for separations printing. This updated driver is functionally equivalent to AdobePS 5.1.2. The URL to obtain this updated driver is: <http://microsoft.com/windows2000/downloads/recommended/q252 891/default.asp>

There is currently no facility to create printer instances with the PostScript printer driver using any general user-specified PPD as you currently may with the AdobePS PostScript printer drivers with Windows NT 4. You must use the "Add Printer" wizard within the Printers window. The Microsoft-provided, abbreviated PPD files may or may not directly correspond to the PPD files you currently have and/or really need. Further, not all printer models may be included with the wizard. "Fixing" the wizard to correct this problem requires hacking around with .inf files. We recommend that you "don't try this at home!"

To address the very severe shortcomings of (4) above, Adobe is currently completing the testing of a comprehensive Windows PostScript printer driver installation package for ALL "current" versions of Windows (Windows'9x, Windows NT 4, and Windows 2000). Based upon the version of Windows detected, this installer installs the latest version of the driver (AdobePS 4.x for Windows'9x, AdobePS 5.x for Windows NT 4, or uses the system driver for Windows 2000), and provides the capability of creating new printer instances based on user-specified PPD files.

Installation of Acrobat 4.05a under Windows 2000 does automatically create a printer instance for the Acrobat Distiller printer using the correct Distiller PPD along with the system PostScript driver.

For users upgrading a Windows NT 4 system to Windows 2000. existing driver instances using AdobePS 5.1.x actually continue to work under Window 2000, but with a different user interface than the native Windows 2000 driver. However, new printer instances using AdobePS 5.1.x cannot be created once the system is upgraded to Windows 2000.

Type 1 font support in terms of simple installation, screen display, and driver integration is now provided natively by Windows 2000. ATM (Adobe Type Manager) now has only two functions under Windows 2000:

- The full version of ATM provides true font-management functions in terms of activation, deactivation, etc. of fonts and sets of fonts. (These functions are not provided by the "lite" version of ATM.)

If you produce a PostScript with the individual device's PPD, then distill that PostScript, is there an advantage to using the Distiller PPD? The major reason not to use a device PPD is that it may not work at all. Some device-dependent stuff is not understood by Distiller. But the other reason is that the "device" is really Distiller.

The resolution should make no difference to what goes into the PostScript, in real-world cases. There are quite a few applications that try to second guess what screens your output device can manage at specific resolutions—Illustrator, PhotoShop and InDesign among them. If your RIP is configured to override some aspects of screening (frequency, angle, spot function), but not all of them, then you can end up with unexpected results on the plate. Overriding spot function but not angle or frequency, for instance, can produce a very coarse screen at 0 degrees.

AdobePS 5.1.2 PostScript Driver for Windows NT 4.0.

It is available now for downloading in English and eleven other languages from:

<http://www.adobe.com/ support/downloads/pdrv win.htm>

This driver version provides the following key fixes:

1. PostScript from FrameMaker 5.5.x is now correctly generated when using either the "separations" or the "generate Acrobat data" options.

2. Certain PostScript errors no longer occur when PostScript is sent to certain Heidelberg printers.

- Multiple Masters font instances are not supported natively via Windows 2000. ATM continues to provide such support.

The existing current version of ATM for Windows NT 4, ATM 4.0, is reported to work as a font manager under Windows 2000 although a new version of ATM, specifically tested for Windows 2000, will be available in a few months.

InDesign 1.0 for Windows does not support the native Windows 2000 PostScript driver. A version that does fully provide such support will be available within a few months.

Importing

There are many other ways to enter documents and images into PDF files. The Import menu in the File menu of Acrobat will allow you to import several items directly into the PDF file format. Supported menu options are

- Scan
- Import Images
- Annotations
- Form Data

Perhaps the most exciting feature listed is the ability to scan directly into Acrobat. This allows users to perform OCR capabilities on files via the Acrobat Capture plug-in. Additional advances made in drag-and-drop capabilities make the Import Image feature one to really consider in advanced PDF workflows.

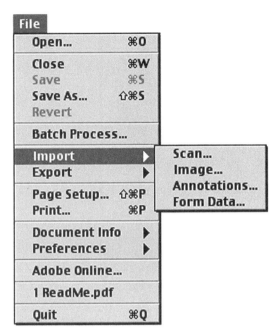

Figure 10-3
The Acrobat Import submenu.

Importing Images   Acrobat 4 supports the automatic conversion of several bitmap image types directly into PDF. This will bypass Distiller. Using the new TouchUp tools, you can then move these images to any PDF file. The following are file types supported:

- GIF
- TIF
- PNG
- JPEG
- BMP
- PCX

Images can be imported directly into Acrobat via the Import Image selection in the Import submenu of the File menu. This will bring you to the Import Image dialog box.

All users of AdobePS 5.1.1 and earlier versions of AdobePS 5.x are most strongly encouraged to update to AdobePS 5.1.2 at their earliest possible convenience.

Check whether a PPD disk was included with your printer (most PostScript printers include a disk that contains the PPD file for the printer). If you cannot find this disk, contact your printer manufacturer for a replacement or visit your printer manufacturer's Web site or FTP site to obtain the PPD file. Visit Adobe online services such as the Adobe Web site, which may have the PPD file you need.

This printer driver is not for use with PostScript Level 1 devices. Owners of PostScript Level 1 devices should use the Microsoft PostScript printer driver included with Windows NT 4.0 instead of AdobePS 5.1.2. To determine what level of PostScript is included with your printer, see your printer's documentation or contact your printer manufacturer. The installer does not run on Windows 2000.

If you have a Quark EPS and then bring it into Illustrator and resave it as an Illustrator EPS, will Distiller embed the fonts?

1. *If the same fonts that were used in making the Quark file are still active on the system when you bring the Quark EPS into Illustrator, they should be recognized and when saving as an .eps back out of Illustrator in Illustrator 7 or 8 format, you'll have the ability to tell Illustrator to include the fonts in the EPS.*

2. *ALAP's XTension package includes one that will generate an EPS with fonts included.*

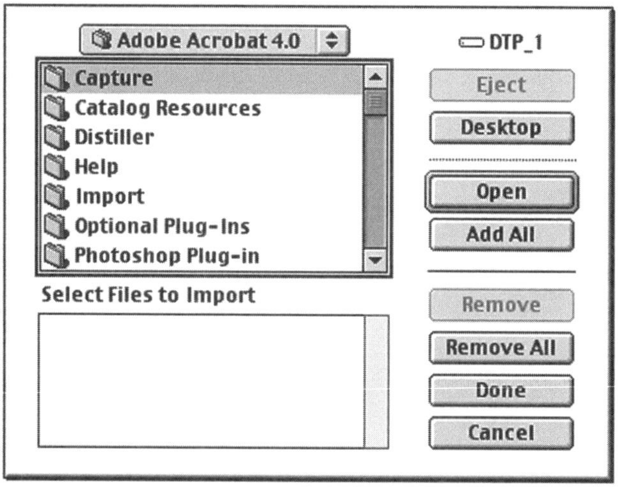

Figure 10-4
The Import Image dialog box.

To add files to the import list, find them using the top navigation box and either double-click on them, or highlight them and click the Add button. Then, click the Done button. You will be brought to a dialog box asking for a destination of the new images. The choices will be to create a new page for each image in the currently open document, or to create a new PDF file that will contain just the images.

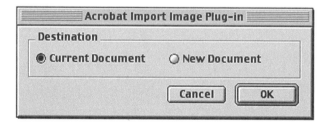

Figure 10-5
The Import Image Plug-in dialog box.

After you decide where the images will reside, there will be a status bar indicating the progress of the file import. This bar will provide you the feedback you need to insure that the process is working properly.

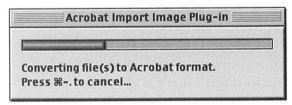

Figure 10-6
The Import Image Plug-in dialog box status bar.

After the image imports, it will be scaled to 100 percent on the resulting page. The page size will be the size of the image area. You will have full cut-and-paste capabilities with these images

Import Annotations   Annotations to files (Notes, attached sound links, attached file links, attached text, and attached stamps) can be imported and exported from PDF file to PDF file. This usage comes in very handy in large documentation markup. If everyone in a group of reviewers has the base PDF file, the smaller file containing just the annotations can be imported and exported by users.

This new exported FDF file (Forms Data Format to be discussed later) is very small (maybe 20 K for an average document) and is ideal to be attached to an e-mail. Then the receiver of this mail can import the notes back into the main PDF file, and all the placement and note information is intact.

To import a PDF file of just Annotations, Open the Main document that the Annotations came from (the base document), then go to the File menu, then to the Import submenu, then to Annotations. When you do this, you will be prompted by a selection dialog box. All you have to do is select the file that contains the Annotations, and you will Import them into your file.

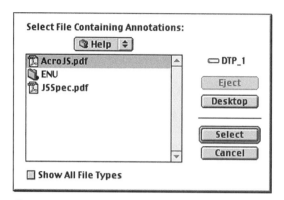

Figure 10-7
The Select Image dialog box status bar.

Importing Form Data   The process of importing forms data is similar to that of importing Annotations. Both processes operate on the FDF (Forms Data Format) file. This file is a uniquely structured file used to exchange data pertaining directly to any forms created in a document. In order for this transfer to be seamless, the base PDF file must reside at both the originating site and at the receiver's site.

11

Distiller

The Acrobat Distiller is the converting engine from PostScript to PDF. By using Acrobat Distiller, significant control over the final attributes of the document are configured. Distiller should be used over PDFWriter when

- The PDF file will enter a high-end print workflow
- Fine adjustments are made to image compression
- EPS images are used
- Grayscale images are being converted

The building block of all PDF files created with Acrobat Distiller is PostScript. The key to a good PDF file from Acrobat Distiller is a good input stream of PostScript code; or garbage in will equal garbage out.

Once you have the PostScript file on your computer, you launch Acrobat Distiller, set the parameters, and then distill away. The process is deceptively simple. When you open Distiller, you come to a simple dialog box.

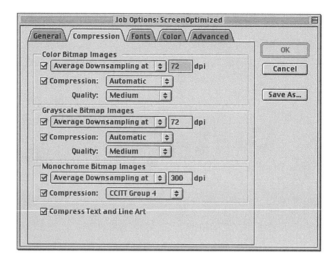

Figure 11-1
Compression Settings tab.

Stored Distiller Job Options   Acrobat Distiller 4 lets you predefine and store Distiller Job Options. These preferences files are saved to a file located in Settings in the Distiller folder. Adobe has predefined a set of three Job Options. These settings define every parameter that can be set in Distillers Job Options for Compression, Fonts, Color Management, and other options.

Screen Optimized

The goal of these settings is to create a file that is as small as possible, for use in digital distribution on the Web. Image compression is set to very high levels, and all images are converted to a CalRGB color space.

Print Optimized

These settings are used for PDF files that are intended to be output on desktop printers and color copiers. The goal is a relatively small file size that still maintains all the characteristics of image integrity. These settings can be thought of as "middle of the road."

Press Optimized

The goal of these settings is to maintain the highest image quality for output. The objective of these settings is to create a PDF file suitable for output by a service bureau or commercial printer. The settings aim at preserving the maximum amount of print-based information about the originating document.

Review the actual settings made by these definitions by selecting a setting, then going to the Job Options and looking at them. You can establish variants of these, or you can create entirely new settings and store them for use. This command center seems simple, but it is your gateway to completely controlled PDF workflows. The two main menu bar items are:

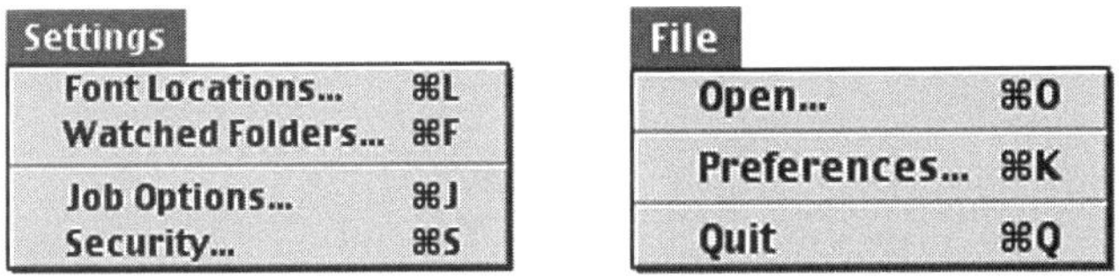

Settings	
Font Locations...	⌘L
Watched Folders...	⌘F
Job Options...	⌘J
Security...	⌘S

File	
Open...	⌘O
Preferences...	⌘K
Quit	⌘Q

Figure 11-2
Distiller menu choices.

All of the action and controls are set in the Distiller menu. Your areas of concentration are

- Preferences
- Font Locations
- Watched Folders
- Job Options
- Security

Distiller Preferences The three choices within the Distiller Preferences dialog box are set once and are always active. Choices here are for general overall feedback mechanisms associated with Distiller jobs.

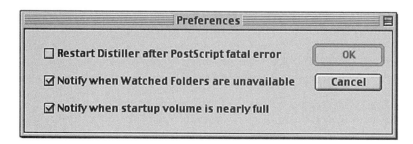

Figure 11-3
Distiller Preferences warning about watched folders.

Restarting after Errors Distiller should be restarted after a fatal PostScript error. Checking the Restart Distiller after PostScript fatal error will restart Distiller when this happens.

Notification of Watched Folders When operating in a watched-folder environment, if a link to that folder breaks for some reason (such as a deleted watched folder), this function will alert you. This feature is very important because if one of these links breaks, you may not be distilling on the schedule you thought you were.

Warning for Full Startup Volume Acrobat Distiller needs approximately 1 megabyte of disk space on the resident drive of Distiller. This space is needed as a temporary hold in the conversion of the PostScript stream. Checking this box will prompt you if this space is not available.

More Preferences for Windows Users Users of the Windows version of Distiller have additional choices to make in the Preferences dialog box. Here is a list of the additional options:
- Ask for PDF file destination will display a dialog box that lets users specify a destination of a PDF file in a drag-and-drop situation or from the print command.
- Ask to Replace Existing PDF File will warn users when an existing file of the same name will be overwritten.

- View PDF when using Distiller Printer automatically displays a converted PDF file when the print command is used from an authoring application.
- View PDF when using Distiller automatically displays a converted PDF file when Distiller is used.

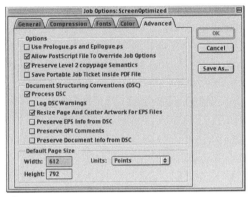

Figure 11-4
Distiller Preferences dialog box showing the Advanced tab.

Font Location Folder   This feature tells Distiller where to find the font files on your system. In the Settings menu under the Font Locations option is the Font Locations choice. By default this folder includes Acrobat Distiller Fonts folder.

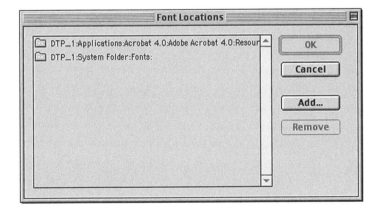

Figure 11-5
Font Locations dialog box.

This dialog box is located in the Distiller menu in Font Locations. Distiller looks in these defined folders for fonts as they are called for. It is important that you specify all possible locations of fonts on your system to avoid replacements. You can add folders to this location by clicking on the Add Folders button. Add the folders that may have fonts on your system.

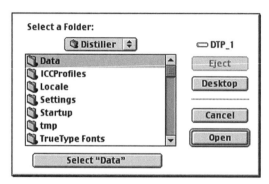

Figure 11-6
Find the location of the fonts to be used.

By doing this, you will be insured that all the fonts on your system are available to Distiller in the conversion process. When you are finished, click OK to accept the changes.

Job Options   This section reinforces the reason to convert Post-Script to PDF with Distiller. The main controls are found in the Job Options choice in the Settings menu. The options are presented in five tabbed folders:

- General
- Compression
- Fonts
- Color
- Advanced

General   The settings in this box provide the ability to set the values for file compatibility for Acrobat 3 or 4. This is the most important setting that is made in Distillers Job Options.

The decision to have compatibility with earlier versions of the Acrobat software imposes serious limitations on the resulting PDF file. When the choice is made for compatibility to Acrobat 3, all output from Distiller 4 will conform to the PDF file format version 1.2. In order to gain the advantages of the version 4 release (PDF 1.3), choose to have Acrobat 4 compatibility.

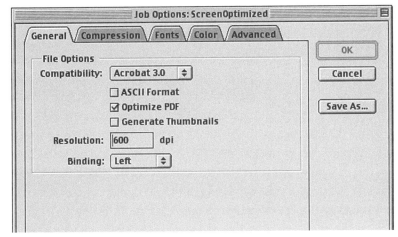

Figure 11-7
Job Options for Screen Optimized.

Some differences between Acrobat 3 PDF files (PDF 1.2) and Acrobat 4 PDF files (PDF 1.3) are summarized below. Some of these features are latent to the user, and others are easier to spot.

- Acrobat 3 files (PDF 1.2) are based on PostScript Level 2. Acrobat 4 files (PDF 1.3) are based on PostScript 3.
- Smooth shading is supported in Acrobat 4.
- DeviceN color space is supported in Acrobat 4.
- Pattern fills display and print correctly in Acrobat 4.
- ICC profiles and CMS are part of Acrobat 4.
- Double byte-fonts are supported in Acrobat 4.

Specify ASCII encoding of page contents, sample images, and embedded fonts by checking the ASCII Format checkbox. If this box is left unchecked, you will generate binary code, which is more compact and desirable. Acrobat 4 enables the Optimization of the resulting PDF file from Distiller. Optimizing a PDF file works to further reduce file size by eliminating duplicate sets of data and/or compressing text and line art. In addition, optimizing a PDF file enables byte-serving, which is used in some Web applications.

Another new feature in Acrobat 4 is the ability to generate document thumbnails during the distilling process. This was a feature in earlier versions of the software and has been brought back.

The default resolution is a setting for some conversion needs. This setting is used by some special PostScript operators (such as a blend operator in FreeHand) that ask Distiller, "What resolution are you?" This setting should be set approximately to the same as your output device, or else banding may become visible in some cases. This setting has no effect on the resolution of other images.

The choice for binding style will determine the way in which a PDF file is displayed in Acrobat. Depending on whether a left- or right-side binding is chosen, display of facing pages and thumbnails will adhere to the specification entered for the binding style. Most documents are designed to have a left-hand binding style.

12

Fonts

Would you buy a font that came with the warning: "This font is restricted and cannot be embedded in PDF documents"? Yet, this is now a common occurrence for two reasons: First, some font makers want to protect their intellectual property and have printout services buy every font every customer will ever use; and second, because one of the programs that makes fonts has a bug in it. Thus, the major workflow solution of the new millennium is being stymied just as it is gaining acceptance.

Adobe Portable Document Format (PDF) is the open de facto standard for electronic document distribution worldwide—a universal file format that preserves all of the fonts, formatting, colors, and graphics of any source document, regardless of the application and platform used to create it. PDF files are compact and can be shared, viewed, navigated, and printed exactly as intended by anyone with a free Adobe Acrobat Reader—that is, unless you want to embed certain fonts limited by intentional or unintentional licensing restrictions. The inability to embed certain fonts in PDFs with Distiller 4, especially some TrueType fonts, which had been embeddable with Distiller 3, is now disallowed. Adobe changed the architecture of Distiller 4 to recognize and force compliance with font licensing information.

We should be able to output film or plate or print from a file made with our fonts. Most users don't ask whether the font can be embedded when they buy it. There is a concern with some font creators that if their font is embedded in a document, someone is going to steal it. For a printout service to buy every font every customer uses would be ludicrous. There is certainly a middle ground.

Fonts that are embedded properly with Distiller 3 now get file creation errors. Depending on settings, the distilling process may cancel, the font may be substituted with Courier, or one may end up with a PDF that looks correct on the computer where it was created, but on another machine is viewed and printed using Adobe's Multiple Master font emulation approach. When PostScript files are created, TrueType fonts are converted to a PostScript version called Type-42. Adobe now honors the font creators' licensing information that Distiller sees in a font, and we get "no embedding allowed." The inability to embed fonts in a prepress workflow is a very serious problem. The advantage to PDF was the fact that it contained everything in one compact file so that jobs could be communicated to graphic arts professionals for printout.

Fonts may have licensing codes inserted by the creator or erroneous codes generated by the font-making program, Macromedia's Fontographer. "fsType" codes allow embedding or not. In the True-Type specifications, defined fsType codes specify degrees of font use: 0002, restrict a font from being embedded; 0004, preview and print embedding; and 0008, editable embedding. Distiller 4 will obey these fsType codes. Macintosh Fontographer, however, uses one-bit code: 0 for embedding, 1 for no embedding, and 2 for print and preview embedding. Thus, Fontographer creates fonts with fsType at 0001, essentially undefined. Distiller treats this as 0002. Fontographer used these embedding bits when Acrobat ignored the fsType parameter, but with Acrobat 4, Fontographer is now a part of the problem.

This "bug" avoided detection until Distiller 4 began to detect and respect. All Fontographer 3.5.1 generated fonts need to be updated, and there is a gigantic user base of the old fonts that can't change the embedding bit. Fonts do not get upgrades (thank goodness), although now they may. Emigre's font license allows you to provide PDFs to service providers for processing if all fonts are embedded and subset, and if you follow other rules like mandatory subsetting and having the PDF security set to allow only printing and viewing and both prohibit changing, selecting, or adding.

Fontographer has not been upgraded since 1996, and much has changed in the industry, especially with the overwhelming acceptance of Acrobat/PDF, including worldwide download of more than 102 million copies of the Acrobat Reader. Linotype, Agfa, Corel, and others do not seem to fear embedding. Smaller companies like Emigre have reservations and restrictions.

All of Adobe's fonts allow embedding, as do their upcoming OpenType fonts, one of which shipped with InDesign 1.0. One recommendation to solve this problem: Distiller should allow the embedding of all fonts for viewing and printing only. If a font has an 0001 or 0002 fsType, Distiller would allow embedding only if the font is subset. Distiller could then indicate that a font was being embedded and subset due to font licensing. We could also use a Font Checker to look at any font and report on copyright information. Some foundries (particularly with Hebrew, Arabic, Chinese, Japanese, etc. fonts) need to ease embedding restrictions.

You may want to consider PitStop, a PDF editor and preflight tool, which will allow you to make text changes to any PDF, including embedding and subsetting restricted fonts, as long as the font desired resides on your system. Most users have no clue about PostScript Type-1, Type-3, Type-42, TrueType, OpenType. They just want everything to work. OpenType finally brings Adobe and Microsoft together, and then Apple has to get weird and do something different. OSX will be full of surprises.

Heck, just convert all fonts to outlines and be done with it. Fonts were a problem when the desktop era started—they will probably be a problem until it ends.

Fonts and Font Embedding   Acrobat Distiller will include a compressed and encoded version of a font for accurate use in the final file. This is the essential benefit of Acrobat PDF.

- Acrobat Distiller must deal with all font types.
- If you use TrueType fonts, be aware of all problems you are introducing into the process.
- As a general rule, if you use any font, embed it in the PDF file.
- The new OpenType fonts may alleviate many font problems.

If you are unsure about fonts, embed them in your PDF file—they do not add significant file size and assure accurate rendering of the file by all users. When you distill the PostScript file, you have the ability to embed the fonts from your computer system in the PDF file. However, do you need to include the font in the PostScript code to get the fonts embedded in the PDF file? Technically no, if you are creating the PostScript stream and converting that PostScript to a PDF file on the same computer. If you do this, then you will have access to the font description files at the distilling process, and the fonts will wind up in the finished PDF file.

It is a requirement on a Windows computer that you embed a TrueType font in the PostScript stream. You also must embed this TrueType font in the PDF when you convert the PostScript file with Acrobat Distiller.

PostScript   In the early 1980s, Adobe Systems developed a way to describe typographic images as vectors, or outlines. This gave type an elasticity that allowed more sizes and variations from the same electronic image. Before that, type for digital output was stored as bitmaps—sets of dots—for each typeface and point size. At the same time, they invented a page-description language called PostScript, which was made up of over 300 verbs and commands that could describe type and pages, fill boxes, select typefaces, etc. The third thing they needed to design was something to interpret this new format, and they created a PostScript interpreter or RIP.

When the RIP receives the PostScript file, it needs to convert it to bitmapped data. PostScript printers use the interpreter to translate the PostScript code into the bitmapped information needed to print a file. The RIP plots out the page as a grid of spot locations. All spots can be located based on the x,y coordinates it sits on. The image can be thought of as having a spot, or not having a spot (one or zero). When only two values are used, it is called binary.

PostScript is a page-description language and is expressed as plain text. PostScript is commonly used for both line art and text. In the former, it is often referred to as encapsulated PostScript (EPS). An EPS is a PostScript file with a preview. There are two EPS types, ASCII, which is text-based, and binary, which is hexadecimal. Vector-based programs that allow the user to save in EPS format usually use the ASCII format.

In the EPS ASCII format, there are two versions of the graphic. One version is the resolution-independent PostScript description for printing on a PostScript device. The other is a low-resolution bit-mapped PICT or TIFF preview, which can be displayed without using PostScript interpretation. With this feature, page-layout programs like QuarkXPress can import, crop, and scale graphics while using the preview image. If there is no preview file attached to the EPS, the application will display a gray box. This makes it very difficult to position or crop the EPS.

When saved as an EPS, the file will not be able to be ungrouped, refilled, or recolored. The only functions that can be done are re-cropping, resizing, and adding distortion. Most programs that do any color separations accept EPS files since they are self-contained. EPS files do not include fonts, which has caused more than one job to print incorrectly. However, the trend is for programs that output EPS to save fonts with the EPS. Illustrator and InDesign do this, among others.

Binary EPS is similar to ASCII versions, containing the PICT preview and the actual graphic. The difference is that instead of saving the file as a PostScript description file, it saves it as a list of numbers that represent pixels. Binary EPS files are used very successfully for outputting bitmapped color images for four-color separation.

It starts with a Bézier curve.

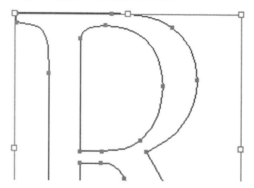

It becomes an outline.

The interpreted character is then filled and converted to spots.

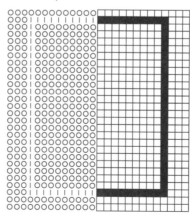

Figure 12-1
Fonts make the metamorphosis from outline to bitmap.

Example of a raster, as zeroes and ones become spots.

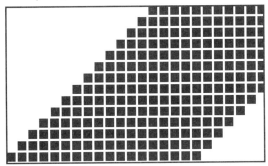

PostScript Type 1 fonts are compressed since they require only one file to create all sizes of a single type style. To display these fonts, the Macintosh needs the outline, a 10-point bitmapped (screen) font of the typeface, and Adobe Type Manager (ATM). The outline file contains information required to render the typeface, and the information is encrypted. PostScript Type 1 uses Bézier mathematics to describe the shape of the curve. This type of math uses less control points to extrapolate the outline of the letters.

Hints maintain the look of type when printing below 600 dpi and in type below 14 point. Hints include making sure all the letters line up, creating visually accurate curves and strokes, and adjusting overall quality. A hint may shift a letter so that it fits in with the other letters that are near it. Font manufacturers are the ones that control hinting, and not all fonts have the capability to use it.

PostScript Level 2 was created in 1990. In 1998, Adobe announced the release of Adobe PostScript Level 3. The big change in this version was to allow customers the ability to print complex graphics and Web content, when and where they needed it. With new digital technologies, Level 3 was created to support digital document creation processes. With enhanced image technology, documents print faster, with optimal quality. PostScript Level 3 also supports direct processing of Web content, including HTML and PDF.

Outline Fonts   In an outline font, each character is described mathematically using lines and Bézier curves. Since these fonts use mathematics in the description, they are scaled up or down with no image integrity problems. Basically, outline fonts come in two major kinds: PostScript and TrueType. Both font types will display and print as well as the other. Acrobat Distiller 3 offers full native TrueType support, so many historical font issues (or misnomers) are solved using the PDF and Acrobat workflow. When an outline font is sent to a PostScript interpreter, it has to ultimately be rasterized (converted to a bitmap) for output.

PostScript Type 1 Fonts   PostScript fonts came into use with the introduction of the PostScript language in 1985. The description of a Type 1 font is done by describing the outline of the font itself using Bézier curves. The outline is then filled in with a solid. This process is the basis for the letter formation, and it works best with higher-resolution output devices such as imagesetters. However, on today's lower-resolution devices, which are proliferating the market, outline fonts count on a technique known as hinting, which completes the font rendering process. Hinting is the miracle worker that makes small fonts on these devices look good, actually better than that; it makes them readable.

In the AdobePS 4.2.x driver for Win9x, if you choose the last radio button option, "Always use TrueType fonts," it will not affect Type 1 fonts, only TrueType fonts that may be in the document. If you choose this, then Type 1 and TrueType will be handled independently according to your preferences in the "Send Fonts As..." dialog.

TrueType   Apple had been developing what was to become TrueType from late 1987. At that time there were many competing font-scaling technologies, and several would have been suitable for the Macintosh. It was by no means certain, according to lead engineer Sampo Kaasila, that Apple would adopt TrueType. In the end though, it proved itself on performance and rendering quality (at high and low resolution) against the others. Kaasila completed his work on TrueType, though it didn't yet have that name, in August 1989. The following month Apple and Microsoft announced their strategic alliance against Adobe, where Apple would do the font system, Microsoft the printing engine. Apple released TrueType to the world in March 1991—the core engine in much the same form that Kaasila left it back in 1989. Microsoft introduced TrueType into Windows with version 3.1 in early 1992. Working with Monotype, Microsoft developed a core set of fonts that included TrueType versions of Times New Roman, Arial, and Courier. These fonts showed, just as Apple's TrueTypes had, that scalable fonts could generate bitmaps virtually as though each size had been designed by hand.

With nonfancy fonts, the system generally worked well. However, since Windows 3.1 had to run on machines with slow 16-bit 286 processors, the TrueType system had to be reconfigured as a 16-bit implementation of Kaasila's fundamentally 32-bit architecture. Memory allocation did not work all of the time, though it did on occasion. There were major problems with the PC version of TrueType. One major flaw was that complex characters would sometimes fail to display at all, or they'd appear on screen but not on the printer. Only in August 1995, with the release of Windows 95, did Microsoft's TrueType engine become 32-bit, which allowed True-Type to be used in the form it was created in. Now it features grayscale rasterization (anti-aliasing), which makes the text on the screen look much nicer than it did before.

These fonts can be used for both the screen display and printing, thereby eliminating the need to have two font files (screen and printer) for each typeface. This format uses square B-spline mathematical formulas (quadratic) to extrapolate type outlines. By using these formulas, it allows the computer to create the characters at any size or resolution.

On the Macintosh, TrueType fonts are made up of the SFNT resource, and a FOND resource. The two resources are combined into one file and contain all the data to create the characters. These were originally designed to work on non-PostScript printers, but work on PostScript printers as well. On the Macintosh list of fonts, the TrueType fonts do not have a number for point size after them. These fonts must be stored in the fonts folder on the Macintosh, unless a font manager is being used. In the PC format, TrueType fonts have the extension TTF.

OpenType   The OpenType font format is an extension of the TrueType font format, adding support for PostScript font data. The OpenType font format was developed jointly by Microsoft and Adobe, primarily to support the Web. OpenType fonts and the operating system services that support OpenType fonts provide users

It turns off the substitution of any TrueType font with a Type 1 font. If you request Type 1 font Glurbish Roman in your document, the driver will download Glurbish Roman, unless Glurbish Roman is one of your printer's resident, permanent fonts. If you request TrueType font Inebriated Oblique in your document, the driver will download Inebriated Oblique (Type 42, Type 1 unhinted outline, or Type 3 bitmap dependent upon driver settings and printer capability —printers with native TrueType support default to Type 42 download), again unless Inebriated Oblique is one of your printer's resident, permanent fonts.

with a simple way to install and use fonts, whether the fonts contain TrueType outlines or CFF (PostScript) outlines.

OpenType addresses the following goals: broader multiplatform support, better support for international character sets, better protection for font data, smaller file sizes to make font distribution more efficient, and broader support for advanced typographic control. OpenType fonts are also referred to as TrueType Open v.2.0 fonts because they use the TrueType "sfnt" font file format. PostScript data included in OpenType fonts may be directly rasterized or converted to the TrueType outline format for rendering, depending on which rasterizers have been installed in the host operating system. Users will not need to be aware of the type of outline data in OpenType fonts; and font creators can use whichever outline format they feel provides the best set of features for their work, without worrying about limiting a font's usability.

OpenType fonts can include the OpenType Layout tables, which allow font creators to design better international and high-end typographic fonts. The OpenType Layout tables contain information on glyph substitution, glyph positioning, justification, and baseline positioning, enabling text-processing applications to improve text layout. As with TrueType fonts, OpenType fonts allow the handling of large glyph sets using Unicode encoding. Such encoding allows broad international support, as well as support for typographic glyph variants. Additionally, OpenType fonts may contain digital signatures, which allow operating systems and browsing applications to identify the source and integrity of font files, including embedded font files obtained in web documents, before using them. Also, font developers can encode embedding restrictions in OpenType fonts, and these restrictions cannot be altered in a font by the developer.

The most current version of the Unicode standard, The Unicode Standard, Version 3.0, contains 49,194 distinct coded characters derived from the Supported Scripts. These characters cover the principal written languages of the Americas, Europe, the Middle East, Africa, India, Asia, and the Pacific Basin. Some modern written languages are not yet supported or only partially supported due to a need for further research into the encoding needs of certain scripts.

Multiple Master Fonts   As the name implies, this kind of font uses a single model (or master) font matrix, and alterations are made to this single letter. The letters are changed according to design axis. A Multiple Master description can include up to four design axes. These axes may include WEIGHT (light to black) and WIDTH (condensed to expanded).

Using these axes (weight and width), a four-point polar design can be constructed and result in four different designs:

- light condensed
- light expanded
- black condensed
- black expanded

The capability to create variations along each axis exists. You may end up with something like a not-so-black semi-condensed font. Whatever the case, these fonts can be sent to a PostScript interpreter.

Type 42 Fonts   Type 42 is a PostScript font format that allows TrueType fonts to be interpreted by a PostScript RIP. A Type 42 font is a PostScript wrapper around a TrueType font; a RIP resident TrueType rasterizer then interprets this font directly. A Type 42 font was designed specifically for this use of TrueType fonts with a PostScript interpreter; therefore, this method works better than a conversion of the TrueType to a Type 1 or Type 3 format for output.

Bitmap Fonts   A bitmap font is nothing more than a series of arranged spots in a predetermined grid. The bitmap data is binary in nature; it defines which spots should be on or off for the particular letter. When these fonts are printed, it is a matter of transferring the data to the output device for interpreting. A major drawback to this method of describing fonts is a limit on the size and scaling of the font. Whenever you make a change to this type of font either in size, shape. or resolution, there is some loss of image quality. The positive side to these fonts is the ease in which a shade or fill can be applied to the character set. Bitmap fonts in PostScript are referred to as Type 3 fonts.

You really don't want to ever create PDF files with "bitmaps." These are device-resolution dependent-causing problems for display and also for printing at any device other than that for which the PDF file was originally created. For creation of PDF, ALWAYS use "Send Fonts as Type42" (AdobePS 4.x) or "Send Fonts as Native" (AdobePS 5.x). At print time, Acrobat properly sends either Type42 (native TrueType support for PostScript) or unhinted Type 1 (for printers without native TrueType support) fonts, depending upon the printers' capabilities.

Why are AdobeSansMM or AdobeSerifMM the default fonts that are substituted in the PDF? Because these are the default fonts used by Acrobat when the actual fonts cannot be found. These are special multiple master fonts that try to emulate the missing fonts. Sometimes the emulations are fairly good, sometimes not. In either case, however, they really shouldn't be used for final output.

A PS RIP identifies fonts by their "long" PS name exclusively. Two versions of the same font will share the same long PS name. We wish there was a scheme to allow RIPs to distinguish that different versions of the same font are present. Type 1 fonts and some other types include a key called UniqueID and it is supposed to be unique to every font. The value is an integer, which limits things slightly— there are almost certainly more versions of fonts out there than there are available numbers. Adobe allocates numbers below 4 million to font vendors. Larger numbers should only be used for "in-house" fonts where they shouldn't clash. Most shareware fonts use numbers in that range. To help with the problem there can also be an XUid (extended unique ID), which is an array of numbers, effectively infinite variety, but most fonts don't use that. The larger font vendors use registered numbers and use different numbers for different versions of the same font.

A RIP identifies characters in its cache by UniqueID and by size/resolution. Thus, as long as two fonts with the same name use different UniqueIDs, they will be recognized as dif-

Legal Issues with Embedded Fonts   When you embed a font into a PDF file, a compressed and encoded version of the font file goes directly into the final PDF file. This being the case, only certain vendors and type developers have been given the go-ahead to embed their fonts in the file. The list includes

- Adobe Type Library and Adobe Originals
- Linotype-Hell, AG (now Heidelberg)
- International Typeface Corporation (ITC)
- Agfa-Gevaert (which acquired Monotype)
- AlphaOmega
- Bigelow and Holmes
- Fundicion Tipografica Neufville

Fonts from other vendors may require permission for complete legal distribution of the fonts. Your best bet to be 100 percent sure is to check with the font vendor.

Simulated Fonts   If fonts are not embedded in the PDF file and not available on the host system, Acrobat will use a simulated font in its place. A simulated font requires about 1K of memory in the final PDF file, so if file size is a concern, you may want to consider using this technique for certain fonts. The simulated font is created from the font style, matrix, and name. The approximation or simulation is then generated using the font information and apply it on the fly to the Adobe Sans Multiple Master or Adobe Serif Multiple Master font. The font will be approximated in the viewing and printing.

This Faux or Substitution font will work for standard fonts. However, when PDFWriter or Distiller encounters a symbolic font or a font with nonstandard glyph names, that font will automatically be embedded in the PDF file under the assumption that that font or glyph cannot be fauxed accurately. If you are targeting a typographically correct audience, you should not rely on this simulation of fonts.

Fonts used to bring up some very tricky situations. Using Adobe Acrobat to package your document, fonts are no longer an issue. A challenge to us all is the use of pirated fonts that have been manipulated so that they are no longer original fonts. These fonts can and will cause problems down the road. However, if you stick with pure and native fonts, there should be no real problems with fonts and the resulting PDF files.

Font Embedding

Embedding a font will place an encoded compressed version of the font in the PDF file. This embedded font insures that the look and feel of the document is carried through to the PDF file. In order to embed a font, the font file needs to be available to Distiller at distilling time. There are two options for font embedding in Acrobat Distiller:

- Embedding the whole font
- Embedding a font subset

If you use a font in your document that is destined for print, embed the whole font. This will insure that you carry the font all the way through the process from application file to PDF. You will have the ability to edit this font later on in the process if the need arises.

Font Substitution

Some facts about Acrobat 4 and its substitution of Arial and TimewNewRoman for Helvetica and Times: The font substitution occurs only if a document uses Helvetica or Times but these fonts are not embedded in the document. Adobe now recommends subsetting and embedding all fonts when using Acrobat 4; this is the default behavior of the PrintOptimized and PressOptimized settings.

The Monotype versions of Arial and TimesNewRoman are used only for on-screen viewing and when printing to non-PostScript printers. When printing to PostScript, Acrobat will use the printer-resident versions of Helvetica and Times.

The Monotype versions of Arial and TimesNewRoman are not TrueType fonts. They are Type 1, and their metrics exactly match those of Helvetica and Times, so the only differences seen are slight changes in character shapes for viewing and non-PS printing—no differences in character placement are introduced.

ferent. In the RIP the sequence is:

1 RIP encounters request for a font, named /X.

2 RIP checks to see if X is embedded in job file.

3 If it is embedded, then load it, if not, look elsewhere, in ROM, on disk etc.

4 For every character to be rendered, check to see if that character is already in the font cache at the right size. This check does not use the font name at all, just the UniqueID, which it will compare with the UniqueID read from the font that was selected in 3.

5 If the required character is in the cache then use it; otherwise generate (and cache) it from the font selected in 3).

Some fonts don't have unique IDs. In those cases most RIPs won't cache the fonts at all. In a few RIPs, fonts in ROM take precedence over fonts in the job or on disk. Typically this only means the base 13. RIPs will use a cached character in preference to building a new one from an embedded font in the job. That is unlikely to mean printing the wrong version of a font if you are using fonts from the larger font foundries.

There is no real valid reason in prepress not to embed all fonts, change the font name via subsetting, but include all characters, just in case someone needs to make a last-minute change. If you subset, you subset. 100% would mean that you subset every font every time, NOT that you get 100% of characters when embedding. The subset consists of the characters you have used, nothing else.

One conclusion of this thread is that you can have "embed all fonts" unticked and "subset fonts" ticked and set to 100%. That this will always embed everything and will force Acrobat to use the embedded fonts.

If you embed all fonts and subset at 99% (meaning the entire font will be embedded only if 99% of the characters in the font are used—highly unlikely), the Distiller will prepend a six-character random string to the font name it embeds. Thus Adobe Garamond becomes AGKDWU+Adobe Garamond, which means it's not the same font as found on the RIP and will therefore be used instead of the RIP's font.

If you have Type 1 versions of Helvetica and Times installed on your system, you can force Acrobat 4 to use them by removing Arial and TimesNewRoman from Acrobat's Resource/Font folder. Alternatively, you can remove Arial and TimesNewRoman from Resource/Font and drop Type 1 versions of Helvetica and Times in (in which case you don't need to install ATM or the Type 1 fonts in your system). However, it is unlikely that your versions of Helvetica and Times contain the Euro character; if so, this character will appear as a blank during on-screen viewing or when printing to non-PostScript language printers. The Euro character will always print on PostScript language printers.

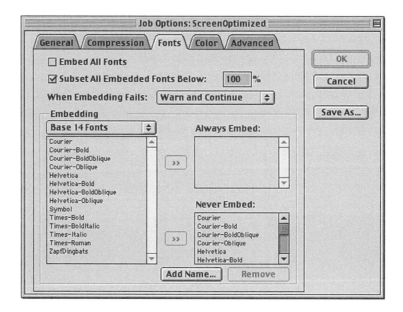

Figure 12-2
Acrobat Job Options dialog for fonts.

Subsetting Fonts   Font embedding will maintain the look and feel of the document during its distribution. Acrobat Distiller offers a choice for embedding all fonts, and for embedding a subset. A font subset is a version of the original font that contains only the characters that you used in your document. This truncated version of the font is ingenious because you can now embed fonts and reduce file size. The advantage to this is that you keep file size to a minimum. The major drawback is you cannot do text touchup on a subsetted font later on in Acrobat if the characters are missing.

There is the ability to set the threshold for when to embed the font subset or to embed the entire font. You have control over this value. It can be set from 1 percent to 100 percent. For example, if the setting is made for 35 percent, the result would be, if 35 percent or less of a font is used in your document, Distiller will select to embed only the used portion of the font that you used. If you used more than 35 percent (or whatever you set this threshold to be), the whole font will be embedded.

When a font is embedded at the original time of creation, it is used for display and print by a host machine if this host machine does not have that font (same name and type) on its system (a host is somebody else's machine, other than the creator's). This is the way that it is supposed to work, but if the creator edited his font a bit and embedded this edited font, a host site (if it had the same font on his system) would not display or print that edited embedded version, it would use the system font. To get around this challenge, you can always embed a subset of the font by setting the threshold to 99 percent (a subsetted font gets a unique name). The host machine will use this embedded subset font with no exceptions. New in Acrobat 4 is the ability to take preference to an embedded font over a host system font; however, this relies on the host computer making an additional preference setting.

By choosing the Embed All Fonts checkbox, all the fonts you used in the file will be embedded in the final PDF file. It is important to note that the fonts still must be available to Distiller when you distill the file. The best way to insure that the fonts are indeed available to you when you distill is to embed all fonts into the PostScript stream or to distill on the computer that you created the document on. This way, you do not have a chance to leave the fonts behind or run the risk of another computer not having the fonts you need.

Embedding Options   Distiller has more flexibility for font-embedding options over PDFWriter. Since Distiller takes PostScript

"Type 42 fonts" are not available as commercial products. This is simply the download/internal format of TrueType when sent to a Post-Script printer or as embedded within a PDF file. OpenType effectively has two "flavors"—one very TrueTypish and the other Type 1ish. Depending upon the "flavor" of OpenType, the driver downloads either a Type 1 or Type 42 font.

code generated by any number of sources, it must get the font from somewhere. You have to tell Distiller where to look for the font files on your system in the Font Location folder.

In order for Distiller to embed a True Type font in a PDF file, the True Type font must exist in the originating PostScript stream.

Font Embedding Failure   Acrobat 4 has the ability to control Distiller when it encounters a font that it cannot find. If Distiller cannot locate a font, the font will either be substituted by Courier, or be created by a Multiple Master instance.

Always Embed List   In the font-embedding tab folder, you have the option to select fonts in an Always Embed list. This overrides any settings made to either embed fonts or not. Another application lets you set up a series of "hot folders" and declare different options in each folder.

Adding fonts to the Always Embed list or to the Never Embed list can be done using the buttons to Add or Remove. Whenever a font in one of these lists is used in a file, the settings in these lists are followed over the Embed All Fonts checkbox.

To ensure Distiller will report missing Type1 fonts, it is recommended that you move the font database file. This file enables Distiller to substitute for missing Adobe Type 1 fonts. While this is a great feature, for high-end output the original font is required, and the user should be made aware when Distiller cannot locate the font. Move the file superatm.db out of the Acrobat Distiller data folder. Do not trash or throw this file away; move it to another location so that it is available if you'd like to use it in the future. To reestablish its use, move it back into the original location.

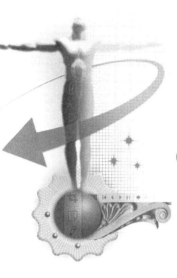

13

Compression

Compression is the heart of the Distiller Job Options. You can compress text, line art, and photos all in one application. Each object is evaluated by Distiller and then compressed on the fly with the appropriate approach. Available options include

- JPEG—Continuous tone photos (no sharp edges)
- Downsampling, which is more accurate than subsampling
- Bi-cubic Downsampling, which is more accurate than Downsampling
- ZIP—Repeating patterns in images (screen captures)
- CCITT—Close balance of black and white
- Run Length Encoding—Large areas of black and white

Color Bitmap Compression The term color bitmap images refers to images that are by definition pixel-based. This includes images from Adobe Photoshop or any other "paint" programs. The options that can be applied to color bitmap images are to downsample or subsample, and to automatically compress or to manually compress. Whatever option you choose for the compression, it is applied only to this type of image. This means that the settings in this area are specific only to this class of images, and no other image classes will be affected by the settings made in this area.

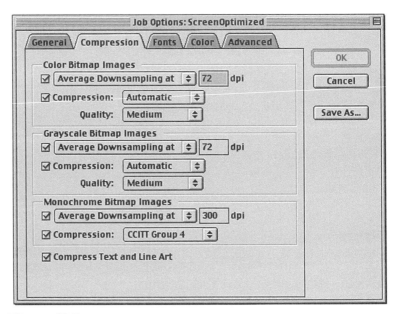

Figure 13-1
Job Options dialog box.

Downsampling and Subsampling   Photographic images are often scanned with more data than may be needed for final printout. Downsampling and subsampling discard unneeded image data. Distiller lets you establish downsampling or subsampling settings:

- Color Bitmap
- Grayscale Bitmap
- Monochrome Bitmap

The value that you plug into the field is a target value. Distiller downsamples or subsamples only to the nearest integer. Depending on the initial resolution of the image, the results will vary, but the final resolution will be at the target (if the math works out) or above it, but never below it.

The difference between subsampling and downsampling is in the approach to data reduction. Both start with a pixel array with various values. The end result in both cases is one value representing the entire array. Downsampling averages the array and uses that average value to represent the area. Bi-cubic downsampling uses a weighted average value, which is applied to the pixel area. Subsampling just grabs the center value and assigns it to the area. Bi-cubic down sampling is the most accurate, but it takes longer to process the calculations.

Subsampling Subsampling is a compression technique that evaluates an array of pixel data and assigns a single value for the entire area. The center most pixel is chosen as the value, the remaining pixels are filled with this value, and the rest of the data is thrown away. You can set the target value for a subsampled image; the minimum is 9 dpi. The importance of this is that you are setting a target value when converting to PDF. This conversion operates on whole numbers for compression. Suppose you have a 600 dpi scanned image and you want to subsample it to 72 dpi (just over a 5:1 ratio) for Web usage. To calculate what the subsample finished value will be (and downsample value as well), take the original resolution and divide it by the closest whole-number ratio that is lower than the actual ratio if a direct ratio was used:

- Original Scan, 600 dpi
- Subsample to 72 dpi
- Actual compression ratio, 8.33:1
- Compression ratio used, 8:1
- Resultant resolution (600/8), 75 dpi

Downsampling Downsampling is a similar technique to subsampling but is more scientific in its approach. Downsampling takes the array of pixels and averages them and then assigns that average to the entire pixel area. This approach, like subsampling, has a minimum value of 9 dpi.

The following samples show the effects of subsampling and downsampling.

Downsampling

Downsampled to 150 dpi
Distilling time: 13 seconds

Downsampled to 72 dpi
Distilling time: 13 seconds

Full resolution 300 dpi
Distilling time: 22 seconds

Figure 13-2
Downsampling examples.

Downsampling averages tone values from surrounding pixels and reproduces the average tone using one larger pixel. This is a method that takes more computing power and is slower than subsampling, although the quality is better.

Because downsampling averages pixels, the picture becomes more fuzzy but looks better compared to that of subsampling, especially with big reductions in resolution.

If Downsample Images is selected in PDFWriter, it will automatically downsample images to 72 dpi or the closest possible value. Distiller allows you to specify the downsample resolution.

Subsampling

Subsampled to 150 dpi
Distilling time: 12 seconds

Subsampled to 72 dpi
Distilling time: 10 seconds

Full resolution 300 dpi
Distilling time: 22 seconds

Figure 13-3
Subsampling examples.

Subsampling takes the center pixel's value and applies it to the larger resulting pixel. This does not produce as accurate a reproduction as downsampling. Subsampling produces a less fuzzy image compared to one reproduced by downsampling, but the pixels are very noticeable when subsampling from high resolution to very low resolutions. The picture begins to look "blocky."

Subsampling can be accomplished only using Distiller. Because subsampling requires less computing power, subsampling takes less time to distill than does downsampling.

Subsampling

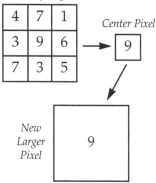

Center Pixel

New Larger Pixel

Average Downsampling

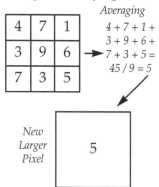

Averaging
4 + 7 + 1 +
3 + 9 + 6 +
7 + 3 + 5 =
45 / 9 = 5

New Larger Pixel

Bicubic Downsampling

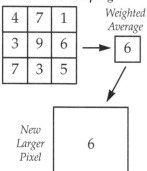

Weighted Average

New Larger Pixel

Subsampling significantly reduces distilling time compared with downsampling but results in images that appear less smooth and continuous. Downsampling reduces the amount of information in the image so that only the image data that the printer can use is included (Distiller never resamples images to a higher resolution, only to a lower one). There are two methods for downsampling: average and bi-cubic. When you select average downsampling, it averages the pixels in a sample area and replaces the entire area with the average pixel color at the specified resolution. When you select bi-cubic downsampling, it uses a weighted average to determine pixel color and usually yields better results than average downsampling. We recommend bicubic downsampling because it is a more precise—though slower—method, and results in the smoothest tonal gradations. You should downsample your images when they contain more image data than your service provider's final output device can use. Higher image resolution is not always the better choice when you're working with images. If their printing device can't use the information, the extra resolution only increases the time it takes the printer to process the image. Smaller PDF files are easier to transmit, take less time to RIP, and need less space to archive.

Printer resolution	Line screen	Image resolution
300 dpi (laser printer)	60 lpi	120 ppi
600 dpi (laser printer)	85 lpi	170 ppi
1200 dpi (image-, platesetter)	125 lpi	240 ppi
2400 dpi (image-, platesetter)	150 lpi	300 ppi

Downsampling images creates a baseline—converting those bitmap image files that have been scanned at a specific resolution, and then scaled smaller in a layout or graphic application, which unnecessarily increases the image resolution and sometimes causes printing problems.

There is a major bug in Acrobat 4.0 that has been corrected in version 4.05. Distiller provides the same compression no matter which compression level you select. Actually, the two lowest are the same and the two highest are the same. Do it and check the file sizes.

Automatic, Manual, and Zip Compression   When assigning the major compression approach for color bitmap images, two choices need to be made: first, a choice for the general method, and then a setting for the specific parameters to be followed.

Distiller can be set to use different general compression approaches for color bitmap images:

- Automatic
- JPEG
- ZIP

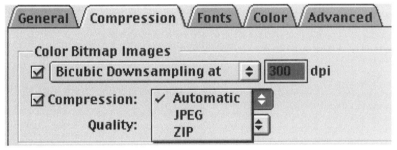

Figure 13-4
Compression alternatives in Distiller dialog box.

The automatic compression option will make Distiller evaluate the images on the fly and apply the appropriate compression scheme to them. Distiller uses these criteria when assigning compression routines to images:

- JPEG applied to images with smooth color changes
- ZIP for images with sharp color changes

Generally, as the bit depth of an image increases and the color shifts are smoothed out, Distiller applies JPEG compression to the image. As the bit depth of an image drops below 4 bits, ZIP compression will be applied to the image. Automatic compression will

Watch out for terminology, it can be confusing—someone may say "JPEG high" but that can be two different things: the level of quality or the level of compression. High quality is just that—high compression is just the opposite: lousy quality. The difference in size can be considerable, especially if downsampling is utilized. The most dramatic we've seen was a 900 Mb PostScript file turn into 4 Mb. The reason was that all the 4-color images in the original were EPS and scaled to about 15% of the scan size. The job looked beautiful and processed far faster than a PS workflow would have done. For the other compression option, stick with 8 bit Zip for grayscale images (this is lossless—no degradation in quality whatsoever) and Group 4 for bitmaps (this is lossless as well). Of course, compress text also.

not be applied to line art, text, or monochrome images. In addition to making the choice for automatic compression, a choice for the amount of JPEG compression needs to be set. Making this setting in Acrobat 4.0 is much akin to the setting in Photoshop, where the setting is in reference to the Image Quality. Setting this value to Minimum will enable the highest amount of JPEG compression.

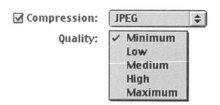

By selecting JPEG compression for color bitmap images, you gain direct control over all compression that is applied to color images. When this setting is made, all color images will be compressed according to the level of JPEG specified in the Quality menu. Again, a setting of Minimum in the Quality menu will result in the highest amount of JPEG on all color bitmap images.

Applying Zip compression to all color bitmap images will apply the Zip algorithm of compression to all color images. When this choice is made, an additional setting of control over the bit depth of the images is selected. In normal circumstances, Zip compression is considered lossless. However, if an 8-bit image is compressed with Zip 4-bit compression, a loss of pixel depth will result. Therefore, verify the type of image you are compressing before you start.

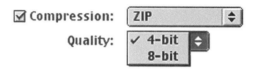

The Zip compression method achieves the highest levels of effectiveness when it is applied to images with relatively large areas of single colors, or repeating image patterns. Refer to the Compression chapter for more information.

Grayscale Bitmap Compression   Compression of the Grayscale Bitmap images in your document is handled much the same way as the controls for color bitmap images. Settings made in this area are applied only to grayscale bitmap images.

Monochrome Bitmap Compression   The compression of monochrome bitmap images is handled with similar menu items to color and grayscale images, except that the option for automatic compression is not available. Additionally, the choices for compression schemes are different. The compression schemes that are available to apply to monochrome images are

- CCITT Group 3 and 4
- ZIP
- Run Length Encoding

The available compression for monochrome images are considered to be lossless. This is to say they accomplish compression by rearranging the individual bits of the images, rather than eliminating pixel data. Refer to the compression chapter for more in-depth discussions of the available compression approaches.

Compress Text and Line Art   To engage the compression of text and line art in a file, simply click the check box to engage the setting. When this checkbox is enabled, the text and line art are compressed with the Zip compression approach. Since this is a lossless technique, no image data will be lost.

☑ Compress Text and Line Art

When you select the Optimize file either in Distillers General tab, or in a Save As in Acrobat, compression of text and line art is performed automatically, regardless of the settings made in this section.

Lossless Compression Schemes   Lossless compression techniques do not eliminate data the same way lossy techniques do. Lossless compression is set up so that none of the original pixel data

The only kind of compression that may be subject to argument is JPEG. JPEG is a lossy compression algorithm. The degree of "lossiness" depends on parameters you can set in Distiller (low/medium/high etc.). Anybody who has tried JPEG will tell you that it is safe to use low-to-medium JPEG compression—no noticeable degradation of images will occur, but a lot of space is saved.

All other compression available in Acrobat Distiller is lossless (except for ZIP/4-bit where the loss though does not come from compressing but from throwing away 4 bits in every byte). As far as technology can be safe at all, these are safe. All these compression algorithms have been part of the PostScript language for nearly 10 years now (they are part of the PostScript Level 2 spec). Any decent RIP should have no problem supporting it. There are some applications though that still cannot handle certain compressed image data, e.g., QuarkXPress still seems to be unable to create separations for JPEG compressed image data. Therefore, whenever you need to turn a PDF into EPSes for import into XPress (and many many other applications) save them as

is lost in the process. This may not result in as a high-compression ratio as found in lossy methods for images, but the image quality will remain. There is a tradeoff involved, image quality versus file size. You saw firsthand the artifacts or noise present in the JPEG compression. In lossless compression, noise is a nonfactor, but image flattening may become one.

The basic approach of lossless techniques is very simple. Each pixel in the document has a value of either on or off (black or white). Thus, if you have 500 pixels that are black, right next to each other, a typical way to store this is by individual pixel. With a lossless compression approach, the file is examined and patterns of like pixels are detected. Once these pixel packets are found, a single value that accurately represents the pixels is assigned. The original string of 500 black pixels, a single value of black, is used to represent those pixels.

Zip Compression   Adobe's implementation of the Zip compression approach is based on the Zlib compression method devised by Jean-Loup Gailly and Mark Adler. This approach is centered on the use of a variant called deflation, which is very effective.

4-Bit and 8-Bit Compression   Zip compression can be applied either in 4-bit or 8-bit schemes. What does that mean? The number represents the bit depth of the image. Bit depth is the amount of bits that are allocated for the description of each pixel of image data. Therefore, a 4-bit image is one that has 4 bits of data to describe each pixel. See how easy it can be?

Each pixel in a 4-bit image can be represented by 16 different colors (2 to the power of 4). An 8-bit image can represent 256 colors (2 to the power of 8). The mathematical model for different colors can also be used for gray levels in a grayscale image.

If you were to look at the results of compression tests on both the ISO grayscale image and the monochrome image—in general, Zip compression is not suited for continuous tone images. This is because there is generally no repeating data for the schemes to be effective. Zip is best used on a line art image, so it is not recommended that you apply Zip compression to continuous tone images.

Other Lossless Techniques   The remaining techniques for compression that are available for usage in Acrobat 3 are

- CCITT Group 3
- CCITT Group 4
- RLE

Level 1 EPS files because all data in the EPS will be written out uncompressed (and then eat up your disk space).

CCITT Group 3 and 4   The CCITT (now known as International Telecommunications Union; ITU) Group 3 and 4 compression schemes have their roots in facsimile transmission. These techniques are used on all modern fax machines. The system works by converting the monochrome information into information packets called pels. These pels are then used in the description of the page. These techniques can be very effective on pages that have a good balance (in terms of percent page coverage) of black and white areas.

Run Length Encoding   Next in the series of compression techniques is Run Length Encoding, or RLE. The concept behind RLE is converting large sequential image data (runs) in a compressed form. RLE is best applied to pages that have large areas of black and white.

Compression Refresher
- JPEG: Continuous tone photos (no sharp edges)
- Zip: Repeating patterns in images (screen captures)
- CCITT: Relatively close balance of black and white (generally the best for monochrome images)
- RLE: Large areas of black and white
- Downsampling: generally longer to process, but more accurate than subsampling

Lossy versus Lossless Compression   There are several compression approaches and techniques available to you when you create a PDF file. Data in a file can be compressed to various levels depending on the image itself and the technique applied to it. Each compression technique has its own place in your file. An overview and basic understanding of each scheme and what that is doing to

There is one specific type of image that we consistently see bad results with jpeg compression: any image that has been silhouetted—that is, has a hard clean edge against a pure white background within a square image. Highest quality JPEG will cause a halo of 1-2% scatter pixels to form around the edge of the subject in the previously pure white background.

You read it here first: jpegging a JPEG is bad news. When making a PDF with .jpg file compression, the original source image files should not be .jpg within the layout program. Otherwise, one is jpegging a jpeg. There is a visible loss of quality.

your images is necessary. In the grand picture, there are two basic compression techniques:

- Lossy
- Lossless

Lossy compression uses algorithms designed to compress the file by selectively removing portions of the images. It selects details that the human eye does not pick out very well, so it does a relatively good job. In doing this some of the image information (detail) is lost, and artifacts or noise may be picked up in some images. This technique is ideal for soft viewing applications (on screen). The compression ratio can be high depending on your settings. When creating a PDF file, the lossy techniques that are available are

- JPEG (low–high)
- Subsampling
- Downsampling
- Bi-cubic Downsampling

Lossless compression is slightly more conservative than lossy techniques. Lossless techniques retain all pixel data for images, byte for byte. Although the compression ratios may not be as large as those for a lossy technique, image integrity is retained. This type of compression is recommended for high-contrast images, line art, and text. Lossless compression approaches including monochrome image compression are

- Zip
- CCITT Group 3
- CCITT Group 4
- Run Length Encoding

JPEG Compression   Joint Photographic Experts Group (JPEG) compression falls into the lossy category of compression. Since this method does lose some of the original pixel data, you are in a trade-off situation when considering file size and image quality. In order to make this choice easier, several levels of JPEG compression are available to you:

- High compression (Maximum)
- Medium-high compression (High)
- Medium compression (Medium)
- Medium-low compression (Low)
- Low compression (Minimum)

Analyzing compression ratios for images compressed with the JPEG technique will vary according to the amount of compressible data available. Images with smooth transitions between tones are compressed greater than images with sharp tone and color shifts. Keep in mind that JPEG compression is designed to compress continuous tone images either in full-color or grayscale (black-and-white) photographs. JPEG is designed to take advantage of known limitations of human vision. The first areas of image deletion are in areas containing small color shifts; then, it moves to the next largest change.

As a general rule of thumb, as the resolution of an image increases, the effectiveness (compression ratio) of JPEG will also increase. This is because the color transitions are smoother, and therefore there are more compressible areas.

Images such as black-and-white line art (1 bit per pixel, on or off) reveal increasing artifacts or unwanted noise in the image with higher levels of JPEG compression. Images such as line art or vector images are not suited for JPEG compression.

JPEG and Line Art   JPEG compression should not be used on images other than continuous tone. Line art (1 bit per pixel) images are not suited for JPEG compression. They have hard edges, with sharp color changes. These attributes are opposite what JPEG is designed to accomplish. Because of this you will encounter noise or artifacts that appear in these types of images as the compression rates increase. JPEG works well on continuous tone images and not well on line art, so do not use JPEG on line art.

Acrobat 3 users: You are familiar with working with JPEG compression schemes, but the names have different meanings with PDF and Acrobat 4. Be advised that what Acrobat 3 used to be set on was the level JPEG compression. With PDF and Acrobat. the settings are made in reference to image quality (more like Photoshop).

Resolution Follies

DPI is the addressability of an output or input device. What input device has any kind of addressability in terms of dots per inch? Input devices such as scanners have a resolution in terms of SPI (samples per inch); when their data is interpreted by scanner software (mostly, the driver), it then becomes pixels per inch. Output devices (most of them) make dots. A dot is a solid thing, not gray. Either you have a dot, or you don't have a dot. This is not the case with either samples (per inch) or pixels (per inch). A sample or a pixel can have shades, or levels. This is how an input device is described—not as having DPI.

- After a scanner scans an image, sampling it at "2400 dpi"—a scanner does not sample in "DPI." They are called samples per inch.
- "At what resolution would you like this scanned?" "I would like it scanned at 2400 spi" is correct usage.
- "I would like a 2400-ppi image" is also correct usage.
- "I would like it scanned at 2400 dpi" is incorrect usage.

PPI implies image file (or some kinds of output devices that don't use dots for halftoning); dpi implies dots or output device, spi implies input device. Technically, there is no such thing as continuous tone reproductions. Even silver photographic images are made up of either black silver or clear film, and they still show graininess. But that is where continuous tone original came from: photographic emulsion.

Let us not equate contone to anything that prints with a dot, be it a conventional halftone dot, or stochastic screening. Dye sublimation can be considered contone. High-resolution inkjet printers can be considered "near continuous tone," but don't give them more than that. Contone is a pretty specific thing. In almost all printing, output of images is based on some kind of spot.

Our industry draws the line between contone and noncontone at the point where little visual structure is present. Resolution can mean different things. Device resolution is used in the context of

Adobe has a special responsibility when picking the compression methods in PDF. They have to not only work, they have to be accessible. That is, not only Adobe, but the many other developers who produce software to work with PDFs all have to be able to work with the compression method. There has in fact been only one change since PDF was first introduced: to replace LZW—troublesome because of patents on it— with ZIP, which was not patented and also had a public domain implementation. If Adobe were to introduce a new compression method which does not have a cross platform, public domain or free-to-use source implementation already available, it would be a major step backwards for PDF.

TIFF-IT is not a unique compression method, nor is it lossy; it is a file format based on an extension of TIFF. MrSID is a proprietary technology, rendering it useless for this purpose.

The next format likely to be considered is JPEG2000, because it has a large standards effort behind it. Once there is a publicly available implementation, as there is for original JPEG, it may be a good candidate.

physical devices, such as scanners, monitors, and output devices (including machines that create halftones, such as laser printers and imagesetters, and machines that create continuous-tone output, such as film recorders and dye-sub printers). Device resolution tells you how small a spot a printer can produce, a monitor can display, or a scanner can "see."

The higher the resolution, the smaller the spot and the better-quality output you'll get—a 600-dpi printer is better than a 300-dpi printer but nowhere near as good as a 2,400-dpi imagesetter or plate-setter.

Image Resolution   Image resolution tells you how many pixels (the small units that make up a bitmap) fit in an inch. While device resolution is always a fixed number, image resolution depends on the size of the pixels. The smaller they are, the more fit into an inch. We mistakenly use the term dots per inch (dpi) when referring to all resolution. The term dpi describes physical output—spots on paper or film or plate.

Bitmapped images are composed of pixels and so should be defined in pixels per inch (ppi). Lines per inch (lpi, or halftone screen frequency) sounds as if it is related to image resolution, but it is not. Laser printers and imagesetters use halftone dots to simulate grays. The term lpi defines how many rows of halftone dots make up a halftone screen—that is, how fine or coarse the screen is. LPI does not apply to contone printers or line-art images because they do not use halftones.

Image resolution and screen frequency are related. The resolution for a scan should be at least 1.5 times the number of lines per inch at which you're printing. For images with fine detail, image resolution should be 1.7 or even 2 times the lpi.

Scaling a Bitmap   When you scale a bitmapped image in a page-layout program, you don't change the number of pixels, so each pixel must get bigger or smaller. Image-editing programs like Photoshop let you change the number of pixels, the resolution, or the size of an image independently. To do this, the program must resample, which entails throwing away or creating new pixels. For instance, if you halve the size of the image but leave the resolution the same, Photoshop downsamples—it throws away half the pixels. That means you lose image detail, though often it's detail you don't need.

If you double the resolution but leave the image size the same, the program has to upsample—it doubles the number of pixels, making them up. Some programs add information more intelligently than others (Photoshop's Bi-cubic interpolation is the best).

14

Color

Make sure all desktop programs are set up to interpret RGB and CMYK colors the same way or you will have color shifts that affect how colors look on screen and how they print. Photoshop, Illustrator, Acrobat, and InDesign do not interpret colors the same way. We suggest that you characterize your monitor, launch Photoshop, and choose File, Color Settings, RGB Setup. Your profile appears next to the word Monitor at the bottom of the dialog box. Select the Display Using Monitor Compensation checkbox, and select Adobe RGB from the RGB pop-up menu. This is Adobe's RGB color space for prepress work. Save this Adobe RGB profile as an ICC (Mac) or ICM (Windows) file. On the Mac, save it to the ColorSync Profiles folder in your System Preferences folder; in Windows 95 or 98, save it to Windows\System\Color; and in Windows NT, save it to WinNT\System32\Color.

Choose File, Color Settings, CMYK Setup. Click the Built-In radio button and select your desired option from the Ink Colors pop-up menu, or define your custom settings according to the output device, printer, or press. Click the Tables button to switch to the ICC/ICM model, and save the CMYK settings as a CMYK profile in the same folder in which you saved the RGB profile.

In Illustrator, choose File, Color Settings. From the Monitor (RGB) pop-up menu, select the Adobe RGB profile that you just created in Photoshop. From the Printer (CMYK) pop-up menu, select the CMYK profile that you created. For soft-proofing, select Simulate Print Colors On Display checkbox.

In Adobe InDesign, choose File, Color Settings, Application Color Settings. Choose a monitor profile from the Monitor pop-up menu and the CMYK profile from the Separations pop-up menu. For soft-proofing, select the Simulate Separation Printer On Monitor checkbox. From the File menu, choose Document Color Settings, and Enable Color Management checkbox. Choose Use Separations Profile from the CMYK pop-up menu and the Adobe RGB profile from the RGB pop-up.

Now, create an image in Photoshop, and save it as a TIFF or JPEG image. Then, import it into InDesign, make a PDF, and print it out. Check it out. The steps are complex, but the effort is worth it.

And Now to Acrobat   Acrobat 4 has a new Color Options tab in the Job Options of Distiller to control how Distiller handles all aspects of color management and color-related issues. The most significant advancement of Acrobat 4 in terms of color is the support of embedded ICC profiles for control of color output.

The most basic definition of color management is the application of software to control the display and/or output of color on a variety of imaging devices so that the result of all device output matches the intended color representation.

It all starts in the Color Tab of the Distiller Job Options (Figure 14-1). Be aware of the ramifications of the settings made in this dialog box. You will adversely affect the final color of the printed piece if proper settings are not made here. Always check with your printer or prepress service bureau for the optimal settings for their color workflow.

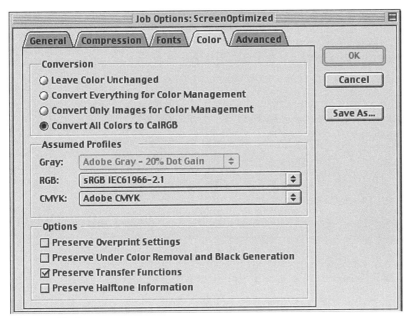

Figure 14-1
The Color tab of the Distiller Job Options.

Color Conversion   When it comes to color management, a serious amount of communication between a client and service provider must take place prior to any file submission. The settings made in the Conversion section of the Color tab should be left to Leave Color Unchanged unless such discussions have taken place. It is also important to note that in the capacity of Distiller settings, you are tagging only images and documents for color-managed profiles. No pixel altering will take place.

If there is agreement and a color-managed workflow exists, then the options to embed tagged information is easily done. Choose the method of tagging and select the source profiles of the various color spaces for the images and embed those tags into the PDF file. In a well-defined color-management system, all images will originate from a single color space. Distiller settings give the options to tag and manage multiple spaces, but only one should be selected.

Color Options

Preserve Overprint Settings   Overprinting of images—either text or graphics—sometimes are on a solid background. If you check this box, all subsequent overprint settings will be ignored. If you foresee the need to have control over the overprint settings at final output time, this selection should not be made.

Under Color Removal/Black Generation   The basis of Under Color Removal (UCR) is to replace a three-color (cyan, magenta, yellow) construction of neutral shadow areas with a dot area of 70 percent or higher. This area is replaced by a single black printer. This is very effective in the reduction of ink costs.

Black Generation is a more recent technique and, also known as Gray Component Replacement (GCR), involves replacing proportionate amounts of cyan, magenta, and yellow with black in areas of desaturated colors in a 10-percent dot or higher. Desaturated colors or grays occur when cyan, magenta, and yellow are overprinted. With this technique, a savings of ink is achieved on press.

These two techniques are used when creating a CMYK separation from an RGB scan at the scanner workstation. This information is carried along with the PostScript file in the same way that transfer functions are. You have two options for the handling of Under Color Removal/Black Generation:

- Preserve—this will keep the settings intact and available for use. The feature will not be displayed on screen; rather, it will be used only when the file is sent to a specific output device that can handle the functions.
- Remove—this will erase the function's associated information with the images. As with transfer curves, if electronic distribution is the intended use of the PDF file, the Under Color Removal/Black Generation settings should be removed. Preserve them for print applications.

Transfer Functions   The PostScript code for some images may include extra data called transfer functions (or curves). This additional data about the image is used when outputting to specific print-ers that support the use of these functions. When creating the PDF file from a PostScript stream, you have only two options for handling transfer curves in the resulting PDF file:

- Preserve—this saves the transfer function along with the PDF file. At the time you need to print, this data is called into use. Photoshop deals with these functions in the same manner.
- Remove—this will delete any associated functions in the PostScript code stream. This option may be the best choice for electronic distribution of documents because transfer functions are meant for a specific output device.

Preserve Halftone Screens   Halftone screen angles of vari-ous sizes, frequencies, and shapes are output for specific imaging reasons from different applications for different devices. It is impor-tant for print applications that this information be retained. If it is discarded in the conversion process, the default settings on the par-ticular output machine will be used. By checking this box in the setup, your desired halftone screen information will be transferred to the PDF file. Now, when you output from Exchange, your desired screen angles and shapes will be used.

Spot Colors   From PDF 1.2 (Acrobat 3) onwards, spot colors (such as Pantone) have been incorporated into PDF. It has been pos-sible only to incorporate spot color vignettes from PDF 1.3 (Acrobat 4) onwards. However, Distiller 3 recognized only spot colors defined with PostScript Level 2. A few programs (including QuarkXPress) continue to use PostScript Level 1 procedures. The resulting files have to be converted in Distiller 3 using an accompanying prologue file. This conversion is now integrated in Distiller 4, and spot colors are now always incorporated in the PDF file. However, this has a dis-advantage in that spot colors can no longer be converted into process colors in Distiller (by disabling the prologue/epilogue function). If such a conversion is required, use other tools such as PitStop, Quite A Box of Tricks, pdfOutput-Pro, and CrackerJack. Individual ele-

Spot colors can be included in a PDF 1.2 document. Define the colors as spot colors in QuarkXPress, generate composite color PostScript using the Distiller PPD (Color Model=CMYK), in Distiller's Advanced Job Options:
1. *Distill with pro-logue and epilogue.*
2. *Color = unchanged.*
3. *Turn off CMYK to RGB conversion*
4. *Distill with pro-logue.ps and epi-logue.ps in the same directory level as the Distiller.*

You can check to see if the spot colors are in the document by checking the inks list in Crackerjack or with PitStop 4 (Acrobat 4 only).

Acrobat supports three
main types of color
space:

Device-dependent
DeviceGray
DeviceRGB
DeviceCMYK

Device-independent
CalGray
CalRGB
Lab
ICCBased

Special
Separation
DeviceN
Indexed
Pattern

ments can also be converted during editing (with Adobe Illustrator). Preflight tools must be used to find out whether a file contains spot color definitions or not. PitStop allows individual spot colors to be converted into grayscale, RBG, and CMYK color models, or into a different spot color. The preflight function also permits automatic conversion of all spot colors into process colors.

Duotones   Until Acrobat 4, the use of duotone images in PDF had always been a problem. Duotones are grayscale images that are output in two colors. The second color, alongside black, is generally a spot color with a different gradation. If three or four colors are used, the images are known as tritones or quadtones. These images are generally created in Photoshop and positioned in a layout in the form of an EPS file. It was only with the introduction of the DeviceN command in PostScript 3 that multitone images could be properly defined. Before this, the required effect was achieved with the grayscale image being positioned on all color separations. The gradation was set to zero for separations that were not to contain the image.

   This PostScript solution no longer works with color PDF files. The PostScript querying functions are lost during the distilling process, resulting in the grayscale image being fully visible on all color separations. The only means of using duotone images in PDF until now has been to use preseparated PDF pages or to convert to CMYK in an image editor like Photoshop. Because Distiller 4 is equipped with a PostScript 3 interpreter, and an appropriate data object has been included in PDF 1.3, duotone images can now be transferred correctly to PDF. Duotone images are defined in PhotoShop by assigning a grayscale image a second color with a different gradation. Photoshop Version 5.02 was the first version to generate duotone images supported by Distiller.

Remote Proofing Is Closer Than You Think   Adobe PressReady is a printing and proofing tool that supports selected color inkjet printers to produce interim color proofs. That means that creative professionals can generate color comps in-house, shorten review cycles, and reduce the chance of mistakes when documents go to press. It is the least expensive approach to remote proofing.

PressReady is, in its heart, a host-based PostScript 3 RIP (raster-image processor) optimized for certain inkjet printers. It also includes a color-management system and tools that help generate and manage color-calibrated PDF files. Thus, the same PDF file that will go to the print professional for printing can be used for a remote proof. This is not a contract proofing system and does not compete at the high end, but often little things tend to change the world more than big things.

The best way to preview a color document prior to final output is to generate hard copy proofs from a device that processes jobs the same way that prepress services and printers—via PostScript RIPs. Most desktop color inkjet printers do not offer PostScript RIPs or produce color that is representative of final output. PressReady allows you to print via Adobe PostScript 3 essentially without a RIP.

Industry-standard color output is now accessible through that little inkjet printer. PressReady supports the ICC (International Color Consortium)-based Adobe color engine, also used by Adobe Photoshop 5 and Illustrator 8. This allows reliable color-composite proofs with acceptable quality on inkjet printers. ICC profiles for SWOP, U.S. Commercial, Euroscale, and Japanese Standard Proofing are supported, as are user-defined press profiles. PressReady also includes ICC profiles for Windows ICM and Apple ColorSync color-management technology and profiles that allow PressReady to emulate press standards.

You can specify the format of RGB data, in AppleRGB, sRGB, Adobe RGB (the 1998 version included with Adobe Photoshop 5.0.2), or the RGB of your monitor. Using the Adobe Gamma control panel that comes with the program, you can color-calibrate a monitor using either a "wizard"-like mode or a more advanced control panel (for the color geeks out there).

This ensures that you get the most accurate display possible. You create and print color-calibrated, print- and press-optimized PDF files, as in Acrobat Distiller 4.0. The "Create Adobe PDF" driver provides PostScript-based (not screen-based) generation of print-

How can a PDF 1.2 workflow handle composite duotone images?

There is no easy way to describe a duotone image (containing one or two spot colors) via PostScript Level 1 or 2 in a composite (nonpre-separated) way. A duotone image is a grayscale image that has two different colors and transfer functions. Why not use two copies of the same grayscale image, which get colorized with the appropriate colors, putting them on top of each other in sandwich style and letting the top one overprint the bottom one? The screen preview lets you see only the top image since PDF browsers do not support transparency yet. If you use the preview feature of Adobe InProduction, which simulates overprints, you see it correctly on screen. What tools allow this sandwich? Agfa Apogee. Creo CopyDot Toolkit with a merging feature. IMPRESSED DCSMerger, which merges any kind of Photoshop DCS 1.0 or 2.0 images to a composite EPS file, which can be distilled to a PDF 1.2 or 1.3 file. The benefit of using a two-channel DCS file instead of a real duotone is that the two image channels can hold totally independent image information for more creativity.

optimized PDF files—like creating a PDF file via Acrobat Distiller, but it takes only one step. It also comes with tools that help you manage PDF files—by combining, printing, or e-mailing them via drag-and-drop. PDF files reduce the possibility of failed print jobs caused by missing fonts, missing graphics, and generally weird application files.

Adobe "Circulate Printer Edition," which is a PDF file-management tool, allows users to scan thumbnail versions of PDF files, navigate through individual pages, and automatically launch Acrobat 4.0 or Acrobat Reader to view files at full size. Designers can e-mail PDF files to clients who can produce calibrated color prints on inkjets supported by PressReady. PressReady includes relatively simple Adobe PDF creation and management tools that help designers minimize job failures as their designs move to prepress and production. Adobe PDF combines layout, fonts, and color information into a single, compact file that streamlines workflow.

PressReady initially supports eight inkjets that offer the quality output that graphic designers may require: Canon BJC-8500; Epson Stylus Color 800, Epson Stylus Color 850, Epson Stylus Color 1520 and Epson Stylus Color 3000; and Hewlett-Packard DeskJet 895C, Hewlett-Packard DeskJet 1120C and Hewlett-Packard 2000C. Adobe expects to expand the number of supported inkjets.

By moving some level of proofing back to the originator, it reduces the volume of proofing at the prepress and printing company. PressReady is no substitute for a contract proof, but many in the industry derive income from multiple iterations of proofing that creative people go through to get what they want. Remote proofing started with Iris inkjets and Imation Rainbows in large customer sites. The Epson 3000 and 5000 brought the price down and expanded the market, but they drove users and printers crazy as we all tried to get the color to match what the press would do.

This little program builds in a lot of power for all those interim proofs. Many of the craft skills of the printing industry are being shrinkwrapped, and that will have a profound effect on the industry as we know it. PressReady is part of that trend.

Color Management

Color management works, and you can achieve color matching between the monitor and the printed page, as well as close color matching between inkjet printers, thermal wax, dye sublimation, and color laser printers as well. But note the following:

- Color management is still a complex process.
- You need rigorous process control.
- You must have accurate device profiles.
- Your workflow is everything.
- There are still issues.

Process control requires calibration. When you calibrate a device, a scanner, monitor, or printing device, you alter its behavior and force it to comply with some known standardized state. When you profile a device, you do not alter its behavior. Profiling a device simply describes or characterizes the behavior of that device. We use a standard format for these profiles, the ICC profile format. It's a very useful part of color management. All modern color-management systems are based on the idea that we can represent the behavior of the device in this ICC profile format. Color management began in 1995 when we eliminated the problem of proprietary formats.

Once upon a time, Fogra color profiles didn't work with Kodak profiles, which didn't work with Agfa, which didn't work with Candela. Once all of the major hardware and software vendors agreed that they would represent the behavior of their devices with this same profile format, it became possible to have vendor-independent color-management systems.

A publisher is using a scanner from one company, a computer from someone else, a monitor from a third company, a proofer, a press, and so on, with fifty different hardware, software, operating system components, print drivers, and so on—all of which affect color. The enabling technology that allowed us to do color management in this open-systems environment is that everyone was describing the devices in the same format, with software tools for building ICC profiles.

Workflow has been based primarily on CMYK. This made sense when everything was going to print and the scanning was being done on high-end drum scanners. We relied on that scanner to capture all the tonal information in the photograph and, on the skill of the operator who adjusts the knobs and dials to analyze the tonal content. It was the skill of the scanner operator that would map the wide range of tonal values into the much smaller range of tones available on the particular output device. The trend today is toward RGB-based workflows for a number of reasons: the World Wide Web, multimedia, what we call N-Color printing or high-fidelity color printing where we're using more than four colorants. This could be Pantone Hexachrome or it could be a low-end inkjet printer that's using cyan-magenta-yellow block plus light-cyan-light-magenta or other colorants. All of these are good reasons for using RGB-based workflows, especially with this idea of "media agility," editing an image once, correcting it once, cleaning it up once, and then moving it across all output conditions.

When the scanner operators had scanned an image for a catalog to be printed on a web press, on uncoated paper, they would have made certain decisions about remapping those tonal values. If you later decided to use that same image in a catalog being printed on a sheetfed press onto coated paper, then it would be possible to remap the CMYK from one to the other, but it would not be ideal. You'd have to either go back and rescan the image or at least have the RGB data so that you could reseparate it for those new sets of print conditions. PDF will be an increasingly important part of color-managed workflows because it is cross-media oriented.

When we build a color-management architecture, we really have three different components:

- The profiles that describe the behavior of different devices
- A color engine or color management module that will do the color conversions—from scanner RGB to monitor RGB or from monitor RGB to printer CMYK or whatever the two color spaces are
- The applications program, operating system, and RIP

Should the intelligence lie in the color management system? Do we need smart profiles and dumb CMMs, or dumb profiles and smart CMMs? We have a little bit of both, and this is an inevitable outcome of the political battles that existed in the ICC as it was coming together three or four years ago. We're moving toward a world where the profiles will essentially be just measurements and where the intelligence will reside in the color engine or CMM.

Take an image in RGB form with a certain pixel in that image with known red, green, and blue values. Apply a profile that describes the scanner that it would scan on or the monitor that it was displayed on, with a printing device, a CMYK printing device, and a profile that accurately describes the behavior of that device. Regardless of how that conversion occurs, make sure that the RGB values get converted into the same CMYK values, no matter who does the separations. The CMYK values that you get as the output of that process are critically dependent on the color engine that is doing those color space transformations.

We should ideally have a single CMM, but we need multiple CMMs. There are some distinct differences between the CMMs provided by Heidelberg, Kodak, Agfa, Imation, Adobe, and other vendors. This is a temporary period of transition while competition makes sure that we get the CMM that really is the best possible engine for conversions.

What a color-management system is all about is device independence, color that reproduces consistently and predictably from device to device, from monitor to monitor, from monitor to proof, from proof to print. A color-management system achieves device independence by integrating three fundamental processes:

- First, we calibrate our devices—we adjust them to a known and stable condition.
- Second, we create a profile of each device, each device's individual characteristics.
- Third, we use a color-management module, a CMM, to translate or navigate from one color space description to another.

Color measuring tools like colorimetry, the measuring of color, are not based on perception. Colors that measure the same may look differently, and colors that look the same may measure differently. The observer is the end user of the product that we're trying to produce. The color that we are ultimately concerned with is always going to be both by the eye and by the machine. Photoshop is a prerequisite because of its ICC-handling characteristics and its working spaces. In our opinion, you must use a monitor calibration package and it must be nonsubjective. It must be "by the numbers."

Viewing Conditions Viewing conditions require a viewing booth that's 5,000° Kelvin. It is extremely difficult to judge or accurately compare color from a reflective print or a transmissive slide or chrome to an emissive monitor unless they have the same apparent brightness. If you can't adjust your viewing booth, it's not going to be easy to make them match. Your working environment is also critical to the perceptual judgment process. The workroom and work surfaces must be neutral in color, dimly and consistently lit, and without windows. Any light that strikes the monitor will alter your perception of the black point, the contrast, and the lightness of the image.

A very useful tool is the image calculations function in Photoshop. Using this method, you can determine the precise difference between two images. Let's say you want to know what the difference is between the Apple CMM and the LinoColor CMM to make your conversion from RGB to CMYK. Take the same file, convert it with one CMM, then convert it with the other, and save the two resulting files. Then in Photoshop you can use the image calculations function and specify one saved file as source 1 and the other source 2.

You set the blending mode to difference and the result to a new document. This will subtract one document from the other, and if the two documents are exactly identical, you will get a completely black square. You should use the image histogram function to give you statistical data on what the difference is. If the difference is only slight, you might not see it lurking in that black square. Now you have some numbers. In this case, the statistical difference is zero.

Profile Tuning   The term "profile tuning" rather than "profile editing" is preferred because one of the first rules of profile tuning is that you should be making only small mistakes as you implement color management. A profile is not necessarily like an image because it represents an entire gamut of all the colors, all the tonal ranges. The relationships within that gamut must be preserved if you're going to maintain the fragile illusion of continuous tone that we're attempting to reproduce using only 256 levels of gray or color. Once you've confirmed that the edits are actually moving you in the direction that you expect them to, then you can go back and make the small and subtle moves required to tune your profiles to perfection. You are tuning a profile, not editing an image.

The edits that you make will have to work on images other than the one that you're using for your evaluation target. Always evaluate results in Photoshop, not in Profile Editor or whatever your editing software might be. The best way to evaluate your results is with the monitor profile, going back and using a reference target print and the target description file pair, such as Kodak's evaluation target and its related digital image files. The reference target print that you're trying to match is a very high quality photo print. Although you're going to be able to match it on the monitor, you're only going to be able to get close to it in a CMYK halftone.

Target description files are essentially in the Lab color space. Open the file in Photoshop without converting it, and then use the image mode profile and profile command to change the data in the file by setting the source profile as Kodak Open Interchange RGB, which is the destination profile as your working RGB space, which is where you're going to use it. This translates the file from its original color space into your working color space. If there's any clipping going to occur, it will occur in that process. Now, name and save this target description file as the TDF file for your working space. Tell Profile Editor where it resides using the Save button in the Photoshop RGB setup dialog box.

In Profile Editor you use View Image command to open this new file in Profile Editor and specify as the source the working RGB profile that you just made. What this does is to translate the file from your working RGB space into Profile Editor space. Now Profile Editor is speaking exactly the same color language as Photoshop is. Rather than starting all over, printing out thousands of patches and measuring them, you can just take that SWOP profile and tune it until it matches. You don't have to go back to square one and start all over again with a new profile if you change paper stocks or ink lots or change the cartridge in your inkjet printer. All you do is tune out the differences.

Thanks to Michael Kiernan and his superb Seybold sessions on color management for helping the industry to apply color in a meaningful way. When you attend his sessions, take good notes.

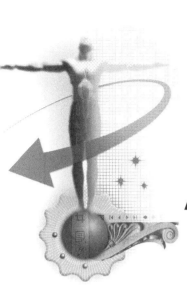

15

Advanced Options

The final folder in the Job Options dialog box is the Advanced tab folder. This folder contains the heart of the high-end print applications in Distiller and some miscellaneous options. The available options are

- Using an Epilogue and Prologue
- Allow for advanced copy page applications
- Save the PJTF inside the PDF
- Process DSC comments
- Preserve OPI comments
- Set the Default page Size
- Set the Default unit value in Distiller

Prologue and Epilogue New in Acrobat 4 is the "Distill with custom prologue.ps/epilogue.ps." This code will be sent before (prologue) and after (epilogue) the body of the PostScript code as it gets converted by Distiller. These snippets of PostScript code are user-definable and can be used for advanced workflows. In previous versions of the software, these snippets of code were used to preserve spot colors. This is now done automatically.

In Acrobat 3, the code files had to be moved to the same folder as the Distiller application file itself; or in a watched folder setup, to the same level as the In and Out folders. A failure to do this will result in Distiller not using your code.

Allow PostScript File to Override Job Options   Since Distiller is a PostScript interpreter, it can be controlled on a command line basis from special PostScript operators embedded in the incoming stream of code. These operators are called Set-DistillerParams (see Adobe Technical Note 5151 for complete details). In some cases, this setup may be unintentional, and therefore a user may opt not to let Distiller be overridden by such commands. If you want to use the commands embedded in the incoming PostScript (if present), then check the box for this to be allowed in the Distilling process.

Preserve Level 2 Copypage Semantics   Since Distiller 4 is a PostScript 3 interpreter, it must fully support all of the functionality of the language. The copypage operator has been redefined to work in some high-end personalization printing applications. If you will ultimately be outputting to a PostScript Level 2 device, choose to preserve the Level 2 copypage semantics.

Save Portable Job Ticket Inside the PDF File   This setting will allow you the opportunity to create a space for the Portable Job Ticket (PJTF) to be stored. The information about specific options on how the job is to be output are specified here. Document Specific information is stored, such as

- Finished Page Size
- Output Resolution
- Trapping Information

The use of portable job tickets is in its infancy, but they will be the major enablers of automated workflows in the future.

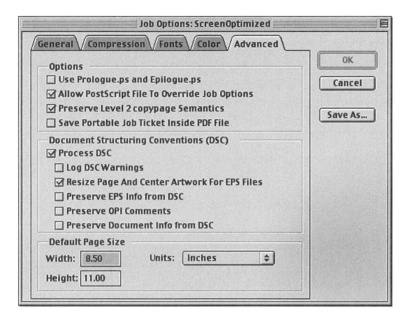

Figure 15-1
Job Options dialog box tabs.

The trap information is based on Adobe's In-RIP trapping module. Check with the service provider for applicability.

Process DSC (Document Structuring Conventions)   The PostScript language provisions have been made so that the code can include important information about the file. Items included can be:

- Origination application
- Time and date of file creation
- The user and owner of the file

In addition to these comments, the page and file structure can be based on these conventions. To maintain these useful bits of information in the PDF file, check the Process DSC (or Process DSC Comments for PC users). In addition to the major comments, the subcategories that are closely related can be individually controlled. To use any of these options, simply click on the appropriate checkbox in front of each option.

Log DSC Warnings   Choose this option to have any encountered DSC warnings that Distiller comes across to be put into a log file. This file is created once for each distilled PostScript stream. This text file can be opened in any text-editing program, such as Simple Text.

DSC-compliant PostScript is irrelevant to "cleaner" PDF files. Thus, DSC options in drivers should make no difference whatsoever in the quality of the PDF file output by the Distiller even for separated PostScript. What References is Distiller using to get the individual plates?

Distiller does look at "some" DSC comments, specifically those related to spot colors, OPI, etc. DSC comments related to fonts and the like are ignored. DSC for OPI and spot colors are NOT a function of the driver (drivers only know about CMYK or RGB, not spot color or hi-fi color or duotones, etc.).

The DSC generated by the driver is generally irrelevant to printing or distillation. Application-generated DSC for special colors, colorspaces, OPI, etc. is highly relevant but is not controlled by the driver options. "Better" PostScript may result in "cleaner" PDF. Generally though, this is a function of the application program as opposed to the driver.

For example, application program generation of PostScript 3 smooth shading operations in the PostScript data stream will obviously create much "cleaner" PDF for Acrobat 4 (PDF 1.3) than application generation of either the equivalent image or multiple polygons to simulate a gradient.

However, for common applications, a Level 3 Rip, which Distiller is, should optimize these blends. For common applications (Windows GDI or MacOS QuickDraw producing applications such as Microsoft Office, etc.), there has been generally no analog to the PostScript 3 smooth shading for purposes of generating gradients/blends. These applications generate GDI or QuickDraw with gazillions of regions of images or filled polygons to simulate gradients/blends. The only "hope" for these applications is under Windows 2000 in which there is now a GDI call for gradients that should translate to the equivalent PostScript 3 smooth shading operations via the PostScript driver (obviously, only for PostScript 3 devices, including

Distiller 4). This of course would require that applications use this new GDI operation. Microsoft Office 2000 under Windows 2000 may do this. This would dramatically increase performance and generally increase quality of Powerpoint gradient slide backgrounds for PostScript 3 printing and for PDF.

Resize Page and Center Artwork for EPS Files Select this option if you desire to have an EPS file centered on a page with a size of the originating EPS bounding box. If this is deselected, then the EPS page will be sized based on the upper left and bottom right elements on the page.

Preserve EPS Info from DSC Choose this option to have the PDF retain information gathered from any EPS information, such as the creation time and date.

Preserve OPI Comments Open Prepress Interface (OPI) is a workflow solution used in the high-end print workflow. The concept is relatively simple: A high-resolution scanned image is represented in the page layout with a low-resolution for placement only (FPO) image. This low-resolution image has a comment attached to it that calls for the high-resolution file during output. It is important to understand that in the grand scheme of things the amount of digital data is not reduced with the use of OPI; rather, you tote around less data in the page layout files and let the server handle the images in real time just prior to sending the PostScript to printout.

Benefits of an OPI based workflow are

- Less transported data
- Faster page display because of low-res images
- Less data volume transfer on networks

If you are in a prepress environment where you are involved with an OPI workflow solution, check this box to preserve OPI comments. Remember, the high-resolution files should stay in storage and are called when needed by the OPI Server.

New in Acrobat 4 is the support of both OPI version 1.3 comments and OPI version 2.0 comments. These advances are welcomed signs in today's workflow. Check with the software manufacturer of your OPI software for support of a five-file DCS version 1.0 file format in a composite workflow.

Preserve Document Info   Choose this option to retain information from the incoming PostScript stream (such as title or creation time and date), and then subsequently populate the General Document Information dialog box in Acrobat.

Default Page Size   One of the final settings made is for the Default Page Size. Most PostScript streams contain a specified page size. However, some EPS files and/or PostScript files may not have such information. When you distill a PostScript file without such information, Distiller needs some point of reference, and as a result will refer to the settings made here. When a PostScript file does have the page size specified, the incoming code overrides the default settings made here.

The Final Step   After all of your custom Job Options have been set, you can save this set of parameters to a file. A new feature in Acrobat 4 allows you to save and distribute these settings to anyone using Distiller 4.

To save the settings, click the Save As button in the Distiller Job Option panel. The file-naming dialog box will open. Name the settings file with an appropriate naming convention and save this setting file in the folder:

Adobe Acrobat 4 > Distiller > Settings

If you do not do this, then Distiller will not "see" this file and it will not be available to you in the pull-down menu of predefined Job Options. You now have a customized set of Distiller Parameters.

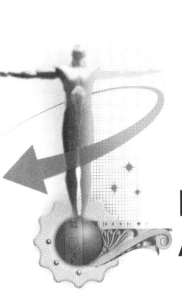

16

Interactive Acrobat

You can make Acrobat pages sing and dance. This can include a significant amount of interactivity.

Setting a Page Action   When a page is viewed on your computer screen, an action can be linked to that page. This Page Action can be set to perform a number of actions. To set a page action, go to the Document menu, then to the Page Action selection. You will be prompted by a Page Actions dialog box.

Figure 16-1
Page Actions dialog box.

Determine the point at which you want the action to occur. Your choices are when the page opens or when it closes. These page actions also work when the Full Screen Mode is being used. After you decide on the timing, select it from the left column of the dialog box. Click on the Add button on the right to open the Add an Action dialog box.

Page Actions   Each action you choose in the main pull-down menu will have a series of choices associated with it. You then make the decision about the exact settings for that particular button. The options for actions are

- Execute a menu item
- Go to a view
- Import form data
- Javascript
- Play a movie
- Open a file
- Read an article
- Reset a form
- Show/hide a field
- Play a sound
- Submit a form
- World Wide Web link

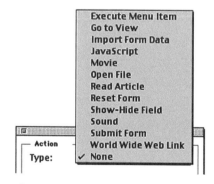

Figure 16-2
Page Actions pop-up menu.

Execute Menu Item   When you choose to Execute Menu Item, you perform any single operation you would perform with a mouse from the menu. You are even given a simulated menu bar. The limitation is that you can perform only one action from the menu.

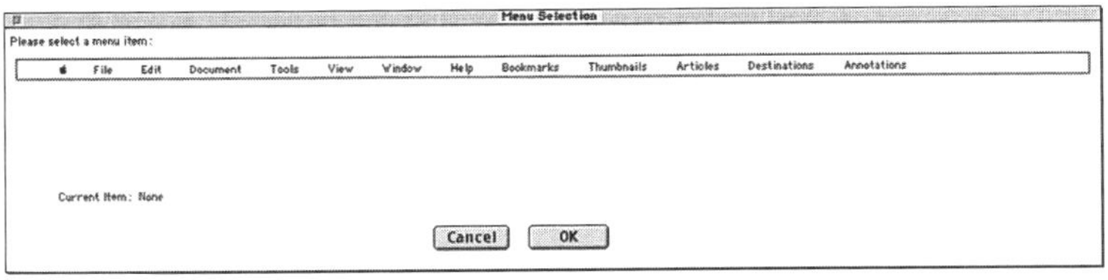

Figure 16-3
Menu selection dialog box.

Go to a View   This allows you to set the zoom factor of the page. You are limited to a fixed zoom, the fit to view, page, width, height or visible, and the inherit zoom available. You cannot change pages when setting the action (use Links for this function). This means that you are limited to altering the zoom on the page you have the icon placed on.

Form Data Import   This option is used when you have a link to a form data file. You also must have the form fields set up to take the data into the correct place. You have to match up the names of the form fields (remember that every form has a name attached to every field). When the page is set up correctly, you can import form data.

JavaScript   This will activate the specified JavaScript and execute it. It helps to know JavaScripting—use the Forms JavaScript Guide found in the Help menu.

Playing a Movie   A movie link must be present in the document on which you are working. If there is no movie, you will be prompted with a message telling you so.

Opening a File   This will open any file that you have resident on the system disk. However, if you move the linked file, Acrobat will not be able to find it. You will then be asked if you want to browse for it. This feature works best if the file that it is linked to is on the same disk; this way the files are always together. QuarkXPress and other desktop users will be familiar with the problem of linked files.

Reading an Article   An Article must be present in the file you are working on. If you have an article in the document, you can choose it.

Resetting a Form   This will clear the data from the form fields that are selected. You will be prompted to select the fields in the document. You can then target specific fields for inclusion or exclusion by clicking the Select Fields button.

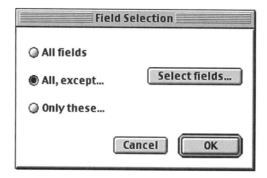

Figure 16-4
Field Selection dialog box.

Showing or Hiding a Field   You can select the actions of all fields in the document when you select this option. You are prompted by the Show/Hide Field dialog box. A possible use of this option is for pop-up help fields that increase the level of interactivity.

Figure 16-5
Show/Hide Field dialog box.

Sound   Setting the button to link to a sound will embed the sound file (either a .wav or .aif file) into the PDF file, and the sound will play when the button is activated. Make certain that the sound is an uncompressed sampled sound.

Sound files take up a good amount of disk space, so use them with a degree of care.

Submit a Form   Define the button so that it is set to Submit a Form. You must have access to a Web Browser such as Netscape or Explorer (because you can only submit forms to a URL, and not to a local disk drive). You can also set the exact fields that are sent to the Web address. This is a great aid in e-commerce since it can link buyers and sellers.

The two options that have to be set are for the format of the data submission, and the Fields to include in the selection. Always synchronize these settings with the expected data format at the receiving end to automate forms processing.

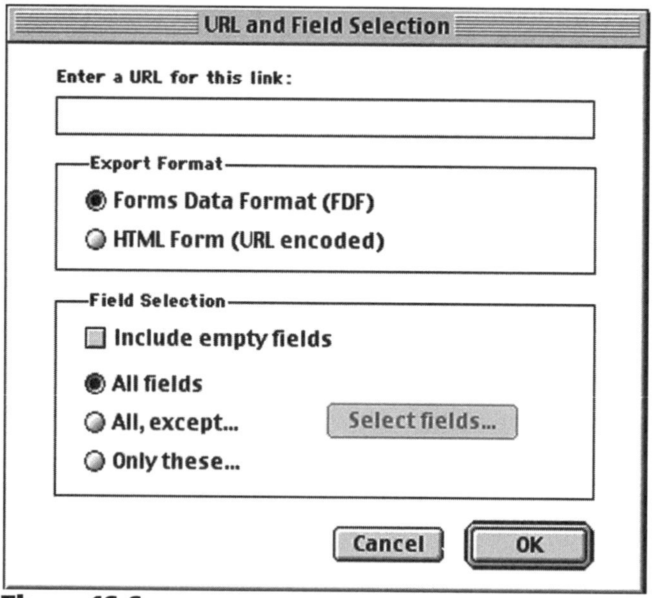

Figure 16-6
URL and Field Selection dialog box.

World Wide Web Links   World Wide Web Links, or hypertext links are also created with the forms tool. You can set the URL that you want to open when the page is opened or closed. This feature works with the Web Browser plug-in that you set in the File menu under Preferences.

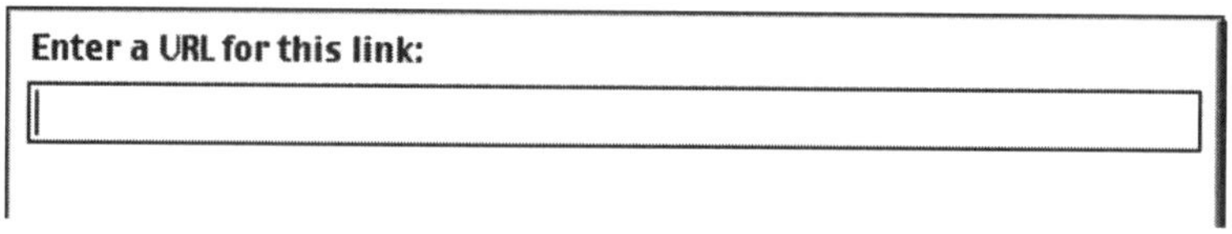

Figure 16-7
Enter a URL for this link dialog box.

Confirming the Action   After you have established the settings for the action, click OK to set that action—it will now be used on every entrance or exit to the page.

Links   Links are similar to Fields in that they can be made to perform an action when activated. Links are designed to provide the ability to cross-reference documents, WWW links, and links to other parts in the current document. Select the Link tool in the side tool bar, or use the shortcut "L." When you select this tool, your cursor will turn to a crosshair icon. Click and define the area—an image, some type, anything that can be defined. You will then be prompted by the Link Attributes dialog box to set the attributes of the linked area.

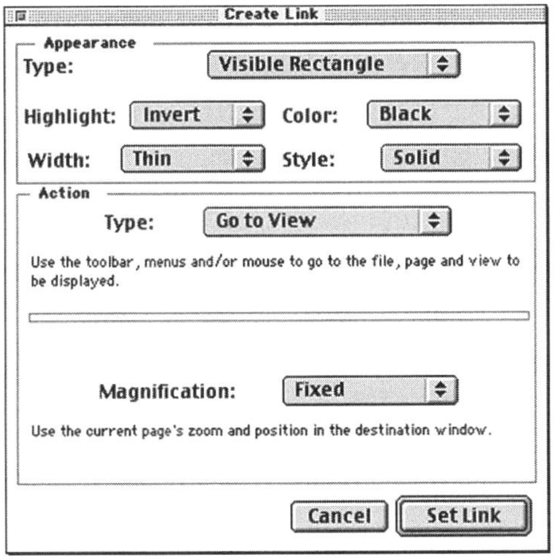

Figure 16-8
Create Link dialog box.

You can control the Appearance of the link. Set the Type (visible or hidden), the Highlight type (none, invert, outline, or inset), the border width, color, and style, and the action that the link will perform. You can make the link look like a button and act like a button.

When you drag across an area to create a link on text, hold down the Option key to highlight only the text and make it a hypertext link. Complete the process with the text selection tool and manipulate the Text Attributes to change the color of the text that is linked.

Forms and Form Fields

Forms let you create documents with the use of buttons and text fields that let you collect and send data in the form of FDF files—Forms Data Format. This FDF file can be exported and sent to a URL for on-line registration or other e-commerce purposes. Users key data into Form fields. They then send this small FDF file for data collection and recording. The approach takes some planning in the page-layout stage.

What Is a Form Field? A Form Field can be any defined field that you enter data into, or it can be an icon or radio button set for a specific task when clicked. It can also be a checkbox that will activate an action. Acrobat also allows for the integration of Java scripting to allow verification and calculation functions to be performed via PDF forms.

Basic Buttons In Acrobat 3 the basic Button was extremely basic. You now have control over every part of the Button, from the button shape to the color. The first step in creating a Button is to go to the side tool bar and choose the Forms button. When you have the Form tool selected, your cursor will turn into a crosshair. Click and drag an area where you want the Button to be.

Don't worry if you do not get the size and position exactly correct, as you will have the chance to go back later on to move and resize the area. After you drag the area, you are immediately prompted by the Field dialog box. This dialog box is the command center for all attributes of the Form.

Forms Dialog Box Once you are inside the Forms dialog box, you need to select what type of form you want to create. Depending on the type of form selected, you will have a dialog box with a series of tabs. In this case, the choice has been made to create a button.

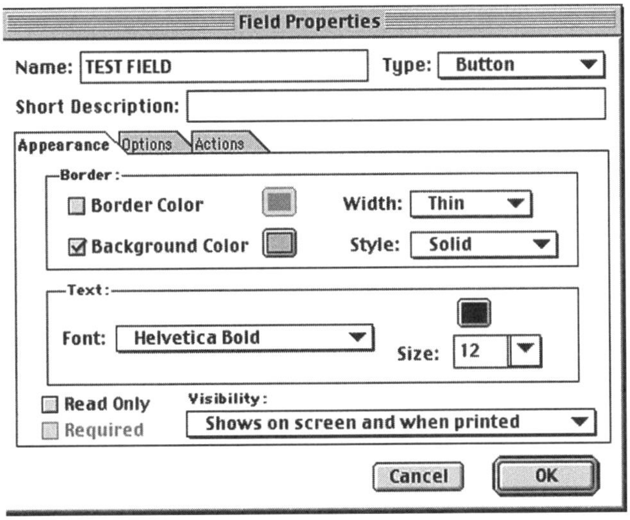

Figure 16-9
Field Properties dialog box with Appearance tab selected.

Set the name of the Field first. Do this by clicking in the Name box at the top of the forms dialog box and key in a name for the current form. Select the type of Field you want to use. To set a form Type, use the pull-down menu. Form types include:

- Button
- Check Box
- Combo Box
- List Box
- Radio Button
- Text
- Signature

Appearance of Form Fields   The Appearance tab folder sets the visual aspects of the button. This folder is common to every kind of form (button, checkbox, etc.). When making the settings for the look and feel of the form field, you can make settings for:

- Borders
- Text attributes
- Icon visibility options

In forms design it is good practice to choose one style (any one will do) and keep it consistent throughout the entire document. In the Border section of the dialog box, there is direct control over the border color and width (thin, medium, or thick), the background color, and the style (solid, dashed, beveled, inset, or underlined) of the border. The border width and style have pull-down menus. The color options are linked via the color swatch to a color picker to create a custom color.

Other settings on the appearance tab folder are for the font, text color, and point size. The text color is linked to a similiar color-swatch table as found in the border section. The font choices include only Courier, Helvetica, Symbol, Times, and Zapf Dingbats, with full control over the point size. The Auto option in the point size menu refers to the automatic sizing of the text that Acrobat will do according to the size of the button placed. The text will be dynamically part of the form if it gets resized.

Form Integration   At the bottom of this tab folder, there are a series of options associated with the form integration icon. These options are for the way in which the form is displayed and integrated into the PDF file.

> Read Only—This limits users to read only for the data in the form field.
>
> Required—This will place a condition on the form indicating that you must do something with the form field in order for the data to be submitted. You may want to set this feature on important data fields that are essential to the success of the data collection.
>
> Visibility Limiters—Viewing and printing conditions can also be controlled in the Appearance tab of the Forms dialog box. Options include
>> • Shows on screen and when printed
>> • Hidden on screen and when printed
>> • Shows on screen, hidden when printed
>> • Hidden on screen, hidden when printed

Button Options Tab   With the button choice selected as the form type, you have additional options for the layout of the button in the Layout drop-down menu:

- Text only
- Icon only
- Icon Top, Text Bottom
- Text Top, Icon Bottom
- Icon Left, Text Right
- Text Left, Icon Right
- Text over icon

Whatever you choose, you can set the appearance of the button to be different either for before or after it is clicked on. If you need to key in text, be careful that the text line does not exceed the width of the button. Acrobat will not limit the line of text according to the button size. The text gets centered on the line, and both the beginning and ends of the line get hidden if the line of text is too long.

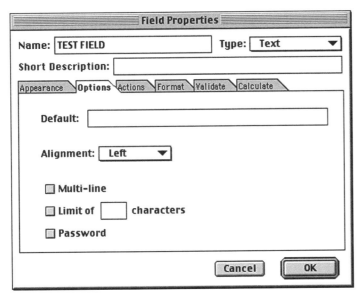

Figure 16-10
Field Properties dialog box with the Options tab selected.

Forms and Icons   Select the Icon choice in the Layout pull-down menu. Click on the Select Icon button in the Button face attributes section. You will be prompted by a dialog box allowing you to select any page of a PDF file as an icon. After you have selected a PDF file page as an icon, click OK at the bottom of the dialog box.

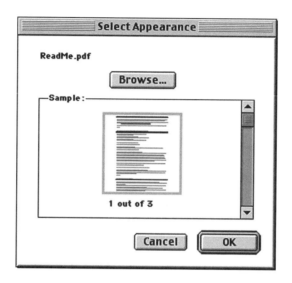

Figure 16-11
Select Appearance dialog box.

If you choose to incorporate text into the button, be sure to input the text into the Text field in the Button Face Attributes area.

More Button Options   The final button options can be set for a higher level of interactivity and greater visual attributes of the button. The first setting selects the appearance of the button when it is pushed. Settings can be made for inverting, outline, none, or pushing. Depending on the Highlight option, the Button face options will change. You can make alterations to the face of the button when it is straight up, or when it is depressed.

Advanced Button Options   When the choice to include an icon is present in the Layout pull-down menu of the Button Options, you have the ability to make additional advanced settings to the icon placement. To enter into the advanced layout options, click on the Advanced Layout button in the Options tab of the form layout.

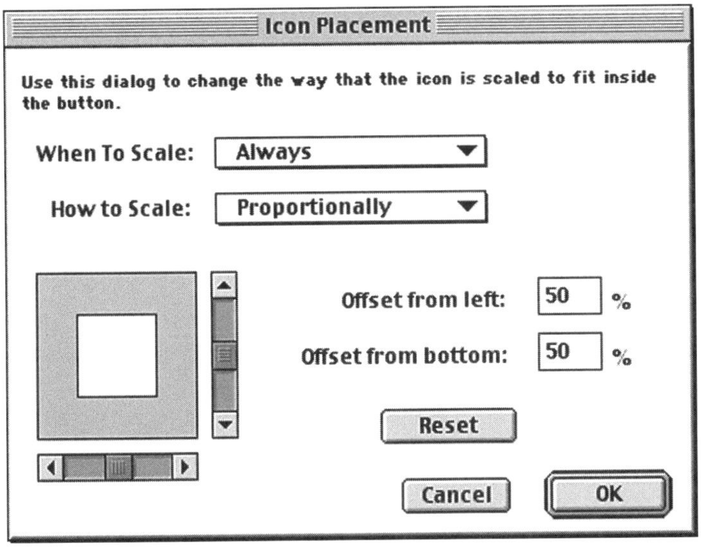

Figure 16-12
Icon Placement dialog box.

The Advanced Icon Placement dialog box is used to customize the way in which an icon is situated inside a button. This new feature in Acrobat 4 allows you to alter just about every aspect of icon spacing and scaling.

The lower left corner of the dialog box is a thumbnail view. It shows the settings dynamically when you set them. In the top two pull-down menus, you can choose when to scale an icon and what approach to use.

The main fields of the dialog box will determine the percent offset for the icon in the button display. Be careful with these settings, and always double-check your work in the PDF file.

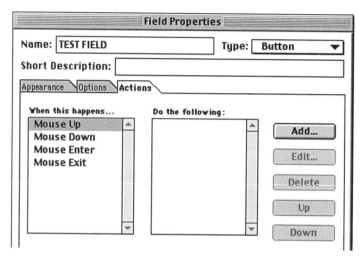

Figure 16-13
Actions defined in the Field Properties dialog box.

Setting Actions

The final tab folder in the set offers the ability to set the Actions of the button—what happens when the button is clicked, or rolled over. The first step is to determine when you want the action to occur. Your choices are

- when the mouse is clicked down
- when the mouse is unclicked up
- when the mouse rolls on a field
- when the mouse rolls off a field

Each of these actions can be configured to trigger another specific action. In order to assign an action to a mouse movement, you choose the mouse condition and then click on the Add button on the right side of the dialog box. When this is done, the Add Action dialog box will open.

Each action you choose in the main pull-down menu will have a series of choices associated with it. You then decide about the exact settings for that particular button.

The options for actions are
- Execute a menu item
- Import form data
- Play a movie
- Read an article
- Show/hide a field
- Submit a form
- Go to a view
- Javascript
- Open a file
- Reset a form
- Play a sound
- World Wide Web link

Checkboxes   Another option for a form fields configuration is the Checkbox. In many applications Checkboxes are used as indicators where valid answers include
- Multiple choices
- No choices at all

The rationale behind this is that the returned value of a checked box is based upon your exported value. If you are in a situation where you need a positive or negative (yes or no) response to a specific question, a better approach is to use a radio button.

You can make a field become a checkbox. To do this, pull down the menu in the upper right corner of the Field Properties dialog box. The Appearance and Actions tab in the dialog box is the same as those set in the Button section. The form options tab will have changed. The two major settings are for the checkbox style and for the Exported value in the FDF file.

Creating Rollovers   When creating a form field, one of the Field Properties is "Short Description:" Whatever is filled into this field is text that will appear in a box of some color whenever the user rolls over the field.

- If you use the forms tool, you can create a button field that can be programmed to perform a "rollover"—move the mouse over it and it is activated. This is appropriate if you have a limited amount of text that will fit on one line and will fill the button or you want the user to see that something is interactive. Rollovers used to require extensive coding in Lingo in the Macromedia Director.
- If you have more text that is required, then create two text fields. One will act as the trigger and while it may not be visible, its APPEARANCE is never HIDDEN. Call it "Barney."
- The other text field is HIDDEN and it contains your message. Call it "Booboo."
- Once you create "Barney" and "Booboo," you program the trigger using the ACTIONS tab—for "mouse enter" and "mouse exit" actions. On "mouse enter" select "SHOW-HIDE FIELD" as the action and specify SHOW "Booboo." Then on "mouse exit" select "SHOW-HIDE FIELD" as the action and specify HIDE "Booboo."

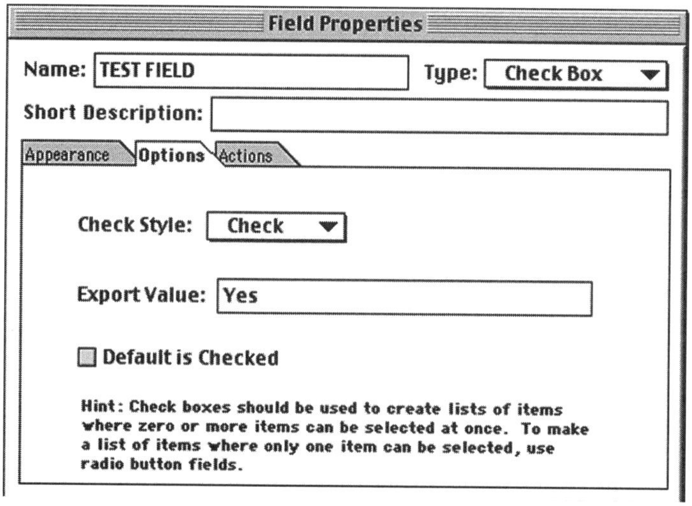

Figure 16-14
Setting up a checkbox.

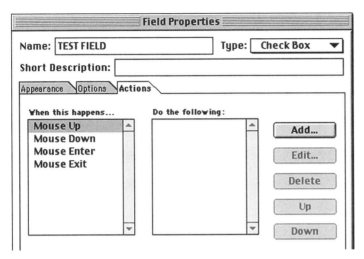

Figure 16-15
Actions for checkboxes.

Choose the checkbox you want to use to indicate a check has been made. In the Choose Style pull-down menu of the Options tab, you can choose from a check, circle, cross, diamond, square, or star.

After you choose what indicator you want to use, you have to give the activated checkbox a value to export. The value that gets exported is put into the FDF file for data collection. Finally, you need to indicate whether or not you want the defaulted value of the checkbox to be on or off.

Combo Boxes   A Combo Box is short for a combination box. This means that there is a combination of a list box and an optional user defined input area. A Combo Box will allow you to set a pull-down menu list of choices for users to choose from. Combo boxes can be created in the same manner as any other form field. Go to the Type pull-down menu, and choose Combo Box. When you set the Form Type to Combo Box, an expanded list of folder tabs appear. In this list of folders, the Appearance and Action tab folders previously discussed are the same.

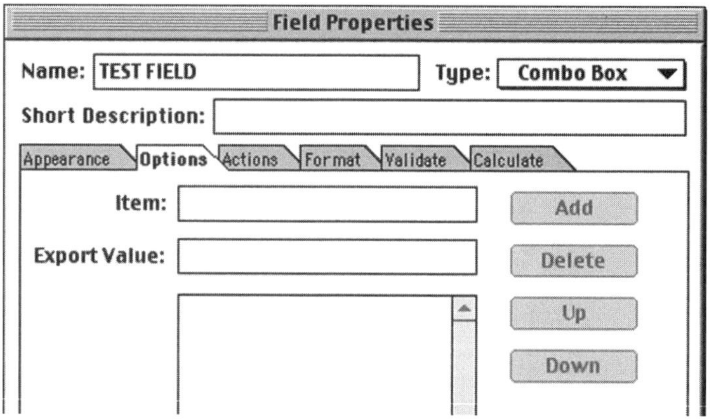

Figure 16-16
Expanded list of folder tabs for Combo Box.

Enter a Value and Export item to create a list. The Value item is viewed by the user, and the Export item is what goes into the FDF file. The user can pull down a menu of the list of items in the PDF document. You can then alphanumerically sort the items on the list by clicking on the sort items checkbox at the bottom of the dialog box. You can also make the field editable by the user. In this situation, the edited text would be placed in the FDF file.

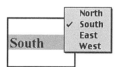

Figure 16-17
A user can pull down a menu of items.

Combo Box Format Tab   New in Acrobat 4 is the usage of formatting in Form Fields. Formatting is forcing input data to adhere to a set of predefined specifications. For example, if the author formatted a Combo Box to be set for the date, all entries to the field would be converted to the specified date format. The first option is to have no formatting applied to the Combo Box. This will work in a normal situation where there is no need to use any one of the predefined formats.

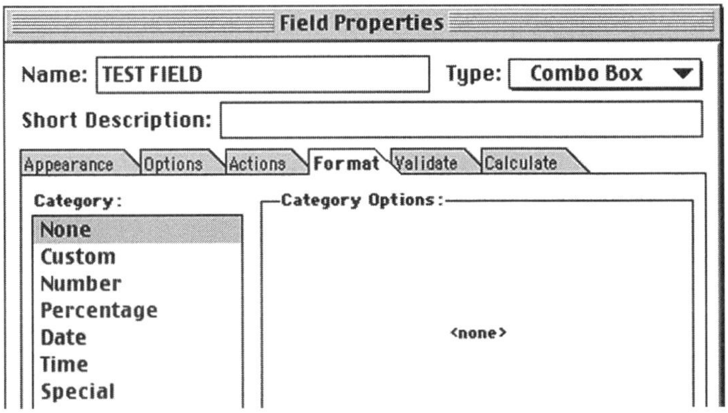

Figure 16-18
Combo box with no formatting applied.

Custom Format   The next selection in the Category list is for a Custom type. A custom format of a particular combo box uses a custom format Javascript and a Custom Keystroke validation Javascript. Each of these scripts can be defined with the Javascript editor launched when you click on the Edit button.

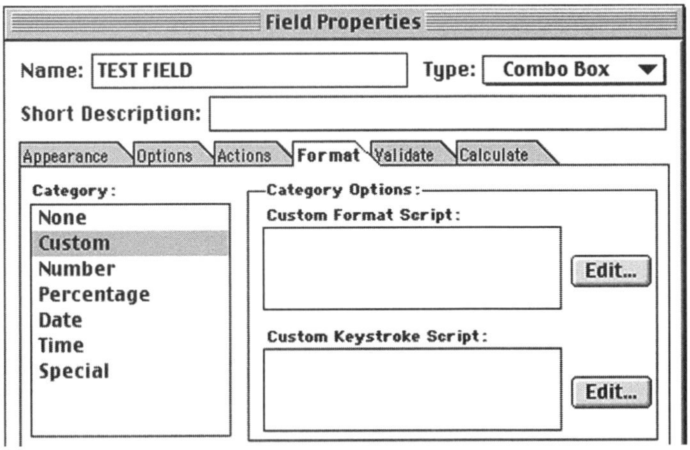

Figure 16-19
Format defined in the Field Properties dialog box.

Javascripts are generated in the integrated script editor, accessed via the Edit buttons in Category Options in the Format tab.

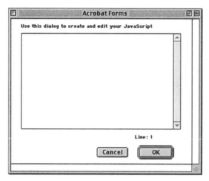

Figure 16-20
Category Options used to access Javascripts.

Numbers Formatting Number types supported are for currency, decimal style, negative numbers, and for decimal places shown.

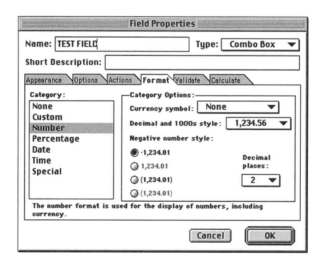

Figure 16-21
Field Properties dialog box.

Uses of PDF forms for pricing and order sheets show the need for integrated support of multiple currency types. The currency symbols listed in the pull-down menu at the top of the Numbers category are

- None
- Deutschmark
- Franc
- Krona
- Peseta
- Pound

- Yen
- Dollar
- Euro
- Guilder
- Lira

You control the decimal and thousands style in the second pull-down menu. The style of display reflects the display of affected numbers with decimal points, commas, or no space holders at all. You also have control over the number of figures displayed for the decimal placeholder. Negative numbers are formatted using the radio buttons in the Category Options. Choose the display that best represents how you want negative numbers to be viewed on screen.

Percentages Formatting   If the numbers in a particular form field are formatted as percentage values, you are telling Acrobat to perform two functions, a mathematical one and a formatting one. The mathematical function will take the input value and multiply it by 100, and it will display the result with a percent sign. For example, if you key in the value 0.5, the result will be 50%.

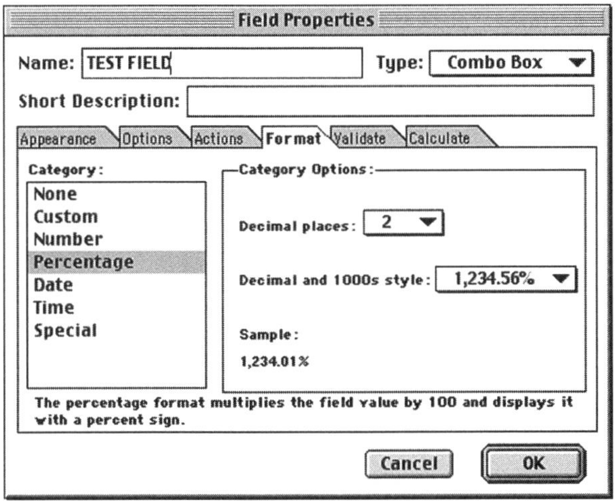

Figure 16-22
Percentage formatting defined in the Field Properties dialog box.

You can also control the number of decimal places displayed in the form in the pull-down menu at the Decimal Places choice in the Category Options window. You can make decisions to the way in which decimal and thousands are styled. This is controlled in the pull-down menu in the Decimal and Thousands style option.

Date Formatting   To format a form field to display the date, choose the Date feature in the Category list of the Format tab and choose the display style in the Date Format Category Option.

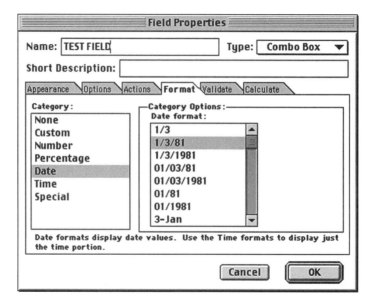

Figure 16-23
Date formatting defined in the Field Properties dialog box.

When specifying a date format, you can choose to display the date and time of day that the form was populated. If you desire just the time to populate this field, see the next section. Remember that this field can pull the time from the host system it is opened on, and all users may not have their date and time correct on their computer.

Formatting Time Form Fields   In a similar fashion that the form fields can be formatted to display the date and time values, a form field can display just the time value. Simply choose the style that you would like to use for time display, and you are off and going.

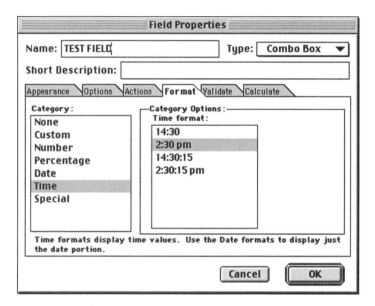

Figure 16-24
Time formatting in the Field Properties dialog box.

Specially Formatted Forms   A cool new feature in the format tab of a Form field is the addition of special categories. These selections allow for the specific needs of these special situations. Each of the categories listed require unique formatting. The list includes
>   • Zip Code {02117}
>   • Zip Code + 4 {02117-3333}
>   • Phone Number {(716) 555-1212}
>   • Social Security Number {123-00-6789}

   Each of the listed number formats can be input in contiguous number strings. The form will add the necessary ancillary characters and spaces.

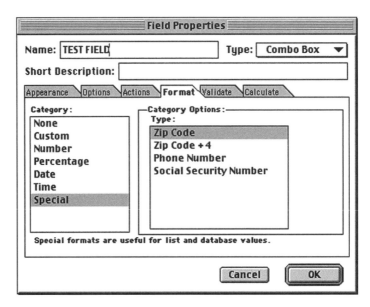

Figure 16-25
Setting categories and category options.

The software is looking for a specific type of data in this field. If it does not receive that specific type, it will prompt users and tell them that the entered data is not conforming to the chosen standard.

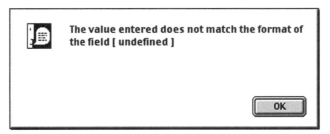

Figure 16-26
Prompt about field data.

After this dialog box is presented, the form value will be automatically reset to the the value prior to the invalid data.

Validation of Form Fields   Acrobat 4 has the ability to use a Javascript to perform a validation of input values placed in a form field. This validation will allow creators to expect certain data input from fields. The validation process is controlled by the same Java editor as in previous sections.

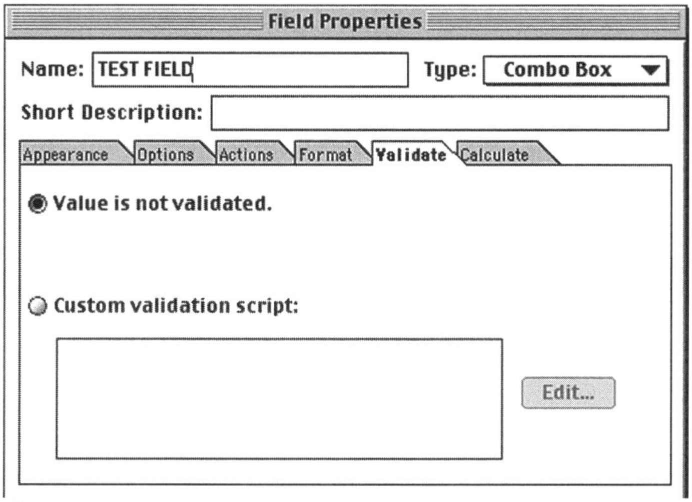

Figure 16-27
Validations checked in the Field Properties dialog box.

Calculations   An important feature of Acrobat 4 is the ability to perform calculations with Javascripts. These calculations are created in the Javascript interface window. For information on Java and Java-scripting in Acrobat 4, see the on-line help document outlining Java-scripting in an Acrobat environment. Put your mind in geek mode.

List Boxes   The next choice in the Type pull-down menu in the Field Properties dialog box is to create a List Box. A list box is very similar to a Combo Box; the only difference is the List Box enables users to scroll through the listed options.

The Options Tab   To make a list of display values, you have to enter an Item and Export a Value. Typically these two items are one and the same, but they do not have to be. The Value item is viewed by the user, and the Export item is what goes into the FDF file. The user can then view the list of items going to the PDF document.

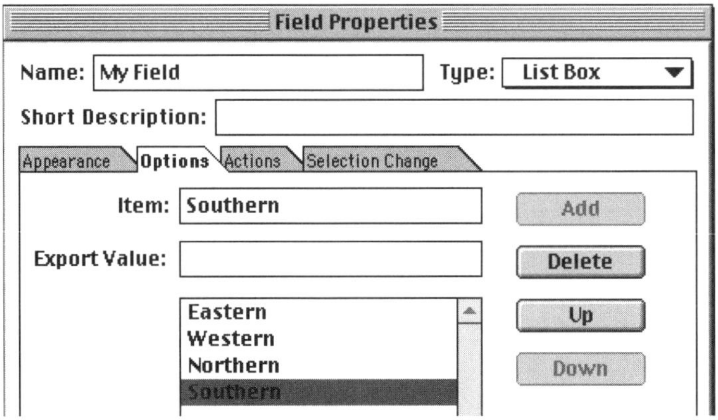

Field Properties	
Name: My Field	**Type:** List Box ▼
Short Description:	

Appearance \ Options \ Actions \ Selection Change

Item: Southern   [Add]

Export Value: [Delete]

Eastern   [Up]
Western
Northern   [Down]
Southern

Figure 16-28
List of items going into List Box.

You can alphanumerically sort the items on the list by clicking on the sort items checkbox at the bottom of the dialog box.

List Boxes in a PDF   The major difference between a List Box and a Combo Box involves viewing. The Combo Box makes a pull-down menu, and the List Box gives you a Scroll Menu.

Figure 16-29
The List Box uses a Scroll Menu.

The size of the field when you created the form field determines the amount of choices shown. Resize the box if necessary.

List Box Selection Change Tab   The List Box options is the Selection Change Tab of the List Box control dialog box. This tab section will allow users to enter a custom Javascript to be enabled when a particular choice in a list box is chosen. This script is edited in the same Java editor found in other sections of the program.

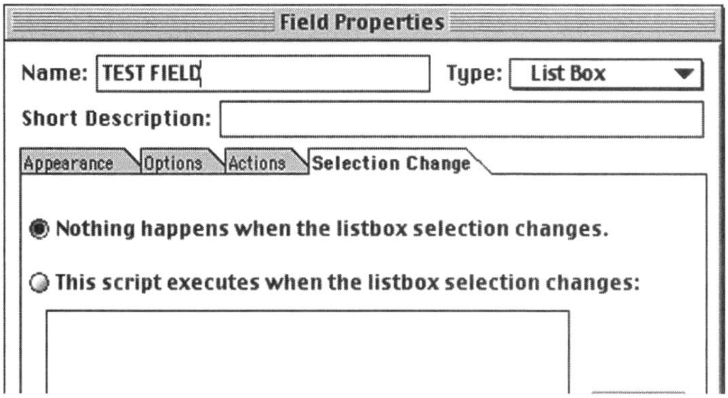

Figure 16-30
Selection Change in Field Properties dialog.

Radio Buttons To switch a field to a Radio Button, go to the Type pull-down menu in the Field Properties dialog box. After you choose Radio Button, Radio Button Options will appear. A Radio Button is similar to a Checkbox.

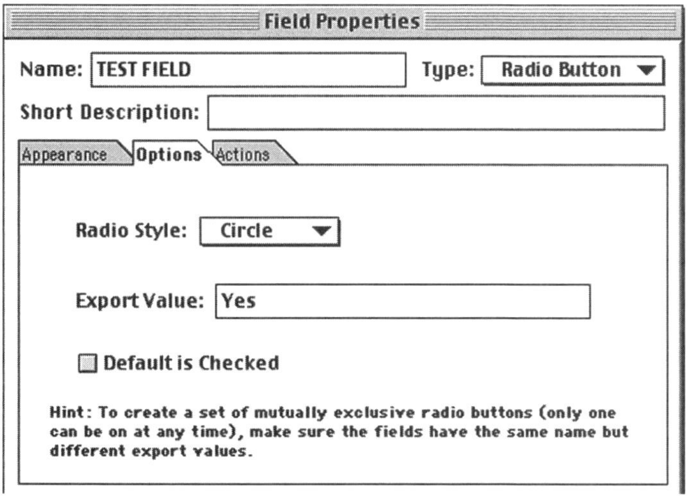

Figure 16-31
Setting up a radio button.

Radio Buttons are usually reserved for a pick-one-of-two-choices response to a selection. The On-Off nature of the Radio Button is perfect for this type of function. You can specify a Value to be exported to the FDF file when the Radio Button is selected.

Text Fields   Another option in the field type menu is for a Text Field, which is used to collect information of some kind. This means that the user will input the data. The tab folder for a Text Field is the Options tab.

In the Text Options folder tab, you have control over the default text that is in the text box. In addition, you can change the alignment of the text inside the box. Your choices are right, left, and centered. You can also set the field for a multiple-line format. This means that if the box is narrow, the lines of text will wrap in the box. If multi-line is not selected, then there will only be a single contiguous line of text, like you get in some of those e-mails.

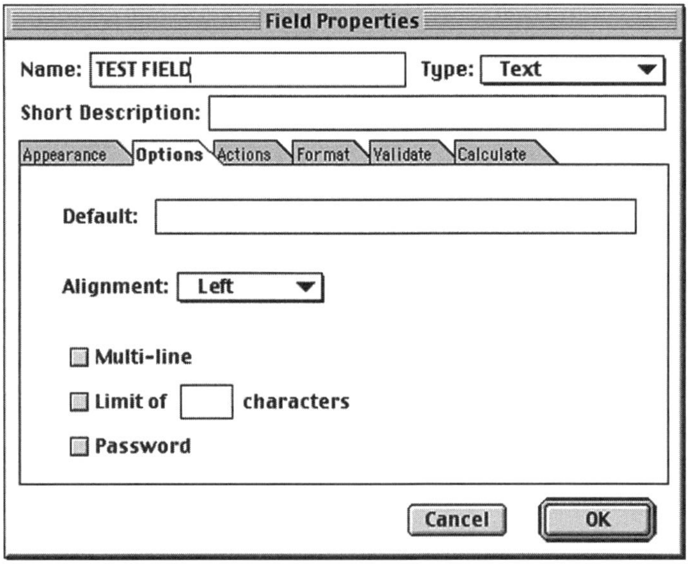

Figure 16-32
Specifying alignment of the Text Field in Field Properties dialog box.

You can also limit the number of characters that the Text Field will accept in the Limit section. Make provisions for the use of a Password protection. If you choose to protect editing of Form Fields, see the section on setting the passwords on a PDF file. The password used for the Form Fields is drawn directly from the PDF file password setting. There is no pull-down menu or list to choose from. A text field should be planned for in the page layout of a PDF file. Leave spaces for the Text Field.

Signature Form Field   Digital Signatures are becoming popular because of the Web. They assure that each user of Acrobat will have his or her own unique identifier. Using a Form Field to manage the Digital Signatures will provide a method of approving a PDF file. To set a field for a Digital Signature, pull the Field Type menu down to the Signature option. The Tab series of options is reduced to two:

* Appearance
* Actions

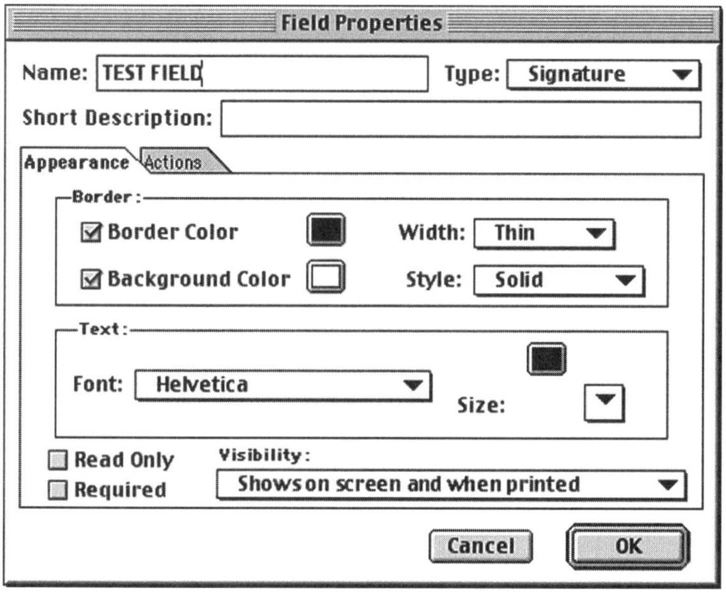

Figure 16-33
Appearance and Actions tabs for Digital Signature.

The digital signature module has been available only under Windows, but Acrobat 4.05 brings the Mac version up to the same level. It was released in Spring, 2000.

Managing Form Fields   After you have created fields, you may have to alter them. You can always go back to the Forms tool and double-click on the field you want to edit.

Forms Menu Option   The Forms option holds the key to successfully editing and arranging existing form fields. This menu is your home base for all editing needs.

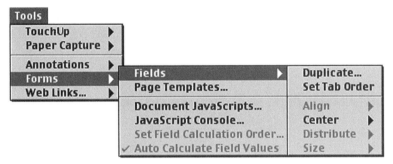

Figure 16-34
Forms sub-submenu choices.

Duplicating a Field   You have the ability to make a duplicate of any field. To do this, use the Form tool to select any existing field by single-clicking on it. Next, go to the Field's submenu of the Forms menu in the Tools menu (or while holding down the Control key, click and hold on any Field on the page to get a contextual menu).

Select the Duplicate option in the list. You will be prompted about which pages you want to make a duplicate of. Remember that this will place an exact copy of the form on every selected page. This is useful with items such as running forms buttons, tool bars, and buttons common to all pages.

Copying Form Fields   Form Fields can also be copied. The usual copy-and-paste commands work very well. Hold down the Option key when selecting a form field. You can drag the Field anywhere in the document for placement. If while you are moving the Field, you hold down the Shift key you will restrain the placement to be exactly along either the x- or y-axis of the original.

Setting the Tab Order   If your page has a large number of Fields, the Tab key will allow the user to skip ahead (or Shift + Tab to go in the reverse tab order). As a default, the Tab Order is defined in the order in which the Fields were created. If you want to change this, use the Fields selection in the Forms menu to set the Tab Order. You must be using the Form tool to access the mode to set the tab order. The outlines of the Fields turn to black, and there is a number in the upper left corner of each form on the page, the number in the sequence. The cursor will have a pound sign attached to it to indicate that you are setting the Tab Order (Why a pound sign—who knows?). To reorder the sequence, click once on the field that you want to be first. Go through the page setting in the order of the way you want it.

Setting Templates   Creating a standard template series for use in PDF Forms applications is a new feature in Acrobat 4. This feature allows users to become consistent in the application of Forms to multipage documents. To define a page of Forms as a Template, first you must create all of the forms on the page in the location you want. After that is complete, simply go to the Forms submenu of the Tools menu and choose the Page Template option.

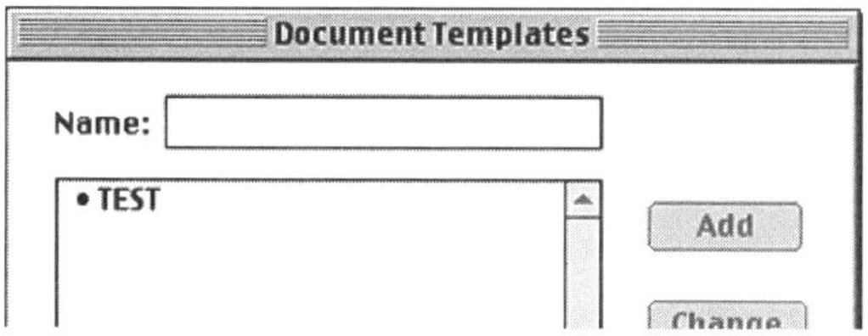

Figure 16-35
Document Template dialog box.

If you have any predefined templates in the list, they will appear in the main dialog box. To add the current page as a Template to the list, simply give the new Template a name in the Name field. Then, click the Add button. You will be asked if you really want to specify the current page as a new Template.

Figure 16-36
Template warning box.

Changing, Deleting, and Applying Templates   If you need to make an alteration to an existing template, highlight it in the Document Template list. Then, click the Change button. You will be prompted and asked if you really want to change the current template. If you really, really want to, do it.

Figure 16-37
Managing templates.

To apply a Template to the current page in the PDF, highlight your choice in the main Document Template list, and click the Go To button. This will apply the template to the current page. To delete a Template from the Document Template list, highlight it, and click the Delete button.

Alignment and the Forms Grid   The alignment functions found in the Fields submenu of the Forms menu in the Tools menu will allow you to better align multiple forms in a document. To use the menu selections for Alignment, Centering, Distribution, and Sizing, you must have the Forms tool active.

By clicking once on a form field *(shift-click for multiple-field selection)*, you can use any one of the options to help with the alignment of the selected forms. Experiment to get the look you desire. An aid to forms layout is the use of a grid. In order to toggle the grid on and off, go to the View Menu. At the bottom of the menu will be the settings to turn the Grid on or off, as well as settings to enable a "snap to" grid function.

Setting Web Links   You set document Web links in the Tools menu item under the Web link option. A Web link will allow you to specify links to World Wide Web (URLs) sites from within the PDF file. These settings work with Web link preferences.

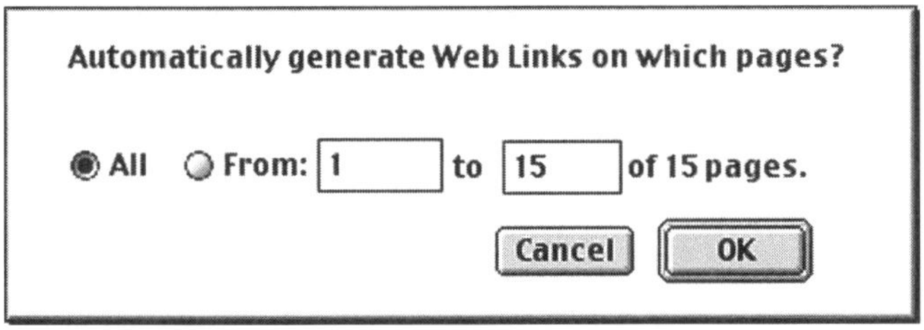

Figure 16-38
Setting a Web link.

Movie Tool   Acrobat allows you to link movies to the PDF file. You do not embed the movie file in the PDF file—you make a link to it. You will need to have a path to the file, as well as the movie file to play the movie. To make a link to a movie, select the movie tool from the Side menu, or use the shortcut key "M." When you do this, your cursor will turn to a crosshair target. Click and drag the area where you want the movie to be located.

After you do this, you will be prompted to look for a movie on your system. Browse to find it and click on the Open button.

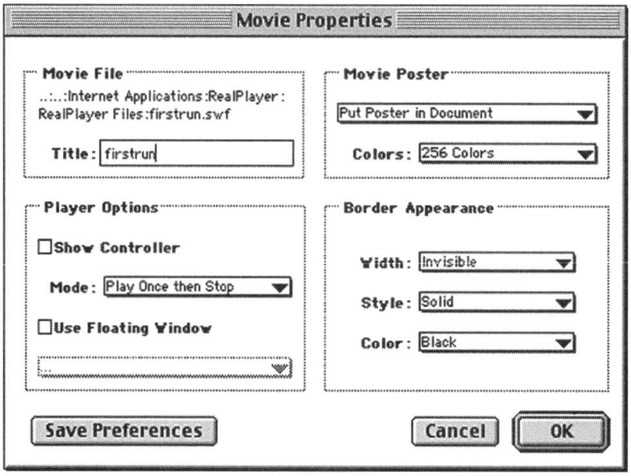

Figure 16-39
Movie Properties dialog box.

The Movie Properties dialog box controls the display of a movie. You can set both the physical appearance of the movie and the way that it is played. You can alter the settings at any time by going back to the movie tool and double-clicking the movie placeholder (or the Control key drop-menu technique). You can set the preferences for the way in which the user sees the movie by establishing a floating window. This will launch a window the size that you specify. Giving the movie a border and placing an image of the movie will define its place on the page. You may want to include the movie control panel for the user to use to start and stop the movie.

Actionable Items   There are three tools in Acrobat for creating actionable items. You can use the Link tool to create hyperlinks, the Form tool to create field buttons, or bookmarks. All of these allow you to apply any one of a variety of Actions to the link, field, or text (Go to View, Import Form Data, JavaScript, Movie, Open File, WWW Link, etc.). Novices usually start off experimenting with the

Link tool, but there is much more that you can do with a field button than there is with a "link" button. For instance:

- A Field button can be copied and then pasted—either within a document or onto other documents
- You can duplicate Field buttons throughout a document by using the Tools/Forms/Fields/Duplicate menu item.
- Multiple Field buttons can be selected for copying, aligning, space distributing, or resizing.
- Field buttons can be named. This means that if you change the characteristic of the button (appearance or action), the changes will be applied throughout the document to any field button with the same name.
- Field buttons can be programmed with multiple actions—including rollovers, hidden/show fields, mouse enter/exit triggering, etc.
- Field buttons can contain icons (other PDF files) or text—ideal for the creation of navigation controls.

PDF for Presentations

Powerpoint has a Save to HTML file menu item that creates a frameset HTML series of pages and .gifs (or .jpg, if specified) with its own navigation controls (Javascript) and bookmarks. The full composite size of the resulting Web site of HTML pages tends to be very small. No fonts are embedded. The same PowerPoint presentation can be saved to PostScript (20 Mb, for example) and then distilled to a font-embedded, vector PDF. The resulting optimized file is only 80 K, for example.

Navigation controls are a part of the Reader interface. Bookmarks and hyperlinks can be added. The big difference is the quality of the presentation images—bitmap images are much bigger and lower resolution than their vector counterparts, which accounts for the size disparity of the two solutions. The JavaScript navigation controls are cleverly implemented but have at least one drawback—they do not work within framesets.

Advantages of PDF for Presentations

- They are totally cross-platform and cross-version.
- PDFs can be uploaded to and played from the Web.
- It is so much better than HTML versions of presentations and just as universal (see comparison above).
- You can create your pages in anything—any size or shape—and tack them together once they are converted to PDF. You can convert existing digital artwork without having to repurpose your old stuff.
- PDFs are smaller, more scalable than Powerpoint, and have better kerning.

17

Watched Folders

You can set up Distiller to watch certain folders on a network server by going under the Distiller Menu and selecting Watched Folders. When Distiller watches a folder, it periodically checks the folder for PostScript files. When a PostScript file is saved or copied into a watched folder, Distiller automatically processes the file and moves it to an Out folder. Sharing Distiller on a network conserves resources, such as memory and disk space, and can automate Job Options settings. Acrobat Distiller can watch up to one hundred folders. You do not create a new folder to watch; you must select an existing folder or create a new folder first.

   You can specify different options for each folder using the Edit Options tool. To add watched folders:

   1. Choose Distiller and Watched Folders; then Add Folder.

   2. Select the folder location for the In and Out folders.

Distiller creates an In folder and an Out folder in the selected folder. Distiller does not create new In and Out folders if folders with those names already exist.

A PDF is a device-inde-pendent file format with good possibilities for compression. In addition, it does not "lose information" and retains the design rich-ness. Depending on the complexity, you will most likely fit a menu in a compressed PDF file on a floppy disk. (Remember floppies).

A workflow feature in Acrobat 4 is watched folders. By setting up a series of watched folders, you can efficiently convert PostScript streams to PDF files with your desired options. Distiller must be open for the folders to be watched. To access the Watched Folders, go to the Settings Menu, then to the Watched Folders option.

The first step is to define the folders you want watched. You can choose any folder that Distiller can "see" through the selection menu (you have to set up an empty folder for this to work). Make sure that once you name a folder, you do not change it after you choose it to be a Watched Folder. If you change a name, Distiller will not know and your folder will be unwatched.

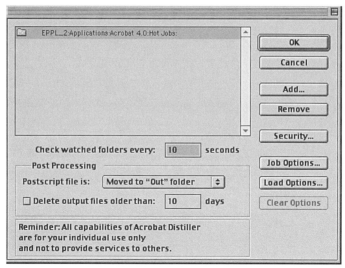

Figure 17-1
Acrobat Watched Folder dialog box.

After you have created a folder, you select it by clicking the Add button. A standard file chooser dialog box will open. Find the select-ed folder and click OK. Your folder will appear in the Watched Folder List. Distiller will add two subfolders to the chosen folder: one named "In," and the other "Out." When you drop PostScript files for conversion, drop them into the "In" folder. Distiller will convert the PostScript and deposit it (that's right—the original file is moved) and the PDF file to the "Out" folder.

Setting the Watched Folder Options   Once you have the folder on this list, you have to set the options for time, disposition of the PostScript after conversion, and disposition PostScript files left in the out folder.

After you have made the basic choices and the folder name is still highlighted in the Watched Folder List, click on Job Options. When you click on this button you come to a custom Job Options dialog box. This set of Job Options applies only to files converted via this folder. If you do not make alterations to the Job Options at this point, the default Distiller settings will be used. After you make any alterations to the Job Options, the folder in the Watched Folder list will have a small icon next to it. This indicates a change from the default settings.

Another option is to load a predefined set of Job Options. To do this, click the Load Options button on the Watched Folder dialog box. You will open a dialog box that contains all of Distiller's known parameters (either Adobe supplied or user defined). Select one of these parameter settings, and click Open.

To clear any Job Options associated with a Watched Folder, highlight the particular Watched Folder in the list, and then click the Clear Options button. You can confirm the deletion of any associated Job Options by the elimination of the small icon next to the folder name in the list.

This feature is best used on a network. With many users in an organization converting PostScript files to PDF, there is room for variation. This is because users might fail to select the right job option, or choose one that is incorrect. If you set up a series of Watched Folders, one for each user, each with the required settings for different end uses, you will assure consistent results. You can set up one folder for high-end printing, one for Web distribution, one for contract proofing, and another for soft proofing. Each folder converts PostScript into PDF using Job Options established for that folder.

After you have specified a Watched Folder, you will notice a preferences file in the Watched Folder. Double-click on it. On the PC, the Job Options will open in a floating window for you to edit.

Any PDF file that is opened and saved by Acrobat 4 will have a version of 1.3. This does not mean the file is automatically incompatible with Acrobat 3. A file created by Distiller 4 with compatibility for Acrobat 3 or for 4 both have Distiller 4 as the creator.

1. Which version of Acrobat was actually used to distill/save the file (2.1, 3.0, 4, etc.) ?

2. Which version of Acrobat is the PDF file compatible with, (a 4 file saved with 3 compatibility or with just 4 compatibility)?

Also, is the second question linked to PDF version (1.2 vs. 1.3)? Is an Acrobat 4.0 file saved with 3 compatibility a PDF 1.2 file or a PDF 1.3 file?

First, PDF 1.0 and 1.1 documents (Acrobat 1.0 and 2.1) should not be considered to be prepress documents. If they behave in your prepress environment, consider yourself lucky. Next, Distiller 3.01 (PDF 1.2) behaved consistently. You know what you were getting. Most people would say that its biggest problem area was fonts. The bulk of prepress functionality was added in PDF 1.2 and Acrobat 3. Many production applications

Opening the PostScript File

If you want to manually distill a file, and Job Options are set with all specifications in order, the next step is to open the PostScript file for processing. As you open the file, you will be prompted by a dialog box for the destination and name of the file. The default name of the PDF is the name of the PostScript file. Click OK. As Distiller is processing the file, you will see a status bar running indicating how far along you are in the process. If you run into any errors, they will be reported to you in the Distiller status box, and also in a log file placed with the final PDF file.

Stored Distiller Job Options

Acrobat Distiller 4 lets you predefine and store Distiller Job Options. These preferences files are saved to a file located in a folder named Settings located in the Distiller folder. Adobe has predefined a set of three Job Options. These settings define every parameter that can be set in Distiller's Job Options for Compression, Fonts, Color Management, and other options.

Screen Optimized

The goal of these settings is to create a file that is as small as possible for use in digital transmission on the Web or disk distribution. Image compression is set to very high levels, and all images are converted to a CalRGB color space. These are the smallest PDF files.

Print Optimized

These settings are used for PDF files that are intended to be output on digital printers, desktop printers, or color copiers. The goal of these options is to create a relatively small file size but still maintain image fidelity for printing with toner or inkjet.

Press Optimized

The goal of these settings is to maintain the highest image quality for output, suitable for output by a commercial printer on a high-quality press. The settings preserve the maximum amount of information about the originating document. These are naturally the largest PDF files.

Suggested settings for digital and high-end distribution:

General Settings Tab—Digital Distribution

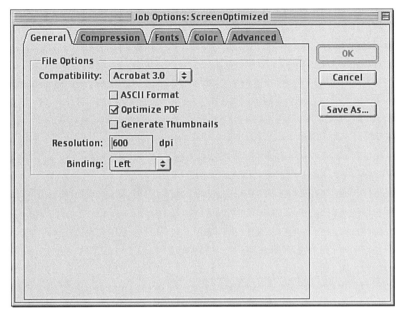

Figure 17-2
General Settings tab.

- Choose Acrobat 4 compatibility.
- Deselect the ASCII Format checkbox.
- Select the Optimize box.
- Deselect the Create Thumbnails checkbox.
- Set the default resolution to 600 dpi.
- Choose Left Binding.

were and continue to be served by this version. One must remeber that Distiller 3 is essentially a PostScript Level 2 interpreter. If you are dealing in PostScript 3 constructs, such as smooth shading, spot color blends, or duo-tones (DeviceN), then you really have no choice but to work with Distiller 4.

Distiller 4 supported new capabilities, but it did not support the pre-press application as expected. It still pro-duced real PDF docu-ments. Some of the issues can be corrected with PitStop. If you are looking to use ICC pro-files, then you definitely want Distiller 4.05 doc-uments. If you are try-ing to avoid ICC pro-files, then you probably want PDF 1.2 docu-ments, unless you are looking for PostScript 3-like features. Then you want PDF 1.3. There are two version num-bers to be aware of: the PDF specification ver-sion and the Acrobat Software version.

PDF version 1 was introduced with Acrobat 1.

PDF version 1.1 was introduced with Acrobat 2.

PDF version 1.2 was introduced with Acrobat 3.

PDF version 1.3 was introduced with Acrobat 4.

All Acrobat software can handle PDF versions at the same and at the lower version number than that which came introduced with them. Acrobat viewer software (formerly known as Exchange) sets the version number to its own version number when it writes a document back, even if the original document was on a lower version number and has not been changed. Acrobat viewer software can read documents with a higher version number correctly if the document does not use any new features of the higher version number. When it encounters an unknown feature, it either ignores that particular object, or it creates an error condition. This is per se not predictable; it all depends on the documents.

Compression Settings Tab—Digital Distribution

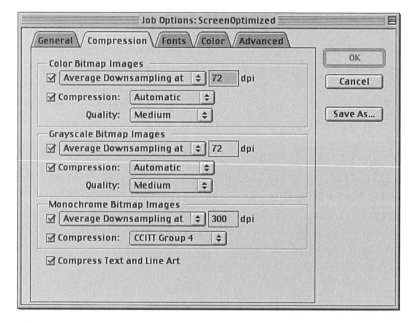

Figure 17-3
Compression Settings tab.

- Select Average downsample color and gray images to 72 dpi.
- Set color and gray images to Automatic Medium JPEG.
- Use Average Downsampling to 300 dpi on monochrome images.
- Set monochrome images to be compressed using the CCITT Group 4 compression.
- Select to have the text and line art compressed.

Fonts Settings Tab—Digital Distribution

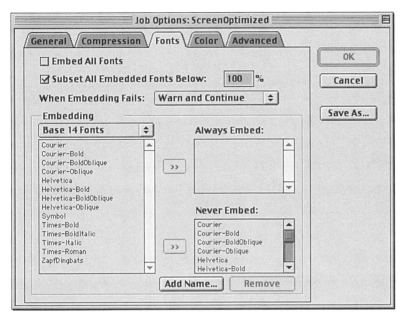

Figure 17-4
Font Settings tab..

- Choose to Subset all Fonts at 100 percent.
- Select to have Distiller warn you when a font is missing, but to continue after that point. Even the 14 standard fonts will be subset.

Generally, PDF files and the Acrobat viewers are safe to use and are not prone to attacks by viruses. Unfortunately, there are several ways in which a malicious individual might create a PDF file that could cause mischief on the recipient's machine. Most of these cases fall into two classes: those using the Open File action and those using File Attachments.

Open File actions allow the author of the document to "launch" or invoke an external application on the user's machine. An Open File action can be attached to a bookmark, a link, a form field, or even to Page Open or Page Close events. This feature was designed for CD-ROM publishers who want to include links to simulations and other example programs. Unscrupulous authors could create an Open File action that accesses a malicious executable that erases the users hard drive, sends system information to a Web site, or any other detrimental action. It is necessary, however, that the end user's machine already have such a program installed and that it be in a known location. Most virus protection software will prevent rogue executables from installing on a user's system. It is

Color Settings Tab—Digital Distribution

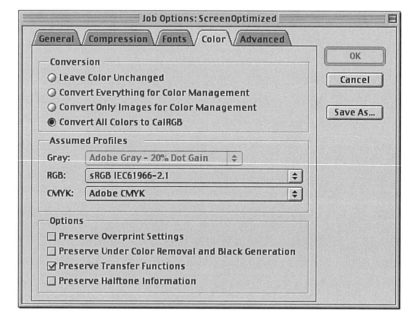

Figure 17-5
Color Settings tab.

- Select Convert all color images to the CalRGB color space.
- Set the Assumed Profiles to:
  RGB: sRGB IEC61966-2.1
  CMYK: Adobe CMYK
- Deselect the option to preserve overprint information.
- Deselect the option to preserve Under Color Removal and Black Generation.
- Select the option to preserve Transfer functions.
- Deselect the option to preserve halftone information.

Advanced Settings Tab—Digital Distribution

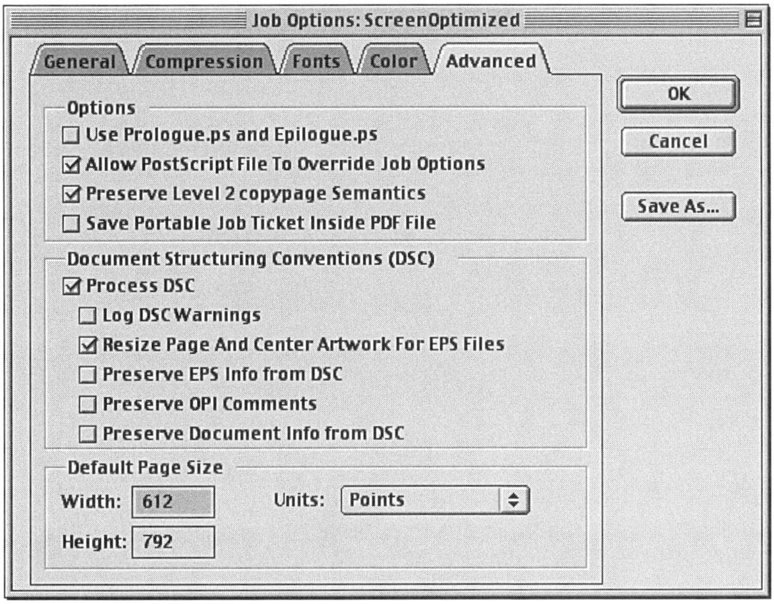

```
Job Options: ScreenOptimized

General  Compression  Fonts  Color  Advanced

┌─Options──────────────────────────────────┐         ┌──────────┐
│ ☐ Use Prologue.ps and Epilogue.ps         │         │    OK    │
│ ☑ Allow PostScript File To Override Job Options │     └──────────┘
│ ☑ Preserve Level 2 copypage Semantics     │         ┌──────────┐
│ ☐ Save Portable Job Ticket Inside PDF File│         │  Cancel  │
├─Document Structuring Conventions (DSC)────┤         └──────────┘
│ ☑ Process DSC                             │         ┌──────────┐
│   ☐ Log DSC Warnings                      │         │ Save As… │
│   ☑ Resize Page And Center Artwork For EPS Files │  └──────────┘
│   ☐ Preserve EPS Info from DSC            │
│   ☐ Preserve OPI Comments                 │
│   ☐ Preserve Document Info from DSC       │
├─Default Page Size─────────────────────────┤
│ Width:  612      Units:  Points  ▲▼       │
│ Height: 792                               │
└───────────────────────────────────────────┘
```

Figure 17-6
Advanced Settings tab.

- Deselect the option to use Prologue and Epilogue functions.
- Select the option to allow the incoming PostScript to override any Distiller settings.
- Select to preserve Level 2 copypage semantics.
- Deselect the option to save the PJTF inside the PDF
- Select the process DSC option.
- Select to process resize and center all standalone EPS's.
- Use the 612 x 792 default page size.

You now have a PDF suitable for efficient electronic distribution.

unlikely that this will occur if a user's system is properly protected with a virus scanner.

There are, of course, safeguards built into Acrobat. Before opening an external file, Acrobat will display a warning dialog. If the user clicks "Yes" then the launch will occur. If the user clicks "No" the application will not be run. If the user clicks "All" then the launch will occur and the warning dialog will never appear again for this application session.

File attachments are actually files embedded within the PDF file, similar to attachments in email messages. File attachments are normally used during the authoring or mark-up and review process to attach auxiliary files to a PDF and package them up with the PDF for easy distribution. Just like e-mail, rogue executables can be file attachments, which can make them potentially more dangerous than Open File actions. Again, there are safeguards; before extracting and launching a file attachment, Acrobat displays the dialog shown below. If the user selects "OK" the application or file will open. If the user checks the box to "Do not ask this question again," the warning will not be dis-

played until the preference to Allow Open File Links is reset ("Are you sure you want to launch the attached file?").

The user can also prevent both launch actions and file attachments from working by unchecking the Allow Open File Links preference in the general preferences dialog.

The Acrobat installer, on the Windows platform, is configurable. A system administrator or IS manager can customize the installer to have the Allow File Open Links preference turned off by default by modifying the ABCPY.ini file in the installer package.

Group1RegEntry1Parentkey=HKEY_CURRENT_USER

Group1RegEntry1Key=SOFTWARE\Adobe\AdobeAcrobat\4.0\AdobeViewer

Group1RegEntry1Value Name=AllowOpenFile Group1RegEntry1Value Type=NUMBER

Group1RegEntry1Value Data=0

This still allows the naïve user to go into the General Preferences and remove the protection put in place by checking the Allow File Open Links checkbox. For even greater security

Suggested Settings For High End Print Printing

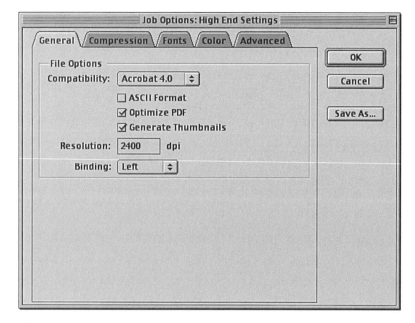

Figure 17-7
General Settings tab.

- Select Acrobat 4 compatibility.
- Deselect the ASCII Format checkbox.
- Select the Optimize box.
- Create Thumbnails.
- Set the default resolution to 2,400 dpi.
- Choose Left Binding.

Compression Settings Tab—High End

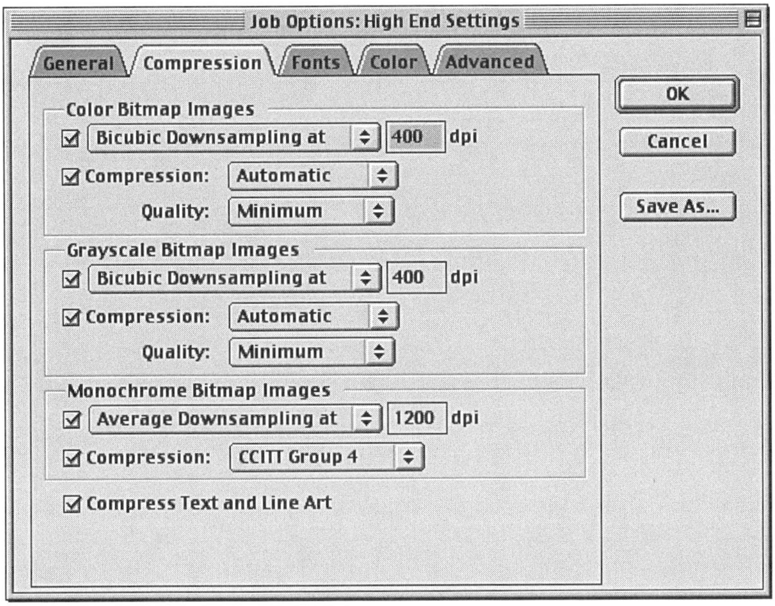

Figure 17-8
Compression Settings tab.

- Select Bicubic downsample color and gray images to 400 dpi.
- Set color and gray images to Automatic Minimum quality.
- Use Bicubic Downsampling to 1,200 dpi on monochrome images.
- Set monochrome images to be compressed using the CCITT Group 4 compression.
- Select to have the text and line art compressed.

*there is a hidden prefer-
ence that makes this
even more difficult to
turn off:*

*Group1RegEntry1
ParentKey=HKEY_CU
RRENT_USER*

*Group1RegEntry1Key=
SOFTWARE\Adobe\
AdobeAcrobat\4.0\Ado
beViewer*

*Group1RegEntry1Value
Name=SecureOpenFile*

*Group1RegEntry1Value
Type=NUMBER*

*Group1RegEntry1Value
Data=1*

*This registry entry
overrides the user pref-
erence. Even if the
Allow Open File Links
is checked, the user can-
not launch external
applications or open file
attachments. However, a
savvy user that has per-
mission to edit the reg-
istry can remove the
registry entry. Acrobat
displays a warning dia-
log to the user whenever
an application is about
to be launched. A user
could, either through
confusion, impatience,
or inattention, dismiss
this dialog and execute
the offending applica-
tion. A system adminis-
trator can preconfigure
the installer to make the
launch action or file
attachment annotation
effectively harmless.*

Fonts Settings Tab—High End

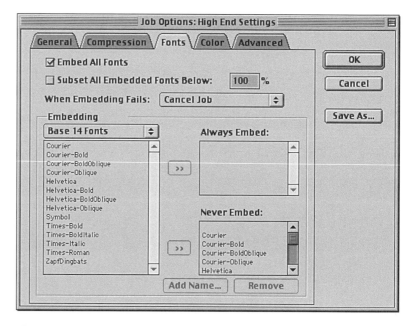

Figure 17-9
Fonts tab.

- Choose to Embed all Fonts.
- Select to have Distiller Cancel the PDF file conversion when a font is missing.

Color Settings Tab—High End

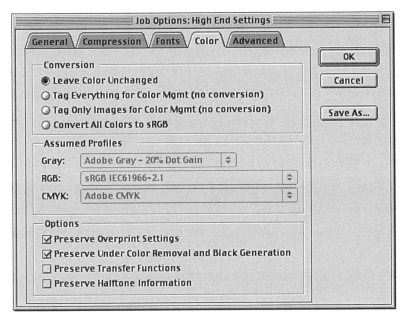

Figure 17-10
Color Settings tab.

- Leave all color unchanged.
- Select the option to preserve overprint information.
- Select the option to preserve Under color removal and Black Generation.
- Select the option to preserve Transfer functions.
- Deselect the option to preserve halftone information.

Advanced Settings Tab—High End

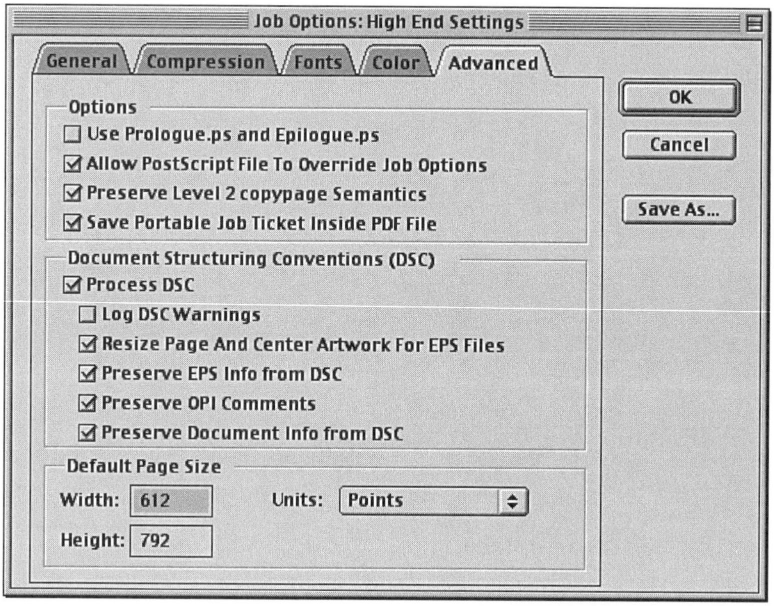

Figure 17-11
Advanced Settings tab.

- Deselect the option to use a Prologue and Epilogue functions.
- Select the option to allow the incoming PostScript to override any Distiller settings.
- Select to preserve Level 2 copypage semantics.
- Select the option to save the PJTF inside the PDF.
- Select to process all DSC except to log DSC warnings.
- Use the 612 x 792 default page size.

You now have a PDF suitable for high-end printing.

18

PDF in InDesign

InDesign exports PDF directly, without requiring the print-to-file and then grind-through-Distiller shuffle you have to perform with any other program. The resulting PDF is the same as what you'd get from Distiller 4 using the same settings, with one exception: It's likely to be a lot smaller than what Distiller would generate. This is due to a bug in the first release of Distiller 4, which should be fixed by the time this book hits the stores. There is also a difference in the way InDesign performs image subsampling from that of Distiller, which we'll get to shortly.

There are two basic export paths for PDF: on-line and for press. With an on-line PDF that will be distributed over the Internet or included on a CD-ROM, the main concern is with the resulting file size. If you want to make a PDF file from an InDesign document that contains high-resolution bitmapped images, and if you want to use the PDF file only for electronic distribution, for on-screen reading, and for printout on basic office and home printers, there's no need to bloat the thing with large images. InDesign can *resample* high-resolution images intended for a printing press to a size more appropriate to screen display or for printing on a basic laser or inkjet printer.

A PDF file generated for press will generally not have image downsampling applied because you need the full resolution of the images for correct reproduction. The resulting file can be huge, but because compression can be applied to all images, the final PDF will usually be smaller than a PostScript version of the same document.

PDF files can be edited to some extent with the Acrobat program. While you cannot easily make major text changes in a PDF file, you can usually correct minor typographical errors. A PDF file also exhibits page independence, meaning you can rearrange the pages in Acrobat without worrying about text reflow. A PDF page is an island, so to speak, and can exist on its own.

Resampling of images can be specified in two ways when exporting from InDesign: by average downsampling, or by subsampling. Distiller adds a third method, called bi-cubic downsampling, which is more accurate than the average downsampling method. Let's say you have a 300-ppi image in a document that you want to prepare for on-line viewing, so the ideal image resolution should be 72 ppi. Here's how resampling works:

- Average downsampling takes the average color level of all the colors in a group of 300-ppi pixels and replaces the group with a single big pixel of the average color. This usually produces pretty good results.
- Subsampling takes the one 300-ppi pixel at the center of a group that would occupy a single 72-ppi pixel, and replaces the entire group with a big version of that pixel. Subsampling will usually produce a more "jaggy" looking image than downsampling will, but it's a lot faster.
- The bi-cubic downsampling option available in Distiller takes a weighted average to determine the replacement pixel's color and can produce a better downsampled image than the average downsampling method, but in order to use it, you need to save a file as PostScript and run it through Distiller.

However, if you need to resample images that are intended for a printing press, you should always use the average downsampling method, or the bi-cubic method if you are going to use Distiller. This might occur if an image is scanned at a higher resolution than your output device can use effectively. For example, if you scanned an image at 400 ppi, but are printing only it at 85 lines per inch, then the optimum resolution for that image would be 170 ppi.

By downsampling that image, you'll significantly decrease processing time at the imaging device because the excess data in the 400-ppi image is simply thrown away. Excess resolution will also result if you place an image into InDesign and then reduce it. Placing a 300-ppi image and then scaling it 50 percent will result in an effective resolution of 600 ppi. This will slow things down only at the imaging stage. You can specify a resampling resolution when exporting. This resolution should be at least 1.5 times the screen ruling of the final print job, preferably two times. If a job is to be printed at a screen ruling of 150 lpi, then your image resolution should be 300 ppi. InDesign won't resample anything if the object's resolution is less than 1.5 times the specified resampling resolution.

Font Issues

You can choose to embed a document's fonts for proper display and printing at another location, even if the recipient doesn't have the fonts. Some font vendors prohibit embedding. You can embed a *subset* of a document's fonts, which means that only the character outlines for those characters actually in the document will be embedded. This has a minor benefit of slightly reducing the final file size, but it has a major benefit because any subset font will have a new, custom name assigned to it, which means that even if the recipient has the same original font loaded, only *your* version will be used for display or printing. This is important because like any other type of software, digital typefaces are revised on occasion, and the metrics and kerning data may change.

By embedding a "subset" of your font into a PDF file, you ensure that your version is the one used by everyone else. Setting the subset percentage to 100 percent is recommended. Setting it much below that might cause problems later if a particular character's outline is missing from the resulting PDF, and if it later turns out that you need it to fix a typo prior to printing, you can't do it. If you don't embed any fonts, and the recipient doesn't have them, then the resulting PDF is displayed and printed with special Adobe substitution fonts. These are designed to emulate the spacing characteristics of any missing characters, but they are bland, generic typefaces that cannot reproduce a missing typeface exactly, and if the missing typeface is a script or display face, the results will look nothing like the original. It's always a good idea to embed fonts.

PDF for Print   Before preparing a PDF version of a document to be printed on a press, always ask your printer or service provider about any special needs they might have for the processing of PDF files, such as composite (RGB/LAB) vs. preseparated (CMYK), OPI or no OPI, color management or no color management, and the final screen ruling of the print run. While PDF is relatively device-independent, the screen ruling will be used to determine the amount of resampling, if any, that you should apply. Once the images are resampled for a particular print run, the resulting PDF can't really be considered device-independent.

PDF for On-line Use   The difference between PDF for print and PDF for on-line use is that you will resample your images to 72 ppi (Mac) or 96 ppi (Windows), and specify that all images be converted to RGB space if they aren't.

Exporting PDF

Open the file you wish to convert, and then press Command/Control + E. Choose Adobe PDF (as if there were more than one type of PDF), name the file, append .pdf to the end, and then click Save.

You'll see the options shown in Figure 18-1, many of which are very similar to those we've already seen in the EPS and prepress export dialogs. The PDF Export process has four dialogs, though few people will probably use the fourth, which offers security options.

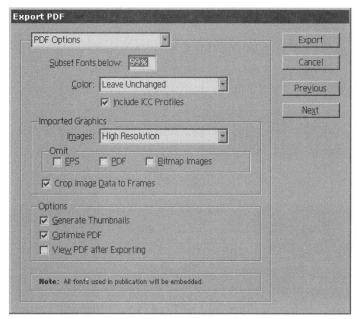

Figure 18-1
Export—PDF Options.

The first dialog wants to know about font, color, and some other options.

- Enter a percentage for the Subset Fonts field. Ninety-nine percent is usually the preferred setting.
- Color lets you specify any color space conversion. These options are exactly the same as for the EPS and Prepress export methods.
- Choosing Include ICC Profiles is selectable if color management is enabled for the document. Choose this option if you are sending the PDF through an ICC-aware workflow and plan to use in-RIP separations. Otherwise, you really needn't bother.

- Images are the same as for EPS and Prepress.
- OPI are the same as for EPS and Prepress.
- Omit—Sorry, same as for EPS and Prepress.
- Crop Image Data to Frames—This eliminates image data that falls outside of an image's frame. Some prepress applications, such as a trapping program, might use this information, so you need to experiment with this option.
- Generate Thumbnails—Acrobat can display a thumbnail view of a PDF file, but only if you create them when exporting a PDF file.
- Optimize PDF—This should always be on for on-line PDF. The option eliminates redundant data, resulting in smaller files, and allows one page at a time to be served up from a Web server. This option really makes no difference when generating a PDF for print.
- View PDF After Exporting—Pretty easy to figure out. You can designate a specific application to view the resulting PDF, but your choices are pretty much limited to Acrobat or Acrobat Reader. InDesign always exports version 1.3 PDF, which can be read only by Acrobat 4. You can't save a file for Acrobat 3 from InDesign.

The next dialog (Figure 18-2) is where you specify compression and resampling. For color and grayscale images, you can choose JPEG or ZIP compression. Recall that JPEG compression throws away data it considers to be redundant or unnecessary for proper display, but if you choose the Maximum Quality level, the amount of data discarded by JPEG compression is rarely noticeable.

ZIP compression doesn't work too well for continuous-tone images like photographs, but it preserves all data in the image. Of course, choosing None doesn't apply any image compression, which is probably not really necessary for most PDF files destined for a print shop or if you really don't care about the final file size.

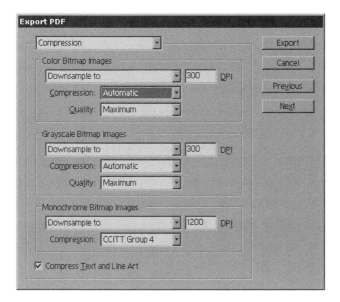

Figure 18-2
Export PDF—Compression.

For Monochrome Bitmap Images (line art and the like), the CCITT Group 4 compression method works well and doesn't throw anything away. CCITT Group 3 compression works the same way, but it'll take longer to compress the image. Choosing Compress Text and Line Art will apply a default compression method to any text and InDesign-native artwork in the document. This type of compression doesn't throw anything away, and there's no harm in applying it since it'll help make the final PDF file a little smaller.

Be sure to choose the correct resolution for the final printing specification. If you know your images are already at the optimum resolution for your reproduction needs, choose None in the Resampling pop-up menus for each image type.

Line art with a resolution much over 1200 ppi won't necessarily reproduce any better, and it'll take longer to process, so it won't hurt to enable resampling of line-art images.

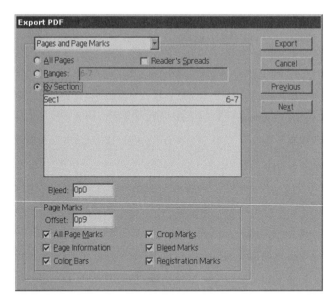

Figure 18-3
Export PDF—Pages and Page Marks option.

The next dialog (Figure 18-3) asks about which pages to export, and whether to apply bleed and printer's marks.

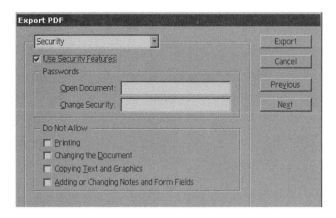

Figure 18-4
Export PDF—Security.

Entering a password in the Change Security lets someone else alter the security settings as long as he or she has the right password.

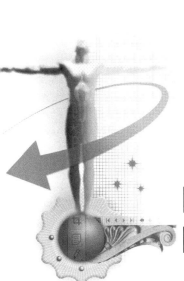

19

High-Resolution Printing

Quality printout of high-resolution PDF files is a five-step process:

1. Composite PDF versus Preseparated PostScript   Decide whether to create a composite PDF file or traditional preseparated PostScript file. Adobe recommends choosing a composite PDF workflow because it offers

- On-screen viewing (or soft proofing): You can review the file in its final form before it's printed; you can double-check graphic placement, wording, and other file details; you can catch problems before going to press.
- Simple text and graphics editing: You can edit the PDF file if you find a problem or last-minute change.
- Device-independent color: Acrobat 4 lets you preserve device-independent CMYK color information, so that you can print your document to a variety of output devices.
- Faster, more efficient file transfers: Composite PDF files are teeny in comparison to typical, high-resolution

PostScript files. A typical PostScript file with an 8-up imposition and embedded high-resolution images can occupy 600 Mb to 1 Gb of disk space. A service provider has to transfer it over its network multiple times, once for each separation. A PDF file offers a compact, one-shot transfer, making it simpler for everyone.

* The right use of in-RIP functionality: A service provider can perform trapping, separations, and late binding and file editing, all at the RIP. Page-independence in PDF files supports the Adobe PostScript Extreme workflow.

If the service provider uses a PostScript Level 2 RIP to color separate in-RIP, then you must use a preseparated PostScript workflow for documents that contain certain graphics file formats or features such as duotone EPS files, colorized TIFF files, and spot-color-to-spot-color gradients. DCS images were designed to support a preseparated PostScript workflow and don't include the information for color separation from a composite PostScript file. Adobe Photoshop 5.0.2 and later resolves the multitoned image (duotone EPS) issue, as long as you use Distiller 4/PDF 1.3 file format and an Adobe PostScript 3 RIP to correctly interpret and color separate (in-RIP) the duotone EPS. These provisions are necessary because this version of Photoshop uses the DeviceN colorspace operator (a PostScript 3 construct) to define the multitoned color information.

Preseparated PostScript Workflows

If you use duotone EPS files, colorized TIFF files, DCS images, or spot-to-spot color gradients in your workflow, then you'll need to create a preseparated PostScript file instead of composite PDF files.

If you're using Adobe Photoshop 5 and Acrobat Distiller 4 (with 4 compatibility selected in the General Job Option tab), and the service provider has an Adobe PostScript 3 RIP, then you do not need to preseparate your PostScript files when the document contains one or more duotone EPS files. They should color-separate properly from a composite PDF file to an Adobe PostScript 3 RIP.

If multitoned EPS files were not created and saved from Photoshop 5.0.2 or later, they will not color-separate properly when included in a document printed to disk as a composite PostScript file. Photoshop 5.0.2 uses the DeviceN color space operator, so Distiller 4 (when set to Acrobat 4 compatibility) can interpret and later color-separate these images in-RIP (PostScript 3).

You can create colorized TIFFs in a variety of applications. Check with your software vendor to ensure that these TIFF images use the DeviceN color space operator so that they can be color-separated properly in-RIP to an Adobe PostScript 3 RIP.

DCS files, by nature, are not intended to be used for final output in a composite PostScript workflow. Instead, DCS files will print the low-resolution composite placeholder EPS on the black plate. Here are your options for handling most DCS files:

- Create a preseparated "fat" PostScript file with all image data separated into the four process-color channels.
- If you want to use a composite PostScript/PDF workflow with your DCS images, open the DCS file in an image-editing program like Photoshop and save it as a CMYK TIFF or EPS file. Then, link the new image to your document. This will allow you to maintain a composite PostScript workflow.
- In QuarkXPress 4 and earlier, use the SmartXT XTension from Total Integration (http:// www.totalint.com) to recombine the DCS file into a single file when creating a composite PostScript file. You can then maintain a composite PostScript workflow. No similar plug-in is available for PageMaker that we know about.
- Check with your service provider to see if its OPI server can handle the picture replacement of a five-file DCS 1.0 image in a composite PostScript workflow.

Today, there are many workflow alternatives. They start with someone creating file. If that is you, check with the service first.

Custom Color Gradients or Blends   Gradients or blends of two custom/spot colors in vector EPS files will be converted to process colors when you create a composite PostScript file. They will then separate on the process color plates at the RIP.

Preserving High-quality Printing Information in PDF
Earlier versions of Acrobat presented challenges in consistently creating PDF files (fonts, color, links to high-resolution images, and overprint settings) for high-resolution printing. In Acrobat 4, this process is made much easier by including predefined Job Option Settings and by providing the ability to create, name, and save customized settings.

The PostScript imaging model is at the heart of PDF files. Acrobat Distiller 4 and earlier accepts only PostScript or Encapsulated PostScript (EPS) files. Like a PostScript printing device, Acrobat Distiller interprets PostScript code. Instead of creating printed output on paper, film, or a printing plate, as a PostScript printing device would, Distiller creates a PDF 1.3 file. Just as a document printed from a PostScript printing device is an exact representation of the original document, so too is a PDF file. While Acrobat Distiller 4 is an Adobe PostScript 3 interpreter, Distiller does not actually "rasterize" the file, and it isn't a pure PostScript RIP.

PDF files represent text and graphics using the imaging model of the PostScript language. Like a PostScript language program, a PDF page description draws a page by placing small drops of "paint" on selected areas. The quality of the page-description drawing process is directly related to the quality of the PostScript file that Distiller interprets. If, for example, the PostScript does not include required fonts, proper paper sizes, or custom/spot color information, neither will the resulting PDF file.

2. Preflighting the Application File   Before creating a PostScript file for distilling, you must start with a "print-ready" application file. This is a file that adheres to a service provider's specifications for high-resolution printing. For example, the file:

- doesn't include any RGB images or RGB colors in a four-color process printing job.
- maintains links to placed graphics and images.
- includes all document fonts.
- contains only high-resolution image data (no 72-dpi images).
- includes paper size with bleed-and-page-mark allocation.

3. Creating Efficient Composite PostScript files   Preparing composite PostScript files for high-resolution printing is not as simple as deselecting color separations in the application's Print dialog box. Here is a list of variables you need to consider:

- Printer driver and PPD selection
- Paper size
- Font inclusion
- Spot-color information
- Trapping information
- OPI workflows

Selecting a Printer Driver and PPD   For optimal results, use the Adobe PostScript printer driver (AdobePS) and the Acrobat Distiller PostScript Printer Description (PPD) file. This will ensure the creation of consistent, device-independent PDF files for printing on more than one device. When you create PostScript files for distilling, make sure you're using the latest version of the AdobePS driver (vAdobe PS 8.6 for Macintosh, Adobe PS 5.1.1 for Windows NT, and Adobe PS 4.3.1 for Windows 95/98). You can download the latest versions of the AdobePS printer drivers from the Adobe Web site:

http://www.adobe.com/supportservice/custsupport/LIBRARY/4cea.htm Windows 95 and 98
http://www.adobe.com/supportservice/custsupport/LIBRARY/5066.htm Windows NT 4
http://www.adobe.com/supportservice/custsupport/LIBRARY/52d6.htm

Acrobat 4 Installs a PPD File　The file is either Acrobat Distiller (Macintosh) or ADIST4.PPD (Windows). Earlier versions of the Acrobat software installed a PPD, which included default settings not appropriate for high-resolution printing, such as RGB for the default color space. The new 4 PPD includes appropriate default settings for high-resolution print-publishing—so you no longer have to edit the PPD. Use the Distiller 4 PPD because it doesn't write device-specific information in the resulting PostScript file, yet it allows you to select certain high-end controls, such as custom paper sizes for oversized jobs.

If the page size (usually specified in an application's Document Setup dialog box) does not account for image bleeds or printer's marks, you must create a custom paper size using your application's Print dialog box. The Acrobat Distiller PPD, like an imagesetter PPD, supports custom paper sizes. Increase paper size by one inch when printing with crop marks.

Including All Document Fonts　When you create a PostScript file for distilling, make sure you include all PostScript Type 1 and TrueType fonts to ensure that fonts are available for viewing and printing. Unlike Type 1 fonts, Acrobat Distiller 4 can embed True-Type fonts in a PDF file only if they're included in the original PostScript or EPS file.

If you plan to use TrueType fonts for high-resolution printing, discuss it with your service provider. It may have printing devices or post-processing applications that do not contain a TrueType rasterizer, which is required for printing these fonts, and your document fonts will then print in (gulp) Courier.

QuarkXPress 4 and earlier versions do not include document fonts when you save pages as EPS files (rather than printing a file to disk as a PostScript file).

Spot-color Information　Some page-layout applications, such as Adobe PageMaker and QuarkXPress, preserve spot colors applied to their native elements when you output composite PostScript files. However, files from other page-layout applications or certain graphic files containing spot colors may not color-separate properly from a resulting composite PDF file.

For Acrobat Distiller to preserve trapping information in a PDF file, that information must be included in the composite PostScript file. The page-layout application you are using determines what document trapping information you can include in a composite PostScript file. "Document trapping" does not refer to line art created in a graphics application and placed in a page-layout application. Instead, it refers to trapping applied to native application elements, such as text and drawn elements.

QuarkXPress 4 and earlier versions include document-trapping information only when creating preseparated PostScript files. On the other hand, Adobe PageMaker 6.01 and later include document-trapping information in both composite and preseparated PostScript files. If you are using QuarkXPress, you may need to modify your workflow (e.g., use a preseparated workflow, a post-processing application to trap the file, or an output device that supports in-RIP trapping). If your service provider is using Adobe in-RIP Trapping, trap information can be specified using the in-RIP Trapping plug-in for Adobe PageMaker 6.52 (available for downloading from the Adobe Web site).

When you distill a PostScript file that contains Adobe in-Rip trapping specifications using Distiller 4, those trapping instructions are stored in a Portable Job Ticket Format (PJTF). This workflow is supported by Distiller 4 and the Adobe Normalizer within an Adobe PostScript Extreme Printing System.

Preserving OPI Comments   Acrobat Distiller 4 will now preserve Open Prepress Interface (OPI) 1.3 and 2.0 comments in the resulting PDF file. Earlier versions of Distiller preserved only OPI 1.3 comments. If you are using OPI proxy files, preserving OPI comments in Distiller 4, and then replacing OPI images on a traditional OPI server, you cannot use Direct PDF Printing to your PostScript 3 printing device. Direct printing is available only on certain RIPs from certain suppliers.

4. Acrobat Distiller Job Options for High-resolution Printing   The next step is to evaluate the Acrobat Distiller 4 predefined job-option settings with your service provider and decide whether to use those or to create a custom set based on the provider's prepress and post-processing requirements. The selections you make affect how Distiller interprets PostScript or EPS files, determining, for example, whether the document fonts will be embedded, how graphics and images will be compressed and/or sampled, and whether the resulting PDF includes high-end printing information such as OPI comments.

When you prepare PDF files for high-resolution printing, use Acrobat Distiller, not PDFWriter. PDFWriter enables you to convert documents to PDF files quickly, but it uses the on-screen display (QuickDraw commands on the Macintosh or GDI commands in Windows). Acrobat Distiller supports PostScript technology-based applications and can preserve high-resolution printing and color information. Acrobat Distiller 4 now provides three predefined sets of default job options appropriate to final output:

- PressOptimized (printing press)
- PrintOptimized (digital printers)
- ScreenOptimized (Internet/other electronic publishing)

You can also use a predefined set as a baseline for customizing options to suit specific printing devices, processes, or workflows. The PressOptimized settings are designed to maintain all the necessary high-end printing information so that your service provider can process and print the document. To evaluate the PressOptimized settings, click the pop-up menu for Job Options and select PressOptimized. To access specific settings, choose Settings > Job Options, or press Command + J (Macintosh) or Control + J (Windows). A dialog box appears with five tabs: General, Compression, Fonts, Color, and Advanced.

General Job Options   The General tab includes file-settings and device-settings options for compatibility, resolution, and binding. Select Acrobat 4 from the Compatibility pop-up menu, so your PDF file can support these new Acrobat 4 features:

- Adobe PostScript 3 operators like DeviceN, smooth shading, and masked images
- ICC-profile color management
- Page sizes up to 200 inches (Windows 95/98 has a maximum page size of 129 inches because of a 16-bit addressing limitation.)
- Double-byte font embedding
- TrueType font searching
- PDF 1.3 file format

When you select Acrobat 4 Compatibility, ask your service provider what level of PostScript device it uses. In some cases, your composite PDF file will properly color-separate in-RIP to a PostScript 3 RIP, but not to a PostScript Level 2 RIP. For example, if your composite PostScript or EPS file contains a duotone EPS file from Photoshop 5.0.2 and you've selected Acrobat 4 Compatibility, then a Level 2 RIP will not correctly separate the duotone.

ASCII Format   Leave the ASCII format option deselected so that Distiller saves the PDF file in binary format, creating a smaller file. This format is used for older DOS-based systems.

Optimize PDF   Select this setting to reduce the PDF file size by removing repeated background text, line art, and images and replacing them with pointers to the first occurrences of those objects.

Generate Thumbnails   Select this option to create a thumbnail preview of each page. Then, use the thumbnails to easily preview the resulting PDF file.

Default Resolution   Enter the resolution (dpi) of the PDF file's final output device in the Default Resolution text box. The value you enter here affects only vector (object-oriented) EPS files. Distiller may use this value to determine the appropriate number of steps for a blend in an EPS file.

Binding   Select Left or Right from the pop-up menu, depending on your final binding method.

Compression Job Options   The Compression tab contains settings for compressing images, graphics, and text. The settings you select can have a significant impact on the quality of your final printed results. The settings recommended below can serve as a baseline, but you should also consult the service provider.

Compress Text and Line Art   Make sure the Compress Text and Line Art option is selected (it is the default). The compression method Distiller uses for text and line art, such as vector EPS graphics, is lossless, so it doesn't affect the quality of these elements in your PDF file.

Color Bitmap Images   If you want Distiller to downsample color images, select the Bicubic Downsampling At option and specify the appropriate dpi value. If you enter a value such as 300 dpi, Distiller downsamples the image only when its resolution exceeds 1.5 times the value specified here. If all your images contain the appropriate amount of image data and the images have not been scaled smaller, deselect the downsampling option. For compression, choose Automatic, and set Quality to Maximum.

Setting sampling and compression options has a significant effect on the quality of final printed output: You want to reduce your file size as much as possible without losing crucial data that your images, graphics, and text need to print correctly on higher-resolution printing devices. Acrobat Distiller 4 gives you various sampling options and a range of lossy and lossless compression options for images, graphics, and text.

Grayscale Bitmap Images   If you want Distiller to downsample grayscale images, select the Bicubic Downsampling At option and specify the appropriate dpi value. If you enter a value such as 300 dpi, Distiller downsamples the image only when its resolution exceeds 1.5 times the value specified here. If all your images contain the appropriate amount of image data and the images have not been scaled smaller, deselect the downsampling option. For compression, choose Automatic, and set Quality to Maximum.

Lossy versus Lossless Compression   Compression decreases the file size of images and produces smaller PDF files, but it also causes an image's quality to decrease. The ZIP compression method is lossless (it does not eliminate data to reduce the file size and will not affect the image's quality), while the JPEG compression method is lossy (it does eliminate image data and may decrease the image's quality). Because it will eliminate image data, JPEG compression achieves smaller file sizes than ZIP compression. To apply compression to color or grayscale bitmap images, select the compression option for color or grayscale, and choose a compression method (Automatic, JPEG, or ZIP) and quality setting. Acrobat applies the compression to all color or grayscale bitmap images in a PDF file.

If you select the Automatic option, Acrobat determines the best compression method (JPEG or ZIP) for your color or grayscale bitmap images. JPEG is applied to 8-bit grayscale images and to all 8-bit, 16-bit, and 24-bit color images when the images have continuous, smooth tones; ZIP is applied to 2-bit, 4-bit, and 8-bit grayscale images, to 4-bit color images and indexed 8-bit color images, and to 16-bit and 24-bit color images when the images have sharp color changes. Choosing the Automatic option does increase the time to distill the file as Distiller must first examine each image to determine the proper compression method to apply.

Monochrome Bitmap Images   Select the Bicubic Downsampling At option and enter the resolution of the final output device. Then, select CCITT Group 4 for the greatest lossless compression. Acrobat Distiller 4 provides CCITT Group 3 and Group 4 compression options.

CCITT Group 3, which is used by most fax machines, compresses monochrome bitmaps one row at a time. Another option, Run Length, is a lossless compression option that produces the best results for images that contain large areas of solid white or black.

If you want to control the downsample threshold for Acrobat Distiller, you can create a custom Prologue.ps file that overrides the Distiller 4 default at 1.5 times the specified sampling value. To override this default, do the following:

1. Open the PressOptimized file or your custom job option settings file in a text editor.

2. Locate the lines of text that read:

   /ColorImageDownsampleThreshold 1.50
   /GrayImageDownsampleThreshold 1.50
   /MonoImageDownsampleThreshold 1.50

3. Edit the value 1.50 to be the desired ratio. For example, enter 1.0 to set your downsampling threshold to a 1:1 ratio with your downsampling resolution.

Font Job Options   Font Embedding lets you specify which fonts to embed in a PDF file to prevent font substitution at print time. Distiller 4 can now embed ITC Zapf Dingbats and Base 14 fonts (Helvetica, Times, Courier, and Symbol font families), whereas the previous version did not allow you to embed these fonts. When you select the Subset All Embedded Fonts Below option, Distiller embeds only the font characters (glyphs) used in the document. It ensures that your fonts and font metrics are used at print time by creating a custom font name—so your version of Adobe Warnock (a new font) will always be used for viewing and printing, not your service provider's.

Subsetting fonts may limit your ability to do late-stage editing. However, you can use the improved TouchUp tool in Acrobat 4, or a third-party plug-in such as Enfocus PitStop plug-in, to add font characters for late-stage editing as long as the font is installed on your system.

The value you enter for the Subset Fonts Below option determines the point at which Distiller will include the entire font. For example, if you specify Subset Fonts Below 25 percent, and more than 25 percent of a font's characters are used in the document, Distiller will embed the entire font. If you always want to subset fonts, enter a higher value, such as 100 percent.

Embed All Fonts   Select this option to prevent font substitution at print time. (Distiller embeds all PostScript fonts used in the document and all TrueType fonts included in the PostScript file.) This option also enables Distiller to subset fonts.

Subset Fonts Below   Select the Subset Fonts Below option and specify 100 percent so that Distiller will embed only the font characters used in the document. Distiller also renames the subsetted fonts in the PDF file to prevent an available font with the same name from being used for viewing or printing.

When Embedding Fails   Select Cancel from the pop-up menu to ensure that a PDF file will not be created when distilling a PostScript or EPS file with one or more missing document fonts. A log file is created indicating which fonts are missing. With earlier versions of Acrobat Distiller, you were instructed to rename the font database (Superatm.db for the Macintosh and Distsadb.dos for Windows) to avoid the possibility of font substitution. In Acrobat 4, you no longer need to rename these files: Simply select Cancel from the When Embedding Fails pop-up menu, and rest assured that Distiller 4 won't substitute missing fonts.

Color Job Options   Most problems associated with accurate color reproduction stem from reconciling the differences between the gamut produced by the red, green, and blue phosphors of a computer monitor and the restricted gamut produced by the cyan, magenta, yellow, and black inks of a printing press. To minimize these color-reproduction issues, Acrobat 4 supports color management using ICC profiles. The high-end print-publishing industry has not yet adopted a complete, device-independent color-managed workflow. Here are some common scenarios and solutions:

- If you are color-managing and embedding device profiles when you save color images in Photoshop 5, then Acrobat Distiller 4 will use your images' color-source information when it distills the PostScript or EPS file.

- If you're not embedding device profiles when you save your color images, you can still color-manage images that are produced from one consistent color space. Simply select the device profile that characterizes the color space in the Assumed Profiles section for RGB or CMYK in Photoshop 5. This will "tag" the untagged images or the entire document with a source profile, which Distiller can use for color management.
- If your images were not saved with embedded device profiles and they come from a variety of color sources (different RGB monitor color spaces or Separation Tables for CMYK images), then we recommend not tagging or converting your color images or documents.

Conversion   Select Leave Color Unchanged for conversion so that no color conversion takes place when you're in a noncolor-managed workflow. If you tag your images or entire document, check with your service provider.

Preserve Overprint Settings   If the PostScript or EPS file includes overprint settings and you want Distiller to include them in the PDF file, select this option. This option will override any overprint settings your service provider may specify at print time. If you want to specify overprint settings at print time, deselect this option.

Under Color Removal/Black Generation   If the PostScript or EPS file includes Under Color Removal (UCR) or Black Generation information, select this option. This option will override any Under Color Removal/Black Generation settings your service provider may specify at print time. If you want to specify Under Color Removal/ Black Generation settings at print time, deselect this option.

Transfer Function   If the PostScript or EPS file includes transfer functions, select this option. This option will override any transfer functions your service provider may specify at print time. If you want to specify a transfer function at print time, deselect this option.

Preserve Halftone Screen Information   If the PostScript or EPS file includes custom halftone screen information and you want Distiller to include it in the PDF file, select the Preserve Halftone Screen Information option. The halftone screen information will override any halftone screens you specify at print time. If you want to specify halftone screens at print time, deselect this option.

Advanced Job Options   Distiller uses the Advanced job options to specify whether to preserve certain document structuring comments in the resulting PDF file, define a default page size, or set other options that affect the conversion from PostScript. In a Post-Script file, document-structuring-conventions (DSC) comments contain information about the file (such as the originating application, the creation date, and the page orientation) and provide structure for page descriptions in the file (such as beginning and ending statements for a prologue section). DSC comments can be useful when your document is going to print or press.

The default page size is used if a PostScript file does not specify a page size. Typically, PostScript files include this information, except for Encapsulated PostScript (EPS) files, which give a bounding box size but not a page size. Therefore, if you're distilling EPS files, make sure you adjust the default page size to ensure that your file does not clip your original EPS file. Overall, it's best to accept the defaults for Advanced job options. Change it only if you know what you are doing.

Use Prologue.ps and Epilogue.ps   Select this option to send a prologue and epilogue file with each job. These files have many purposes. For example, prologue files can be edited to specify cover pages or custom watermarks; epilogue files can be edited to resolve a series of procedures in a PostScript file. Acrobat Distiller 4 does not require you to select this option to preserve spot or custom colors—they're preserved automatically. A sample Prologue.ps and Epilogue.ps file is located in the Distiller/Data (Windows) or Distiller/Data (Mac OS) folder. Be sure to place your prologue and epilogue files in the appropriate location for your workflow. If you're using a Watched-folder workflow, place these files in the Watched folder at the same level as the In and Out folders. If you're doing a non-Watched-folder workflow, put the prologue and epilogue files in the same folder as the Distiller application.

Allow PostScript File to Override Job Options   Select this option to use settings stored in a PostScript file rather than your current job options. Before processing a PostScript file, you can place Distiller parameters in the file to control compression of text and graphics, downsampling and encoding of sampled images, and embedding of Type 1 fonts and instances of Type 1 multiple master fonts. See the Acrobat Distiller Parameters, Technical Note 5151 (DST_PRM.PDF) on the Acrobat 4 CD.

Preserve Level 2 Copypage Semantics   Select this option when printing to a PostScript Level 2 device if you want to use the copypage operator defined in PostScript Level 2 rather than that in PostScript 3. The copypage operator has been redefined in Postscript 3. Now you can use this operator to "copy page" elements for personalized or forms printing. If you have a custom PostScript 3 file and select this option, Distiller will make the copypage a show-page to ensure Level 2 compatibility; otherwise, the copypage elements will image on top of one another.

Save Portable Job Ticket Inside PDF File   Select this option to create a portable job-ticket "placeholder" in your PDF file. A portable job ticket contains document-specific information, such as page size, resolution, and trapping information, rather than content. For example, you must select this option to preserve trapping information in your composite PostScript or EPS file for post-processing. Then, the trapping information is stored in a portable job-ticket placeholder. You can include trapping information only when using the Adobe in-RIP Trapping plug-in with Adobe PageMaker 6.52.

Process DSC Comments (Windows) or Process DSC (Mac OS)   Select this option to maintain particular document structuring information from a PostScript or EPS file, along with these related options: Log DSC Warnings. Select this option to display warning messages about problematic DSC comments in a PostScript or EPS file during the distilling process, and then add that information to a log file for further reviewing.

Resize Page and Center Artwork for EPS Files Select this option to center an EPS file and subsequently resize the PDF page to closely fit the original bounding-box dimensions of the EPS file. If you deselect this option, the EPS page is sized and centered based on the top left corner of the top left object and bottom right corner of the bottom right object on the page.

Preserve EPS Information from DSC (Windows) and Preserve EPS Info from DSC (Mac OS) Select this option to retain information such as the native application and creation date for an EPS file. Preserve OPI Comments. Select this option to retain OPI version 1.3 and 2.0 comments needed to replace low-resolution proxy files (FPO images) with the high-resolution images located on an OPI server. Preserve Document Information from DSC (Windows) and Preserve Document Info (Mac OS). Select this option to retain information such as the title, creation date, and time in the resulting PDF file. When you open a PDF file in Acrobat, this information appears in the General Info dialog box (through File > Document Info > General).

Default Page Size If the PostScript file you're distilling includes paper-size information (and most do), you can ignore the Default Page Size option. On the other hand, if you're distilling an EPS file, enter a page size for the EPS file. EPS files include a bounding-box size, but not a paper size. Distiller uses the values you enter in these text boxes when a PostScript file, such as an EPS file, doesn't include a paper size.

Using a Custom Prologue.ps for Scitex APR Files Scitex Corporation provides a custom prologue file to prevent Distiller from removing low-resolution APR (Automatic Picture Replacement) proxy-file information as it distills PostScript files. (This prologue file is available on the Brisque CD.) Scitex provided the information below about installing and using this prologue file.

The ScitexDistillerStartup.ps file contains PostScript Code that enables distilling of PostScript files with Scitex PSImages in the Acrobat Distiller. PSImages are the base for Scitex's Automatic Picture Replacement (APR) workflow. If this file is not used, a PostScript file with encapsulated PSImages will lose the PSImages information once it is distilled. If you want to preserve the PSImages in your resulting PDF, you must install this Startup file before distilling.

To install the 'ScitexDistillerStartup.ps':

- Make sure that the Acrobat Distiller application is NOT running.
- Place the 'ScitexDistillerStartup.ps' file in the Distiller Startup folder (right next to the Example.ps file).
- Launch the Distiller application. You should see the line "(Loaded Scitex Distiller Startup)" in the Distiller's messages window.

Once these steps are complete, you'll be able to distill PostScript files containing Scitex PSImages. The resulting PDFs can be output directly on a Scitex RIP that supports PDF, or they can be exported back to PostScript and ripped on any Scitex PostScript RIP. Known limitations:

- If the PDF file contains Spot CT, it cannot be output directly. You must first export the PDF back to PostScript through the Adobe Acrobat ExportPS plug-in.
- Direct Rip of a file with LW APR (Low res created by the Brisque translator pointing at a LW high res) is not supported. You must first export the PDF back to PostScript through the Adobe Acrobat ExportPS plug-in.
- A PostScript file containing both OPI comments printed with Omit Tiff or Omit Tiff&EPSF in QuarkXPress and a PSImage file (.e) is not supported.

PDF/X

PDF/X is not an alternative to PDF; it's a focused subset of PDF designed specifically for reliable prepress data interchange. You can do a lot of things in PDF that are not appropriate for graphic arts use, and that can cause problems when outputting for high-quality reproduction. PDF/X can be thought of as a shorthand way of specifying most of what you need to tell somebody in order for them to create a file that's likely to print correctly when they send it to you, even if they don't understand the details of what it's doing for them. That's looking ahead a little to a point where applications include a "PDF/X" checkbox on their PDF export dialogs, but signs are that is not going to be too far in the future.

Phrased slightly differently, think of all file formats used for file transfers as being compromises between flexibility and reliability (where reliability is defined as the final printed piece looking like you expected it to).

At one end of the scale are application files like QuarkXPress documents. You can change those in whatever way you like if you have the application. Unfortunately the receiver of a file can also change them accidentally rather too easily, and the results you get when printing are dependent on many factors in the environment in which that copy of XPress is running.

At the other end of the scale you have copydot scans. Those will print absolutely as you expect, given the necessary provisos about resolution and calibration; that's partly why they are inflexible.

In between, in order of decreasing flexibility and increasing reliability, other options include PostScript, EPS, PDF, PDF/X, and TIFF/IT. When we use "PostScript" in that list we mean the format in an otherwise unspecified way. It's always possible to push such a format towards the reliable end of the scale by using appropriate software to create it. In northern Europe, many people use Pro-Script, which limits the options used in EPS files. A "ProScript EPS" file might be placed on the scale somewhere between PDF and PDF/X. In the same way, appropriate use of preflight tools on PDF can give you a "reliable PDF" much closer to where PDF/X is on that

Converting Raster Images to PDF files. http://www.calpha.com/ ~apex/imagepdf.html
This software converts most TIFF or JPEG images (including CMYK) to PDF.

scale. The point of PDF/X is that it gives you a convenient and well-specified label to use when asking for such a "reliable PDF" file.

Every transfer of files from one place to another, whether it's between designers sitting at adjacent desks, or from an ad agency to a magazine publisher, has an optimal position on this compromise scale; that is, there's a file format appropriate to that optimal compromise. In some cases there will be additional selection pressure for a specific format, for example, for compatibility with other processes, but as a general rule the optimal compromise for the supply of print-ready files between organizations will be toward the reliable and less flexible end of the scale.

That doesn't mean ads and other print-ready files should be sent as copydot files—that's too inflexible for most general transfers, although there are some instances where it's the right thing to do (typically between publishers and print sites). For inter-company print-ready transfers where the sender and receiver do not have a strong relationship in place, either TIFF/IT-P1 or PDF/X-1 will probably work equally well.

The PDF/X standard was worked on by Subcommittee 6 of the Committee for Graphic Arts Technical Standards (CGATS SC6) at the request of the DDAP Association (Digital Distribution of Advertising for Publications). CGATS has been tasked by ANSI (the American National Standards Institute) to generate standards for the graphic arts in the United States.

CGATS SC6 covers digital-advertisement exchange, but that does not mean that PDF/X is useful only for advertisement—the committee recognized that it should make the standard more general and have deliberately not limited it in that way. The active members of CGATS SC6 vary slightly with time but have included the following companies over the last year of the development: Young & Rubicam, Western Laser Graphics, Webcraft Direct Mail, Time Inc., Scitex, R.R. Donnelley, Newspaper Association of America, Iris Graphics, Hewlett-Packard, Heidelberg, Harlequin, Graphic Communications Association, Fuji Photo Film, Eastman Kodak, DuPont Electronic Imaging, the DDAP Association, Dainippon Screen, Creo, Barco, Agfa, and Adobe Systems.

The standard has been split into two. PDF/X-1 is a file format for what's known as "blind interchange," where all technical information and content are held within one single file and nothing needs to be supplied alongside it. It's expected that publishers will make their specifications available to ad agencies and prepress houses. These will include page sizes, bleed allowances, number and types of hard copy proofs to be sent alongside digital files, and file formats that will be accepted. No further technical discussion will be required in order to make a PDF/X-1 file suitable for delivery.

PDF/X-2 will address exchanges where there is more discussion between the supplier and receiver of the file—the receiver may have certain fonts available that would therefore not need embedding, or maybe the receiver already holds high-resolution images to replace FPOs (low-resolution previews) in the supplied file.

What's PDF/X-1:1999? The graphic arts never stand still, and the organizations working on PDF/X expect to have to release new revisions of PDF/X-1 in the future to support additional functionality appropriate for the graphic arts community. In order to allow users to be sure that an application creating PDF/X-1 files is making files that a consumer of PDF/X-1 files can read, it's important to be able to distinguish between different revisions. CGATS SC6 recommends that the version that has just been approved be referred to in all literature describing product capabilities as PDF/X-1:1999.

Many publishers and printers are represented on CGATS SC6, either directly or through associations and trade organizations. Their representatives have worked hard to ensure that the standard will be suitable for their use. Once PDF/X-1 compliant tools appear, these companies will begin testing the use of PDF/X-1 to parallel similar workflows using TIFF/IT.

PDF 1.3 is not PDF/X, and files created by Acrobat Distiller 4.0 will not be PDF/X-1 compliant. Tools that are specifically PDF/X aware are just beginning to appear, including a PDF/X-1 verifier from the DDAP Association.

Acrobat Distiller versions 4.0 and earlier cannot create PDF/X-1 compliant files. It may be possible to coerce Acrobat Distiller 4.05 into generating PDF/X-1 compliant files. For the technically minded, that would probably involve a combination of specific Distiller job options, care in construction of PostScript files to be distilled, and a few PostScript fragments calling pdfmark, possibly added into a PPD file or the Distiller prolog.

Isn't PDF/X raster only? It's just a wrapper for TIFF/IT, isn't it? Although it's possible to use PDF/X as a wrapper for TIFF/IT files, that is not the intent of the design. A PDF/X file can, and usually will, include vector objects (such as rules, fills, and text) using normal PDF constructs. It can also include image data, whether scanned or computer-generated. In this sense PDF/X is very similar to both PostScript and PDF. Unlike PostScript, it can make references to TIFF, EPS, DCS, and TIFF/IT-P1 files and actually have those "external" files embedded within it.

Where it differs from PDF is in limiting some options (such as the colorspaces that may be used) to ensure that it will print reliably and consistently through all devices with PDF/X compliant readers.

PDF/X-1 as currently approved is based on PDF 1.2, plus those few pieces of PDF 1.3 included in Adobe Technical Note 5188 (PDF 1.2 is the native version for Acrobat 3, PDF 1.3 is the native version for Acrobat 4). Those few pieces do not include the DeviceN colorspace.

PDF/X-1 is in the same position with respect to duotones and bump plates as PDF 1.2—it's possible to encode duotones and bump plates in PDF 1.2, but very few applications that do that encoding have ever become available. In addition, such encoding is not appropriate for use in all output environments because of spot color and overprint issues, raising questions about its suitability for blind interchange, which requires predictability of output without prior discussion. There are no duotones in the current revision of PDF/X-1.

CGATS is well aware of the problems that this might cause some users and is basing PDF/X-2 on PDF version 1.3, probably including additional features that might finally appear in a PDF version 1.4. Duotones and bump plates will be fully supported in PDF/X-2. A revised PDF/X-1, also based on PDF 1.3, is being developed alongside the PDF/X-2 specification.

PDF/X-1:1999 limits the color spaces used to CMYK, grayscale, and spot colors. It cannot, therefore, be used in many workflows that might be referred to as color-managed, although it's possible to produce color-managed output from a PDF/X-1 file, typically by applying a DeviceLink ICC profile.

The PDF/X-1:1999 standard received final ANSI approval on October 14th, 1999, and will probably be printed ready for distribution around the end of December 1999. CGATS SC6 has also created an application note covering some issues that were not appropriate for inclusion within the standard itself but that are designed to assist developers and systems integrators. That application note is available on the NPES Web site and will be distributed with the standard.

The final published PDF/X-1 is almost identical to all drafts released since December 1998. Tools to work with PDF/X-1 are beginning to appear, and more have been announced. These include creators, editors, verifiers, RIPs and conversion tools. CGATS SC6 has also started work on PDF/X-2, assisted by an ISO task force.

The fact that PDF/X is being developed by CGATS means that the people working on the standards are either American or working for organizations with significant activities in the United States. CGATS SC6 has, however, been more than happy to take comments and other input from people and organizations around the world during development.

At the international level, the relevant working group in the International Standards Organization (ISO/TC130/WG2) is eager to assist in creating a PDF/X standard and has set up a task force to feed international requirements into, and to review the work of, CGATS SC6. This move has been warmly welcomed by CGATS SC6. Remember that TIFF/IT was developed first as an ANSI/ CGATS standard and then converted into an ISO standard.

Now that PDF/X-1 has been adopted as an ANSI standard, ISO/TC130/WG2 has started the process to adopt it also as an ISO standard. Although PDF/X-2 (along with a revised PDF/X-1) is being developed by CGATS SC6 it will likely be prepared, with the help of the ISO PDF/X task force, for approval as an ISO standard without being processed by ANSI first.

CGATS information is available at the Web site for NPES, The Association for Suppliers of Printing, Publishing, and Converting Technologies
www.npes.org/standards/cgats.htm.

Information on current work in progress may be obtained from
www.npes.org/standards/workroom/cgats.htm

The CGATS site includes copies of draft standards. Drafts are available only here while a standard is in development or ballot.
Once published, CGATS standards may be obtained from NPES for a small charge
www.npes.org/publications/index.htm

ISO standards may be obtained from NPES, or from the national standards bodies in other countries. The DDAP Web site
www.ddap.org
maintains a list of software either already available or being developed to support the PDF/X standards.

InProduction

Adobe Acrobat InProduction provides the bridge between design creation and reliable Adobe Portable Document Format (PDF) output. Built for print production professionals, Acrobat InProduction features tightly integrated tools for preflighting PDF files, managing color separation and color conversion, specifying trim and bleed settings, and defining trapping parameters. You can efficiently prepare PDF files for color printing using tools designed to work together.

Until now no single product has offered integrated tools for reliably processing color PDF files for printing. Instead, print-production professionals have had to piece together disparate tools, which have produced undesirable results. Acrobat InProduction solves this issue, providing the tools you need to exercise control over a PDF-based print-production workflow.

With Acrobat InProduction, you can handle problems processing PDF files for color printing. That's because Acrobat InProduction provides comprehensive tools for identifying and correcting production-specific problems, creating imposition-ready PDF files, managing color settings, specifying trapping parameters, and more. Together, these tools streamline PDF print production and deliver a highly productive, cost-effective workflow.

To prepare color Adobe PDF files for output, you need to manage color conversion and separations, spot-color mapping, preflight, and other tasks. With Acrobat InProduction, you can convert RGB, LAB, and CMYK colors using ICC profiles. You can review color separations on-screen, and map one color to another, as well as define, save, and share production parameters to automate processes. Media, trim, and bleed boxes to prepare PDF files for imposition can be defined, and you can set up art boxes for placing PDF art in layouts. InProduction also supports print standards, such as ICC, PDF/ X-1, and Portable Job Ticket Format (PJTF). The following functions are included:

- Preflight tool
  - Create, share, and reuse preflight profiles for consistent results.
  - Locate and view errors in context on your screen.
  - Fix certain errors during preflighting, such as font-embedding or image-resolution issues.
  - Generate detailed preflight reports.

- Separator tool
  - Specify, preview, and create color separations.
  - Map spot or custom colors to specific printing plates.
  - Produce host-based or in-RIP color separations of Adobe PDF files.

- Color conversion tool
  - Convert CMYK, RGB, and LAB colors in individual or batch modes using industry-standard ICC profiles.

- Tag and untag CMYK images with ICC profiles for specific output devices.

- Trim/bleed tool
  - Define media, bleed, and trim specifications within 1/1000 of an inch to prepare PDF files for page positioning and imposition.
  - Specify art boxes around graphics or layouts to accurately place PDF pages or images into other applications.
  - Preview media, bleed, trim, and art boxes on screen.

- Trapping tool
  - Specify page and regional zone-based trapping parameters.
  - Define trap parameters and execute them in an Adobe PostScript 3 RIP with Adobe in-RIP trapping.

Q. What is Adobe Acrobat InProduction?

A. Acrobat InProduction is a new set of tools from Adobe for managing, manipulating, and processing PDF files through a color print-production workflow. Based on Adobe Acrobat 4.0.5, InProduction features a tightly integrated toolset offering improved productivity, increased reliability, and enhanced control over PDF preflight, color separation and conversion, trim/bleed settings, and Adobe in-RIP trapping parameters.

Built for print-production professionals, InProduction enables PDF files to be easily, efficiently, and reliably processed through a color printing workflow. Prior to InProduction, users had to rely on a piecemeal solution of tools to complete their PDF workflow. With InProduction, the tools needed to gain control over PDF files are integrated within Acrobat. InProduction provides the bridge from design creation to reliable Adobe Portable Document Format (PDF) output.

Q. What is included when I purchase Adobe Acrobat InProduction?

A. The complete InProduction product consists of Adobe Acrobat 4.0.5 and a set of five tightly integrated PDF print-production tools:

- Preflight, which lets users create reusable preflight profiles for finding errors, then analyze their files based on those profiles, view errors on screen and in context, and correct certain problems.
- Separator, to specify, preview and create color separations, map spot colors to process colors and spot colors to spot colors, and output files for color separation.
- Trim/Bleed, which gives users the precise control they need to define imagable areas and specify or alter the media, bleed, trim, or art boxes for accurate page positioning or imposition.
- Color Converter, for managing CMYK conversions from LAB, RGB, or CMYK using industry-standard ICC profiles.
- Adobe in-RIP Trapping, which enables users to specify page and regional zone-based trapping parameters for later execution in an Adobe PostScript 3 RIP that uses Adobe in-RIP Trapping.

In addition to InProduction's tools, there is also an on-line resource for preflighting PDF files—called InProduction Preflight On-line. Go to preflightpdf.adobe.com.

Q. If I already own Acrobat 4 why should I purchase InProduction?

A. Acrobat InProduction provides an integrated set of tools created directly from the many requests from users for Adobe to create Acrobat tools providing control over printing color PDF files. InProduction is built to work with the existing features of Acrobat and takes advantage of the inherent benefits of using PDF files for print. Acrobat InProduction provides improved control and enhanced reliability necessary for managing a productive color PDF printing workflow.

Q. How much does it cost?

A. Acrobat InProduction can be purchased in a number of ways, depending on whether you already own a version of Acrobat 4.0. The InProduction retail price is $899 with Adobe Acrobat 4.05 full version.

Q. Where do I get more information about Acrobat InProduction?

A. Go the Adobe Web site at
www.adobe.com/inproduction.

Be sure to check this Web site regularly for the latest information regarding InProduction and PDF workflows. Also visit
www.prefightpdf.adobe.com

for the opportunity to experience a subset of the Adobe Acrobat InProduction Prefight tool online.

Q. How does InProduction work with Acrobat?

A. Acrobat InProduction is an integrated set of tools that works within Acrobat 4.05. The Acrobat 4.05 interface, buttons, menus, and functionality are all the same, with the addition of the InProduction tools. Users can access the InProduction toolset from the Acrobat Tool Menu > InProduction > Preflight, Separator, Color Converter, Trim/Bleed, Adobe in-RIP trapping.

Q. How does InProduction fit into a PDF workflow?

A. It is a good portion of a workflow. It is a set of tightly integrated tools that has been developed to fulfill the specifc needs of a PDF print-production professional. Before taking a PDF file to press, the print-production people need to preflight, make color conversions, define trim, bleed, and trapping settings; then preview and complete color separations in order to finish the file output process. InProduction provides these tools with the control and reliability necessary when working in an efficient PDF workflow.

Q. Who is the target user of Acrobat InProduction?

A. InProduction is designed for two types of users: the print service providers who prepare and output PDF files for their clients; and the production specialists at graphics-related departments or businesses who generate PDF files for high-quality color printing. Prepress and print production professionals would most likely use all five InProduction tools as they take documents to final output. The second group, production specialists, would typically use Preflight to check for errors and Separator to preview color separations before delivering PDF files to print-service provider.

Q. How does InProduction help me process files for printing?

A. The tools in Acrobat InProduction have been specifcally built for print production professionals. The tools have a great range of detail for print output. Look at the preflight profiles and see the signifcant range of items looked for and reported on—all specific to the variety of printing environments, manufacturing paths, and workflow requirements that might be encountered in a printing environment. This level of detail and sophistication goes into each tool, providing an integrated and customizable PDF workflow that gives you the control and reliability necessary to accurately process PDF files for print.

Q. Is the InProduction serial number overwriting my Acrobat serial number? Can I use my old Acrobat serial number?

A. InProduction uses its own serial number, which overwrites Acrobat's serial number.

Q. Can I load just the InProduction tools if I already have Acrobat?

A. Yes, if you are already running Acrobat 4.05, you can install InProduction into your version of Acrobat. Use the InProduction installer on your CD or purchase and download InProduction tools from Adobe.com.

Q. Will Preflight fix all the problems found in my PDF file?

A The Preflight tool cannot fix all the problems found in your PDF file. Low-resolution images, for example, can only be fixed in the original graphic file. InProduction's Preflight can embed a missing font (provided you have the embeddable font loaded on your system), fix image resolution problems, overprint settings, and transfer functions. Other problems can be fixed using Separator and Color Converter.

Q. Can I trap a PDF file using InProduction?

A. While InProduction does not actually perform trapping, it does provide tools for creating and setting trapping parameters within a PDF file. These trapping parameters are then processed in an Adobe PostScript 3 RIP that uses Adobe in-RIP trapping.

Q. Why should I use Trim/Bleed?

A. The Trim and Bleed box tools are essential for accurate positioning of pages. By creating a Trim box of the correct size and positioning, you can be assured that when that PDF page is imported into InDesign or an imposition program, the page size and position will be accurate. Once you have defined your Trim box, you can then use its position and measurements to add printers' marks to your PDF file.

Q. What are art boxes and why are they important?

A. By drawing an art box around a graphic (or any content on a PDF page), you are essentially creating a clipping path (like in Photoshop) for placing that graphic into a page layout program. When that PDF page is imported into InDesign, the Art box is recognized and only the content of the art box is placed into InDesign. An art box is a part of the PDF/X-1 standard for PDF ad delivery.

20

The Digital World

Now that you can create, view, and edit PDF files, we're going to bring it all together and discuss PDF in the job-workflow environment. There's no doubt that changing customer demands are driving markets toward completely digital workflows. Every technology involved in the production and reproduction of information on paper is now electronic.

Short-Run Market   Digital press technology is driving short-run, on-demand jobs, which are the ticket to the future. Printing trends are leading towards full-color printing, which is faster and cheaper. Entire markets have sprung up seemingly overnight. Digital-color presses like the Xerox Docucolor, Agfa Chromapress, and Indigo E-Print 1000 are making inroads where traditional lithography once reigned. Making money in printing requires keeping the presses running. This is even more so for digital-color presses. In order to keep them running, data must come in a reliable self-contained package that is easy to process. Because the runs are smaller, the profit margins are very tight. To make money on 300 copies of a color brochure, the workflow must be easy-in, easy-out. The workflows must be virtually snagless. PDF files have the most to offer this market. No other file format can accurately render a page in such a compact and efficient manner—font-formatted text, vector objects, and contone images all packaged into one neat, viewable file. United Lithograph, a commercial printer in the Boston area, uses PDF files this way to keep its Xerox Docucolor and computer-to-plate system running three shifts a day.

Sending PDF for On-demand   You've received approval for the menu from the client and want to send a PDF file to the print shop for reproduction. Instead of e-mail, though, you are going to send the file on some type of media.

> **Q:** Should PDFWriter or Distiller be used to create the PDF?
> **A:** Distiller is the best choice.

> **Q:** What compression options apply?
> **A:** Since the PDF is going to be sent via removable media, file size is no longer critical. Image quality is the deciding factor. The designer wants to insure that all of the illustrations and images in the menu reproduce at the highest possible resolution. Downsampling is probably not a good idea. JPEG-Medium compression won't degrade image quality to unacceptable levels.

> **Q:** Should the fonts be embedded?
> **A:** Since this is the final output for the PDF, the designer wants to make certain of all of his/her typeface choices. Embedding the fonts is the only option.

The work is ready to be proofed; however, instead of sending the QuarkXPress files with the illustrations, you send the "okayed" PDF file to the reproduction company contact person. The reproduction company now receives the single PDF file and does not need to load the typefaces or to have your version of the creating application. Instead, Acrobat Exchange is used. From here, the proof is output through the OPI system, where the low-resolution images are exchanged with the high-resolution versions. The proof is then sent back to you for you to show the client. Of course, the client will be eager to make even more corrections, but the initial soft proofs are managed with PDFs.

Digital Growing Pains   While the entire graphic arts industry experienced these digital growing pains, the effects were especially hard on newspapers. If a printer had a problem with a digital file, he/she could reschedule the job. If a newspaper couldn't print a digital file, that revenue was lost for that edition. If the ad was about a "One-Day-Only" sale, the revenue was irrevocably lost. Thus, both the newspaper and the advertiser lost. Why not send PostScript files? This is also impractical because PostScript files are generally written for a specific output device. If an advertiser has to generate customized PostScript streams for each newspaper, it might as well send films. Sending films would be more productive and certainly more reliable than sending huge customized files to newspapers. On top of file-format problems, delivering the ads was still a problem, when sending veloxes or removable media. The ad still had to be shipped through expensive ground or air delivery. The newspaper industry needed a file format that was self-contained, cross-platform, reliable, and compact enough to be transmitted quickly. (Can you see where this is headed?)

The PDF format provided the newspaper-advertising community a reliable way to economically and quickly reproduce digital newspaper ads. With reliability, fast turnaround, and cheap reproduction out of the way, inexpensive distribution became the focus. The Associated Press was the first to really tackle this issue.

AdSend   Beginning in 1993, the Associated Press began offering a digital-ad-delivery system to newspapers. Since most newspapers were already receiving some type of AP data, either photo or copy, why not send ads using the same distribution system? Associated Press chose to use PDF as the file format.

Associated Press is now sending 70,000 ads a month to newspapers in PDF form. The 955-member newspapers either print the pages directly or use the "Export to EPS" to place their ads in their pages. At peak, 2,000 ads a day are handled. Included in the AdSend workflow is a job ticket that gives the newspaper information regarding the size, placement, and run dates for the ad.

While being used mostly for black-and-white ads, some retailers have used color. Boscov's, a retail-store chain centered in Reading, PA, began sending preseparated color ads in early 1996 using Distiller 2.1. This is even more effective now because Distiller 3.0 can embed halftone screen information. The workflow is identical to traditional workflows until output. At output, the advertiser or agency generates a PDF file instead of film. This PDF file is sent along with a job ticket and a list of selected newspapers to the AdSend site. Once received, the PDF is distributed to the desired newspapers.

Delivery Criteria   To be successful, a digital-ad-delivery system must be able to meet three criteria—low material and transportation costs, fast-turnaround time, and reliability. PDF meets all of these criteria:

- Low Material Costs: Films or veloxes are generated at the printing site instead of the distribution site.
- Low Transportation Costs: Sending data via telecommunications, be it ISDN, modem, or satellite, is much cheaper than sending hundreds of overnight packages.
- Fast Turnaround: Ads can be sent at the last minute and still be relatively on time.
- Reliability: Because fonts and images can be embedded, all necessary components are available for output.

The Archiving Market   How many times have you wished you hadn't trashed a file or a document? Archiving is critical for a printer. It serves as a history of completed work. After a job has been printed, it is not just thrown away. What if the client needs a reprint? In traditional workflows, archiving stores the physical consumables such as the films or plates.

Stacks of films and plates pile high, and soon you have rooms fully consumed by this archival method. Space is real estate and real estate is money. Since markets are driven by making money, printers are looking to digital archiving.

Digital archiving is the way to go for archiving documents that are electronically composed, as most are today. As magazines and newspapers migrate to complete electronic pagination on systems that support PostScript, they have the opportunity to create an archive of pages for printing, faxing, reprinting, or viewing on the screen. The real question is what format should be stored?

Some may choose the original application file, such as Quark or PageMaker. This raises longevity concerns since application versions are constantly being upgraded. The other choice is to store the PostScript file. This can also be messy due to the huge file size and the near impossibility of editability. The goal of archiving is to save the file that can be repurposed or reprinted.

PDF Archiving   Using PDF as the storage medium for archiving print jobs allows the customer, the printer sales rep, or the printer to see a history of past jobs. Some commercial printers have been archiving PDF versions for use by print sales reps. The files are kept on a central server, which allows the reps to view a history of jobs printed for a given client. Instead of having a huge file cabinet of printed jobs in a storeroom, the rep can access a copy of the job from his/her desk.

Other Archiving   PDF is a natural file format for archiving digital documents. They are not only predictable, but they are considerably smaller in file size than other digital options. Books in PDF form could be connected to a text-retrieval system and used for research purposes. With an Acrobat-based approach, users could retrieve whole pages, with graphics in place, not just text. Reference publishers who need to keep an archive of revisable text might also want an Acrobat archive for reprints, but they would probably maintain that archive alongside an editorial database.

As commercial (and even corporate) printing and publishing worlds migrate towards increasing reliance on digital methods, what are and where are the markets going to be? In a landmark study of digital workflow, visionary industry analyst Mills Davis predicted a new world order where automated information factories churn out new products and deliver them in new ways.

Core markets for printing and publishing will remain substantially intact into the twenty-first century. While the quantity of commercial printing and publishing may gradually level over the next decade, the quality of demand will change rapidly. Networked interactive media and information will grow rapidly over the next five years, but measured by advertising revenues, digital media will still be less than 10 percent of print media. Most categories of printing and publishing now have print, digital media, networked printing, and networked-interactive product alternatives. The most important change is not the displacement of print to nonprint media, but the evolution of printing and publishing processes from craft-based manufacturing to computer and communications-based services. New categories of demand are emerging as key attributes of printing and publishing products are redefined. The dynamic of market demand is about new ways to reach the right person, with the right content, at the right time, in the right place, in the right form for intended uses.

Changing Business Conditions   The printing and publishing business environment is changing. An emerging digital economy is restructuring the industry as well as transforming relationships both within and among customers, service providers, and suppliers. The need for rapid innovation and rapid response to changing markets is a fact of life. The emerging digital infrastructure will propel interbusiness communication, workflow, and content management to new levels of performance, flexibility, and service. The business of printing and publishing wants to be real-time, with zero lag time between identification and fulfillment of need. Advantage will go to companies that, together with their customers, providers, and suppliers, move information better and respond more quickly to changing market needs than their competition.

The need for more rapid response to changing markets, better service, higher quality, lower costs, and greater flexibility is driving businesses in the printing and publishing industry to restructure and to reinvent the way they do business. To drive out costs and reduce processing latency, industries and businesses must take steps to compress their value chain.

Networked Digital Workflows The focus is on process reengineering to achieve rapid response, short cycle time, quality fail-safing, on-line customer service, low transaction costs, low materials usage, minimum inventory costs, and minimum distribution costs. Networked digital workflows introduce new forms of printing and publishing, conducting all business over inter/intranets, establishing print networks for distributed printing, publishing and document management services, and supporting both "push" and "pull" demand models.

Content can be either "pushed" or "pulled" through the network from databases. High-performance networked systems with links to databases make variable page, personalized, and custom content an option. Through printing networks, the distribute-and-print model emerges as an alternative to print-and-distribute.

Internetworking business enables lean, flexible printing and publishing with just-in-time, on-demand delivery. As customer, provider, and suppliers internetwork and make information and systems interoperable, they can molecularize to achieve minimum inventories and processing costs, as well as more rapid response to changing market conditions.

Specific networked workflows will vary depending on the type of business, its markets, technology base, the roles it chooses to play in the networked digital process. Networked digital workflows support a richer and more coordination-intensive information logistics, in which content, workflow, and business-information streams are fully integrated. Digitization begins sooner in the process, ends later, and encompasses more of the total communication and information flow between businesses than has ever possible with analog or digital-analog workflows. All business-to-business communication and as much work-in-process as possible is handled across networks.

Customers can inquire through the net, learn how to prepare jobs, obtain estimates, submit work, determine status, and conduct business transactions. Workflow quality failsafing begins by aligning processes across the value flow to head off problems, by communicating preliminary specifications to all affected parties before ever producing the job. Prepress services, printers, binderies, and fulfillment services, for example, could simulate the job, suggest alternatives to customers, estimate and quote production, provide job-specific instructions, plug-ins, color profiles, business forms, and applets to handle preflight at the customer site. Before transmitting a job (such as a digital advertisement), the source files could be prechecked to ensure not only that the PDF would process correctly, but also that content elements had been made to the correct specifications for the application, medium, and reproduction process.

Networked digital-content creation adds digital photography to the repertoire of digital-analog techniques. All input capture devices will evolve into color-managed network appliances. As the price performance of desktop tools to manipulate image and graphic content and master pages continues to improve, new levels of capability emerge for feature-based content editing, cross-media authoring and meta-design, and variable and custom data merge, to name a few. Many applications will be reengineered to function as software objects across inter-intranet front-ends.

Prepress, printing, and post-press functions will become increasingly automated processes across networks. Incoming work will be digitally logged into content, workflow, and business transaction databases, triggering credit checks, content file preflighting, scheduling, and resource allocation. Digital job specifications will provide the information needed to program individual prepress, press, and post-press operations. Networked digital-process steps will be threaded, multitasked, or concurrently executed as needed, with status updates posted to a common database visible to everyone concerned. Even off-line functions will be coordinated digitally.

One of the hallmarks of networked digital workflows will be color-managed digital printing, proofing, and remote proofing. The defining application will be digital advertising in newspapers, magazines, and catalogs. Pigment-based inkjet printing may provide a near-term breakthrough towards direct proofing on actual stock with colorants that behave like inks on press. Prep will move from files, imagesetters, and imposetters toward databases; variable and custom data merge; and computer-to-film, computer-to-plate, and computer-to-press.

The benefits of moving to an integrated content, workflow, and business database are major, impacting operations upstream as well as downstream. The benefits of computer-to-anything are basically incremental and depend on successful front-end integration of the digital workflow that feeds the prep-step.

Changing Workflows

It is now well known that the integration of PDF into current prepress workflows will streamline those workflows.

Network digital workflow leverage all kinds of printing output—analog sheet-fed, web offset, gravure and flexo presses, and hybrid presses, as well as digital ones. Specifications have been developed for digitally-driven press rooms and digitally-coordinated binderies. These workflows enable multiple distribute-and-print and on-demand printing models as well as print-and-distribute. Networked digital workflow management is based on new control structures. Digital insourcing and outsourcing is common place.

Integration across multiple businesses is achieved through open-network infrastructure standards, shared-process semantics, application-level content specifications, standard file and database formats, and industry standards for electronic data interchange. Distributive workflows are coordinated through network communications to common (synchronized) databases containing evolving content and product information, workflow schedule and current job status, business relationship and financial data, and management information.

Networked digital-content management involves efficient file formats, standard page-description languages, and digital archives with dedicated librarian applications to index, search, and retrieve data. Multipurposing requires maintaining multiple versions of source content. Networked digital business systems are fully integrated with work-in-process and content management. Electronic data interchange and, in some instances, electronic commerce are standard operating procedure.

Quantum improvements in printing and publishing workflow are possible by combining principles of business-process reengineering with architectures for distributive workflow, integrated business systems, and media-independent content management. The PDF is unique in that it is both the product and the enabler of this new world order. As a product it is the view file delivered on disk or over the Web. The information consumer receives his or her content in a format-rich form where type and image are preserved. As an enabler, the PDF is the raw material of new workflows that reengineer the way we print or present. In the history of human communication, there has never been a method that could be so totally repurposed, reused, replayed, and even regurgitated on demand.

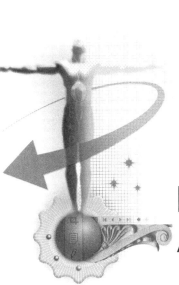

21

Plug-ins Extend Acrobat PDF

Plug-ins are a significant development in the use of application software. A plug-in is an accessory computer program that extends the functionality of a "host" program. On its own, a plug-in can do nothing since it needs the host program to operate.

Plug-ins can be programmed to perform exceptionally simple or complicated tasks. They can be configured to appear when certain conditions are met, such as a particular file being open. They can even cause the Acrobat interface to be completely modified.

Creating plug-ins is a job for software-development professionals. The Acrobat Software Developers Kit is a set of C Language routines, which can be called by other programs. Plug-in developers have used these tools to create dozens of useful Acrobat extensions. If you are thinking of integrating Acrobat into your business, you'll need a plug-in or two.

The plug-ins are in subfolders in the Acrobat3\Goodies folder. Application Programming Interface files are used to develop plug-ins (extended features) in accordance with the information in the

Acrobat Software Developer's Kit (SDK) and provide automatic access to features of an Acrobat application. There are now about one hundred developers developing PDF plug-ins, with about fifty products actually out in the market.

Crackerjack

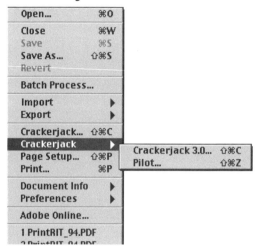

Figure 21-1
Crackerjack appears under the File menu in Acrobat.

Adobe Acrobat outputs composite files. That means that all four colors are contained in one file. This kind of file will drive a color laser printer or digital color press, but it will not drive an imagesetter or platesetter—any device that requires preseparated files. There was a need for a mechanism to do this from within Acrobat.

Extended Print Services was the first major plug-in, and it has been refined and introduced as Crackerjack by Lantana. Because of its importance in printing, we have more detail on it. This plug-in adds print-related features to Acrobat Exchange. With this plug-in the user is able to print separations to an imagesetter or platesetter. The dialog box has four tabs: Pages, Output, Page, and Color. Print-related information is edited and sent to the RIP in four monochrome separations, or if spot colors are used, either separated into CMYK or printed as the spot colors.

The Benefits of Crackerjack   Crackerjack is installed in the Plug-in folder in the Acrobat folder. When Acrobat is opened, Crackerjack will be found in the File menu. Even though the normal Page Setup and Print options are still available, all the controls, and more, are found in Crackerjack. The following are main functions that can be set and or modified with Crackerjack:

- The range of pages in the document to be printed
- The PostScript Printer Description file to use
- Resolutions supported
- Print or save the file as PostScript or EPS
- The Page format
- Offset of page on media
- Offset of image on page
- Crop marks, color names
- Mirrored output
- Negative output
- Composite CMYK or separations
- Screen ruling, screen angle, and halftone pattern
- Screening as specified in document or EPS images
- Control over the rendering if separations will be made in the RIP
- Convert spot color to CMYK process colors
- Specify GCR and UCR

Crackerjack Functions   The settings that relate to how the document will be printed on the page are interactively shown in a second window, Current Page Fit, that is brought up as soon as Crackerjack is chosen. In this window, paper size (as specified in the PPD), page size of the document, crop marks, etc. are shown as they are changed.

Crackerjack and PostScript Level 1 RIP   Crackerjack was designed to work with PostScript Level 2 (or above) applications and devices. This allows a broader array of screening solutions and enables composite color workflows so that the same data can be used for printing, CD-ROM creation, and on-line distribution.

Document

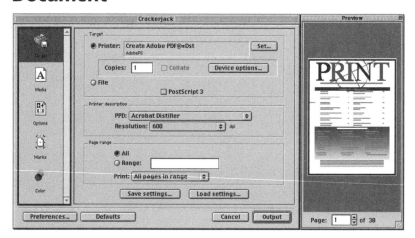

Figure 21-2
Crackerjack Target Options area.

Crackerjack makes it possible to set the PPD file directly from the print dialog box. This function makes it easier to have control over the setting even though there is no difference than if it were specified in the Chooser. The Current Page Fit window changes the printable output size as the PPD is changed. Instead of printing the document to a printer, it can be saved as a PostScript or EPS file, with or without font inclusion. The other document functions are very similar to other printer dialog boxes. Either all of the pages or a range is printed.

Separations from Word or Excel   It is possible to print separations from a document created in Microsoft Word, even if it has embedded graphics, and even if the graphics were created in Microsoft Excel. First, use Type 1 fonts—avoid TrueType. The next step is to create "good" PostScript output from Word by using a high-end PostScript Printer Description (PPD) file. By high-end, we mean a PPD for a device like an imagesetter. When printing from Word you must choose the high-end device and specify "print to file." The resultant PostScript file is then fed into Distiller to create a PDF file. On most PCs, the PostScript file will have a .prn file suffix. You can either edit the file name to give it a .ps suffix or simply let Distiller open the .prn file. Once you have distilled the PostScript file into a PDF document, you can now use Crackerjack to create separated output on your PostScript RIP.

Pages

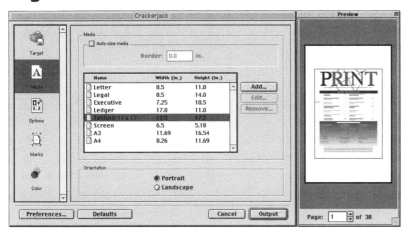

Figure 21-3
Crackerjack Media Options.

For each PPD there is a set of predefined output sizes. These are found in the Media Size pop-up menu. If none of them is suitable for the document that will be printed, it can be customized in a dialog box that appears if the last option in the pop-up menu, Custom Page Size, is picked. All the Page Size choices are shown on the Current Page Fit window. The user can determine from this window whether the document will fit on the available page size. If the page needs to be offset on the output media, the Page to Media option is used in x-y direction. The new preview is very helpful.

No Screen Angle or Frequency Saved in a PDF File
Grayscale TIFF images in an Adobe Acrobat PDF (Portable Document Format) file do not have the same screen angle and frequency as they do in the original file.

- Download the free AddPS Plug-in module (AdDiskR2. sit.hqx "Acrobat Ad Sample Disk"), which is available on the Adobe BBS (206-623-6984) and Adobe's FTP site ftp://ftp.adobe.com/pub/adobe/acrobatdistiller/mac/addis kr2.sit.hqx. The AddPS Plug-in lets you set screens and angles as well as lighten and darken images.
- Print the PDF file to disk as an EPS graphic; then place that EPS into an application in which you can change screen parameters (e.g., PageMaker), and print it from there.
- Create a custom printer file and change the default screen settings for the printer.

Because screen-angle and screen-frequency information are considered device characteristics, Acrobat does not include that information within a PDF file. Doing so reduces the intended portability of PDF files. When Acrobat Exchange or Reader prints PDF files, it adheres to the default screening of your printer. If your printer driver uses a PPD, you can modify it to include the screen settings from the original file.

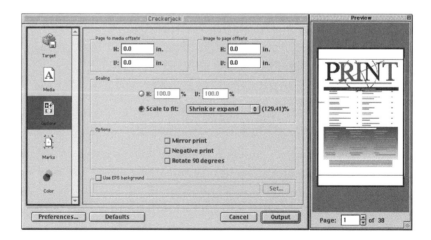

Figure 21-4
Crackerjack lets you position the page image in relation to the sheet size as well as change the proportion in the Options area.

A similar function is the Options setting, but here the document information is offset relatively to the page. This function will change the position of the page as the margins will be changed. If the customer has made a mistake and specified a larger size than available on the output device, there are two options on how this can be solved, without making new PDF files. The document may have enough margins to cut off some of these so that the page need not be reduced to fit the paper size.

Printer Not Printing Separations   Desktop laser printers are not enabled to do in-RIP separations. Therefore, they are unable to process Crackerjack's commands to create separated output. Here the position function in the Options window becomes important. The preview images occupies the same amount of space relative to the media as the objects on the page do. The margins can, however, easily be seen and no guesses have to be made whether the information fits on the smaller page size. For further control of the reproduction of the document, use the options in the Output tab.

Output

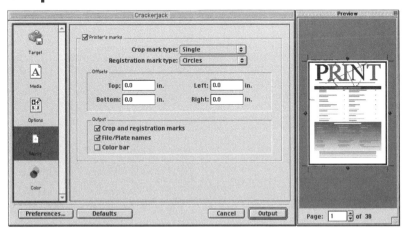

Figure 21-5
Crackerjack Mark Options lets you add printer's marks.

There may be times when the document has a page size that is larger than the possible output size on the imaging device. If the client accepts the page to be scaled in size to fit the maximum page size available, this is easily done by choosing the Shrink to Fit Page option. The user then has a combination of offsetting the document on the printed page and a reduction x and y percent, which can be entered.

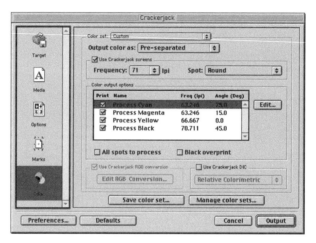

Figure 21-6
Crackerjack Color Options area.

Adobe Acrobat now includes a "job ticket" with your print job—this feature will be expanded in a future version of Adobe PostScript Extreme as more PostScript 3 features are incorporated into the architecture. These "job tickets" let the print job carry a set of instructions for its handling at various stations along the way. They can also convey device-specific information, so the same job can be delivered to two different output devices. Eventually, job tickets may provide a method for tying jobs into job-management databases and perhaps tracking jobs through the work sequence, or even attaching post-press instructions for devices like automated binderies. Many companies are implementing this technology.

The results that can be created with the scaling function in the Output folder tab and the Image Area to Page setting in the Pages folder tab are quite special and give the printer and customer more options when the deadline is close and there is no time for re-creating the design and PDF files. Usually the Current Page Fit window will serve only as an informative guide on how the document will be imaged. Further options in the Output folder tab let you choose whether the output is to be printed mirrored and/or negative depending on the printing requirements. Printers' marks will image crop marks, registration marks, and color names.

Color

This is the important part of Crackerjack where the most benefits are enabled—separations. Without Crackerjack, color separations can not be output from Acrobat. In the Color tab this is an easy procedure: Choose separations and you can also choose whether any spot colors used should be printed as spot color or converted to process colors.

When it comes to screening, there are some further decisions. Depending on the creator of the document, there may be a demand for multiple-screen rulings on the same page. This may have previously been defined in a image application like Photoshop. If these customized screen rulings should be saved, one has to change to Use Document in the top of the Color tab dialog box.

Crackerjack Pilot   Lantana Research Corporation Crackerjack Pilot is an automation option to Crackerjack. PDF print production can be streamlined to a drag-and-drop operation as a plug-in to Adobe Acrobat and is available in Macintosh and Windows versions. Crackerjack Pilot allows the user to set up "hot folders" that are associated with a different output device and/or application-specific output parameters. Folders can be established for an imagesetter or plotter, for brochures or data sheets, for client Jones or Lee, or combinations of these. Once folders are set up, the user needs to drop PDF documents into the appropriate folder(s). The Pilot plug-in scans folders and insures that each document is processed using Crackerjack, which includes professional control over positioning, scaling, separation, screening, and more.

If the page will be reused for a different printing process that can not reproduce the same screen ruling it is a good idea to override the document setting by choosing dialog instead of document. In the Color tab dialog box, the screening and screen angle can thus be specified. When dealing with halftone screens, it must be remembered that you can specify any screen angle but not all screen angles can be used. Screen angles are in almost all cases restricted to 15, 75, 45, and 0 degrees. The screen rulings available depend on the RIP. The same thing is true for the raster shape. The RIP has to be set up to use certain shapes, and there is not much visual result to change the shape on the screen.

Crackerjack   Lantana Crackerjack 3 can be used for both the Macintosh and Windows (95/98/NT) platforms. Crackerjack enables color production workflows using PDF. Crackerjack is the link between the natural preflighting environment of Adobe Acrobat and production printing equipment, such as imagesetters, digital proofers, and color printer/copiers. Crackerjack 3 is released in US English, German, French, and Japanese versions. Release 3 adds to Crackerjack's list of professional controls. New features include

- Preseparated output allowing laser proofs on desktop printers
- Black text overprint to ease trapping and multilanguage work
- New color-management options to tune output to your specific print conditions
- Improved bleed and crop support
- Inclusion of Crackerjack Pilot's watched folder automation (by itself, a $295 savings)
- Auto-size media selection
- Optional backgrounds
- Dynamic page preview capability, and more

The Crackerjack 3 plug-in is compatible with either Acrobat 3 or Acrobat 4. When used in conjunction with Acrobat 4, Crackerjack 3 supports larger and smaller page sizes, smooth shading, PostScript 3, duotones/tritones/quadtones, spot color gradients, and Asian language output. Crackerjack 3 will be included in all future deliveries of PDF PowerPack, a bundle of the leading PDF production plug-ins.

Crackerjack DCS, an optional module for Crackerjack 3, allows generation of DCS 2 files directly from PDF documents. Quark established Desktop Color Separations (DCS) to standardize usage conventions for color separations. Crackerjack DCS supports either one file or multifile output modes, including spot color plates.

Crackerjack 3.1 includes a number of new capabilities, such as tiled output with user-definable overlap, all text to black, and printing and separation support for PDF-based MrSID images. DCS 2.0 output, either single file or multifile, including spot colors, is now included in Crackerjack 3.1 as a standard option.

MrSID, LizardTech's image compression and expansion format based on wavelet technology, permits the same PDF to be small for Web usage, but high quality for production printing. Crackerjack can now automatically output more high-quality image source data for larger formats and higher resolutions.

PDF ImageWorks Is an Image Editor for Acrobat   Lantana ImageWorks is the first native image-editing program for Acrobat. PDF ImageWorks permits image editing and manipulation of PDF images where they appear in the PDF document. PDF ImageWorks does not require any additional external applications. PDF ImageWorks is designed to meet user need for control over image selection, integration, appearance, and usability. Its capabilities address different aspects of PDF images from the various PDF image types, to color spaces, to different image output formats, such as TIFF, EPS, and JPEG. Users can edit image content, perform operations on entire images, and even update OPI-related information. Some functions, such as color conversion and resampling, may be automated. A brief list of additional capabilities provided by PDF ImageWorks includes

- Defect removal
- Compression options
- Color-space conversions
- PDF image replacement
- Extraction of PDF images
- Trim-area specification for bleeds
- Contrast tonal range
- Color balance
- Inclusion of MrSID images in PDF

Q: What is Crackerjack?

A: Crackerjack is a plug-in to Adobe Acrobat for Macintosh or Windows (95/98/NT). It provides a direct link between Acrobat and production printing equipment, such as imagesetters, color proofers, platesetters, digital presses, color printer/copiers, plotters, and high-speed laser printers—from black and white to full color plus spot colors. It drives PostScript Level 2 and PostScript 3 devices.

Q: What need does Crackerjack satisfy?

A: Crackerjack satisfies a number of different needs. First and foremost, it permits PDF documents to be used directly for production printing, that is, "print for pay" applications. It does this independent of platform, vendor, RIP (Adobe, Harlequin, others), and output technology. Many customers use Crackerjack to separate PDF files, particularly those created from Microsoft applications. Crackerjack allows you to drive production printing equipment directly from PDF. Using Crackerjack Pilot you can automate your high-quality PDF printing via "hot folders."

Q: What does it do?

A: Crackerjack delivers professional level control over printed PDF output. It provides handling of target device, screening, separations, fine positioning, scaling, rotation, media and background selection, printer marks, rendering, color control, automation, and much more. Crackerjack takes the PDF and this control information, converts it into sophisticated PostScript, and sends it to the device or destination file. The best way to understand what Crackerjack does is to download the free Demo version and try it.

Q: How can I try Crackerjack?

A: Macintosh and Windows Demo versions of Crackerjack are available at the Lantana web site (http://www.lantanarips.com). The free Demo versions are full working versions with one extra feature: It prints the word "Demo" on the output.

Q: Where can I buy Crackerjack?

A: The Lantana web site (http://www.lantanarips.com) provides listings of domestic and international resellers of Lantana products.

Q: I have a rush job and I need Crackerjack right away. Can I license a serial number to convert my Demo version into a fully licensed version?

A: Yes. Rush orders are processed for an additional $25 handling fee. After your rush order has been successfully processed, the deliverable has been prepared, and a serial number has been assigned, the serial number will be e-mailed to you.

Q: Is volume pricing available for Crackerjack?

A: Yes. Contact sales@lantanarips.com with your specific needs.

Q: Are localized versions of Crackerjack available?

A: Yes. German, French, and Japanese versions are available from Lantana distributors in the corresponding regions.

Q: What is the part number for Crackerjack?

A: For the Macintosh version, the Crackerjack part number is 630-MAC-US. For the Windows version (95/98/NT), the Crackerjack part number is 630-WIN-US.

Q: How can I get support questions about Crackerjack answered?

A: Send an e-mail with your questions to support@lantanarips.com and you will receive a reply promptly.

Plug-ins from EnFocus

PitStop 4 PDF Preflight and Repair   Enfocus Software has added major features to its PitStop 4.preflight, editing, and automated correction application for paper and Internet PDF document with new advanced Action List capability allowing operators to set and employ, in "macro" fashion, recurring changes and corrections.

Action Lists are the way users can implement highly-detailed editing "macros," in conjunction with the Job Profiles that have been available in PitStop 4.0 since its launch. Previously, with Job Profiles and PitStop 4's global change capability, users could make changes on all objects, on one or many pages in a document. Now, with Action Lists, users have the flexibility to make changes to specific objects based on their positions and attributes. In addition, an Action List can contain many of PitStop's editing functions.

PitStop 4's unlimited "undo" function allows users to reapply any portion of a series of steps as part of an Action List process. These can be applied interactively, document by document, or saved as an Action List with "Hot Folder" (batch processing) capability, to be used with new PitStop Server. PitStop 4 includes on-screen editability, guided correction, graphic search and replace, paragraph editing with text reflow and, reusable action lists (e.g., recurring changes/ corrections can be made into automated "macros").

The Navigator Panel is the interface through which users get both standard preflight reports with hyperlinks back to each problem in the original document(s), and "on-the-fly," viewable preflight annotations indicating problem areas. The Navigator Panel opens with just the press of a button, and then either reports that a page is "okay," or "steps" the user through reported problems, one at a time.

PDF editing includes improved text editing and font management, plus editing of higher-end attributes such as spot color and overprint.

- Global conversion of RGB to CMYK or spot colors is possible.
- Control over the ability to automatically move odd and/or even pages to allow for gutter leeway is an option.

- Text editing can be done per complete paragraph with word reflow, or line by line.
- Sophisticated viewing capabilities allow users to see and edit bleeds (and other views saved within the document).
- Changes can be made to any object and/or its attributes, without affecting any other objects in the document.
- Recurring corrections will become part of PitStop 4's auto-correction functionality via reusable (macro-type) action lists. Existing PitStop 4 users will be able to download this feature upgrade at no charge.

Enfocus DoubleCheck   Enfocus DoubleCheck (formerly known as Ferrari) is a unique application and core technology guaranteeing correct document output in client-to-service provider PDF and Adobe PostScript workflows. DoubleCheck accomplishes this by providing a robust verification application engineered to detect the broad range of issues that can impede successful file output.

The Enfocus DoubleCheck Client and Server modules work in concert to greatly enhance productivity throughout the workflow. Four key benefits:

- Offers quality assurance for client-to-service provider print workflows
- Allows creators to verify documents before submission
- Makes PDF and PostScript files production-ready by checking and automatically correcting
- Generates comprehensive preflight and correction reports

DoubleCheck verifies documents before they leave the creator, and then autocorrects them on arrival at the production site, regardless of the originating application or computer platform. Creators utilize rules, or profiles as defined by their service provider using the DoubleCheck Client verification module, to ascertain the exact status of their PostScript or PDF files relevant to the output workflow. Printers and prepress shops, by setting these "rules" (the profiles) for their workflows, allow creators to utilize the DoubleCheck Client verification module so that they can receive files that are fully compliant with their particular workflow. In this way the burden of preflighting is shifted away from the service provider and back to the document originators, who are in a better position to make the necessary corrections to the file.

In addition to automatically detecting and correcting typical errors, DoubleCheck automatically generates a preflight report that pinpoints any other problems within the document that have not been autocorrected.

Supported formats and functions:
- PostScript Level 2
- EPS (Encapsulated PostScript)
- PDF (Portable Document Format)
- OPI (1.3, 2.0, Helios, Color Central, DCS 1.0)
- Produce clean DSC 3.0 PostScript or EPS
- Substitute and embed fonts
- Change spot color to process
- Set black text to overprint
- Statistics on fonts, color, images, OPI
- Errors and warnings; correction log

Tailor 2　With Enfocus Tailor you can open and visually edit any PostScript or Encapsulated PostScript (EPS) file from any source. The document appears in a window exactly as it will print and can be directly manipulated on screen. Simply click-and-drag to move or resize images, paths, or text; open a text line to correct a spelling mistake; use the color mixer to apply a new color. You can move between pages at random, or zoom in to check and edit in detail.

When placing artwork in a layout or preparing a document for prepress production, Enfocus Tailor is the tool to help you meet all requirements. You can add a missing font, change a spot color to process colors, or set the overprint attributes. Before you separate a PostScript job, use the power of Enfocus Tailor to make corrections: an incorrect price, a missing logo, a color problem, etc. Enfocus Tailor cleans up questionable PostScript and always produces normalized PostScript output (Adobe Document Structuring Conventions, DSC 3.0). PostScript or EPS files can also be converted to other popular layout, prepress, and on-line formats such as Adobe Illustrator 3, PDF, PICT, TIFF, and GIF.

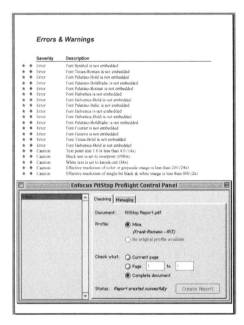

Figure 21-7
Pitstop Control Panel and the report that is generated.

Features found in Tailor Workflow 2.0:

- Move, scale, or rotate any object
- Edit text lines; convert text to outlines
- Edit nodes and Bezier control points
- Modify object attributes using floating inspector, color mixer and font picker
- Save as DSC 3.0 compliant PostScript or EPS with PICT or PC-TIFF preview
- User defined font substitution table
- Export to PICT, TIFF and GIF
- Export text to RTF or ASCII
- Recognize, edit, and create spot colors, names of spot colors from incoming files are maintained
- Support for the major OPI formats (OPI 1.3,
- OPI 2.0, Color Central, Helios and DCS 1.0)
- Batch processing via AppleScript and Luminous OPEN

Third-Party Plug-ins   The next few pages list almost fifty plug-ins (or products that work very closely with Acrobat). With a list this extensive, we cannot guarantee 100 percent accuracy. We have tried to get as much contact information as possible.

5D Solutions Ltd.

Guardian House, Borough Road, Godalming, Surrey, GU7 2AE, UK

Tel: (44) 1483 426 421 Fax:(44) 1483 419 541

www.five-d.com

Niknak's sole purpose is to offer efficient and low-cost creation of PDF 1.2 files compatible with Adobe Acrobat products, or third-party PDF tools. Niknak operates in two modes: Installs as a printer in the Windows Printing System allowing users to print to a PDF file directly from any application. Niknak combines the simplicity of Adobe PDF Writer with Distiller's ability to interpret arbitrary Post-Script and EPS files. Appears as an icon on the desktop allowing drag and drop conversion of any PostScript or EPS file directly to PDF.

ODDJOB is a PostScript and PDF workflow product offering for viewing PS, PDF, EPS files with optional anti-aliasing-translation between any combination of PDF v. 1.0, 1.1, 1.2, PS level 1,2,3,EPS-option to output low resolution GIF/JPEG/TIFF-file splitting and merging, page reordering, watermarking-mailmerge facility using Acrobat Forms plus simple imposition (2- and 4-up, step and repeat)—color separation—batch scripted processing and watched folder processing where appropriate.

Alliant Techsystems

13133 34th Street, North Clearwater, FL 33762

Tel: (813) 572-2200or 1-800-HELP-102 Fax: (813) 572-2658

http://ais.atk.com

InfoLinker is an Acrobat Exchange plug-in that adds navigational capabilities to PDF documents through the generation of automated hyperlinks and bookmarks. Hyperlinks can be created based on a set of user-defined rules or through the use of an automatic rule generator called the Maestro. InfoLinker provides the ability to link from one document to another or to incorporate multimedia or other software applications into your PDF document. It also supports URL links.

Library Manager is a front-end user interface tool that organizes PDF files by a descriptive title. The descriptive name can include up to sixty characters. A search on a portion of the title will yield a list of matching documents. Alias path names and volume labels are used for variable pathing to repositories, such as CD jukeboxes, disk arrays, and networks for easy document retrieval.

Link Manager is used for easily modifying links in PDF files. It allows users to selectively modify manual or automated links by changing attributes, or deleting specific links, notes, and threads. Link Manager also can refresh hyperlinks in documents that have had minor revisions and can change the color of hyperlinks.

Atlas Software BV

Buys Ballotstraat 17-193846 BG Harderwijk, The Netherlands
Tel: (+31) 341 426700 Fax: (+31) 341 424608
www.atlassoftware.nl
PrintShop Mail is a production tool for Variable Data and personalized printing. PrintShop Mail lets you create all kinds of personalized documents, from simple labels and newsletters to complex (variable images) color mailings. Sophisticated PDF and PostScript technology is used to realize a short process (SPOOL + RIP) time.

BCL Computers

990 Linden Dr., Suite 203, Santa Clara, CA 95050
(408) 225 2679
Fax (408) 249 4046
Hanyen@bcl-computers.com
http://www.bcl-computers.com
Freebird 2.01 Creation/Conversion. Freebird allows you to easily convert your PDF file archives to graphical archive. Freebird supports output resolutions up to 600 dpi. Supported platforms: WinNT/95/98.

Magellan 2.0 Creation/Conversion. Magellan 2.0 allows you to easily convert your PDF to HTML format. Magellan 2.0 preserves the page structure, presenting information accurately. Supported platforms: WinNT/95/98.

Jade 1.0 Creation/Conversion. Jade 1.0 is a plug-in for Acrobat Exchange 3.0 and 3.0J that allows users to accurately extract data from Adobe PDF files that would be unobtainable.Supported platforms: WinNT/95/98.

Freebird 4.0 Creation/Conversion. Freebird 4.0 allows for easy conversion of your PDFs to graphical archives. Resolutions up to 600 dpi are supported, giving high-clarity archives. Supported platforms: WinNT/95/98.

Jade 4.0 Creation/Conversion. Jade 4.0 is a plug-in for Acrobat 4.0 and 4.0J that allows users to accurately extract data from PDF files that would otherwise be unobtainable. Supported platforms: WinNT/95/98.

Magellan 4.1 Creation/Conversion. Magellan 4.1 allows for easy conversion of PDFs to HTML format. Magellan preserves the page structure, allowing for accurate presentation. Supported platforms: WinNT/95/98.

Drake 4.0 Creation/Conversion. BCL Drake 4.0 is an application that automatically converts PDF documents into RTF documents utilizing the MS Word drawing features. Supported platforms: WinNT/95/98.

callas software
Pappelallee 9D-10437, Berlin, Germany
Tel: +49 30 443 90310 Fax: +49 30 441 6402
www.callas.de
pdfToolbox:
—pdfBatchMeister applies predefined Distiller settings for pre-press/CD-ROM/Internet to EPS/PostScript in batch mode
—pdfOutput is for cross-platform EPS file-generation with preview and embedded fonts
—pdfInspektor for preflighting PDF files for output: resolutions colors, embedded and subsetted fonts etc.

—pdfCrop&Measure for crop and measure areas and distance of PDF files

—Batch preflight and convert PDF files into RIP-friendly EPS from a single dialog box.

—pdfCropMarks to your PDF file.

—Preflight OPI and compression information with pdfInspektor

—Full separation output for Level 1/2 RIPS.

MadeToPrint XT 3.1: Batch-printing workflow tool now creates PDF files from QuarkXPress.

—MadeToPrint's preconfigured PDF settings mean you don't need to touch the Distiller settings.

—integrates Distiller settings and destination folders into MadeToPrint jobs

—MadeToPrint can now launch PDFDesign XT (TechnoDesign) for user-defined placement of directives automatic generated book-marks within QuarkXPress.

—Flexible options to create one PDF document per page/document and hot folder locations

—Creates PostScript/perfectly cropped EPS files, calls up Distiller and PDF Design XT directly for PDF files for prepress/Internet/CD-ROM use in one print job

—Updates modified picture without printing

—Prints to single or multiple devices simultaneously with different print settings

—Fully automated when used with AutoPilot XT.

Computerised Document Control Ltd.

PO Box 5, Chepstow, Monmouthshire NP6 6YU, UK

Tel: + 44 (0) 1291 641 715 (direct) USA: 1-888-240-1752

Fax: + 44 (0) 1291 641 817

www.docctrl.com

Document publishing software to enable the assembly, dissemina-tion, and distribution of critical business documents. Forging the link between document systems and Adobe Acrobat, CDC's products offer solutions for:

—Dossier compilation and publishing

—Database publishing for customized documents on demand

—Controlled printing for regulated document environments

—"Intelligent" PDF creation

Products are available either as integrated solutions for document management systems or System Integrator tools for Web-based publishing solutions.

Data Technology Group, Inc.

221 E. Main St. Milford, MA 01757

Tel: 508-634-1099 Fax: 508-634-0898

www.dtgsw.com

Publisher is the first software package created specifically for the generation of FDA compliant electronic submission of Case Report Forms (CRFs) in Adobe's Portable Document Format (PDF). The software performs on-the-fly PDF generation, including Tiff conversion, bookmarking, and Table of Contents generation without the use of Adobe Capture, Distiller, Plug-Ins, or print drivers. The comprehensive functionality provided by CRF Publisher virtually eliminates the problems that can be introduced with the manual steps required by other solutions. The software is designed for unattended operation.

Digital Applications, Inc.

215 E. Providence Rd., Aldan, PA 19018-4129

Tel: 610-284-4006 Fax: 610-284-4233

www.digapp.com

Redax for Text and Redax for Text and Images are plug-ins that allow the user to edit PDF documents in compliance with Freedom of Information Act and Privacy Act Requirements.

DateD is a set of plug-ins that add dynamic date/time information as well as a static message to documents when opened and printed.

TimedOut adds additional security features and expiration dates to documents. Expired documents can be accessed only with the proper passcode established by the System or Document Administrator.

SecurSign adds digital signatures to PDF documents using public/private key pairs.

AppendPDF is a server application that appends PDF files or page ranges within files.

StampPDF is a server application that adds text messages, page numbers, or other static information to numbers of PDFs in an automated process.

Dionis

167 Milk Street, # 478, Boston, MA 02109-4315
(617) 738 7806 Fax (617) 738 5879
info@Dionis.com
http://www.dionis.com
Ari's Power Bundle Management. Ari's Power Bundle includes Ari's Ruler, Ari's Print Helper, Ari's Link Checker, and Ari's Crop Helper. Supported platforms: Mac/WinNT/95/98.

Ari's PDF Splitter Management. Ari's PDF Splitter splits your large PDF files into smaller PDF files, automatically adjusting and maintaining your links and bookmarksSupported platforms: Mac/WinNT/95/98

Ari's Print Helper Print. Ari's Print Helper gives you an expanded print dialog box. Page ranges can include even or odd numbered pages or pages in reverse numerical order. Supported platforms: Mac/WinNT/95/98.

Ari's Ruler Management. Ari's Ruler lets you measure your PDF documents on screen. Check out your file before going to film. Supported platforms: Mac/WinNT/95/98.

Ari's Link Tool Management. Ari's Link Tool, is a plug-in for Adobe Acrobat Exchange that provides powerful tools for editing links in PDF files. Supported platforms: Mac/WinNT/95/98.

D Soft
(ADA 823)Sparrestraat 24B-9920, Lovendegem Belgium
Tel: + 32 9 372 70 41 Fax: + 32 9 372 41 66
www.dsoft.be
The company develops plug-ins for clients (mostly publishers) that provide a unique navigation interface for the user giving direct access to the requested information. They wrote an alternative for the Acrobat Search engine. By using this plug-in, a user can limit the search to certain chapters within a PDF file rather than the file itself. You can browse through a complete table of contents that is extracted for the PDF files. These are plug-ins for special CD-ROM purposes.

Dynalab Inc.
41900 Christy St., Fremont, CA 94538
Tel: 408-735-0774 Fax: 408-735-9070
www.dynalab.com.t or www.dynalab.com.hk
or www.dynalab.co.jp
DynaDoc/PDF plays back documents with Chinese or Japanese characters through the reader into the English Windows environment. It allows users to view and print Asian character documents across a varying range of platforms. DynaDoc utilizes the convenient print-driver option to generate the formatted document. Offers two ways of generating PDF formatted documents—through the Adobe PDF printer driver or through a PostScript file to a PDF converter. Generates and reads PDF documents across platform, application, and software version. Handles two-byte data, embedding CJK fonts.

Electronics for Imaging, Inc.

2855 Campus Drive, San Mateo, CA 94403

Tel: (650) 286-8556 Fax: (650) 286-8686

www.efi.com

Fiery DocBuilder Pro is an optional upgrade to the standard Fiery Command WorkStation application. It features the industry's first server-based imposition by way of Adobe's Portable Document Format (PDF) architecture. In addition to imposition, Docbuilder Pro also contains all of the classic DocBuilder capabilities, now at a pre-RIP stage. This includes the ability to view thumbnails and full-screen previews, full-page editing by way of third-party plug-in support, as well as delete, duplicate, and combine of pages between multiple source PDF documents. All changes are retained in the original PDF file, so they may be archived or re-RIPped.

Enfocus Software

234 Columbine Street, Suite 3008, P.O. Box 6410, Denver, CO 80206

Tel: (303) 393-7282 or (888) 363-6287 Fax: (303) 393-7290

Technologiepark-Zwijnaarde 3B-9052 Gent, BELGIUM

Tel: +32 9 241 57 05 Fax: +32 9 245 03 04

www.enfocus.com

Enfocus PitStop is a plug-in for Adobe Acrobat to visually edit PDF documents inside Acrobat Exchange. You can edit any PDF-document in Acrobat Exchange no matter where it was originally created. Open any PDF document in Acrobat Exchange and click on the Enfocus PitStop button in the toolbar. A PitStop window pops up with the page ready for editing. Simply click-and-drag text or graphics to select, edit, move, scale, rotate and/or change color. It is a tool for PDF editing.

CheckUp lets you preflight and check any PDF document in Acrobat. Verify whether the document is properly created to suit the intended use. Does it contain embedded fonts? Are the images in the desired resolution and color space? Compression? The rules on how and what to check in a PDF document are defined and saved in preflight profiles. Just select the preflight profile of your choice and click on the Check button. Enfocus CheckUp generates a comprehensive preflight report divided into four main areas: fonts, images, color, and general information. The report lists warnings and errors, and hyperlinks point you to the flagged objects in the checked PDF document.

Enfocus "Ferrari," now DoubleCheck, is a server application for print production. Normalize and preflight PostScript to a reliable format and also convert it to PDF and EPS if needed. There are numerous automatic-correction functions such as spot to process and font inclusion. Optimize your PostScript and PDF workflow. With Enfocus Ferrari you can preflight, correct, convert, and normalize your PostScript, PDF and EPS files before going into prepress production.

Extensis Corp.

1800 S.W. First Ave., Suite 500, Portland, OR 97201
Tel: (503) 274-2020 Fax: (503) 274-0530
www.extensis.com
Preflight Pro automates the preflight process, finds errors in all leading page-layout and illustration programs, and helps correct problems with the unique Pilot feature before the job is output. After preflighting, the job can be distilled into a clean, error-free PDF file, increasing the speed and reliability of digital workflows.

Preflight Designer eliminates rework by allowing designers to prepare error-free files for printing. Inspects files and displays key information related to RGB images, missing fonts, and more. Users can then collect all the elements needed to print, including embedded fonts and graphics. An electronic Job Ticket helps streamline communication with service bureaus. Additionally, users have the option to distill a PDF directly from Preflight Designer, and collect it with a job for output.

FileOpen Systems Inc.
101 W 85th St. #1-4, New York, NY 10024
Tel: 212-877-3183 Fax: 212-712-9543
www.fileopen.com
FileOpen PDF is a system for publishing secured PDF files on the Web or CD-ROM. The system allows publishers to define access privileges for collections of PDF documents, set rules for document expiration at an absolute or relative date, embed the copyright owner's contact information in the file, embed Digital Object Identifiers (DOIs) for copyright management and usage tracking, and automatically create an installer for the client software and PDF collection.

The FileOpen client, at the user end, invisibly stores permissions data in the user's operating system and opens files for users without any password entry. The FileOpen PDF security system blocks unauthorized users from accessing FileLock'ed or expired files.

HAHT Software
4200 Six Forks Road, Raleigh, NC 27609
Tel: (888) 438-4248 Tel: (919) 786-5177 Fax: (919) 786-5250
www.haht.com
The HAHTsite Enterprise Solution Module (ESM) for Adobe Acrobat provides a rapid and powerful way to connect Adobe PDF documents to server-side data and applications over the Web. The ESM for Adobe Acrobat is a wizard that runs in the HAHTsite Integrated Development environment to allow developers to point and click to associate PDF form fields with databases and applications.

PDF forms can now quickly and easily be integrated in any Web application. The ESM for Adobe Acrobat requires the HAHTsite IDE and is available as a free download from the HAHT Web site.

HELIOS Software GmbH

Steinriede 3, D-30827, Garbsen, Germany

Tel: +49 5131 709320 Fax: +49 5131 709325

www.helios.com

US distributor EMC, www.ugraf.com

Helios PDF Handshake is an extension for EtherShare and/or EtherShare OPI servers. It allows the user to print PDF documents with proper colors to any PostScript device and to use PDF as hi-res input format for the OPI workflow. PostScript Type 1 and 3 as well as TrueType fonts are supported. It comes with the standard PostScript fonts, about 340 Berthold font faces, and about 30 Mb high-quality ICC profiles.

Users can print PDF documents with a Helios supplied Acrobat plug-in or Unix tool: separated for final print or matched for proof print, to any PostScript device, including Level 1 RIPs, with optional merging of spot-to-process colors, and with registration marks. In case of OPI, PDF Handshake generates color-correct EPS lo-res images of PDF originals. These lo-res representations can be used like any other EPS.

During output the Helios server swaps EPS lo-res by PDF hi-res and sends it as color attached/separated PostScript to the printer. PDF Handshake gives prepress and printing customers all the benefits of PDF as a universal exchange format for their existing applications and their currently installed output devices, without any need for costly and time consuming upgrades.

Iceni Technology Ltd.

82 St Philips Road, Norwich, Norfolk UK NR2 3BW

Tel: 44 (0) 1 603 474 831 Fax: 44 (0) 1 603 474 832

www.iceni.com

This software enables the repurposing of the content of PDFs, both text and images. It uses an intelligent content recognition engine to automatically determine the different content component parts of a document. This information is then used to tag and extract the content from the PDF page. For example, it is able to identify and link together the heading, by line, caption, and body text of an article on a page of a newspaper or magazine. It can automatically associate captions with images to enable searching of images using the caption within an asset management system. This process is automatically carried out for each separate article on the page. Thus, the different articles on a page are identified, tagged, and extracted as separate files from the same PDF page. The tags that are applied to the content components are user-configurable for different end uses such as XML, HTML, RTF, or input for search engines.

AdStract: extracts and tags the content of ads that have been supplied in PDF format, distilled into PDF from EPS files, and/or been converted to PDF from camera-ready artwork using Capture. Software has been optimized for auto and job ads. For example, the software is able to extract and format lists of autos, with their prices, from dealer ads. The tags that are applied are user configurable for different uses, such as for HTML output and Web ad sites, such as Auto Hunter and Job Hunter.

TEP extracts text from PDFs and formats it into XML, HTML, RTF, or user-defined Tagged Text format. It supports automatic embedding of PDF image links in XML and HTML. Software is also used as a front end to provide search engines with high quality and very structured input. It recognizes and separately tags headings, paragraphs, footnotes, title, page number, author, and creation date. Gives more accurate and relevant captions in search results fields. Uses hot folders and/or standalone process.

PEP extracts images from PDF as Progressive JPEG, EPS, or TIFF. It is able to preserve or convert color spaces and supports image-compression schemes. It comes supplied with macros for automatically naming images and embedding information into image-header files. It can be used in combination with TEP software to provide full PDF to XML or HTML output including images, with links. PEP is available as a plug-in to Acrobat, which uses hot folders and/or standalone process.

Imation Publishing Software

1011 Western Avenue, Suite 900, Seattle WA 98104

Tel: (206) 689 6700 Fax: (206) 689 6701

http://ips.imation.com

Imation PressWise produces plate-ready signatures in minutes, for use on web or sheet-fed presses. It includes the ability to RIP files to screen, which allows detailed, on-screen review of font, ink, and page specifications. PressWise comes with customizable sets of page, form and sheet marks, including the option to use EPS art as a mark. PressWise imposes PDF files, allowing you to mix PDF, EPS, and PostScript pages within the same signature. PDF support allows PressWise users to benefit from the application independence and small file sizes of PDF.

With Imation OPEN software, you can automate time-consuming, repetitive tasks within a distributed server environment. OPEN can automate repetitive steps in a PDF workflow, such as creating PDFs on a server, converting PDF to PostScript, or distributing PDF files to multiple recipients. Users can send files into the Pipeline from anywhere on the network, letting OPEN control their progress each step of the way. Whatever your production needs, OPEN can scale up to handle the heaviest workload.

Cross platform with Microsoft SQL Server. Imation Media Manager spares the tedium of managing valuable digital resources. As a client/server database system, Media Manager manages text, image, sound, video, and other digitized media files from a high-performance server, while users control operations from the comfort of their own workstation. With the Media Manager PDF I Piece plug-in, users can transparently catalog, preview, locate, and retrieve their PDF documents from the Media Manager database.

Infocon America

620 Newport Center Dr. Suite 1100, Newport Beach, CA 92660

Tel: (714) 721-6662 Fax: (714) 759-8391

www.infoconamerica.com

The InfoLink Publishing Enhancement Software converts to PDF, greatly enhances with many navigational capabilities, bookmarks and links, edits, preflights, indexes for full text search, and secures for sale and distribution to subscribers and customers.

Infodata Systems/Ambia Corporation

12150 Monument Drive, Fairfax, VA 22033
Tel: (703) 934-5205 Fax: (703) 934-7154
www.infodata.com
Virtual File Cabinet (VFC) is a family of client/server, intranet-based products that allow users to collaborate on mixed-file documents across the enterprise. Utilizing a familiar Web Browser interface, VFC allows workgroups to annotate and share Acrobat PDF documents in real-time.

Infodata's Acrobat division, Ambia, is one of the market's leading developers of Acrobat products and services, has a full line of Acrobat tools for publishers (Compose), workgroups (Re:mark), and individual end users (Aerial). Ambia also develops custom solutions for organizations needing specialized Acrobat features, or integration of Acrobat software into a systems solution.

Ivy International

270 West Center St., Orem, UT 84057
Tel: (801) 227-3447 Fax: (801) 227-3478
www.virtualt.com
Java/Internet server version VBShelf enables publishers to create complete publishing solutions by allowing both control of documentation presentation and the contextual organization of every electronic document. Using VBShelf, an Acrobat plug-in, PDF files are programmed with information that makes them "Intelligent." They are arranged by date, collection, volume, issue, or article. Being Intelligent, these documents can reside anywhere: hard drive, CD-ROM, floppy disk, corporate Intranets, or the Internet. The end result is that readers no longer need to remember cryptic file names, where files are located, or their relationship with other documents you've published or will publish in the future.

Kuehling Buerokommunikation GmbH
Schleefstr. 2e44287 Dortmund, Germany
Tel. and Fax: 0049-213-45991-0
www.kuehling.de
This is a server application for archiving and printing spool files from
UNIX or IBM (converting their native formats) or Windows (using
PDF). It features document separation, page handling, long-docu-
ment splitting, thumbnail insertion. It permits tunneling of index
info to the archival system. It does text extraction for full-text indexing. It can control import into an archival system. It offers text-field-
extraction capabilities like in classical COLD document, and type
classification based on content used for deciding where the document goes.

Lantana Research Corporation
39560 Stevenson Pl. #220, Fremont, CA 94539
Tel: (510)744-0282 Fax: (510) 744-1307
www.lantanarips.com
Crackerjack Version 3.0 contains a host of new features and capabilities. Crackerjack is a powerful plug-in that enables PDF-based color
production printing. Crackerjack extends the usability of Acrobat and
PDF by providing expert control over print output and associated
devices, such as imagesetters, proofers, platemakers, digital presses,
and plotters. With the new preseparated output option, you can also
proof separations on PostScript desktop laser printers. Crackerjack
employs a simple to use, and visually intuitive, user interface, which
is unique in that it provides the user with controls to tune the position, scaling, separations (including spot colors, and duotones),
screening, color management, black overprint, stored settings, etc. of
all output. It also includes Crackerjack Pilot, the automation option
for Crackerjack.
   OPI Doctor cures what ails your OPI information within a PDF
document. Typically, OPI information comes into PDF as comments
only, as a low-resolution or placeholder image only, but rarely with all
the right information to both preview/proof correctly and to eventually print the high-resolution version. With OPI Doctor, you can

include or substitute images (skinny PDF to fat PDF, or vice versa), verify and update links, and perform other OPI related functions. You can also extract images for editing and later replacement; move and resize images; or resample images to repurpose the PDF file.

PDF Bellhop uses a PDF document to provide full suitcase services. In addition to fonts, you can include images, QuarkXPress, PageMaker, or other digital files. This Acrobat plug-in turns a PDF file into a portable container for prepress delivery. PDF Bellhop's easy-to-use features speeds inclusion and extraction of files. Not restricted to graphic arts applications. Suggested retail price US $95.

PDF Librarian turns a PDF document into an archiving environment. With this Acrobat Exchange plug-in, you can store digital files within a PDF file. PDF Librarian also provides a complete tool set for managing, extracting, and launching these files. PDF Librarian has capabilities for compression, encryption, versions, revision control, auto backup, and logging. Great for engineering projects, Web site management, graphic arts projects.

PDF Valet is an easy-to-use royalty-free plug-in to Acrobat that unpacks digital files that were inserted within PDF documents by PDF Librarian or PDF Bellhop. Suggested retail price is free.

PDF PowerPack is a bundle of the leading graphic arts tools for PDF production. The bundle includes PitStop 4.0 (preflight and editing) from Enfocus, Imposing Plus (imposition) from Quite, Crackerjack (output control), Crackerjack Pilot (output automation), and OPI Doctor (OPI and image management) from Lantana, all plug-ins to Acrobat 4.0. This collection of software is an excellent way to get started doing PDF print production. The price for the bundle represents more than $200 savings over the packages purchased separately.

PDF Essentials is a bundle of the two most important PDF production plug-ins to Adobe Acrobat. PDF Essentials contains

Enfocus PitStop and Lantana's Crackerjack. These products extend Acrobat from a mere graphical viewing environment to an editing and print-production environment. PDF Essentials makes the difference between working with PDF and worrying about it.

MapSoft Computer Services
Hunters Moon, Idstone, Loddiswell, Kingsbridge, TQ7 4 EJ
Devon, UK
+44 1548 550047
Fax +44 1548 550267
sales@mapsoft.com
http://www.mapsoft.com
Mapsoft PDF Explorer Management. Mapsoft PDF Explorer enables you to look at the internals of PDF files. Supported platforms: WinNT/95/98.

Mapsoft Impress Management. Impress allows you to mark the pages of a PDF document with various kinds of impressions, such as watermarks, date and time stamps, page numbers etc. Supported platforms: WinNT/95/98.

Mapsoft MediaSizer Creation/Conversion. Mapsoft PDF Explorer enables you to change the media (page) size of a PDF file. Supported platforms: WinNT/95/98.

PageForm Creation/Conversion. PageForm dramatically improves the PDF creation workflow by enabling the creation of interactive PDF forms from within PageMaker. Supported platforms: WinNT/95/98.

Mapsoft Impress Pro Management. Impress Pro contains the features of Impress: AND batch functionality. Security, open defaults and document information can also be set. Supported platforms: WinNT/95/98

Muscat Limited

St. John's Innovation Centre, Cowley Road

Cambridge CB4 4WS UK

Tel: +44 (0) 1223 421222 Fax: +44 (0) 1223 421223

www.muscat.com

This is a Web-server based UNIX- and NT-scalable PDF indexing and search product that indexes large collections of PDFs either—document by document, or page by page—and preserves positional information for term highlighting. Natural language searching with relevance ranking with Search by Category (Dates, Authors, Sections).

OneVision

Florian-Seidl Strasse 11, D-93053, Regensburg, Germany

Tel: +49-941-78004-0 Fax: +49-941-78004-49

438 Division Street, Sewickley, PA 15143

Tel: (412) 741-4811 Fax: (412) 741-4818

www.onevision.de

DigiScript opens, checks, and corrects digital data and enables you to pass it along as error-free PostScript or PDF files to your production environment. It offers the capability to amend image, text, and graphic elements without regard from which system environment the files originate. It accepts and edits EPS, PDF, separated and unseparated PostScript files. It zooms up to 80,000 percent, may also be set in dpi (WYSIWYG). It offers processing of image, text, and graphic elements and changing colors for selected elements, selected pages, or entire documents. Extraction of all embedded fonts is also a feature.

DigiServer software enables you to proof data files from customers in PDF, EPS, AI, TIFF, and PS format for a fully automated and error-free production process, from order entry to the final print. A log file gives you detailed information about the incoming files. Faulty files can be rejected. Necessary corrections and enhancements for image, text, and graphic elements can be done using DigiScipt.

There is automated interpretation of PDF, EPS, AI, TIFF, and separated PS files. Data formats are independent of hardware architectures and applications. It rejects files containing PS errors before entering the production process and will not disturb your workflow. There is automated order processing and controlling. It logs faulty datafiles, which can then be amended with DigiScript. Both DigiScript and DigiServer allow you to use OneVision Imposition to impose documents from any hardware architecture and/or application, making it possible to process data that has entered the production in PS, EPS, PDF, AI, or TIFF format. It also supports OPI. No import filters required. There are folding schemes.

PenOp Inc.

One Penn Plaza, Suite 2407, New York, NY 10119
Tel: (212) 244-3667 Fax: (212) 244-1646
www.penop.com
Provides secure electronic sign-off, approval, and authentication for documents and forms within Acrobat Exchange. PenOp technology enables the safe and legal execution of electronic documents through the innovative combination of cryptography and biometrics. It's designed to be the legal equivalent of a handwritten signature on paper. PenOp captures the signing event using an inexpensive digitizer and links it to an Acrobat Exchange document or form, creating a Biometric Token— an evidentiary record of who signed what, when, and why.

PenOp allows users to sign Acrobat documents and forms using the PenOp plug-in for Acrobat. PenOp's Software Development Kit, as well as a number of other plug-ins or PenOp-enabled document management and workflow solutions, are also available for customization of the particular environment.

Quite Software Ltd.

105 Ridley Road, Forest Gate, London E7 0LX UK
Tel: +44 181 257 1044Fax:+44 181 522 1726
www.quite.com
Quite A Box Of Tricks is a new plug-in for Adobe's Acrobat from Quite Software, for Macintosh and Windows 95/98/NT. Features

include conversion to CMYK or grayscale, shrinking images to reduce PDF file size, thickening "hairlines," transformations, integrating form fields with documents, all text to black, and detailed info on text and images. In Windows 98 and on the Macintosh, ICC profiles can be used for CMYK conversion.

The aim of Quite A Box Of Tricks is to make easy commonly needed PDF functions that were difficult, time-consuming, expensive, or just impossible. The functions come under five headings: shrink, color, transform, fields, and info. The plug-in is extremely easy to use, but also comes with a forty-eight-page on-line guide to give extra insight into PDF and get the most out of the plug-in.

- Subsample and/or recompress images without any need to redistill
- Can produce dramatic space savings
- Ideal for Web page preparation, proofing, or fixing bad distiller settings
- Offers "JPEG extra," stronger compression than Distiller will allow
- Easy access to compression settings through named profiles
- See the results immediately: If you compress too much just hit Restore and try again with different settings
- NEW! Can offer savings over Distiller 4.0
- Converts any PDF file to CMYK by converting all RGB and Lab data to CMYK
- Optionally converts all spot plates to process (CMYK)
- On MacOS and Windows 98 (only), use ICC profiles for precise, accurate color conversion
- Converts to grayscale, or all text to black
- Choose a minimum line thickness to make "hairlines" print on high-res devices; fix an entire file at once
- Scales pages
- Free rotate by any angle
- Mirrors pages, e.g., for film or for fabric transfers
- Combines form fields into document so they cannot be modified or lost

- Removes all form fields to shrink files
- Makes annotations a part of the document, or removes them all
- Gets information on text and images in a PDF file
- For text, shows the exact font used, and whether it is embedded and/or subsetted
- For images, shows exact dimensions, how well they are compressed, JPEG method, DPI, and more
- Searches document for the largest images or for RGB image to identify troublespots
- Shrinks or recompresses individual images

Quite Imposing and Quite Imposing Plus are plug-ins. Quite Imposing combines pages onto larger sheets to make books, booklets, or special arrangements. A particularly important feature of the plug-ins is that the combined pages are a new PDF document. Quite Imposing Plus also has options to add numbers to pages, to cover things with "masking tape," or add a page from a PDF file over any other page at any scale. Both plug-ins can also reorder pages, split or merge even and odd pages, and more. The most popular feature may be an easy-to-use booklet maker, which can make a foldable booklet from just about any PDF file. Both are available in a version for Windows (NT or 95 only), and for Power Macintosh. Quite Imposing and Quite Imposing Plus have the same core features.

- Create booklets: Create 2-up booklets from any PDF file (The result is a PDF document ready for printing.) Arrange pages on a larger sheet, e.g., 2 x 2.
- N-up pages… Can add margins, crop marks, frames; can arrange onto a background PDF file; trim from the edge of pages; or add space at the edge of pages; or shift the contents of pages by a fixed or variable amount. Also shift for "creep" in a folded booklet.
- Shuffle pages for imposing: Rearrange pages to any order by defining a imposing simple rule.
- Shuffle even/odd: process even and odd pages separately; can split into separate files, and merge together.

- Reverse pages: reverses order of pages.
- Insert blank pages: inserts blank pages or creates a blank document.
- Create sample document: useful for testing imposition.
- Remember last action.
- Give a name to almost any of the above functions.
- Playback action: Step back through a saved action.
- Preferences: Define background templates containing printers marks etc.

Quite Imposing Plus has the following features plus above.
- Step and repeat: fills sheets with multiple copies of the same page (e.g., for business cards, labels).
- Manual imposition: total manual control; places page over any other page, at any scale.
- Defines bleeds: allows pages to be imposed with contents reaching over the edge, for trimming; adds numbers to pages or imposed sheets; can also add arbitrary text with or without numbers.
- Peels off page numbers; defines a layout for "tape," sticks on one or many pages; removes numbers or text added by Quite Imposing from one or many pages, or from imposed sheets; removes crop marks, etc. added by Quite Imposing marks and Plus.
- Imposition info: view origin of imposed pages for full accountability; also extracts imposed pages for reuse, and deletes pages from imposition; allows additional plug-ins.

The limitations of Quite Imposing are mostly those of the current releases of Acrobat.
- Acrobat 3 does not allow page sizes smaller than 1 inch (25.4 mm) or larger than 45 inches (1143 mm), and Quite Imposing naturally cannot support sizes outside this range. Acrobat 4 increases the limit to 200 inches (5080 mm).

- Quite Imposing will not impose files for which any security attributes have been set. This is a deliberate prohibition built into Acrobat.

Radtke Consulting
4707 140th Avenue N., Suite 103, Clearwater, FL 33762
Tel: (813) 531-8205 Fax: (813) 531-9141
rradtke@gte.net
This is a PDF Comparison Plug-In. Using P/Comp will build bookmarks and links that describe the differences between two PDF files. P/Comp uses different colors of links to highlight differences in font types, size, position, and most importantly, new or missing words. Bookmarks are organized into New Words and Missing Words by page in the PDF.

P/Comp allows a user to select fonts, sizes, attributes, and/or strings to be used to create Bookmarks in a PDF document. The Bookworm searches through a document and when a match is found, it creates a bookmark to the location of the Match in the document.

RC:Splitteris an Automated PDF Splitter and Combiner Plug-In. Based on selected criteria, this plug-in searches a PDF, and when the criteria changes, the plug-in creates a new PDF document with all the pages up to the changed page. The tool can optionally recombine the newly created PDFs into a reorganized complete document.

PDM: PDF Document Manager allows a collection of PDFs to be organized for delivery. The PDM keeps track of where PDFs are located: network drives, removable CDs, jukeboxes. Selection criteria can be searched to find PDFs. When the documents are selected, the proper device and location are automatically selected or requested, and the document is opened. This can be used for controlling links across devices or for delivery on CD-ROM.

A Round Table Solution

Level 10, 114 Albert Rd, South Melbourne, 3205, Victoria, Australia

+61 (3) 9530 6715 Fax+61 (2) 9475 0464

karl@roundtable.com.au

http://www.roundtable.com.au/

ARTS PDF Workshop Management. PDF Workshop extracts and collates PDF document and file info (title, subject, keywords, pages) into a spreadsheet to simplify managing your PDFs. Supported platforms: WinNT/95/98.

ARTS Joust Management. ARTS Joust is a flexible workflow tool for people who send PDFs via e-mail. Supported platforms: WinNT/95/98.

RTSJoust is a streamlining plug-in for Adobe Acrobat providing three powerful functions, including Send Mail, Save and Edit/ Transfer. RTSJoust makes editing, annotating, and sending a Web-based Portable Document Format document a simple, one-click process. This plug-in runs only in Acrobat and Reader.

ARTS Import Creation/Conversion. ARTS Import automates the conversion of your images (BMP, GIF, DCX, PCX, TG4, TIFF, RLE, PNG and JPEG) to PDF. Supported platforms: WinNT/95/98.

ARTS ThumbOpt Management. ARTS ThumbOpt allows you to create thumbnails and optimize PDFs from command line. New to ThumbOpt is the ability to process individual PDFs. Supported platforms: WinNT/95/98.

ARTS Duplex Print. ARTS Duplex allows the printing of odd and even pages independently on a nonduplexing printer. Supported platforms: WinNT/95/98.

Double-sided printing is made easy, and moreover, it halves the amount of paper you would normally use. RTSDuplex doubles your printing options in Acrobat. RTSDuplex will allow you to print odd, even, and double-sided copies from any printer, even the most archaic, whether in Acrobat or a Web Browser. This plug-in runs only in Acrobat and Reader.

ARTS Special Management. ARTS Special is in fact ARTS Import and ARTS PDF Workshop bundled together for only US$349. Supported platforms: WinNT/95/98.

ARTS Import (Upgrade Only) Creation/Conversion. ARTS Import 2.0 automates the conversion of your images (BMP, GIF, DCX, PCX, TG4, TIFF, RLE, PNG, and JPEG) to PDF. Supported platforms: WinNT/95/98.

ARTS Split & Merge Wizard Management. ARTS Split & Merge Wizard is the easiest way to split and merge PDFs. Supported platforms:WinNT/95/98.

ARTS Security Developer. ARTS Security is an OLE Server plug-in that allows you to use OLE and Acrobat to work with secure PDFs programmatically. Supported platforms: WinNT/95/98.

Solimar Systems Inc.
3940 Fourth Avenue, Suite 300, San Diego, CA 92103
Tel: 619 294 4960 Fax: 619 294 5973
www.solimarsystems.com
LegacyXCHANGE is a Windows NT-based print server solution that converts print data intended for Xerox LPS production printers to PDF, PostScript, and PCL.

The print server connects directly to legacy host systems including IBM mainframes, AS/400s, RS/ 6000s, Unisys A-series, and Unix hosts. The emulation is modular and allows automated conversion in a production environment.

LegacyXCHANGE translates Xerox resources to the desired output format on-the-fly, providing accurate, simple conversions that can be installed and maintained by the user. Converted data can be delivered to destinations by file, Internet, print queue, or direct connect.

Sys-Print, Inc.

4151 Memorial Drive, Suite 111-D, Decatur, GA 30032

Tel: 404-296-7812 or1-888-698-4767 Fax:404-296-0884

www.sysprint.com

This is high-speed transformation software to convert mainframe, legacy data to PDF, and/or PostScript. It accepts a variety of data input types, including Xerox DJDE and Metacode, IBM AFP, HP PCL, TIFF, and "sys-out" line data. Mainframe and PC operating versions are available, allowing organizations to easily retrieve and view documents for selective printing and archiving. Sys-Print converts mainframe "Sys-Out" data to either a PostScript file for printing or a PDF file for viewing and storage. The system provides automatic indexing, forms merge, font changing, and graphics.

The conversion is accomplished on-the-fly, without distillers, and is up to forty times faster than alternative methods. Sys-Print software accepts a variety of data-input types, including Sys-Out, Xerox DJDE, Xerox Metacode, IBM AFP, and HP PCL. Sys-Print software also offers automatic creation of an index for use as a navigational tool, also referred to as bookmarks. Three levels of indices may be extracted on-the-fly. Users may define the "zoom" variable and the geometric position of the viewable data on the screen.

Tumbleweed Software

2010 Broadway, Redwood City, CA 94063

Tel: 650-369-6790 Fax: 650-369-7197

www.tumbleweed.com

Posta is an Internet document-delivery solution that allows business users to control and protect the delivery of their important, time-sensitive documents. Posta offers real-time tracking capabilities and several levels of security to the delivery of documents, including encryption, authentication, and password protection. Posta converts files to PDF automatically while sending to let recipients easily view document, regardless of what applications or OS they're using.

Ultimate Technographics

1 Westmount Square, Suite 1700, Montreal,

Quebec Canada H3Z 2P9

Tel: (514) 938-9050 or 1-(800) 363-3590 Fax: (514) 938 5225

www.ultimate-tech.com

The Ultimate Server is a new concept in PDF workflow for prepress. The Ultimate Server uses the technologies of Impostrip, UltimateFlow, and Trapeze and combines them into a single powerful PDF workflow. The Ultimate Server is designed to have multiple processes on one machine, with load balancing in mind (Mac or NT). The Ultimate Server's main concept is to move the data only once by processing the data through an integrated workflow stream. The benefits of this workflow will have a revolutionary impact on time saving, productivity, and prepress resources.

xman Software

350 Pacific Ave., 2nd Floor, San Francisco, CA 94111

Tel: (415) 986-1773 Fax: (415) 438-4905

http://www.xman.com

xToolsOne Plug-ins for Acrobat aim to enhance productivity and save valuable work time. It creates a floating window that provides detailed information about each annotation in an Acrobat document. It can assign creation dates to all annotations and export lists of document annotations; bend a page's corner for reference; copy text to clipboard in footnote format; mark a page as a home page for future reference; quickly and easily create links and bookmarks; put marks on a page with nonprinting ink; and focus print area to a user-defined rectangle.

While every attempt has been made to make this list accurate, we apologize for errors or omissions.

22

Adobe Capture

Acrobat Capture software lets you easily convert one scanned page or thousands to Portable Document Format (PDF), while preserving all the original fonts, formatting, and images. Acrobat Capture is compatible with all the leading scanners. You can use the new Software Development Kit (SDK) to customize Acrobat Capture for your own paper-to-PDF conversion system. Document-capture vendors can help you automate big paper-to-PDF conversion projects.

Convert Paper to PDF Turn printed documents into instantly accessible resources instead of artifacts awaiting rediscovery. Adobe Acrobat Capture software makes it fast and easy to put paper documents on-line. Acrobat Capture lets you convert paper documents to electronic files in the Adobe PDF, which accurately reproduces the look and feel of the printed page, complete with fonts, graphics, formatting, and color, black-and-white, or grayscale images. PDF files are searchable, and you can add annotations, cross-document links, and bookmarks to help readers navigate quickly using Acrobat.

How Capture Works

The Acrobat Capture, Import, and Scan plug-ins for Power Macintosh were not available when Acrobat 3.0 was released but are included in Acrobat 3.01. The Acrobat Import and Scan plug-ins can be used within Exchange to create PDF Image Only documents. The Capture plug-in converts PDF Image Only documents to PDF Normal document. The Macintosh Import plug-in supports PICTas well as TIF, GIF, PCX, and BMP formats on Windows.

1. Scan a printed page of any document—from contracts and spreadsheets to brochures, books, or magazine articles. Acrobat Capture supports many scanners. The image is captured right in Acrobat Exchange.

2. Acrobat Capture converts the scanned image to an electronic copy in PDF.

3. Once your document is in PDF, it is completely platform- and application-independent. Now, here is the magic: Capture converts the scanned image into OCR'd text that underlays the scanned image.

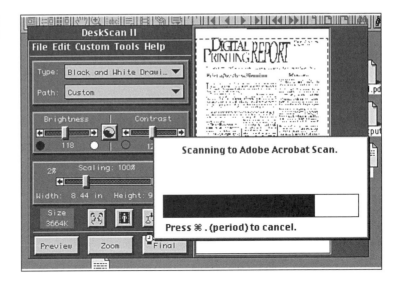

Figure 22-1
The sliding bar shows that Capture is scanning the page.

Capture includes a Software Development Kit with information on how to integrate Capture with other products. The Application Programming Interface (API) gives you direct access to the Capture server, which converts TIFF, BMP, and PCX images to PDF and other formats.

As an enterprise market application, you can use Capture in any number of workflows:

- Network Fax Server Connect Capture connected to your network fax server converts incoming faxes to PDF. You can easily distribute PDF files so that others can read them from a variety of computer systems. Distribution of faxes converted to PDF Normal format requires less network bandwidth than distribution of fax images.

- Network Scanner Use Capture with the software for a network scanner (e.g., HP Network Scanjet 5, or Kofax Netscan) can convert files from TIFF to PDF before attaching them to e-mails or posting them to a network drive or departmental Web server.

- Database Integrate Capture with a document workflow or management application automatically converts TIFF files to PDF, and then store the PDF files in a document system or database so that you can retrieve them using a full-text search.

Automated Page Recognition Acrobat Capture offers improved page recognition, including support for black-and-white, grayscale, and color documents—which means improved searchability on highly formatted content such as tables and forms. Acrobat Capture also provides automatic downsampling of photos and artwork. The Acrobat Capture Reviewer has been improved to include more tools for customers to enhance and alter converted documents, giving them options such as changing text fonts and colors, or importing and placing images. Acrobat Capture captures documents in eight languages (U.S. English, U.K. English, German, French, Swedish, Dutch, Spanish, and Italian). Capture 3 features include

- Accurately perform optical character recognition (OCR)
- Recognize documents in sixteen languages: U.S. English, U.K. English, Brazilian Portuguese, Danish, Dutch, Finnish, French, German, Italian, Norwegian, Nynorsk, Portuguese, Spanish, Castilian Spanish, Swedish, Swiss German

- Recognize specialized documents with legal, medical, scientific, and large user-defined dictionaries
- Improve page decomposition, which lets you convert forms, tables, and visually rich color pages with lines and graphics into Adobe Portable Document Format (PDF) files that need less cleanup before publication
- Automatically create intradocument links that make your intranet or Web libraries easy to navigate (Included are tables of contents with nested bookmarks, cross-references, indexes, e-mail links, and URLs. Linking is supported in both PDF and HTML.)
- Define customized font sets for improved OCR and font mapping
- Automatically identify frequently-used styles such as headers, subtitles, and body text
- Automatically store suspect words as bitmapped images in PDF Formatted Text and Graphics files (The suspect word bitmap density is adjusted to closely match the visual appearance of the surrounding text.)
- Achieve smaller file sizes for color documents with color segment recognition
- Enable efficient searching with keyword recognition
- The new deskew agent automatically straightens the page to improve OCR recognition
- In-the-box agents connect to TMSSequoia and Kofax image enhancement software to enable a wide variety of high-quality image cleanup
- PDF Formatted Text and Graphics: for compact, searchable files with only one layer (The layer reproduces graphics and replaces bitmapped text with formatted text based on OCR. This file type (formerly known as PDF Normal) is smaller than any other Adobe PDF option, so it is the ideal Web format.)
- PDF Image Only: for a cross-platform image of the entire scanned page

- PDF Searchable Image (Exact): for an image of the entire scanned page with OCR'd text hidden behind, creating a searchable bitmap (This file type (formerly known as PDF Image+Text) preserves the look of the original scanned image, making it the ideal format for meeting legal requirements.)
- PDF Searchable Image (Compact): for a searchable image of a scanned color page, with small file sizes (This is the ideal format for full color documents.)
- HTML: for Web publication with support for frames and cascading style sheets
- ASCII: for text-only output

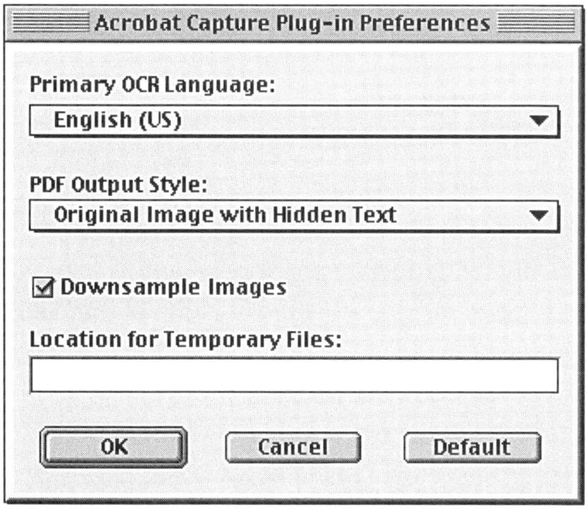

Figure 22-2
Acrobat Capture Plug-in Preferences dialog box.

You specify the language for OCR and the level of PDF output in a Preferences dialog box.

Adobe Acrobat Capture uses a hardware key to monitor throughput (i.e., the conversion of paper to electronic documents). When Capture processes a page, the Acrobat Capture server window opens and displays the number of pages that can be processed with the current hardware key. When you anticipate running out of pages, order another hardware key (page pack).

The Capture plug-in uses the current PDFWriter settings for font embedding and subsetting when it creates PDF files. To avoid problems when correcting a captured document, be sure that font subsetting is not selected in PDF Writer before capturing the document.

Most popular desktop and high-volume scanners are supported through ISIS and TWAIN drivers. Convert documents to PDF from common image formats, such as TIFF (including G3, G4, and LZW formats), PCX, BMP, and PDF Image. Scan and convert pages up to 27"x27". Scan and convert up to 20,000 pages in batch-processing mode.

Increase available memory to process complicated grayscale or color images: Necessary memory = Uncompressed Image Size x 3. During Capture processing, versions of your document will also be stored as temporary files on your hard disk.

OCR, Font, and Page Recognition   Convert paper documents to PDF Normal; for compact, searchable files—the ideal Web format PDF Image; for a cross-platform image of the entire scanned page PDF Image+Text; for an image of the entire scanned page with OCRed text hidden behind, creating a searchable bitmap—the ideal format for meeting legal requirements to preserve the original scanned image.

Other formats (HTML, ASCII, Rich Text Format (RTF), Microsoft Word version 6 for Windows, and WordPerfect versions 5 and 6 for Windows) convert paper documents to black-and-white, grayscale, and color files. Schedule scanning and conversion at your convenience with delayed processing.

During installation the Microsoft C Runtime Library, Microsoft Controls Library, and Microsoft Portability Library are placed in the Extensions folder within the System folder and are necessary for the Capture, Scan, and Import plug-ins to load and function. Have your scanner's TWAIN driver installed prior to scanning. Some TWAIN drivers have a default setting to store a copy of the preview scan. You may have to increase the memory allocation for Exchange to accommodate the TWAIN driver's stored preview image. Scanning via ISIS drivers is not available on the Macintosh. The Capture plug-in launches the application "Adobe Acrobat: Capture: Capture Server." The Capture plug-in will not function if the overall path name to the application is longer than 128 characters. Do not nest Exchange in a folder that will cause it to exceed this limitation.

View, Navigate, and Print PDF Files   Portable Document Format PDF Web libraries place volumes of important business information just a mouse click away. With free Acrobat Reader software, users on any computing platform can navigate, scale, zoom in on, and print PDF files directly within their Web Browsers. PDF files can be indexed and searched with the leading intranet search tools. Experience high-quality printing on the Web with PDF! Because they aren't limited to 72-dpi resolution, PDF files will print at the maximum resolution of your black-and-white or color printer.

The Capture plug-in is installed from the Acrobat CD-ROM. Use the Capture plug-in to convert small numbers of paper documents to PDF. If you need to convert large collections of paper documents or electronic images to PDF, upgrade to the full Acrobat Capture product with automated processing features.

Choose Capture Pages in Acrobat. The plug-in uses optical character recognition (OCR) to convert bitmap text to text that can be corrected, indexed, searched, or copied to other files. The text it converts is in PDF image documents that were scanned directly, or imported, into Acrobat. The Capture plug-in can recognize any of eight languages, hide recognized text behind a document image, and downsample images to minimize file size. After you capture a document, you can use the touch-up tool in Acrobat to review and correct text.

Capture produces three styles of PDF documents:

1. PDF Normal contains text that is scalable and can be indexed, searched, and copied. Page formatting and images are preserved. Create this kind of file with Acrobat Distiller, PDF Writer, or the Capture Pages command in Exchange. Normal files are significantly smaller than PDF Image Only files.

2. PDF Image Only contains only a bitmap picture of the original document. PDF Image Only files are produced by the Scan and the Import commands in Exchange.

3. PDF Original Image with Hidden Text combines features of PDF Image Only and PDF Normal documents. They contain a bitmap picture of the page, but with OCR-recognized text hidden behind the picture. This provides the advantages of searchable text while ensuring that a document is identical in appearance to the original. This is great for for legal or archival purposes. PDF Original Image with Hidden Text files are created only with the Capture Pages command in Exchange.

The last format is the most desirable since it preserves the visual integrity of the page while providing an underlying searchability.

When you capture a PDF Image Only file, it usually reduces file size significantly. In most cases, PDF files captured with the PDF Normal setting are smaller than those captured with the PDF Original Image with Hidden Text setting.

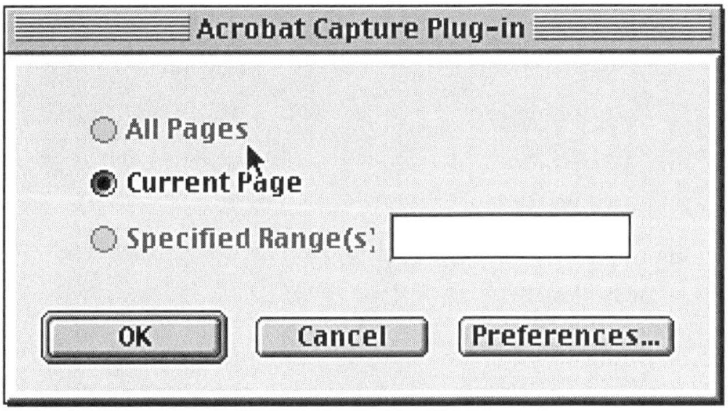

Figure 22-3
Acrobat Capture page-selection dialog box.

Capturing Documents   Documents that you capture are image files that are scanned or imported into Acrobat—PDF Image Only files

1. File > Scan. Choose a scanner and document type; click Scan.
2. After the page has been scanned, choose Document > Capture Pages.
3. Determine which pages you want to capture by selecting All Pages, Current Page, or Specified Range and entering page numbers in the text box.
4. To change the Capture preferences, click Preferences. The document will be captured with the new settings.
5. Click OK. The Capture progress window shows the page, character, and word-recognition process. In order for the process to be successful, the resolution of the captured PDF Image Only file must fall within the following ranges:
   - Monochrome images, 200–600 dpi
   - Grayscale or color images, 200–400 dpi

Text should be dark against a light background. Text on a dark or shaded background, or on a page with complex color gradients, may not be recognized.

Acrobat Capture is available at the suggested retail price of $895 and includes the ability to convert up to 20,000 pages. Additional page packs are priced at $595 for 20,000 pages and $4,995 for converting 200,000 pages. Customers will be able to purchase Acrobat Capture from Adobe Authorized Resellers or directly from Adobe by calling (800) 272-3623. Registered licensees of Adobe Acrobat Capture will be able to upgrade to Acrobat Capture at the suggested retail price of $169.

Watching Capture work is quite amazing. After the scan is done you select Capture Pages. Figure 22-4 shows the information box that comes up and indicates each step in the process of OCR'ing the page. Each area of the page is highlighted as it is being read (OCR'd).

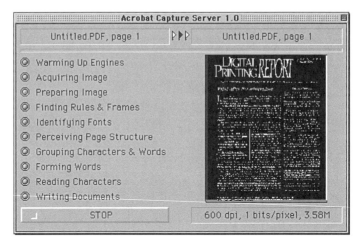

Figure 22-4
The scanned page is displayed on the screen.

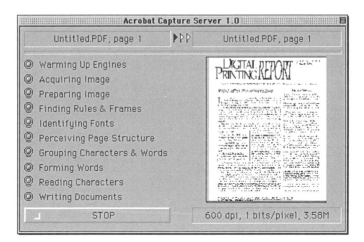

Figure 22-5
The scanned page is OCR'd.

Correcting Captured Documents   When Capture suspects it has not recognized a word correctly, it displays the bitmap image of the original word in the document and hides its best guess for the word behind the bitmap. This ensures accurate reproduction of the original, even without correction. You can review and correct suspect words in Exchange with the text touch-up tool. This is useful when you want your document to be fully searchable.

Remember, you are creating two files in one: the scanned bitmap of the page and the underlying text for searchability. File sizes can get a bit high. Here are some sample file sizes for comparison purposes with Downsampling off and on. The examples are at 300 dpi but OCR and image quality are best at 600 dpi.

Downsampling Off

300 dpi	TIFF File	PDF Image	PDF Normal	PDF Image	Original + Text
Black and White	1043 K	202 K	161 K	213 K	*190 K*
4-bit Grayscale	8335 K	421 K	222 K	328 K	*606 K*
8-bit Grayscale	8333 K	1183 K	756 K	884 K	*796 K*
24-bit RGB Color	2499 K	2531 K	1832 K	2044 K	*3085 K*

Downsampling On

300 dpi	TIFF File	PDF Image	PDF Normal	PDF Image	Original + Text
Black and White	1043 K	202 K	61 K	94 K	*190 K*
4-bit Grayscale	8335 K	421 K	222 K	325 K	*606 K*
8-bit Grayscale	8333 K	1183 K	113 K	309 K	*796 K*
24-bit RGB Color	2499 K	2531 K	500 K	616 K	*3085 K*

The italic number is LZW Compression. Group 4 Compression is even greater.

Build a Business   Here's an example of Capture in action:

Figure 22-6
The First Folio as displayed in Acrobat.

The illustration is the Shakespearean First Folio in all its glory—scanned, OCR'd, and PDF'd by Octavo (www.octavo.com). You can buy the book on CD-ROM in PDF form.

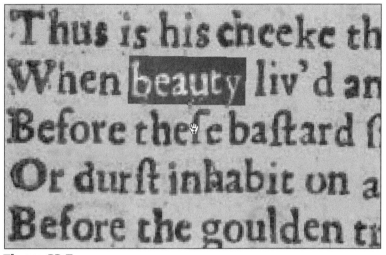

Figure 22-7
Underlying the scanned image is the text, which is fully searchable.

Even at 800 percent zoom you can read the text, which is the exact replica of the first folio. But when we searched for a word, the underlying OCR'd text matched up with the image and both were highlighted. Think of the new market this technology opens for archival materials in paper form. Now they can be electronic.

Key Features

	Acrobat Capture 2.01	Acrobat Capture 3.0 Personal Edition	Acrobat Capture 3.0 Cluster Edition
Platform Support	Win 95/98/NT	Win NT	Win NT
Language Versions English	•	•	•
Dutch, French, German, Italian, Spanish, Swedish	•		
Licensing			
Searchable PDF page limit	20,000°	20,000°	unlimited°°
Image Only PDF page limit	included in 20,000	unlimited	unlimited°°
Reviewer license	5 users		
Capture Assistant license		1 user	5 users°°°
Scalability			
Multiprocessor support (at additional cost)			dual or quad
Workload balancing			•
Robust error handling		•	•

OCR Dictionaries

Multiple languages	8	16	16
Legal, medical, and scientific		•	•
User-defined	•	large	large

Other Types of Recognition

Page, character, and word recognition	•	•	•
Automatic creation of intradocument links		•	•
User-defined font sets		•	•
Table and color segment recognition	•	improved	improved
Keyword, link, table, color segment, and zone recognition		•	•

Image Cleanup

Deskew agent		•	•
Support for TMSSequoia and Kofax image-enhancement software		•	•

Output File Formats

PDF image only, PDF Searchable Image (Exact), PDF Formatted Text and Graphics, ASCII	•	•	•
PDF Searchable Image (Compact)		•	•
HTML	•	with frame + cascading style sheet support	with frame + cascading style sheet support

Productivity Tools

Workbench user interface to create, submit, and track jobs		•	•
Reusable workflows with 22 step templates	•	•	
Reviewer for document cleanup	•	with link editing + global font style replacement	with link editing + global font style replacement
QuickFix tool for OCR suspect correction		•	•
Zone tool for image, text, and keyword area identification		•	•
Capture Assistant for distributed workflows	•	•	

Integration

ODMA support		•	•
API (Application Programming Interface)	standard	robust	robust
Index key support	•	•	•

Scanning

ISIS and TWAIN support with over 150 scanner configurations included	•	•	•
LZW and CCITT Group 4 compression supported directly from scanner		•	•
Reusable scanner settings		•	•

Notes:

   ° Additional 20,000 or 100,000 page dongle packs purchased separately.

   °° Cluster Edition uses an unlimited page serial number, not a dongle.

   °°° Capture Assistant includes the Reviewer.

Acquisition Alternatives

- Adobe Acrobat Capture Personal Edition is ideal for users who need to create high-value documents, have low-volume requirements, or have occasional batch processing needs.
- It processes up to 20,000 PDF Searchable or Formatted Text and Graphics pages (dongle included).
- It processes an unlimited number of PDF Image Only pages.
- Additional 20,000 and 100,000 page dongle packs may be purchased separately.
- Personal Edition runs on a single computer as a stand-alone application.
- Acrobat Capture Cluster Edition is scalable for high-volume requirements, letting you complete big paper-to-PDF conversion projects in less time.
- It processes an unlimited number of any type of PDF pages.
- Cluster Edition lets you do workload balancing.
- You can install additional licenses of Cluster Edition to enable workload balancing across multiple workstations. *N* number of Cluster Editions point to a common task database and share the workload.
- Acrobat Capture Assistant software allows up to five additional workstations offload labor-intensive tasks that require human intervention such as Zoning, QuickFix, Reviewer, and Archive (ODMA). In addition, it provides the flexibility to submit and modify workflows.

INDEX

D

Back	Forward	Home	Reload	Images	Open	Print	Find	Stop

http://www.phptr.com/

What's New?	What's Cool?	Destinations	Net Search	People	Software

P R E N T I C E   H A L L

Professional Technical Reference

...th

...e!

DATE DUE

ILL-PALCI-55516
Due 3-23-02

GAYLORD   PRINTED IN U.S.A.

We... ...pening in
pro... ...e's a bit of what
you...

@ **Sp**... ...ok series, software,
fea... ...l information to
he...

De... ...on for the latest
ba... ...s.

$ **Ne**... ...okseller near you
tha... ...Magnet bookstore
ne...

! **Wh**... ...s for the professional
co... ...ntion schedule, join
an... ...ases on topics of
int...

✉ **Sub**... ...**l newsletter!**

Wa... ...? Choose a targeted
cate... ...l of the latest PH PTR
pro... ...your interest area.

Visit our mailroom to subscribe today! **http://www.phptr.com/mail_lists**

www.phptr.com